A Research Agenda for Public–Private Partnerships and the
Governance of Infrastructure

Elgar Research Agendas outline the future of research in a given area. Leading scholars are given the space to explore their subject in provocative ways, and map out the potential directions of travel. They are relevant but also visionary.

Forward-looking and innovative, Elgar Research Agendas are an essential resource for PhD students, scholars and anybody who wants to be at the forefront of research.

Titles in the series include:

A Research Agenda for Space Policy
Edited by Kai-Uwe Schrogl, Christina Giannopapa and Ntorina Antoni

A Research Agenda for Event Impacts
Edited by Nicholas Wise and Kelly Maguire

A Research Agenda for Urban Tourism
Edited by Jan van der Borg

A Research Agenda for Manufacturing Industries in the Global Economy
Edited by John R. Bryson, Chloe Billing, William Graves and Godfrey Yeung

A Research Agenda for Global Higher Education
Jeroen Huisman and Marijk van der Wende

A Research Agenda for Real Estate
Edited by Piyush Tiwari and Julie T. Miao

A Research Agenda for Political Marketing
Edited by Bruce I. Newman and Todd P. Newman

A Research Agenda for Public–Private Partnerships and the Governance of Infrastructure
Edited by Graeme A. Hodge and Carsten Greve

A Research Agenda for Public–Private Partnerships and the Governance of Infrastructure

Edited by

GRAEME A. HODGE

Adjunct Professor, Monash University, Australia

CARSTEN GREVE

Professor, Department of Organization, Copenhagen Business School, Denmark

Elgar Research Agendas

Edward Elgar
PUBLISHING

Cheltenham, UK • Northampton, MA, USA

Published by
Edward Elgar Publishing Limited
The Lypiatts
15 Lansdown Road
Cheltenham
Glos GL50 2JA
UK

Edward Elgar Publishing, Inc.
William Pratt House
9 Dewey Court
Northampton
Massachusetts 01060
USA

Paperback edition 2023

A catalogue record for this book
is available from the British Library

Library of Congress Control Number: 2022932112

This book is available electronically in the **Elgar**online
Political Science and Public Policy subject collection
http://dx.doi.org/10.4337/9781839105883

ISBN 978 1 83910 587 6 (cased)
ISBN 978 1 83910 588 3 (eBook)
ISBN 978 1 0353 2741 6 (paperback)

Printed and bound by CPI Group (UK) Ltd, Croydon, CR0 4YY

Contents

Figures

Tables

Contributors

Marta Almeida, Assistant Professor, Nova School of Business and Economics, Lisbon.

Anthony M. Bertelli, Sherwin-Whitmore Chair of Liberal Arts, Professor of Public Policy and Political Science, Pennsylvania State University and Senior Research Fellow, Institut Barcelona d'Estudis Internacionals.

Carter B. Casady, Lecturer (Assistant Professor) in Economics and Finance, Bartlett School of Sustainable Construction, University College London.

Lene Tolstrup Christensen, Post Doctoral scholar, Copenhagen Business School.

Sarah Maria Denta, Assistant Professor, CBS Law, Copenhagen Business School.

Richard Foster, Director, Foster Infrastructure, Australia.

Carsten Greve, Professor of Public Management and Governance, Department of Organization, Copenhagen Business School.

Graeme A. Hodge, Adjunct Professor of Law, Monash University.

Erik-Hans Klijn, Professor of Public Administration at the Department of Public Administration and Sociology, Erasmus University Rotterdam, The Netherlands.

Moritz Liebe, Trier University.

Micaela Mihov, PhD graduate, King's College London.

Dónal Palcic, Department of Economics, Kemmy Business School, University of Limerick.

Eoin Reeves, Department of Economics, Kemmy Business School, University of Limerick.

Elena Shadrina, National Research University Higher School of Economics, Russian Federation.

Matti Siemiatycki, Professor, University of Toronto.

Stewart Smyth, Professor of Accounting, Sheffield University Management School, Sheffield University.

Anne Stafford, Professor of Accounting and Finance, Alliance Manchester Business School, University of Manchester.

Sophie Sturup, Associate Professor, Xi'an Jiaotong-Liverpool University, China.

Christina D. Tvarnø, Professor of Law, CBS Law, Copenhagen Business School.

Dmitri Vinogradov, University of Glasgow, and National Research University Higher School of Economics, Russian Federation.

Rianne Warsen, Assistant Professor, Department of Public Administration and Sociology, Erasmus University Rotterdam.

Eleanor F. Woodhouse, Lecturer (Assistant Professor) in Public Policy, Department of Political Science, University College London.

Sebastian Zwalf, Doctoral scholar, Monash University.

Preface and acknowledgements

Our scholarly community has come a long way in thinking about how to best govern infrastructure and in employing public–private partnerships (PPPs). How the public and private sectors in Western liberal mixed economies can work better together has been a central theme in our quest. But new themes for inquiry have also arisen as our infrastructure practices and governing mechanisms have expanded, and the infrastructure field has become a meeting place for commentary and analysis across disciplines. Philosophically, we are both grateful for this. It has always struck us that the strength of individual disciplines to search for solutions which more accurately serve the values of that discipline has also been a critical, but too often unspoken, weakness of each when it came to providing and governing public infrastructure. To our minds, the positive role of politics in governing well has too often been treated as a distraction and an irrelevance next to more important disciplinary matters!

Today's marketplace is awash with new PPP- and infrastructure-oriented publications heading off very different directions. With this book, we aimed to look through a cross-disciplinary lens towards some of the most crucial research matters in the international PPP domain. We have been heartened by the wonderful contributions of the chapter authors, and to the extent that this book succeeds, it is a testament to them. We are particularly thankful to these authors for their willingness to contribute their energy and intellect to this edited volume in an era when many learned institutions are risking becoming obsessed by journal rankings rather than the more difficult task of acknowledging the many ways through which we all learn. Their involvement in our project has been affirming. And for the record, all chapters in this volume were peer-reviewed prior to acceptance.

We thank Edward Elgar for their invitation to produce this edited volume and for the faith that both Alex Pettifer and Finn Halligan put in us to develop a book of substance. Thanks for believing in the book, and for your diplomatic yet effective email reminders to keep us on track.

Furthermore, we would like to thank both of our universities, Monash University and Copenhagen Business School, for being our institutional homes, along with our university colleagues for being a true source of strength.

Finally, we would like to extend the biggest thank you to Stephanie and Birgit, for their continued patience and love. Having previously awarded them each 'Nobel patience prizes' in 2019, it only remains to say 'thank goodness'. Thank goodness that neither Stephanie nor Birgit have ever asked to see the long-term contract under which they entered their marriage. Nor have they asked for major revisions to be made to this (non-existent) contract. Perhaps successful marriage projects do indeed rely more on trust, supportive interactions and collaboration than any contract.

We trust that readers will find the contributions made within this book as exciting and as stimulating as we have found this project.

Graeme A. Hodge and Carsten Greve
Monash University and Copenhagen Business School
July 2021

PART I

Introduction

1   The PPP research terrain in a contested era

Carsten Greve and Graeme A. Hodge

Introduction

Public–private partnerships (PPPs) for infrastructure sit at the nexus of multiple professional and scholarly disciplines – that is what makes them so profoundly interesting. Coming out of politics and public policy, our interest has long been in the political economy of PPPs, but it is fair to say that one must cross disciplines and learn from others if we are to understand what makes PPPs tick and why the partnership narrative remains so globally relevant (Hodge et al. 2010). This book aims to contemplate new research frontiers for PPPs, and this requires us to articulate just what we know at present. Our introduction here sets out some frontiers which will be discussed more in the subsequent chapters.

We have also witnessed a broader interest in 'infrastructure governance' where the PPP model is but one of the options of organizing and governing infrastructure (Weigrich et al. 2017). The Organisation for Economic Co-operation and Development now simply calls the topic under which PPPs belong 'infrastructure governance' (www.oecd.org/gov/infrastructure-governance/). In this book, we also therefore deal with recent approaches to governing infrastructure with a stronger state role. Interest in the 'public–private mix' goes right back to the 1970s–1980s work of the Working Group of the International Schools of Administration (IASIA) and the subsequent Working Group on Public Enterprise Management and the Public-Private Mix through the 1990s reported by Wettenhall and Thynne (1999, 158). They noted the emergence of 'public-private partnerships as an issue deserving much greater attention' and 'a series of [five] international conferences on public and private sector partnerships' prior to 1999, along with publications such as Thynne (1995). The work in this book builds on these foundations.

The aim of this book is to bring together some of the state-of-the-art knowledge in the domain of PPPs and the governance of infrastructure. Looking back over the past three decades or so at the various questions that have been asked by PPP researchers, there is much reason to be proud – and yet there is also considerable room for humility. So, what questions have we been asking to date? How has PPP research expanded over the past three decades? And how might we summarize what we now know? We aim to articulate both priority research frontiers for the future as well as potentially rewarding arenas. We are therefore going to explore some of the most important continuing research themes to which scholars have long devoted their energies, and then look forward.

The PPP global research agenda lineage

Overview articles on a research agenda for PPP and infrastructure governance have occupied minds for some time. One place to start is the global research agenda developed by Hodge and Greve (2018). We sketched the lineage of the global PPP research terrain over the two decades since Broadbent and Laughlin's (1999) seminal early research agenda, and articulated a future international PPP research agenda. Our analysis built on the literatures of mega-projects and project finance as well as previous international research agendas from Hodge and Greve (2008), and Wall and Connolly (2009). Our 2018 review noted that Broadbent and Laughlin initially posed five central questions for Britain's private finance initiative (PFI) program. They questioned whether PFI was a form of privatization, how matters such as value for money (VfM) and risk transfer were operationalized, who was regulating PFI's application, how PFI decisions were made, and what the overall merit and worth of PFI was. This 'first generation set of questions' was built on through the work on mega-projects from Flyvbjerg et al. (2002) and Flyvbjerg (2007). Flyvbjerg observed that with mega-projects overwhelmingly coming in over time and over budget, our historical understanding and control of project risks was pitiful, and a stronger empirical base for estimating project economic risks was desirable. An increasingly dominant 'on-time and on-budget' discourse amongst practitioners, academics and the polity was born. Into this context, a 'second generation' set of public policy research issues was injected, by viewing PPP as both a socio-political issue as well as a technical issue (Hodge and Greve 2008, 17). Central to this was the role of language. We argued that PPP projects themselves were regulated by ad hoc long-term contract regimes rather than by parliaments, and as a consequence there was a serious question as to whether citizens viewed these new arrangements as legitimate. The notion of VfM was also viewed as purposely vague, re-orienting discussion away from project unit costs towards broader notions of whole-of-life costs, risk transfers and risk-adjusted discount rates. The observation was also made that Broadbent and Laughlin's last two questions concerning PFI decision-making and its merits are not at all straightforward to answer. This second-generation view was that PPPs were 'innate matters of government preference as policy' involving 'matters concerning governance, political economy and power' (Hodge and Greve 2008, 13) rather than solely being a technical matter of engineering project management or finance. The central focus here was towards the political governance and regulation of PPPs, because 'determining the real merit of infrastructure partnerships requires more attention to how they solve problems for governments', as well as any technical merit they may have (Hodge and Greve 2008, 22).

Along with this perspective was the research agenda proposed by Wall and Connolly (2009). They called for increased empirical research through the eyes of stakeholders outside the public sector, as well as matters such as the practice of PFI including on/off balance sheet asset recording, and the calculation of scheme benefits. The lineage of questions highlighted thus far is shown in Figure 1.1. Also included in this figure are the five research agenda questions posed in 2018 relating to project financialization, international PPP market and multilateral actors, PPP promotion and transition countries.

Hodge and Greve (2019, 220) commented that many other research contributions could be added to this list. More importantly, though, we articulated several big shifts in PPP scholarship. First was 'a move from PPPs as meaning only a project or its delivery towards … PPP at the broader governance levels'. Second was the observation that studies had moved from being UK/anglophile-centric or having a single country focus to reporting well beyond the nation state. Third was the move 'from studying PPPs solely through a set of technical, formal and utilitarian objectives towards more socio-political as well as informal objectives'. Fourth was the transition of PPP research 'coming from an increasing number of academic disciplines', including psychology, geography, linguistics and political science as well as the traditional fields interested in the management of public works. To our minds, PPP studies were striving to become 'a truly multidisciplinary field'. Fifth, we observed that the views of many commentators had shifted 'away from an optimistic and positive glow prior to the GFC [global financial crisis] towards a more sceptical view' that not only should PPP itself be 'rethought', but so should the 'advice of private finance experts promising public gains but taking hefty commissions'. Lastly, we observed that the range of PPP research topics had exploded over

	Broadbent and Laughlin (1999)	Hodge and Greve (2008)	Wall and Connolly (2009)	Hodge and Greve (2018)
Project / Project delivery level	• How is PFI VfM and risk transfer operationalized?	• When do PPPs give highest VfM and innovation?	• What are the effects of rising transaction costs? • How has the financial crisis affected PPPs?	• What are the impacts of the financialization of infrastructure projects?
	• Is PFI privatization? • What is PFI's merit / worth?	• When does PPP promotion succeed in different jurisdictions? • What is PFI's merit / worth?	• Is PPP the only show in town? • Why are PPPs promoted in some jurisdictions and not others? • What are the impacts of various policy changes on PPP? • Are PPP decisions affected by cash or accrual systems?	• How does the presence of global PPP market actors influence PPP projects?
	• What is PFI and who regulates it? • How are PFI decisions made?	• When can PPPs best act as a governance tool? • How can we regulate PPPs in the public interest? • What have auditors found globally? • What is the nature of the global PPP industry? • How do PPPs assist development? • What is the next PPP chapter?	• Who are the PPP stakeholders?	• What are the consequences of international organizations promoting specific recommendations for PPPs? • How do governments govern their complex portfolio of PPP deals? • Why and how are PPPs becoming a preferred way of doing business in developing countries?
Broader governance levels				

Source: Hodge and Greve 2018

Figure 1.1   The evolving research agenda

the past two decades and yet many of these continued to deserve attention. Our comment was that:

> There is clearly a multiplicity of long-term arrangements possible for infrastructure, so questions as to how they are evolving, the merit of each PPP approach, and the political rationales being pursued for PPPs in different contexts will all no doubt remain important research topics. There is also little doubt that PPP VfM and PPP affordability will both remain highly contested. In the midst of Boardman and Vining's (2010) comment that no government has yet performed rigorous evaluations of PPP, there is significant technical complexity inherent in this calculus and some even doubt that accurate VfM calculations are possible (Yescombe 2013; Hodge 2013). Notwithstanding these observations, it should equally be said that major infrastructure projects will continue to capture our political imagination and the use of private finance allied with the flexibility of the private contract form will ensure its continuation as a delivery option. (Hodge and Greve, 2019, 218)

Overall, then, our judgement was that over time, the research agenda had broadened (with more issues and domains being tackled), had deepened (with many sub-questions being asked through deeper and more rigorous analyses) and had sharpened (through the use of new analytical lenses as well as conventional research methods).

Following the research agenda through special issues of journals

The publication of special issues in academic journals is one indicator of how the evolution of the research agenda has occurred. Special issues are often the product of academic conferences, and influence evolving thought. The International Public–Private Partnerships Scholars' Network (IP3SN) was started in 2012 by the editors Graeme A. Hodge and Carsten Greve together with Professor Anthony Boardman from the Sauder Business School at the University of British Columbia, Vancouver. The network has convened a selected number of participants at a conference on PPP research every year since 2012. The first conference took place at Copenhagen Business School in 2012, followed by the University of British Columbia, Vancouver in 2013 and Monash University in Melbourne in 2014. Subsequent conferences have followed: New York City in 2015, hosted by Cornell University; Antwerp in 2016, hosted by the University of Antwerp in collaboration with Erasmus University in the Netherlands; Limerick in Ireland in 2017; the University of Toronto in 2018; and the University of Central Florida in 2019. Many of these conferences have produced special issues documenting the progress of research on PPPs, as shown in Table 1.1.

The *Journal of Comparative Policy Analysis: Research and Practice* published a special issue on 'Comparative analyses of infrastructure public-private partnerships' (Vol. 17, No. 5) in 2015, edited by Boardman, Greve and Hodge. After an introductory piece by the editors, five articles were included: Ross and Yan compared PPPs to traditional procurement; Albalate, Bel, Bel-Piana and Geddes compared the transfer of different types of risks in transportation PPPs using countries from South America and Europe; Acerete, Gasca, Stafford and Stapleton investigated organizational and financial arrangements of two healthcare PPPs in Spain; Hellowell and Vecchi analyzed agency problems that led to budgetary problems with PPP in hospitals in the UK and Spain; and Reeves reviewed the Irish PPP experience. The cross-disciplinary and cross-country spread of experience and analyses here was impressive.

A Special Issue (Vol. 76, No. 3) on 'Infrastructure public-private partnerships' was published in 2017 by the *Australian Journal of Public Administration* and edited by Hodge, Greve and Boardman. The editors' introductory article focused on 'PPPs: the way they were and what they can become'. Sturup focused on the risk of deep partnerships that could lead to mercantile government.

Table 1.1　　　Recent selected journal special issues on PPPs

Journal	Year	Theme	Editors
Journal of Comparative Policy Analysis	2015	Comparative analyses of infrastructure PPPs	Boardman, Greve and Hodge
Australian Journal of Public Administration	2017	Infrastructure PPPs	Hodge, Greve and Boardman
Public Management Review	2018	Roundtable on PPPs	Klijn, Koppenjan and Verhoest
Annals of Public and Cooperative Economics	2019	The performance potential of PPPs	Palcic, Reeves and Siemiatycki
Public Works Management and Policy	2020	PPPs for social infrastructure	Martin
Journal of Economic Policy Reform	2019–2021	Several articles on PPPs	Siemiatycki

Zwalf, Hodge and Alam examined the problem of finding a suitable discount rate for evaluating PPP proposals. Willems and colleagues provided ten lessons from ten years' experience with PPPs in Belgium. Hodge, Boulot, Duffield and Greve explored what happened to PPP contracts after the ribbon had been cut. De Martinis and Moyan discussed Melbourne's ill-fated 'East–West-link', which got scrapped. Stafford and Stapleton focused on the accountability shortfalls of corporate governance arrangements in PPP. The mix of both international and interdisciplinary knowledge was again a highlight.

Public Management Review published a Special Issue with a 'Roundtable on public–private partnerships' in 2018 (Vol. 20, No. 8) edited by Klijn, Koppenjan and Verhoest. The first article, by Hodge, Greve and Biygautane, examined if PPPs work and what we have learned so far. Hussein and Siemiatycki discussed the role of private capital in infrastructure PPPs and how this role was being rethought in Ontario in Canada. Their standout paper noted that by decreasing the proportion of private capital at risk after construction, savings were gained by government without undermining performance. They put the matter of mixed capital squarely back on the agenda. Soecepto and Verhoest focused on contract stability in European road infrastructure PPPs and how governmental PPP support can prevent contract renegotiation.

Warsen, Nederhand, Klijn, Grotenbreg and Koppenjan used survey research to explore the outcomes and quality of cooperation in PPPs. This paper was another standout contribution, analyzing the influence of soft factors such as trust and network management. They concluded that both mattered. Indeed, such relational characteristics were seen as important, maybe even more important, than contract characteristics.

Annals of Public and Cooperative Economics published the 'Special Issue on the Performance and Potential of Public Private Partnerships' 2019 (Vol. 90, No. 2), edited by Palcic, Reeves and Siemiatycki. The introductory article by the editors argued that performance was the missing 'p' in PPP research. In this context, Petersen's systematic literature review was a highlight. He evaluated the costs, quality and VfM of infrastructure PPPs. O'Shea, Palcic and Reeves discussed two decades of DBFO (design, build, finance and operate) roads in the UK and Spain and evaluated their financial performance. Whitfield and Smyth presented research on the emergent PPP equity market. Marques and Geddes analyzed the use of PPP arrangements in street lighting from an economic perspective. Boyer examined the influence of PPPs on disaster resilience. Vecchi and Cascalini discussed infrastructure PPPs and social impact bonds. Lember, Petersen, Scherrer and Ågren debated the relationship between PPPs and innovation. Siemiatycki explored the diversity gap in the PPP industry and examined women and visible minorities in senior leadership positions.

Public Works Management and Policy published its 'Symposium Issue: Public Private Partnerships for Social Infrastructure' (Vol. 25, No. 3) in July 2020. The symposium's guest editor was Larry Martin from the University of Central Florida. The symposium contained eight research articles on PPPs. O'Shea, Palsic and Reeves examined 20 years of experience with PPPs for social infrastructure in Ireland. O'Neill, Sands and Hodge delved into three decades of prison reform in Victoria, Australia. Agyenim-Boateng, Stafford and Stapleton focused on finance trusts in the UK health service. Vecchi, Casalini, Cusumano and Leone discussed PPP in Italy's healthcare system. Hussein and McKellar presented a case of a healthcare PPP in Canada. Casady and Geddes analyzed asset recycling for social infrastructure in the US. Levey, Connors and Martin looked into public universities' use of the PPP model. Greve and Hodge contemplated learning perspectives for social infrastructure in light of the global diffusion of PPP policy.

The *Journal of Economic Policy Reform* carried several articles related to a conference on PPPs held at the University of Toronto organized by Matti Siemiatycki. Greve et al. presented findings on PPPs in the Danish healthcare sector. Geddes and Goldman focused on institutional economics and the cost of capital for infrastructure projects. Zwalf discussed the policy for privately financed public infrastructure in Australia. Palcic, Reeves, Flannery and Geddes offered an international comparative analysis of tendering periods for PPPs.

PhD theses as a research agenda indicator

Another important indicator of the PPP research agenda terrain has been the work of doctoral students around the globe. Indeed, a remarkable number of candidates have earned PhDs doing research on PPPs and infrastructure governance throughout the last two decades. In Denmark, Weihe examined 'PPPs: Meaning and practice'. Petersen studied 'Public-private partnerships: policy and regulation', with case studies from Denmark and Ireland. Stelling examined PPPs and trusting. Dam discussed 'Public-private partnerships for innovation and sustainability transformation' through municipal waste management in England and Denmark. Christensen explored 'State-owned enterprises as institutional market actors' in public service markets, Denta examined local government PPPs and regulation, and Brogaard explored public–private innovation partnerships. In Luxembourg, Liebe examined 'The political economy of PPPs in the European Union'. In England, Mihov wrote 'Making it fit: The role of institutional work in the transplantation of the Anglo-Saxon PPP model to Germany'.

Interestingly, Hueskes et al. (2019) articulated some 14 doctorates coming out of the Dutch network and partnership school led by Erik-Hans Klijn, Joop Koppenjan and others. These covered a range of topic areas, including:

- Political decision-making and public policy: Eversdijk on politics (2013), Sanders on policy legitimacy/decision-making (2013), Raeyners on public values (2015) and Willems on democratic accountability (2014)
- Success factors/management/conflicts: Lousberg on conflict prevention (2012), De Schepper on success factors (2014), Aerts on management and knowledge transfer (2015) and Verweij on management (2015)
- Contracts/negotiations/tenders: Hoezen on competitive dialogue negotiations (2012), De Clerck on the tender process (2015) and Van den Hurk on standardizing contracts (2015)
- Markets and planning: Lenferink on integrating markets and planning (2013), Verhees on adaptive planning (2013) and Leendertse on markets and infrastructure networks (2015)

And in Australia, several relevant doctoral theses on PPPs were completed, including those of Davies, who investigated the governance of alliances in terms of accountability, stewardship and transparency; Sturup on urban mega-project governance and decision-making; Kabir on successful PPP management in Australia; Atmo on private financing of Asian power-generation projects; and Biygautane on sense-making and power structures in PPP implementation.

These doctorates are listed in Table 1.2. This table illustrates the diversity, vibrancy and depth of PPP doctoral research familiar to the authors of this chapter. However, these represent only a small sample of all doctorates undertaken around the globe.[1] Indeed, there have probably been hundreds of doctoral theses completed on PPPs in the past decade alone.[2] Some of these scholars will continue into academic careers and see their research interests blossom, whilst others venture into industry work. This makes the future influence of any particular doctoral thesis or specific research approach tricky to predict. What we can say, though, is that although this table is not a systematic review, it is fascinating that the PPP arena is now clearly so rich in scholarship, contested in research priorities and crowded in possibilities for the future.

A gallery tour of key PPP publications

As our brief illustration of doctoral examples over the past decade or so indicated, there is clearly now a vast literature on infrastructure PPPs. But as with any research field, there are a number of well-cited articles that readers return to because of their seminal contribution. Newcomers to a field will often be pointed to these publications to get their bearings and understand what the field is based on. Our own early summary of the performance debate, 'Public–private partnerships: an international performance review', in *Public Administration Review* (Hodge and Greve 2007), seems to have become a reference point for many researchers exploring the elusive question of PPP performance. In the following section, we conduct the reader on our own little 'gallery tour',[3] in much the same way as Michael Barzelay (2019) does in his recent book on public management research, and we highlight those publications that we keep returning to for inspiration and learning.

Stephen Linder's (1999) article on 'the multiple grammars on PPPs' continues to inspire. Linder examined the PPP phenomenon from a language game perspective and showed the different usages of the PPP term early on. Any pieces on the 'public–private mix' from Ian Thynne and/or Roger Wettenhall

Table 1.2   Overview of PhD dissertations from the collegiate networks of the editors

No.	Author	Year	University	Topic	Method
Nordic/European **(other than Dutch and Flemish, below)**					
1	Weihe, G.	2009	Copenhagen Business School	PPPs: meaning and practice	Literature review and multiple case studies
2	Petersen, O.H.	2011	Copenhagen Business School	PPPs: policy and regulation	Comparative multi-level case studies from Denmark and Ireland
3	Stelling, C.	2014	Copenhagen Business School	PPPs and the need, development and management of trusting	Case studies of Danish and German service partnerships
4	Dam, S.	2015	Copenhagen Business School	PPPs for innovation and sustainability transformation	Embedded comparative case studies of municipal waste management in England and Denmark
5	Christensen, L.T.	2016	Copenhagen Business School	State-owned enterprises as institutional market actors in the marketization of public service provision	Comparative case study of marketization strategies for the Danish and Swedish national railway companies
6	Denta, S.M.	2017	Copenhagen Business School	Local government PPPs and regulation	Legal analysis of legislation and rules for PPPs in local government
7	Brogaard, L.	2017	Roskilde University	Public-private innovation partnerships	Survey of 260 Danish public-private innovation partnerships plus eight case studies
8	Liebe, M.	2017	Luxembourg	Political economy of PPPs in the European Union	Quantitative panel analysis of PPP uptake in the European Union 1990-2008 plus two in-depth case studies of the introduction of PPP legislation in Germany and France
9	Mihov, M.	2020	King's College London	The role of institutional work in the transplantation of the Anglo-Saxon PPP model to Germany	Case study of how Germany adopted the UK PPP model through institutional transplantation

No.	Author	Year	University	Topic	Method
Dutch/Flemish					
1	Hoezen, M.E.L.	2012	Twente	Public-private negotiations and commitments in the Competitive Dialogue	Policy analysis, survey, comparative multiple case study, single case study
2	Lousberg, L.H.M.J.	2012	Technische Universiteit Delft	Interventions to prevent dysfunctional conflicts in PPPs	Explorative case study, laboratory experiment, multiple case studies
3	Eversdijk, A.W.W.	2013	Maastricht	Political decision-making about PPPs	Document analysis, multiple case studies
4	Lenferink, S.	2013	Groningen	Market involvement in integration of the road infrastructure planning process	Four different multiple case studies
5	Sanders, M.	2013	Twente	Legitimacy in policy- and decision-making on PPPs in the energy sector	Three single case studies
6	Verhees, F.	2013	Groningen	Adaptive planning in PPPs	Literature study, multiple case studies
7	De Schepper, S.	2014	Brussels	Success factors of PPPs, focusing on the role of stakeholder management and transaction costs	Multiple case studies, statistical analysis
8	Reynaers, A.M.	2014	Amsterdam	Safeguarding public values in PPPs	Mutiple case studies
9	Aerts, G.	2015	Brussels	Knowledge transfer and management in PPPs	Multiple case studies, non parametric statistical analysis
10	De Clerck, D.	2015	KU Leuven	The tender process in PPPs	Game theoretic computer simulation experiments
11	Leendertse, W.	2015	Groningen	Market involvement in the management and development of public infrastructure networks	Single case study
12	Van den Hurk, M.	2015	Antwerp	Standardizing contracts in PPPs	Two single case studies

No.	Author	Year	University	Topic	Method
13	Verweij, S.	2015	Erasmus	Management of PPPs after contract close	Two single case studies, qualitative comparative analysis (QCA)
14	Willems, T.	2016	Antwerp	Democratic accountability in PPPs	Single case study
15	Pennink, C.	2017	Erasmus	Trust-building processes in PPPs	Comparative case study analysis of urban generation partnerships in the Netherlands, Poland and US
16	Warsen, R.	2021	Erasmus	Combining contractual and relational governance for successful PPPs	QCA
Australian					
1	Davies, J.P.	2008	Griffith	Governing alliances, accountability, stewardship and transparency	Case studies
2	Sturup, S.	2011	Melbourne	Urban mega-project governance and decision-making	Case studies
3	Kabir, H.M.	2012	Monash	Successful PPP management in Australia	Case studies
4	Chung, D.	2012	Sydney	Modelling and measuring risk toll road risk perceptions	Risk survey, triangulation of three theoretical lenses adopted, supported by multiple statistical analysis methods
5	Atmo, G.U.	2015	Melbourne	Private financing of Asian power-generation projects	Case studies
6	Biygautane, M.	2019	Monash	Power structures and sense-making in PPP implementation	Case studies in UAE, Saudi Arabia, Qatar and Kuwait

are always worth reading. They wisely remind us that partnerships are not in fact new, and that much public–private collaboration and plenty of 'mixes' have been going on for centuries. Tony Bovaird's early seminal work (Bovaird 2004a, 2004b), which he later expanded in our 2010 handbook (Hodge et al., 2010), covered the evolution of the PPP concept in its manyfold configurations. These also provide sure companions to go in our 'gallery', too, as the reader comes out much more enlightened and able to view the PPP phenomenon within a larger context.

From an economic perspective, the writings of Aidan Vining and Anthony Boardman have long inspired us. Their 2008 articles 'Public–private partnerships: Eight rules for government' and 'Public-private partnerships in Canada: Theory and evidence' discussed the promises and the many pitfalls that governments face when choosing PPPs. They later summed up their approach in our 2010 handbook when they discussed 'assessing the economic worth of PPPs'. Boardman and Vining's strong disciplinary expertise and cross-disciplinary and accessible communication demonstrate the way economists can, and should, contribute to interdisciplinary public policy debates in our view. Another publication from an economics perspective was Geddes and Wagner's 2013 article 'Why do U.S. states adopt public–private enabling legislation?' Geddes and Wagner explored which U.S. states had adopted legislation for PPPs and what that meant for the uptake of PPPs.

The question of performance of PPPs has haunted researchers for several decades now, and many fine empirical articles on the performance of PPPs and the effects of PPP policy have been coming out of Reeves and Palcic's work in Ireland. They continue to successfully marry economics perspectives to public policy challenges. The early provocative assertion of Erik-Hans Klijn (2008) that 'It's the management, stupid' encouraged a stimulating and rewarding debate about what determined PPP performance as well as emphasizing the language game connected to PPPs. And in later works, for example in 'Mix and match: How contractual and relational conditions are combined in successful public–private partnerships' with colleagues Warsen and Koppenjan from 2019, Erik-Hans and the Dutch and Belgian researchers systematically assessed and compared performance of PPPs empirically.

Crossing over to the subject of planning and geography, Matti Siemiatycki's article on how mega-projects for PPPs have evolved in Canada was influential and gains a spot in the gallery. His article from 2009 in the *Journal of the American Planning Association*, 'Delivering transportation infrastructure through public-private partnerships: planning concerns', provided important insights.

We could add many contributions to our gallery here, but we will note only a few more. Chris Skelcher's work (for example, Skelcher 2010) thinking about PPP governance has always been insightful, as has that of Mark Hellowell and Allyson Pollock in documenting the UK experience (for example, Hellowell and Pollock 2009). Added to this could also be the warnings of Shaoul,

Stafford and Stapleton (for example, Shaoul et al. 2012). And no gallery tour of infrastructure governance would be complete without the seminal work of Flyvbjerg on mega-projects and planning rationality (Flyvbjerg et al. 2003).

Whilst we finish our small gallery tour here, we anticipate that there will be other additions to the gallery of inspirational PPP research, and we also encourage special exhibitions in the future on particular themes within PPP research.

Reflections on the PPP and infrastructure governance research terrain and its evolution

In retrospect, the depth and width of the intellectual terrain now carved out in PPP research is perhaps not surprising. Conceptually, we have at least five intellectual domains to wrestle with as researchers. We first ask what precisely do we mean by 'public', by 'private', or by 'partnership'? This can vary wildly. The 'public' sector carries with it very different meanings if we compare the Arab Gulf states, China and Western liberal democracies. Second, the history of our PPP inquiry, whether focusing on words, infrastructure delivery methods or the role of private finance, can be revealing. Toll roads have formed a relatively uncontroversial subject of history going back thousands of years, but we also know that some issues (such as domestic violence, for example) can jump the boundary and cease being viewed as a private concern to become a prominent public concern demanding government action. Third, the jurisdiction and culture in which we dwell both matter. Governments direct their power and can implement very different solutions in different cultures with varying degrees of legitimacy. Fourth, when commenting on or analyzing PPP, scholarly disciplines each adopt very different theories of cause and effect and use different lenses, emphasizing particular values over others with vastly different background assumptions as to what matters most. Judging the relative success or failure of a PPP therefore can depend very much on the eyes through which we are looking, our values and our criteria for success. We know engineers usually emphasize completing the construction project, accountants emphasize accurate recording of resources, project managers emphasize staying within budget and delivering on time, economists emphasize doing this all with maximum efficiency, political representatives emphasize timely and high-profile delivery before the next election, public managers and leaders emphasize encouraging a more innovative public sector, and so on.

Figure 1.2 shows these dimensions, and illustrates the growing number of research questions possible as we traverse all of these domains. The number of possible questions is magnified five times if we recall that PPP has been conceptualized as meaning an infrastructure project to some people, a project delivery system to other people, a policy to others, a governing mechanism to yet others and even a label for other diverse meanings in other cultural contexts. If we look back at the recent questions we asked in setting our future research agenda (in Figure 1.1) they included five focal areas for future research:

1. What are the impacts of financializing infrastructure projects?
2. How does the presence of global PPP market actors influence PPP projects?
3. What are the consequences of international organizations promoting specific recommendations for PPPs?
4. How do governments govern their complex portfolio of PPP deals?
5. Why and how are PPPs becoming a preferred way of doing business in developing countries?

Figure 1.2   Expanding research interests

Our suggestions therefore covered project financialization, the global PPP industry, the influence of international actors, their application to developing countries and how governments govern the PPP portfolio. Each of these topics remains worthy for a global agenda. But the choice of these topic areas has also clearly been somewhat arbitrary. The world of research is unlimited, and our intellectual passions are different. Added to this complexity is also the temptation to extend the world of PPP and include other members of the extended PPP family into our research endeavours. This is admirable, but it clouds the 'evaluand'.[4] Examples of such inclusions in the past have been privatization (Broadbent and Laughlin 1999), economic development (Brinkerhoff and Brinkerhoff 2011) and asset recycling (Casady and Geddes 2020).

This all leaves us with a problem. How do we determine the highest-priority research questions for a future research agenda? Our answer is to provide some up-front conceptual frameworks, principles and provocations before we then ask the experts to define their continuing priority research areas along with new future themes. So, *what* do we now know, and *how* do we know these things?

What do we know now about PPP performance?

There is now a vast PPP knowledge base from which to draw international lessons. Articulating every one of these would be an intractable task though. A brilliant summary of our knowledge was put forward by Hueskes et al. (2019, 171). Their review of 14 PhD theses observed that PPPs had 'mixed results in terms of legitimacy and accountability', and they warned that 'PPP-projects do not automatically live up to their prospected advantages'. To their minds, 'it is not so much the PPP-arrangement (i.e. the contract) by itself that leads to high performance ... To a large extent, the success of PPP depends on how its users apply the arrangement in practice, on their skills, commitment, and on their collaborative behaviour.'

One particular recurring theme for many research agendas has concerned the relative performance of PPPs compared to 'traditional infrastructure delivery techniques', however construed. Much has been written trying to answer this simple question of PPP VfM (Hodge and Greve 2017). Despite the VfM criteria being central to the rationale of contemporary PPPs for almost three decades, there remains fierce contestation over the relative efficiency and value of PPP infrastructure delivery methods. The standout empirical reviews of Boers et al. (2013), Sarmento (2014) and Petersen (2019) are the 'go to' references here.

Boers et al. (2013, 470) reviewed 48 audit reports on DBFM(O) (design, build, finance, maintain (operate)) PPPs across 13 countries as their research base. They commented that their study did not give an opinion on, or question the use of, PPPs, but quoted the UK National Audit Office, saying that 'added value tests are prone to mistakes, manipulation and misuse (UK NAO 2009: 20)'. Equally, they commented that there is nonetheless no reason to believe that PPP projects are based on flimsier arguments or less reliable data than other types of contract, and that PPPs were now subject to greater scrutiny than other types of projects. Importantly, their overall assessment of PPP adoption was measured; 'there is still no hard evidence to show that DBFM(O) projects represent the most efficient form of government procurement'.

The outstanding academic research of Joaquim Sarmento (Sarmento 2014, Sarmento and Renneboog 2014) analyzed PPP risk allocation, valuation and VfM analyses from around the world. His review revealed major disparities between how academics assessed PPPs compared to the assessments of governments and auditors. Of the 40 academic papers reviewed, 25 studies concluded that PPPs generated VfM (whilst four concluded the opposite and 11 were unsure). Six of the seven government studies, though, concluded that PPPs generated VfM, whilst state audit offices were equally divided over VfM.[5] Sarmento's overall story here was clear: 'academics are sceptical concerning PPP ability for VfM generation, whereas governments are not'.

Petersen (2019) took a meta-analytic approach[6] to his review of global PPP performance findings, drawing on social science, engineering and economics databases. His data on PPP cost, quality and VfM was limited to peer-reviewed whole-of-life comparisons of PPPs against similar projects. He acknowledged the absence of control-group studies and experimental designs, but drew on 21 empirical studies in advanced industrialized countries from an initial potential list of 804 PPP publications. Only three of the 17 studies investigating PPP costs concluded that PPPs were less costly than traditional procurement, so his conclusion on this aspect was clear: 'the international peer-reviewed literature suggests that PPPs tend to be more costly than the conventional public procurement alternative' (p. 234). He also found extremely thin and mixed evidence on quality. And on the matter of PPP VfM, the strongest finding (in 12 studies) was that information for proper VfM evaluation was missing, whilst the remaining studies had mixed conclusions. Petersen's overall conclusion (p. 239) was that PPPs 'provide approximately similar VfM as conventional procurement'. Fortunately for the editors on this book, these VfM findings were to his mind 'broadly in line with the findings of previous assessments of the international experience (Hodge and Greve 2007, 2009).'

So, can we now simply go to the meta-reviews and believe them? Unfortunately, no. Systematic reviews such as Petersen's can be clear and transparent, but they equally rely on data which, as has been acknowledged, is far from the gold standard. Second, those simple matters of economy and efficiency turn out to be not so simple. Economists still argue amongst themselves as to the 'correct' way of evaluating PPP VfM and social value (Hodge and Greve 2019, 122).[7] We have even gone as far as arguing that 'it is almost impossible to judge the degree to which the promises of better PPP performance are actually delivered' and that relative efficiency and VfM will never be resolved as a consequence (Hodge and Greve 2019, 223). Continuing research will confirm whether this pessimistic assessment is true or not. Third, there are a wealth of other interesting characteristics of PPP planning, performance and operations which have attracted the attention of researchers. Many additional informed commentaries on these broader matters exist: Klijn et al. (2010), Verweij (2015), Kort et al. (2016), Warsen (2019) and Reynaers (2014). And there is clearly just as much contestation around these PPP issues as there is around the so-called 'simpler' matters of efficiency and economy.

Recent systematic literature reviews on how we know

Perhaps just as important as what we think we know is the matter of just how we think we know these things. Again, there have been a wealth of contributions from across the globe as to who is doing what PPP research, and the methods being adopted. If we again focus on one or two references here, we might build on the extensive review of Wang et al. (2018) as well as our own work in *Public Management Review* (Hodge et al. 2018). Wang et al.'s systematic review investigated how scholars from the public administration (PA) perspective look at PPP. Specifically, they asked two questions: what are the prevailing PPP themes in the PA journals, and what are the main contributions of those themes? They found 186 peer-reviewed articles in 22 PA journals and characterized this data by country, year, journal and author citations. They also analyzed the major theories adopted over the past 34 years to study PPP and articulated the 'main PPP issues' being studied.

They reported three major theoretical approaches in studying PPPs:[8] public management/public policy, economics and organizational management. The combined perspectives of public management and public policy scholars was the largest group and incorporated network-oriented theories (11 per cent), governance theories (8 per cent), New Public Management ideas (8 per cent), public choice theory (3 per cent) and policy transfer ideas (3 per cent). The economics perspective was almost as large, but included fewer theories: transaction costs theory (14 per cent), principal–agent theory (11 per cent) and property rights theory (5 per cent). The organizational management dimension included, for instance, institutional/neo-institutional theory (11 per cent), stakeholder theory (5 per cent) and organizational sense-making theory (3 per cent). This systematic review clearly shows that there have been a wide variety of lenses applied by PA scholars to analyse PPP thus far.

By analyzing the frequency with which various keywords co-occurred with the PPP phrase, Wang et al. (2018) also saw 35 main issues being addressed in the PA discipline. The highest-frequency issues were found to be 'performance'-related (for example, VfM, benefits, cost and public value) (frequency = 33), 'risk'-related (for example, risk allocation, risk types and risk-sharing) (n = 25), 'types of PPP'-related (n = 16), and 'drivers of PPP'-related (for example, motivation of the adoption of PPP policies) (n = 15). Again, this review points to the fact that PPP performance, its ambiguities and definitional concerns, the matter of risks and the motivations for adopting PPP have all formed important threads to date in our global PPP research.

The research agenda and the disciplines covered in this book

In this book, we are contemplating the issue of underpinning logics behind various research efforts given the knowledge that many disciplines have been contributing to PPP research. We nominated several of these logics for this book: public administration/public policy, political science, management/ business/project delivery, accounting and public finance, economics, psychology, geography/planning, law and behavioural science. Table 1.3 builds on the style of Hodge et al. (2018), but is developed for this book's content in order to show many of the relevant disciplinary domains, the underlying rationale and logic of each domain, typical performance criteria and examples of published research studies.

Again, this table also shows clearly that there is a wide variety of logics being applied to study PPP phenomena as well as a range of methodological techniques.

Getting to know more

So, how might we best bring together our reflections on what we now know and set some future directions and methodologies that PPP researchers should take? Again, can we simply turn to these 'go to' reviews to learn who is doing what research and what methods are being adopted to learn at the forefront of knowledge? Perhaps yes, but with much balance and care! Analogously to the Etzionian mixed scanning tradition,[9] we need to 'employ two cameras: a broad angle camera that would cover all parts of the sky but not in great detail, and a second one which would zero in on those areas revealed by the first camera to require a more in-depth examination' (Etzioni 1967, 389). This enables a synoptic view to be achieved – of being aware of specific empirical findings, but never losing sight of the overall picture. So, like the sailors of old times, PPP researchers always need to keep one eye on the horizon as we look through the telescope with the other in order to discern the details or the research topic on which we are focusing. Our research task has always been to gather as many clues from as many sources as possible, and put these together synoptically – with both eyes open. Like a good detective, multiple avenues are needed through which we can discern how the world behaves and why. Relying on one review, one method, or one author is likely to lead to less reliable conclusions.

The adoption of multiple methods makes sense. But we also ought to be simultaneously excited by new results as well as being wary of them. There is still a real need to carefully synthesize the research published to date and learn from the many empirical studies already completed, as well as undertaking new empirical work. Equally, there is also a need to adopt new research methods given the vast preponderance of case studies in Table 1.3. These challenges are as serious as they are unsettling.

Structure of this book

Throughout this introduction, we have tried to appeal to scholars to acknowledge different PPP logics and rationales, to welcome multiple research approaches from across many disciplines and to invite new views on 'what matters' in PPP research. After this initial scene-setting, this book wrestles immediately with two eternal issues. Chapter 2 (Klijn) tackles relevant theories and Chapter 3 (Warsen) deals with methodologies. We have invited all chapter authors to consider matters which they regard as not only currently important or 'state of the art', but also those issues which are likely in their judgement to be relevant for future scholarship. In other words, authors will be aiming to articulate matters of both current import as well as trends and likely future priorities.

Part II of the book aims to tackle head-on some of the new frontiers emerging from key PPP disciplines. Of course, any attempt at defining (or should we say 'divining') new research frontiers is more art and judgement than science. But in Part II, entitled 'New frontiers in a contested world', we took courage and decided that there were several areas with exciting future prospects. These

Table 1.3   Examples of various infrastructure PPP research approaches taken across the disciplinary bases of this research agenda book

Disciplinary base	Rationality/ overarching logic	Performance criteria/analytical contributions	Discipline examples	Typical research approaches adopted
Public administration/ public policy	Democratic governance and legitimacy	Sustenance and protection of the public interest Public accountability Risk prices paid Public governance Policy decision-making Complexity and capacity	Osborne (2000)	Multiple case studies
			Hodge and Greve (2013)	Case study
			Johnston (2010)	Survey study
			Van Gestel et al. (2012), and Delhi (2014)	Survey, and QCA
			Sayadat (2018)	Case studies
Political science	Democratic process Power and its use	Political success, interest groups, and private versus public influence	Greve (2003)	Case study
			Roberts (2010)	Case studies
			Flinders (2010)	Case studies
			Skelcher (2010)	Case studies

Disciplinary base	Rationality/ overarching logic	Performance criteria/analytical contributions	Discipline examples	Typical research approaches adopted
Management/ business/project delivery	Project delivery effectiveness and efficiency	Trust, co-ordination, teamwork Managerial strategy Institutional change On-time delivery On-budget delivery Risk allocation Critical success factors Sense-making and power	Alam et al. (2014)	Case studies
			Klijn (2008)	Case studies
			Kort et al. (2016)	QCA
			Steijn et al. (2011)	Survey
			Matos-Castaño et al. (2014)	Case studies
			Grimsey and Lewis (2004)	Case studies
			Yescombe (2007, 2013)	Policy analysis
			Hellowell and Vechi (2012)	Case studies
			Liu et al. (2016)	Survey
			Biygautane (2019)	Case studies
Accounting and public finance	Financial accountability	Balance sheet health (public and private) Finance costs and accountability Taxation impacts	Broadbent and Laughlin (2003)	Financial analysis of multiple case studies
			Demirag and Khadaroo (2013)	Case studies
			Shaoul et al. (2011, 2012)	Case studies
			Lehman and Tregoning (2004), Chung (2017)	Case studies
			Baker (2005)	Policy analysis

Disciplinary base	Rationality/ overarching logic	Performance criteria/analytical contributions	Discipline examples	Typical research approaches adopted
Economics	Efficiency Contract structure	Net economic gains Unit economic cost Total economic value	De Bettignies and Ross (2010)	Mathematical modelling from first principles
			Blanc-Brude et al. (2006)	Econometric analysis
			Geddes (2011)	Case studies
			Boardman and Vining (2010)	Multiple case studies
Psychology	The art of governing	Foucauldian mechanisms of control	Trapenberg Frick (2014)	Case study
			Sturup (2013)	Case studies
Geography, planning	Spatial and population relationships	Urban planning outcomes Mega-project planning	Siemiatycki (2013)	Case studies
			Gil (2017)	Comparative case study design
Law	Legal mechanisms of control	Legislative structure/ effectiveness Contractual sophistication/ characteristics	Hodge and Bowman (2004)	Case study
			Tvarnø (2010)	Legal analysis
Behavioural science	Personal decision-making	Arbitrary and unreliable decisions	Hodge and Greve (2019)	Policy analysis/ review

Source: Adapted from Hodge et al., 2018

included new frontiers in economics (Chapter 4 by Vinogradov and Shadrina), politics (Chapter 5 by Bertelli and Woodhouse), psychology (Chapter 6 by Sturup), behavioural science (Chapter 7 by Zwalf), PA (Chapter 8 by Christensen and Greve), city planning (Chapter 9 by Siemiatycki) and law (Chapter 10 by Tvarnø and Denta). We would be happy for much discussion and debate on these choices – particularly as many of the world's recent disruptors were not foreseen by older academics!

Having said that, of course, wisdom from political science and public policy – and indeed many disciplinary arenas – is likely to remain crucial for some time yet in governing well. This was the basis for Part III, which focuses more on a series of themes which we as editors believe are worthy of closer examination in future. These themes include financialization (Chapter 11 by Stafford, Smyth and Almeida), pension funds (Chapter 12 by Foster and Hodge), market maturity (Chapter 13 by Casady), the political economy of PPP ideas (Chapter 14 by Liebe), institutional and policy transfer (Chapter 15 by Mihov), and state-owned enterprise (Chapter 16 by Palcic and Reeves). The final part of the book, Part IV, brings together some conclusions.

Although we are pleased with the spread of disciplines and topics, some potential themes were not included due to lack of space. PPPs from other parts of the world is one such example. In this volume we restricted ourselves mainly to Western liberal democratic polities, and the place of PPPs within this context. Given the centrality of political dynamics to PPPs, there is clearly a world of knowledge to be gained from coverage of other political systems and cultures. We have also restricted ourselves primarily to looking at PPPs from the perspective of governments, whereas PPPs as seen from the perspective of employers, employees, the infrastructure users and the citizens are just as important. These are all important topics that will merit future attention.

Conclusions

This introduction has briefly sketched the lineage of the global research agenda over the past two decades, and observed that PPP research has been broadened, deepened and sharpened. There have been many dedicated special issues on PPPs in key journals along with multiple PhD theses written across the globe.

We commented that this is not surprising given our interests in language, history, jurisdictional matters of culture and law, as well as the use of different theoretical lenses and differing values in our search for better understanding the PPP phenomenon and its performance. Fortunately, cross-disciplinary learning has progressively become more routine. Yet, simple issues such as PPP efficiency and economy remain hotly contested, despite the existence now of several global reviews of PPP. Other aspects of PPP operations and performance also remain widely debated. We also looked briefly at some of the key overarching logics governing our PPP research.

We aimed in this introductory chapter to set the terrain for the various chapter authors to build on. Hopefully, it balanced purpose, provocation, promise and praise. Scholarship in this book comes from Australia, Canada, China, Denmark, Ireland, Italy, the Netherlands, Russia, the UK and the US. Bringing together authors from ten countries and as many disciplines is always an exciting and stimulating exercise. We trust that readers from across the globe will find the book just as interesting and rewarding.

Notes

1. Importantly, inspirational and sophisticated studies have sometimes come from far-away places. The doctoral work of Delhi (2014) on Indian PPP institutions and governance, and Sayadat (2018) on PPP decision-making in Bangladesh, are two shining examples.
2. Using the two search terms 'public private partnership' and 'infrastructure' in early 2021, the Proquest database yielded 84 relevant doctorates after 2010. This particular search, however, yielded only a few of the dozens of doctorates over this same period known to the co-authors of this chapter. This suggests that the number of relevant doctorates in the infrastructure PPP field over the past two decades is probably in the order of hundreds.
3. We much prefer Barzelay's visual analogy of the 'gallery' (full of paintings which we will always wish to remember and enjoy) rather than the possible alternative of the 'museum' (full of quaint historical relics and artefacts)!
4. The evaluand is the object of an evaluation (Hodge 2010, 85).
5. The European Court of Auditors' (2018) report four years later was less equivocal, characterizing European Union PPPs as having 'widespread shortcomings and limited benefits'.
6. Hodge (2000) emphasized the unreliability of traditional narrative reviews of past research. He argued that many research areas did not so much need more primary research studies, but 'some means of making sense of the vast number of accumulated study findings'. This is the aim of meta-analysis. Coined through the work of Glass (1976, 3), meta-analysis is 'the analysis of analyses' and seeks to 'discipline research synthesis by the same methodological standards that apply to primary research' (Cook et al. 1992, viii), with clarity, explicitness and openness when integrating findings from multiple studies.
7. Economists still dispute, for example, the discount rate, the calculation of VfM, the valuation of risks and the impacts and importance of contract re-negotiations.
8. Additional minor theoretical perspectives also included regime and coalition perspectives (5 per cent), managerialism, corporatist, low growth and welfare (5 per cent), resource dependency (3 per cent), sustainability (3 per cent) and spatial contagion (3 per cent).
9. Etzioni (1967) contemplated the seminal decision-making models of Herb Simon and Charles Lindblom. On the one hand, he viewed Herb Simon's idealistic 'rational' decision-making model as inadequate because decision-makers neither had the money to collect the information required nor did they possess a single set of agreed values on which to evaluate alternatives. To Etzioni, such rationalistic models were 'unrealistic and undesirable' (Etzioni 1967, 386). On the other hand, though, Lindblom's disjointed incrementalism model (for which 'the measure of a good decision is the decision makers' agreement'), was also viewed as inadequate because this model implied that there could be no one single 'right' decision – just 'a "never ending series of attacks" on the issues at hand through serial analyses and

evaluation' (Etzioni 1967, 387). His solution was to propose 'the mixed scanning approach', employing a broad-angle camera simultaneously alongside a close-up camera for in-depth examination. To him, this approach was 'more realistic and more effective than its components'.

References

Alam, Q., Kabir, M.H., and Chaudhri, V. (2014) Managing infrastructure projects in Australia: A shift from a contractual to a collaborative public management strategy. *Administration and Society*, *46*(4): 422–449. https://doi.org/10.1177/0095399712459728.

Baker, R. (2005) Public policy implications of tax-exempt leasing in the United States. *International Journal of Public Policy*, *1*(1–2): 148–161.

Barzelay, M. (2019) *Public Management as a Design-Oriented Professional Discipline*. Cheltenham, UK and Northampton, MA, USA: Edward Elgar Publishing.

Biygautane, M. (2019) *Institutions and Infrastructure Public-Private Partnerships (PPPs): How Individual and Organizational Actors Affect the Initiation and Implementation of PPPs*, unpublished doctoral thesis, Monash University, Melbourne.

Blanc-Brude, F., Goldsmith, H., and Valila, T. (2006) *Ex Ante Construction Costs in the European Road Sector: A Comparison of Public-Private Partnerships and Traditional Public Procurement*. Economic and Financial Report 2006/01. Luxembourg: European Investment Bank.

Boardman, A., and Vining, A. (2010) Assessing the economic worth of public–private partnerships, in *International Handbook on Public–Private Partnerships*, edited by G.A. Hodge, C. Greve and A.E. Boardman. Cheltenham, UK and Northampton, MA, USA: Edward Elgar Publishing, pp. 159–186.

Boers, I., Hoek, F., Montfort, C.V., and Wieles, J. (2013) Public-private partnerships: International audit findings, in *The Routledge Companion to Public-Private Partnerships*, edited by P. de Vries and E.B. Yehoue. Oxford: Routledge, pp. 451–478.

Bovaird, T. (2004a) Public–private partnerships in Western Europe and the US: New growths from old roots, in *Public–Private Partnerships: Policy and Experience*, edited by Abby Ghobadian, David Gallear, Nicholas O'Regan and Howard Viney. Basingstoke: Palgrave Macmillan, pp. 221–250.

Bovaird, T. (2004b) Public–private partnerships: From contested concepts to prevalent practice. *International Review of Administrative Sciences*, *70*(2): 199–215.

Brinkerhoff, D.W., and Brinkerhoff, J.M. (2011) Public–private partnerships: Perspectives on purposes, publicness, and good governance. *Public Administration and Development*, *31*(1): 2–14.

Broadbent, J., and Laughlin, R. (1999) The private finance initiative: Clarification of a research agenda. *Financial Accountability and Management*, *15*(2): 95–114.

Broadbent, J., and Laughlin, R. (2003) Public private partnerships: An introduction. *Accounting, Auditing and Accountability Journal*, *16*(3): 332–341.

Casady, C., and Geddes, R. (2020) Asset recycling for social infrastructure in the United States. *Public Works Management and Policy*, *25*(3): 1–17. https://doi.org/10.1177/1087724X20911652.

Chung, D. (2017) Private provision of public services: The case of Australia's motorways, in *The Oxford Handbook of Megaproject Management*, edited by B. Flyvbjerg. New York, NY: Oxford University Press, pp. 519–538.

Cook, T.D., Cooper, H., Cordray, D.S., Hartmann, H., Hedges, L.V., Light, R.J., Louis, T.A., and Mosteller, F. (1992) *Meta-Analysis for Explanation: A Case Book.* New York, NY: Russell Sage Foundation.

De Bettignies, J., and Ross, T. (2010) The economics of public–private partnerships: Some theoretical contributions, in *International Handbook on Public–Private Partnerships*, edited by G.A. Hodge, C. Greve, and A. Boardman. Cheltenham, UK and Northampton, MA, USA: Edward Elgar Publishing, pp. 132–158.

Delhi, V.S.K. (2014) *Relating Institutions and Governance Strategies to Project Outcomes: A Study on Public-Private Partnerships in Infrastructure Projects in India*, doctoral thesis, Indian Institute of Technology, Madras.

Demirag, I.S., and Khadaroo, I. (2013) Accountability and public-private partnership contracts: Un mariage de convenance?, in *The Routledge Companion to Public-Private Partnerships*, edited by P. de Vries and E.B. Yehoue. Oxford: Routledge, pp. 439–450.

Etzioni, A. (1967) Mixed-scanning: A 'third' approach to decision-making. *Public Administration Review, 27*(5): 385–392.

European Court of Auditors (2018) *Public Private Partnerships in the EU: Widespread Shortcomings and Limited Benefits.* Special report 09/2018. Luxembourg: European Court of Auditors.

Flinders, M. (2010) Splintered logics and political debate, in *International Handbook on Public–Private Partnerships*, edited by G.A. Hodge, C. Greve and A.E. Boardman. Cheltenham, UK and Northampton, MA, USA: Edward Elgar Publishing, pp. 115–131.

Flyvbjerg, B. (2007) Cost overruns and demand shortfalls in urban rail and other infrastructure. *Transportation Planning and Technology, 30*(1): 9–30.

Flyvbjerg, B., Bruzelius, N., and Rothengatter, W. (2003) *Megaprojects and Risk: An Anatomy of Ambition.* Cambridge: Cambridge University Press.

Flyvbjerg, B., Holm, M.K.S., and Buhl, S.L. (2002) Underestimating costs in public works projects: Error or lie? *Journal of the American Planning Association, 68*(3): 279–295.

Geddes, R. (2011) *The Road to Renewal: Private Investment in U.S. Transportation Infrastructure.* Washington, DC: AEI Press.

Geddes, R.R., and Wagner, B.L. (2013) Why do U.S. states adopt public–private partnership enabling legislation? *Journal of Urban Economics, 78*: 30–41.

Gil, N. (2017) A collective-action perspective on the planning of megaprojects, in *The Oxford Handbook of Megaproject Management*, edited by B. Flyvbjerg. Oxford: Oxford University Press, pp. 259–286.

Glass, G. (1976) Integrating findings: The meta-analysis of research. *Educational Researcher, 5*(10), pp. 3–8.

Greve, C. (2003) When public–private partnerships fail: The extreme case of the NPM-inspired local government of Farum in Denmark. Paper for the EGPA conference, 3–6 September, Oeiras, Portugal.

Grimsey, D., and Lewis, M. (2004) *Public–Private partnerships: The Worldwide Revolution in Infrastructure Provision and Project Finance.* Cheltenham, UK and Northampton, MA, USA: Edward Elgar Publishing.

Hellowell, M., and Pollock, A.M. (2009) The private financing of NHS hospitals: Politics, policy and practice. *Economic Affairs, 29*(1): 13–19.

Hellowell, M., and Vecchi, V. (2012) An evaluation of the projected returns to investors on 10 PFI projects commissioned by the National Health Service. *Financial
Accountability and Management, 28*(1): 77–100. https://doi.org/10.1111/faam.2012
.28.issue-1.

Hodge, G.A. (2000) *Privatisation: An International Review of Performance*. Boulder,
CO: Westview Press.

Hodge, G.A. (2010) Reviewing public–private partnerships: Some thoughts on eval-
uation, in *International Handbook on Public–Private Partnerships*, edited by G.A.
Hodge, C. Greve and A.E. Boardman. Cheltenham, UK and Northampton, MA,
USA: Edward Elgar Publishing, pp. 81–112.

Hodge, G.A. (2013) Public-private partnership: Ambiguous, complex, evolving and successful, keynote address to global challenges in PPP: Cross-sectoral
and cross-disciplinary solutions? Paper presented on 6–7 November, Belgium:
Universiteit Antwerpen, City Campus, Hof Van Liere.

Hodge, G.A., and Bowman, D. (2004) PPP contractual issues: Big promises and unfin-
ished business, in *Public Private Partnerships: Policy and Experience*, edited by A.
Ghobadian, D. Gallear, N. O'Regan and H. Viney. London: Palgrave, pp. 201–219.

Hodge, G.A., and Greve, C. (2007) Public–private partnerships: An international performance review. *Public Administration Review, 67*: 545–558.

Hodge, G.A., and Greve, C. (2008) The PPP debate: Taking stock of the issues and
renewing the research agenda. Paper presented at International Research Society for
Public Management Annual Conference, Brisbane, Australia, 26–28 March.

Hodge, G.A., and Greve, C. (2009) PPPs: The passage of time permits a sober reflection.
Economic Affairs, 29(1): 33–39.

Hodge, G.A., and Greve, C. (2013) Public–private partnership in turbulent times, in
Rethinking Public–Private Partnerships: Strategic Approaches for Turbulent Times,
edited by C. Greve and G. Hodge. Oxford: Routledge, pp. 1–32.

Hodge, G.A., and Greve, C. (2017) On public–private partnership performance: A contemporary review. *Public Works Management and Policy, 22*(1): 55–78.

Hodge, G.A., and Greve, C. (2018) Contemporary public–private partnership: Towards
a global research agenda. *Financial Accountability and Management, 34*(1): 3–16.

Hodge, G.A., and Greve, C. (2019) *The Logic of Public–Private Partnerships: The Enduring
Interdependency of Politics and Markets*. Cheltenham, UK and Northampton, MA,
USA: Edward Elgar Publishing.

Hodge, G.A., Greve, C. and Biygautane, M. (2018) Do PPPs work? What and how have
we been learning so far? *Public Management Review, 20*(8): 1105–1121.

Hodge, G.A., Greve, C., and Boardman, A.E. (Eds) (2010) *International Handbook on
Public–Private Partnerships*. Cheltenham, UK and Northampton, MA, USA: Edward
Elgar Publishing.

Hueskes, M., Koppenjan, J., and Verweij, S. (2019) Public-private partnerships for
infrastructure: Lessons learned from Dutch and Flemish PhD-theses, *EJTIR, 19*(3):
160–176.

Johnston, J. (2010) Examining 'tunnel vision' in Australian PPPs: Rationales, rhetoric,
risks and 'rogues'. *Australian Journal of Public Administration, 69*(s1): S61–S73.

Klijn, E.-H. (2008) *It's the Management, Stupid! On the Importance of Management in
Complex Policy Issues*. The Hague: Uitgeverij LEMMA.

Klijn, E.-H., Steijn, B., and Edelenbos, J. (2010) The impact of network management on
outcomes in governance networks. *Public Administration, 88*(4): 1063–1082. https://
doi.org/10.1111/j.1467-9299.2010.01826.x.

Kort, M., Verweij, S., and Klijn, E.-H. (2016) In search for effective public-private partnerships: An assessment of the impact of organizational form and managerial strategies in urban regeneration partnerships using fsQCA. *Environment and Planning
C: Government and Policy*, 34: 777–794. https://doi.org/10.1177/0263774X15614674.

Lehman, G., and Tregoning, I. (2004) Public–private partnerships, taxation and a civil
society. *Journal of Corporate Citizenship*, 15(Autumn): 77–89.

Linder, S. (1999) Coming to terms with the public-private partnership: A grammar of
multiple meanings. *American Behavioural Scientist*, 43(1): 35–51.

Liu, T., Wang, Y., and Wilkinson, S. (2016) Identifying critical factors affecting the
effectiveness and efficiency of tendering processes in public–private partnerships
(PPPs): A comparative analysis of Australia and China. *International Journal of
Project Management*, 34(4): 701–716.

Matos-Castaño, J., Mahalingam, A., and DeWulf, G. (2014) Unpacking the
path-dependent process of institutional change for PPPs. *Australian Journal of
Public Administration*, 73(1): 47–66. https://doi.org/10.1111/1467-8500.12062.

Osborne, S. (Ed.) (2000) *Public-Private Partnerships*. London: Routledge.

Petersen, O.H. (2019) Evaluating the costs, quality, and value for money of infrastructure public-private partnerships: A systematic literature review. *Annals of Public and
Cooperative Economics*, 90(2): 227–244.

Reynaers, A.-M. (2014) Public values in public-private partnerships. *Public
Administration Review*, suppl. Special Issue, 74(1): 41–50.

Roberts, A. (2010) *The Logic of Discipline: Global Capitalism and the Architecture of
Government*. New York, NY: Oxford University Press.

Sarmento, J.M. (2014) *Public Private Partnerships*, doctoral thesis, Tilberg School of
Economics and Management, University of Tilberg.

Sarmento, J.M., and Renneboog, L. (2014) *Public-Private Partnerships: Risk Allocation
and Value for Money*. Discussion paper 2014-22, CentER, Tilburg University.

Sayadat, N. (2018) *A Study on Process-Based Public-Private Partnership (PPP)
Performance: PPP Policy Implementation Experience in Bangladesh*, doctoral thesis,
Tribhuvan University, Kathmandu, Nepal.

Shaoul, J., Stafford, A., and Stapleton, P. (2011) NHS capital investment and PFI:
From central responsibility to local affordability. *Financial Accountability and
Management*, 27(1): 1–17.

Shaoul, J., Stafford, A., and Stapleton, P. (2012) Accountability and corporate governance of public private partnerships. *Critical Perspectives on Accounting*, 2(3):
213–229.

Siemiatycki, M. (2009) Delivering transportation infrastructure through public-private
partnerships: Planning concerns. *Journal of the American Planning Association*,
76(1): 43–58.

Siemiatycki, M. (2013) Is there a distinctive Canadian PPP model? Reflections on twenty
years of practice. Paper delivered to CBSUBC–Monash International Workshop on
PPPs, 13–14 June, Vancouver.

Skelcher, C. (2010) Governing partnerships, in *International Handbook on Public–
Private Partnerships*, edited by G.A. Hodge, C. Greve and A.E. Boardman.
Cheltenham, UK and Northampton, MA, USA: Edward Elgar Publishing,
pp. 292–304.

Steijn, B., Klijn, E.-H., and Edelenbos, J. (2011) Public private partnerships: Added value
by organizational form or management? *Public Administration*, 89(4): 1235–1252.

Sturup, S. (2013) A Foucault perspective on public–private partnership mega projects, in *Rethinking Public–Private Partnerships: Strategies for Turbulent Times*, edited by C. Greve and G. Hodge. New York, NY: Routledge.

Thynne, I. (Ed.) (1995) *Corporatisation, Divestment and the Public-Private Mix: Selected Country Studies.* Hong Kong: AJPA in collaboration with IASIA.

Trapenberg Frick, K. (2014) Pursuing the technological sublime: How the Bay Bridge became a megaproject. *Access,* 44: 22–27.

Tvarnø, C. (2010) Law and regulatory aspects of public–private partnerships: Contract law and public procurement law, in *International Handbook on Public–Private Partnerships,* edited by G.A. Hodge, C. Greve and A.E. Boardman. Cheltenham, UK and Northampton, MA, USA: Edward Elgar Publishing, pp. 216–236.

UK National Audit Office (2009) Private Finance Project. Paper for the Lords Economic Affairs Committee, October.

Van Gestel, K., Voets, J., and Verhoest, K. (2012) How governance of complex PPPs affects performance? *Public Administration Quarterly, 36*(2): 140–188.

Verweij, S. (2015) Producing satisfactory outcomes in the implementation phase of PPP infrastructure projects: A fuzzy set qualitative comparative analysis of 27 road constructions in the Netherlands. *International Journal of Project Management,* 33(2015): 1877–1887.

Vining, A.R., and Boardman, A.E. (2008) Public–private partnerships: Eight rules for governments. *Public Works Management and Policy, 13*(2): 149–161.

Vining, A.R., and Boardman, A.E. (2008) Public-private partnerships in Canada: Theory and evidence. *Canadian Public Administration, 51*(1): 9–44.

Wall, A., and Connolly, C. (2009) The private finance initiative: An evolving research agenda. *Public Management Review, 11*(5): 707–724.

Wang, H., Xiong, W., Wu, G., and Zhu, D. (2018) Public–private partnership in public administration discipline: A literature review. *Public Management Review, 20*(2): 293–316. https://doi.org/10.1080/14719037.2017.1313445.

Warsen, R. (2019) Explaining trust in public-private partnerships: A qualitative comparative analysis (QCA) of 25 public-private partnerships in the Netherlands and Belgium. Paper delivered at the XXIII Annual Conference of the International Research Society for Public Management, 16–18 April, Wellington, New Zealand.

Warsen, R., Klijn, E.-H., and Koppenjan, J. (2019) Mix and match: How contractual and relational conditions are combined in successful public–private partnerships. *Journal of Public Administration Research and Theory, 29*(3): 375–393. https://doi .org/10.1093/jopart/muy082.

Weigrich, K., Kosta, G., and Hammerschmid, G. (Eds) (2017) *The Governance of Infrastructure.* Oxford: Oxford University Press.

Wettenhall, R., and Thynne, I. (1999) Emerging patterns of governance: Synergy, partnerships and the public private mix. *Asian Journal of Public Administration, 21*(2): 157–178.

Yescombe, E.R. (2007) *Public-Private Partnerships: Principles of Policy and Finance.* London: Butterworth-Heinemann.

Yescombe, E.R. (2013) PPPs and project finance, in *The Routledge Companion to Public-Private Partnerships,* edited by P. de Vries and E.B. Yehoue. Oxford: Routledge, pp. 227–246.

2 Theories of public–private partnerships

Erik-Hans Klijn

The many faces of PPP: emergence and forms

Discussing the theoretical roots of public–private partnerships (PPPs) is more difficult than it appears at first sight. This is because PPP is a hybrid. It contains ideas from various theoretical orientations, and, in practice, arguments are freely used from various different theories to justify PPP use and acclaim its value and effectiveness. To complicate matters even more, we find a wide array of organizational arrangements that are called PPPs and an equally wide range of mechanisms to govern PPPs, and these various governance mechanisms are justified by drawing upon various theoretical literature strands. PPPs can be roughly defined as 'more or less sustainable cooperation between public and private actors in which joint products and/or services are developed and in which risks, costs and profits are shared' (Klijn and Teisman 2003, 137).

The emergence and transformation of PPPs

Although the discussion and the literature may sometimes give the impression that PPPs suddenly emerged in the 1990s – and especially in the UK with the Private Finance Initiative (PFI) scheme – this is of course not true. We have had PPPs for centuries.

A famous example is the VOC (United East Indian Company), which was founded in 1602 in the Netherlands. The VOC (whose connection with the darker sides of colonialism is beyond the scope of this chapter) was founded and financed by a group of private merchants together with the municipality of Amsterdam. Its aim was to undertake trade and shipping activities in the Far East, for which it erected trading posts in several countries, and for a long time it was one of the largest and most important players in trade between the Far East and Europe. The municipality of Amsterdam owned 50 per cent of the company, and, in turn, the VOC was involved in the building and restructuring of the city of Amsterdam. The city's town hall, which was completed in 1662, stands as a symbol of the cooperation between public and private actors.

Thus, PPPs date back a long time, but it is clear that the discussion received a boost in the 1990s. Most authors point especially at the PFI in the UK, which started in the early 1990s and has dominated the PPP discussion in both practical and scientific terms (Osborne 2000, NAO 2002, Ghobadian et al. 2004, Hodge and Greve 2005, Weihe 2008). In the PFI context, long-term, integrated contracts are developed, and, with the help of these contracts, public actors tender out the design, building, financing, maintenance, and possibly the operating of a public project to a private consortium (Hodge et al. 2010). In this version, innovation contracting is the most important element and partnership is translated into a long-term contracting relationship between a public and a private partner. Added value is created because the private partner is able to bid on a more generalized formulated set of requirements, can profit from the long-term contract, and can economize on construction and maintenance.

The PPP idea then spread to other countries and to international organizations and consultants (OECD 2008, World Bank 2017) as a magical idea to 'try at home'. The version that was transferred internationally was the PFI Design-Build-Finance-Maintain-(Operate) (DBFM(O)) version of PPP and the strong economic theoretical ideas behind it; but, of course, as in all policy transfers, the core PPP ideas were, and still are, adopted and implemented differently.

An interesting glimpse at this is provided in the article by Warsen et al. (2020), who analysed the PPP assumptions in three countries (the Netherlands, Canada, and Denmark), using Q methodology, in which statements are presented to a group of respondents to analyze their perceptions on a topic. It turned out that professionals from Canada and the Netherlands in particular had quite different ideas about how to govern PPPs. Whereas in Canada in general professionals tend to favour a New Public Management (NPM) orientation – where performance criteria and monitoring (and rewards and punishment) are more dominant – in the Netherlands professionals tend to emphasize much more a governance approach, characterized by collaboration and adapting the contract to the situation.

This can be interpreted in at least two different ways, which are probably both true. The first one is that, even though countries take the same version (the DBFM(O) version) of it, the PPP idea is transformed in line with the (political) culture in a country – Canada having a more Anglo-Saxon political culture and the Netherlands having a more consensual culture. It is also clear, however, that various different theoretical ideas underpin the PPP phenomenon and that these ideas also lead to different forms and appearances of PPP. This is what we want to highlight in this chapter: the different theoretical ideas and assumptions that seem to underpin the PPP discussion.

Different forms of PPP and their theoretical inspiration

To complicate matters even more, talking about PPP is certainly confusing, as there are many forms and authors refer to many different things when they talk about PPP. This holds both for the practice of PPP, where many varieties of cooperation can be seen, and for the scientific literature, which identifies many forms of PPP. In the PPP literature, two main dimensions underlying the various types of partnership can be distinguished (Osborne 2000, Hodge and Greve 2005, Klijn 2010):

1. The (formal) organization of the partnership: here, the question is the degree to which the partnership is organized in a strongly formalized form (a contract or a newly set-up organization) or through a more loosely coupled cooperation (like a network).
2. The nature of the relationship between the public and the private actors: here, the question is whether the partnership can be characterized as a more vertical principal–agent relation or a more horizontal relation.

Combining these dimensions (Table 2.1) results in four forms of public–private relationships: two forms (1 and 3) where relations between public and private partners are characterized more by vertical relations where governmental bodies, despite the fact that long-term cooperation exists, commission the activities to be performed; and two forms where relations between public and private actors are more horizontal. Although in most of the literature only forms 3 and 4 are generally considered as real PPP forms, the table provides an overview of possible collaborations between public and private organizations.

If we omit the first form (private implementation), which comes very close to ideas of privatization and implementing policy through private organizations and involves less partnership, we are left with three partnership forms that emerge in the literature (and in PPP research). Each of these forms seems to find its main inspiration in different theoretical orientations.

The second type of PPP, network-like partnership, refers to principal–principal relations with a loosely coupled organizational form. This type of PPP has a network-like character with intense interaction between public and private actors in a weakly developed institutional setting. It can be found in complex

Table 2.1   A typology of forms of public-private relationships

Type of relation / Organizational form	Principal-agent relation	Principal-principal relation (partnership)
Loosely coupled	1. Private implementation Interaction between public and private actors in implementing governmental policies and providing public services Limited collaboration Governments determine objectives and conditions for implementation	2. Network-like partnerships Developing policies, planning, or coordinating activities Loosely coupled collaboration. Examples: preventive health networks for obesity, area development, or other networks where public and private or semi-private actors work together on more or less equal terms
Tight organizational form	3. Contractual partnerships Collaboration is to a large extent determined by the contract, mostly in the form of a DBFM(O) contract	4. Consortium Partners form a new organizational entity that implements a service or product (such as urban regeneration companies)

Source: Adapted from Klijn (2010)

and enduring processes of development and decision making in urban restructuring (see, for instance, the literature on brown field development in the US and planning literature about urban regeneration in several countries; ODPM 2004). The theoretical inspiration for this section of the literature comes from various sources but mainly from planning theory, such as the governance capacity literature (see Healy 2003), the collaborative governance literature (Ansell and Gash 2008, Emerson and Nabatchi 2015), and the network governance literature (Kickert et al. 1997). Furthermore, the US literature in particular also taps into different theoretical ideas like negotiating (Susskind and Cruikshank 1987) and frame reflection between public and private partners (Forester 1989, Fischer 2003).

The third type of partnership, contractual partnership, has a fairly tight, contractual organizational form and a principal–agent relationship. PPP projects and services are regulated by a long-term contract, such as a DBFM(O) contract, which is probably the best-known example of this form. These PPPs are inspired by the UK's PFI that gained popularity from the 1980s onwards.

The core idea is that shifting the financial risk to the private consortium will create strong incentives to deliver and maintain the project within time, budget, and scope. The integrated nature of the contract motivates the private consortium to take the full lifecycle into account when designing the project. This, it is argued, allows for innovative solutions and the realization of efficacy gains, thus creating added value. The extended contract periods (20, 25 years and more) allow the private parties to recoup their investments. Collaboration between public and private parties in this type of PPP is strongly regulated by a contract.

Theoretical inspiration for this form of PPP comes mainly from economic theory, especially principal–agent theory, which emphasizes the importance of sanctions and monitoring, but contractual theory and transaction theories are also popular backups to the ideas and claims of the effectiveness of this form of PPP (Williamson 1996, Deakin and Michie 1997).

The fourth type of PPP, the consortium, displays a principal–principal relationship between public and private actors who together create and finance a more or less independent organizational form, like a joint public–private venture. This type of PPP is sometimes also called an institutional PPP (or alliance). Examples include the urban regeneration companies (ODPM 2004, Kort and Klijn 2011) that are emerging in various countries. Here, intensive interactions occur between the two partners that jointly develop and organize projects, services, or policies. In doing so, they share a common goal (or at least a set of goals) and associated benefits and risks.

Theoretical inspiration comes partly from the same theories as network-like partnerships, although related theories like alliance theories and resource dependency theories are also important sources of inspiration (Rogers and Whetten 1982, Borys and Jemison 1989, Provan and Kenis 2008).

So, looking at PPP's theoretical inspiration, we see three main theoretical sources: an economic orientation, a governance/collaboration orientation, and a frame/institutional orientation. The three perspectives are discussed in more depth in the next section.

Three theoretical orientations on PPP

As PPPs are more an empirical phenomenon than a theoretical perspective, it is not surprising to see a number of different theoretical orientations used in

PPP research and analysis. Moreover, as argued in the previous section, three dominant orientations can be distinguished: an economic one, a governance one, and an orientation that emphasizes frames and the different institutional backgrounds of public and private actors.

From the literature, we can see that, in general, the monitoring economic perspective is the most dominant. Wang et al. (2018) conclude in an overview of PPP articles in public administration journals that about 40 per cent have a strong economic flavour regarding theoretical orientation, as opposed to only about 20–25 per cent favouring a governance or collaborative approach (sensemaking and institutional theories make up about 15 per cent). One can expect these figures to be even more in favour of the economic perspective in other (more economics-oriented) journals. We discuss each of the three perspectives first and then compare them.

PPP as a monitoring game: economic perspectives on PPP

In the DBFM(O) version of PPP, partnerships are presented as long-term contracts. Various phases of a project, like the design, building, financing, maintenance, and commercial operation of a public road or a public building like a school, hospital, prison, or governmental office are integrated into one contract (a DBFM(O) contract), with the aim of realizing a lifecycle approach (NAO 2002). The added value lies in the lower costs of coordination between the various components (often expressed as efficiency or value-for-money gains) and in the realization of design optimizations aimed at creating innovations that reduce costs in the building, maintenance, and operation phases. In this vision of PPP, the game is essentially one of monitoring. The public actor agrees a long-term contract with a private consortium, monitors the private consortium's performance, and uses the contract as a potential penalty instrument if the performance is not up to standard.

The core idea: checking for opportunistic behaviour

The core idea for that vision of PPP comes from NPM ideas, which are of course dominated by a strong economic line of reasoning. NPM has been dominant in public administration since the 1980s as a reaction to flaws in traditional Weberian public administration (Hughes 2012). In NPM, the idea is that governments should focus on the formulation of public policy and leave the implementation to other bodies (agencies at arm's length, private organizations, or non-profit organizations) (Osborne and Gaebler 1992). A separation between policy formulation and policy implementation should be encouraged by privatization, outsourcing, agentification, and a stronger emphasis on market mechanisms and the involvement of private actors (Hood 1991). Public actors should control implementation by competition, contracts, and the use of performance indicators and performance measurement. This, of course, is strongly inspired by economic theories like principal–agent theory (Jensen and Meckling 1976) and transaction cost economics (Williamson 1996). In this line of thought, PPPs are seen as relations between a principal (the public actor that initiates and commissions the project/service) and an agent (the private consortium that realizes the product/service). That relation is determined by opportunistic behaviour and (incomplete) information collection. The principal needs to know how the agent is performing but also needs to have information to monitor the agent's behaviour. The agent, however, has more detailed information about the job performed and will try to hide that information, as it provides the agent with a better position and more possibilities to underperform (because the principal cannot correctly judge the agent's performance and monitor that performance).

Another important condition that is very relevant from the economic perspective on PPP is the complexity of the task. When transactions are infrequent and investments are undertaken by specific partners, there is a need either for more complex contracts that specify all eventualities that may occur given the unique and complicated nature of the project at hand, or for additional governance mechanisms (like investment in extensive management efforts). Williamson (1979), one of the godfathers of neo-institutional economics, remarks:

> Whenever investments are idiosyncratic in nontrivial degree, increasing the degree of uncertainty makes it more imperative that the parties devise a machinery to "work things out" – since contractual gaps will be larger and the occasions for sequential adaptations will increase in number and importance as the degree of uncertainty increases.

As a solution, he proposes the following:

> Two possibilities exist. One would be to sacrifice value design features in favor of a more standardized good or service. Market governance would then apply. The second would be to preserve the design but surround the transaction with an elaborate governance apparatus, thereby facilitating more effective adaptive, sequential decision making. (p. 185)

Of course, choosing the first option would imply renouncing the potential of added value (actually it implies choosing another type of solution/product), and the second option entails at least additional transaction costs. The specific investments (knowledge, money, material) made by partners in a PPP make those partners vulnerable (Deakin and Michie 1997, Nooteboom 2002).

Specific investments are investments in activities or products that cannot be used easily in other projects. This makes the investing partner dependent upon the other partner. This dependence may lead to opportunistic behaviour on the part of the other partner during the implementation of the contract. Examples include the other party possibly trying to wriggle out of obligations, taking short cuts, economizing on quality, or changing contract conditions. Information asymmetries mean that clients or principals are especially vulnerable to agents' opportunistic behaviour (in this case, private partners) (Jensen and Meckling 1976). Thus, it is crucial that the contractor (the principal) is able to monitor and sanction the contractee (the agent) if the latter does not deliver the promised product or the promised quality. In an economic perspective on PPP, the contract and the possible sanctions that the contract offers are thus crucial to mitigate opportunistic behaviour.

Causes of PPP failure and how to solve them

Thus, the main causes of failure in an economic perspective on PPP are connected to incomplete information and to the principal's inability to check for and punish the agent's opportunistic behaviour; this is more urgent when the task is complex and the dependence is high. Furthermore, DBFM(O) contracts are usually long-term (some of them 30 years) and of course then entail high interdependence (and complexity).

Most solutions for failures in an economic perspective relate to information collection and the possibilities to correct the agent (Deakin and Michie 1997, Nooteboom 2002), thus improving the monitoring process. Of course, information collection is limited given the bounded rationality assumption in most economic perspectives. Information may simply not be available or too costly to gather and an actor's opportunities to collect information are thus not endless, but the contract and the penalties inherent in the contract are the key management mechanism to govern PPPs in an economic perspective (Savas 2000, Hodge et al. 2010).

In some of the economic literature about relational contracting, much emphasis is laid on limitations of the contract and the necessity to develop relational quality (trust relations between the partners, intensive interaction, and so on) to adapt the contract and manage it throughout the contract period (Deakin and Michie 1997, Poppo and Zenger 2002, Brown et al. 2016). In this literature on relational contracting, the importance of trust is emphasized (Nooteboom 2002, Poppo and Zenger 2002, Warsen et al. 2019), which, among the hardliners of neo-institutional economics, is rejected as a governance mechanism (for a plea against trust, see Williamson (1996), who thinks that trust is a redundant and confusing concept and that it is all about risk-taking). The perspective in that branch of literature comes much closer to the collaborative orientation discussed in the next section.

PPP as complex collaboration: network and collaborative orientations on PPP

In the second theoretical orientation, networks, PPP is seen as a collaborative process. This perspective is very different from the economic perspective. It is not so much opportunistic behaviour that is the central focus (although this perspective would not deny that aspect), but rather the difficulties (and advantages) that a collaboration process brings (Huxham and Vangen 2005, Ansell and Gash 2008, Klijn and Koppenjan 2016a). PPPs are seen as complex collaborative processes that need constant nurturing rather than opportunistic relation of partners that need to control each other by contracts.

The core idea: facilitating cooperation

The core idea of what we would call the governance perspective on PPP is that PPP is in essence a complex collaborative process between various actors. Although the collaboration is guided mostly by contractual obligations, these are in no way enough to foresee all the complex issues and interactions that will occur during the lifetime of the collaboration (Warsen et al. 2019). Thus, even when the PPP is strongly contractually organized (as in the case of a DBFM(O)), PPPs still remain complex projects and complex processes that cannot be controlled by a contract.

The collaborative or network governance perspective emphasizes that collaboration between actors is characterized by a constant tension between cooperation and conflict (Huxham and Vangen 2005, Emerson and Nabatchi 2015, Klijn and Koppenjan 2016a). Cooperation is needed because actors are dependent on each other's resources and only bringing these resources together can realize mutual benefits, or collaborative advantage, as Huxham and Vangen (2005) call it. Conflicts arise because actors have different interests and different perceptions on the partnership and its main focus and content; and, as actors in the partnership are autonomous and choose their own strategies on the basis of their interests and perceptions, conflicts are likely (Klijn and Koppenjan 2016a).

Thus, despite the contractual relationship, partners will constantly strategize (as also recognized in the economic perspective) and react to emerging events during the partnership (Klijn and Teisman 2003). This results in constant dynamics and complexity as one of the main characteristics of all partnerships. Such dynamics and complexity will be enhanced by external events like economic crises, political events, and so forth, and other factors (like technical problems in the case of infrastructural projects). Thus, PPP projects can never be tackled adequately by contracts that are agreed upon at the project's start. No matter how detailed that contract is, it can never foresee the dynamics and complex events that will emerge in a partnership. Even worse, if the contract is too detailed, it is probably an obstacle to tackling the complexity inherent in all partnerships (Huxham and Vangen 2005). The more detailed a contract is, the less likely it is to be able to deal with unexpected events and developments during the partnership (Deakin and Michie 1997, Nooteboom 2002, Warsen et al. 2019).

In this perspective, the importance of trust is emphasized (see Ansell and Gash 2008, Warsen et al. 2018). If innovative products or services or policy outcomes have to be achieved, information exchange between partners is crucial. Of course, opportunistic behaviour and the risk of actors using the information for their own interests are a threat to this. Most authors in the governance perspective emphasize that the development of a minimum level of trust is very important for success because then trust acts as an alternative coordination mechanism to contracts and penalties (Lane and Bachman 1998, Nooteboom 2002, Warsen et al. 2018); and trust facilitates both cooperation and information exchange, which are both crucial for successful partnerships. Research conducted so far seems to support this assumption (see, for instance, Warsen et al. 2018).

Thus, the core idea of the collaborative perspective on PPP is that, for successful partnership, it is necessary to facilitate collaboration and to cope with complexity and new developments in the partnership. It is not the contract and the penalties that are the core of the PPP, but rather the (intelligent) way in which actors deal with the emerging dynamics and how the contract and the daily problems are managed.

Causes of PPP failure and how to solve them

Partnership failures in a governance/collaborative perspective on PPP result mainly from core characteristics of the complex and dynamic elements of partnerships, like the partners having views that are (too) different, problems in coordinating the partners' different strategies, and the complexity of the strategic interaction, all of which make it difficult to keep the partnership alive and focused.

Various preconditions, apart from the abovementioned trust relations, have been identified as important to make partnerships a success, such as a certain convergence of perceptions and/or a shared understanding (the two have much in common, of course), the partners' commitment, intense contact, and ground rules accepted by the partners (see, for instance, Huxham and Vangen 2005, Ansell and Gash 2008, Emerson and Nabatchi 2015, Klijn and Koppenjan 2016a). Probably the most important, however, is intensive (network) management (Ansell and Gash 2008, Klijn and Koppenjan 2016a). If PPPs are complex projects with unforeseen developments, the only way this can be addressed is by intensive management that connects the partners; explores different perceptions with them; and tries to find common ground and connect them, achieve win-win situations, and organize additional ground rules to mitigate problems in interactions (Gage and Mandell 1990, Kickert et al. 1997, McGuire and Agranoff 2011, Klijn and Koppenjan 2016a). Thus, in the collaborative perspective on PPP, partnerships are pictured as complex and dynamic vehicles that need constant nurturing. So, the collaborative perspective will argue that the main success factor is active and effective management of the partnership that:

1. Fosters and enhances the core conditions for success (trust, intensive contacts, shared meaning) and
2. Coordinates the partners' activities and solves problems that occur along the way (like conflicts, unexpected events, additional coordination problems).

PPP as a frame discussion and a language game: sensemaking orientations on PPP

Forester, in his book *Planning in the Face of Power* (1989), analyses cooperation between public and private partners in environmental projects and presents the cooperation between public and private actors as a frame discussion. Each of the partners speaks a very different language and operates from very different frames. So, what is needed is frame reflection, where actors' frames are made explicit and discussed. The message of this third perspective is that partnerships need a lot of discussion and verbal interaction to explicate expectations, ideas, and also stereotypes to make them work.

The core idea: PPPs as sensemaking

Holding that perspective, Forester belongs to an honourable and long-standing tradition of scholars who emphasize the importance of frames over other factors in cooperation. As mentioned, this perspective argues that actors view the world through frames that they have created in their interactions and that are part of their crucial actor characteristics (Schön and Rein 1994, Fischer 2003, Hajer and Wagenaar 2003). These frames (or perceptions, or world views; different concepts are used for this idea) determine how actors in a partnership view the problem that needs to be tackled through the partnership, how partnerships are organized, and so on. Thus, differences in frames between the partners have strong consequences for how partnerships function. It is also a perspective that emphasizes the importance of learning as a means towards organizational performance (Schön and Rein 1994). A distinction is often made between single- and double-loop learning (Argyris and Cohen 1976). Only with double-loop learning do organizations really adapt their way of thinking (and their fundamental goals), whereas single-loop learning concerns only their learning on a strategic level. So, partnerships in this perspective are also vehicles for learning to perform better, for which frame reflection and forms of learning are essential. Interestingly, in this perspective, sometimes various layers of frames are also distinguished. Sabatier and Jenkins-Smith (1993) argue that actors have core beliefs, which are more difficult to change. This reflects other authors who distinguish levels in actors' argumentation structures between more technical (superficial) levels and more fundamental levels, including values and ideologies (Fischer 2003).

With this, a more institutional orientation in the sensemaking perspective comes into view, where actors' frames are related to, and partly shaped by, institutional factors. Jacobs (1992) presents us with a slightly more pessimistic version of this institutional version of the sensemaking perspective. She argues that public and private actors have fundamentally different world orientations that actually clash. Jacobs describes the public and the private domain as two fundamentally different ethical systems with different moral syndromes. According to her, the public domain is characterized by a guardian syndrome. Typically, the guardian syndrome, along with a tendency towards fatalism, includes:

• Avoiding trade and commerce
• Striving for discipline and loyalty
• Respecting tradition and hierarchy.

This contrasts with the commercial syndrome that is typical for the private sector and characterized by:

• Avoiding violence
• Competition

- Honesty
- Achieving agreement on a voluntary basis.

Jacobs argues that moral syndromes belong to survival systems and that these systems are very different. Now, perhaps Jacobs' version of institutional sense-making seems somewhat extreme, but it does point to fundamentally different ways of thinking (rooted in organizations' institutional rules and culture) between public and private partners that might cause serious problems in the partnership.

Klijn and Teisman (2003), for instance, accepting Jacobs' dichotomy, have argued that in PPPs one sees very different public- and private-actor strategies as a result of these actors' institutional backgrounds. Private actors search for certainties about production and try to minimize political and societal risks (and lay them with the public actor). Public actors want to guarantee substantive influence and minimize expectations and the risk of additional implementation costs. Staying within budget and minimizing political risks is important (as, also, is maintaining control) and even more important than efficiency. Both actors' strategies make it very hard to achieve added value, because the clash of the two strategies leads to hesitation and difficulties in cooperation. Public actors focus on limiting risks and on agreements that secure control and safeguard public values. Private partners focus on the certainty of market share and profit and hold back on investments until the contract with public actors is acquired. Thus, institutionally solidified ways of thinking obstruct partnership coordination and have to be overcome.

Causes of PPP failure and how to solve them

In the sensemaking perspective on PPP, failure is the result of different frames between partners and the consequences that this has for daily interaction and understanding. Of course, on the basis of the previous section, there are almost two versions of this – one where failures can be overcome by good frame reflection and interaction between the partners, and one, the more institutional one, that is more pessimistic and emphasizes that partners come from two different worlds and that cooperation will be difficult. This arises because, in the latter situation, forms of double-loop learning are necessary, where actors change some of their core beliefs. Solving the problem of PPP failures, however, is very much a matter of clarifying misunderstandings that originate from different frames.

Comparing the three perspectives

Table 2.2 summarizes the three perspectives and provides an overview of their main differences. Looking at the similarities and the differences, one could say that the first two perspectives both emphasize strategic behaviour and inter-actions between partners. The main differences are that PPP as a monitoring game emphasizes control and punishment, whereas PPP as collaboration emphasizes the need for collaboration and managing that process. PPP as sensemaking shares the idea about collaboration with the second perspective and also the need for intensive interaction. What the collaborative and sense-making perspectives also share is their orientation towards innovation in PPPs. In these two perspectives, innovation should come from sharing information, pooling resources, and enhancing creativity by confronting different ideas. In the perspective of PPP as a monitoring game, on the other hand, innovation comes from the right economic incentives. So, innovation must be rewarded. The economic perspective is present in many publications about the PFI PPP projects in the UK in the 1990s (NAO 2002).

Conclusion and reflection: where to from here in PPP?

In this chapter, we have discussed three perspectives on PPP: a monitoring perspective, which has a strong economic flavour; a collaborative perspective, which has a strong governance flavour; and a sensemaking perspective, which has a strong organizational learning and frames flavour. All three perspectives offer distinctly different views on how PPPs are organized and function, and their main potential problems.

It could be argued that the three perspectives are very different and not com-patible with one another, but they can also be seen as complementary. Thus, each perspective displays an important dimension of PPPs and reveals possible problems that could lead to failure.

What does research tell us?

Case studies seem to be dominant in PPP research and much of the literature is even based on single case studies. Research that uses large number of observa-tions, like survey research that uses larger numbers of respondents or research that uses large numbers of cases for comparison, is scarce. Interestingly, some research seems to indicate that contract characteristics do not correlate significantly with PPP performance (Klijn and Koppenjan 2016b). There are

Table 2.2   Three perspectives on PPP

	PPP as a monitoring game	PPP as collaboration	PPP as sensemaking
Orientation	Economic/ opportunistic behaviour	Complex interactions between partners	Partners' frames
Causes of failure	Incomplete information for the principal	Lack of interaction and complexity of coordination	Different frames and lack of connection between them
Innovation in PPP	Result of right (economic) incentives	Result of interaction and pooling of resources and information; trust essential	Confronting various views and connecting them
PPP process	Opportunistic interactions between partners	Complex interactions of autonomous actors in changing environment	Information and communication between actors
PPP management	Getting the contract right, penalties and incentives	Arranging interactions through organizational arrangements, connecting actors, facilitating information exchange, and so on	Explicating and connecting various frames
Theories used in perspective	Economic and contract theory: Principal-agent theory, transaction cost economics, contract theory	Governance theory: (Network) governance, collaborative governance, alliance theories, resource dependency theories	Organizational theory: Organizational learning, frame reflection, institutional theories

also signs that, in both conditions, the contract and relational and managerial factors are necessary for good performance (Poppo and Zenger 2002, Reeves 2008, Warsen et al. 2019). However, the relational dimensions (trust, managerial activities) are certainly a crucial factor, and the economic perspective alone is not sufficient to explain PPP performance; this much is probably clear after a few decades of PPP research.

Of course, one of the core questions is whether PPPs, in the DBFM(O) version or another version, do better than the classical way of contracting and organizing services and governmental assets like roads, railways, bridges, and so on (Hodge and Greve 2017). Unfortunately, this question is not easy to answer, as we have never implemented an experimental design in which we tendered the service in one area through a DBFM(O) contract and in another area through, for instance, a design and construct (D and C) contract. However, benchmarking, for instance DBFM(O) against more or less similar projects in a D and C context, is probably the way forward in our PPP research (Petersen 2019). A systematic analysis of all 21 infrastructure projects of the Ministry of Infrastructure in the Netherlands and benchmarking them against more or less similar projects in a D and C context showed that DBFM(O) projects did not perform badly (Koppenjan et al. 2020). Based on this research where diverse data were collected (financial project data from the ministry, interviews, and survey data), the financial results show that the DBFM(O) cost overruns seem to be lower (despite the projects being larger than the D and C projects). No significant differences in performance were found in the survey results, but there was a significantly better performance in terms of innovations in the DBFM(O) projects compared to the D and C projects (although the scores for both types of project were fairly low on innovation). This research, however, was conducted in only one country, and we definitely need more of this kind of research for other countries (see also Willems et al. 2017).

Combining perspectives

This brings us back to the discussion about whether the perspectives are mutually exclusive or add to one another. Although the basic assumptions of the three perspectives are fairly different and the economic perspective in particular differs from the other two, it is not impossible to connect them with one another. The empirical results discussed in the previous section also suggest that the perspectives can generate useful insights when combined. In that reasoning, contracts are not so much the only game in town, but rather governance mechanisms that need to be supplemented with a lot of relational management to really work. The perspectives will then be combined more and more to explain PPP processes and outcomes. This will consequently result in the economic perspective having a slightly less dominant position in PPP research.

The future theoretical development of PPP research

The three perspectives tend to focus on the functioning of the PPP itself, although the collaborative perspective also shows some interest in the wider environment surrounding PPPs. So far however, most PPP research has been focused on PPPs as projects and on their performance and characteristics. As already mentioned, these PPP projects and how they are implemented are very dependent on the environment in which they are implemented. This can be the national culture, as mentioned in the introduction, but also aspects like the (national) PPP policy that structures concrete PPP interactions (Soecipto and Verhoest 2018), stakeholder composition (and stakeholders' passion about the issue at stake), and the wickedness of the issue, but also the specific history of the PPP project under study. So, in one way or another, more dimensions must be included in our PPP research, along with research methods that allow for a more in-depth examination of the various conditions that can affect PPP performance. Qualitative comparative analysis (see also Warsen's chapter in this book) could be one of the methods that can be used for this. Very likely, a focus on the environment in which PPP projects take place will lead PPP scholars to add other theoretical frameworks to their research, such as complexity theories, and theories about democracy and participation, but also more institutional theories. The field will be in flux in the coming years, as we will be looking for a more fine-grained analysis that enables us to further uncover the mystery of PPP performance.

References

Ansell, C., and Gash, A. (2008). Collaborative governance in theory and practice. *Journal of Public Administration Research and Theory*, 18(4): 543–571.

Argyris, C., and Cohen, M. D. (1976). Single loop and double loop models in research on decision making. *Administrative Science Quarterly*, 21(3): 363–375.

Borys, B., and Jemison, D. B. (1989). Hybrid arrangements as strategic alliances: Theoretical issues in organizational combinations. *Academy of Management Review*, 14(2): 234–249.

Brown, T. L., Potoski, M., and Van Slyke, D. M. (2016). Managing complex contracts: A theoretical approach. *Journal of Public Administration Research and Theory*, 26(2): 294–308.

Deakin, S., and Michie, J. (Eds) (1997). *Contract, Co-operation, and Competition: Studies in Economics, Management and Law*. Oxford: Oxford University Press.

Emerson, K., and Nabatchi, T. (2015). *Collaborative Governance Regimes*. Washington, DC: Georgetown University Press.

Fischer, F. (2003). *Reframing Public Policy: Discursive Politics and Deliberative Practices*. Oxford: Oxford University Press.

Forester, J. (1989). *Planning in the Face of Power*. Berkeley, CA: University of California Press.

Gage, R. W., and Mandell, M. P. (Eds) (1990). *Strategies for Managing Intergovernmental Policies and Networks*. New York, NY: Preager.

Ghobadian, A., Gallear, D., O'Regan, N., and Viney, H. (Eds) (2004). *Public–Private Partnerships: Policy and Experience*. Basingstoke: Palgrave.

Hajer, M., and Wagenaar, H. (Eds) (2003). *Deliberative Policy Analysis: Understanding Governance in the Network Society*. Cambridge: Cambridge University Press.

Healy, P. (2003). Building institutional capacity through collaborative approaches to urban planning. *Environment and Planning A, 30*: 1531–1546.

Hodge, G. A., and Greve, C. (2005). *The Challenge of Public–Private Partnerships*. Cheltenham, UK, and Northampton, MA, USA: Edward Elgar Publishing.

Hodge, G. A., and Greve, C. (2017). On public–private performance: A contemporary review. *Public Works Management and Policy, 22*(1): 55–78.

Hodge, G. A., Greve, C., and Boardman, A. E. (Eds) (2010). *International Handbook on Public–Private Partnerships*. Cheltenham, UK, and Northampton, MA, USA: Edward Elgar Publishing.

Hood, C. (1991). A public management for all seasons. *Public Administration, 69*(Spring): 3–19.

Hughes, O. E. (2012). *Public Management and Administration: An Introduction* (4th ed.). Basingstoke: Palgrave Macmillan.

Huxham, C., and Vangen, S. (2005). *Managing to Collaborate: The Theory and Practice of Collaborative Advantage*. London: Routledge.

Jacobs, J. (1992). *Systems of Survival*. London: Random House.

Jensen, M., and Meckling, W. (1976). Theory of the firm: Managerial behavior, agency costs and capital structure. *Journal of Financial Economics, 3*: 305–360.

Kickert, W. J. M., Klijn, E.-H., and Koppenjan, J. F. M. (Eds) (1997). *Managing Complex Networks: Strategies for the Public Sector*. London: SAGE.

Klijn, E.-H. (2010). Public–private partnerships: Deciphering meaning, message and phenomenon. In G.A. Hodge, C. Greve and A. E. Boardman (Eds), *International Handbook on Public–Private Partnerships* (pp. 68–80). Cheltenham, UK, and Northampton, MA, USA: Edward Elgar Publishing.

Klijn, E.-H., and Koppenjan, J. F. M. (2016a). *Governance Networks in the Public Sector*. London: Routledge.

Klijn, E.-H., and Koppenjan, J. F. M. (2016b). The impact of contract characteristics on the performance of public–private partnerships (PPPs). *Public Money and Management, 36*(6): 455–462.

Klijn, E.-H., and Teisman, G. R. (2003). Institutional and strategic barriers to public–private partnership: An analysis of Dutch cases. *Public Money & Management, 23*(3): 137–146.

Koppenjan, J. F. M., Klijn, E.-H., Duijn, M., Klaassen, H. L., Van Meerkerk, I. F., Metselaar, S. A., Warsen, R., and Verweij, S. (2020). *Leren van 15 jaar DBFM-projecten bij RWS: Eindrapport*. Rotterdam: Rijkswaterstaat en Bouwend Nederland.

Kort, M., and Klijn, E.-H. (2011). Public–private partnerships in urban renewal: Organizational form or managerial capacity. *Public Administration Review, 71*(4): 618–626.

Lane, C., and Bachman, R. (1998). *Trust Within and Between Organizations: Conceptual Issues and Empirical Applications*. Oxford: Oxford University Press.

McGuire, M., and Agranoff, R. (2011). The limitations of public management networks. *Public Administration, 89*(2): 265–284.

NAO (National Audit Office) (2002). *Managing the Relationship to Secure a Successful Partnership in PFI Projects*. London: NAO.

Nooteboom, B. (2002). *Trust: Forms, Foundations, Functions, Failures and Figures*. Cheltenham, UK, and Northampton, MA, USA: Edward Elgar Publishing.

ODPM (Office of the Deputy Prime Minister) (2004). *Urban Regeneration Companies: Guidance and Qualification Criteria*. London: ODPM.

OECD (Organisation for Economic Co-operation and Development) (2008). *Public–Private Partnerships: In Pursuit of Risk Sharing and Value for Money*. www.oecd.org/gov/budgeting/public-privatepartnershipsinpursuitofrisksharingandvalueformoney.htm.

Osborne, D., and Gaebler, T. (1992). *Re-Inventing Government: How the Entrepreneurial Spirit Is Transforming the Public Sector*. Reading, MA: Addison-Wesley.

Osborne, S. P. (Ed.) (2000). *Public–Private Partnerships: Theory and Practice in International Perspective*. London: Routledge.

Petersen, O. H. (2019). Evaluating the costs, quality, and value for money of infrastructure public–private partnerships: A systematic literature review. *Annals of Public and Cooperative Economics*, 90(2): 227–244.

Poppo, L., and Zenger, T. (2002). Do formal contracts and relational governance function as substitutes or complements? *Strategic Management Journal*, 23(8): 707–725.

Provan, K. G., and Kenis, P. (2008). Modes of network governance: Structure, management, and effectiveness. *Journal of Public Administration Research and Theory*, 18(2): 229–252.

Reeves, E. (2008). The practice of contracting in public private partnerships: Transaction costs and relational contracting in the Irish schools sector. *Public Administration*, 86(4): 969–986.

Rogers, D. L., and Whetten, D. A. (Eds) (1982). *Interorganizational Coordination: Theory, Research, and Implementation*. Ames, IA: Iowa State University Press.

Sabatier, P. A., and Jenkins-Smith, H. C. (1993). *Policy Change and Learning: An Advocacy Coalition Approach*. Boulder, CO: Westview Press.

Savas, E. S. (2000). *Privatization and Public–Private Partnerships*. New York, NY: Seven Bridges.

Schön, D. A., and Rein, M. (1994). *Frame Reflection: Toward the Resolution of Intractable Policy Controversies*. New York, NY: Basis Books.

Soecipto, R. M., and Verhoest, K. (2018). Contract stability in European road infrastructure PPPs: How does governmental PPP support contribute to preventing contract renegotiation? *Public Management Review*, 20(8): 1145–1164.

Susskind, L., and Cruikshank, J. (1987). *Breaking the Impasse: Consensual Approaches to Resolving Public Disputes*. New York, NY: Basic Books.

Wang, H., Xiong, W., Wu, G., and Zhu, D. (2018). Public–private partnership in public administration discipline: A literature review. *Public Management Review*, 20(2): 293–316.

Warsen, R., Greve, C., Klijn, E.-H., Koppenjan, J. F. M., and Siemiatycki, M. (2020). How do professionals perceive the governance of public–private partnership? Evidence from Canada, the Netherlands, and Denmark. *Public Administration*, 98: 124–139.

Warsen, R., Klijn, E.-H., and Koppenjan, J. F. M. (2019). Mix and match: How contractual and relational conditions are combined in successful public–private partnerships. *Journal of Public Administration and Theory*, 29(3): 375–393.

Warsen, R., Nederhand, J., Klijn, E.-H., Grotenbreg, S., and Koppenjan, J. F. M. (2018). What makes public–private partnerships work? Survey research into the outcomes and the quality of cooperation in PPPs. *Public Management Review*, 20(8): 1165–1185.

Weihe, G. (2008). Ordering disorder: On the perplexities of the partnership literature. *Australian Journal of Public Administration*, 67(4): 430–442.

Willems, T., Verhoest, K., Voets, J., Coppens, T., Van Dooren, W., and Van den Hurk, M. (2017). Ten lessons from ten years PPP experience in Belgium. *Australian Journal of Public Administration*, 76(3): 316–329.

Williamson, O. E. (1979). Transaction cost economics: The governance of contractual relations. *Journal of Law and Economics*, 22(2): 233–261.

Williamson, O. E. (1996). *The Mechanisms of Governance*. London: Oxford University Press.

World Bank (2017). *Public-Private Partnerships: Reference Guide*. World Bank. https://openknowledge.worldbank.org/handle/10986/29052. License: CC BY 3.0 IGO.

3 The use of research methods in public–private partnership research

Rianne Warsen

Introduction

In past decades the use of public–private partnerships (PPPs) has increased in many countries throughout the world. It is often considered an efficient way of contracting out and realizing public goods and services, in particular transport infrastructures such as roads and railways, and social infrastructure like hospitals, schools, or prisons. Following the example of the UK and its Private Finance Initiative, many countries have adopted PPPs over the years (Wettenhall 2008). International organizations, such as the European Commission and the World Bank Group, have paid attention to PPP as an instrument to provide public goods and services, even – or maybe in particular – when public funds are limited (European Commission n.d.; World Bank 2018). The interest in PPPs of governmental bodies on various levels is reflected in the research on this topic. Just like the actual use of PPP, research into these partnerships and their performance has been growing as well over the past years. Several reviews exemplify this (for example, Osei-Kyei and Chan 2015, Tang et al. 2010, Wang et al. 2018).

Research into PPPs is diverse in many respects. First, it addresses a great variety of topics, including – but not limited to – the different models of PPP (Hodge and Greve 2013), PPP policy (for example, Ghobadian et al. 2004), performance (for example, Hodge and Greve 2017), and the governance and management of PPPs (for example, Benitez-Avila et al. 2018, Edelenbos and Klijn 2009, Warsen et al. 2020). The variety of topics can be explained by looking at the different disciplines that address PPP as one of their research topics. Scholars from disciplines such as construction and engineering, transport, health, public administration and management, economics, and urban studies undertake PPP research. A second source of diversity stems from PPP being an international phenomenon. Research comes from and focuses on a great range of countries. The countries dominating PPP research are the UK and the US, but also Australia, Canada, and several Western European countries – such as Ireland, Spain, Italy, and the Netherlands – are particularly well represented in PPP research (see, among others, Roehrich et al. 2014, Torchia et al. 2015, Wang et al. 2018). However, PPP research is not confined to Western countries. Cui et al. (2018) identify studies stemming from 56 different countries covering six continents. Quite a substantial part of PPP research nowadays focuses on PPP in Asian countries, including China, India, Korea, and Malaysia, but there is also an increase in studies visible in other parts of the world, including studies on PPP in Egypt, Lebanon, and Uganda (for example, Alinaitwe and Ayesiga 2013, Helmy et al. 2020, Jamali 2004). As such PPP can truly be considered a global research topic.

In terms of both diversity and scholarly attention, there is, however, one aspect of PPP research that seems to be lagging behind. This concerns the use of research methods. Little has been written about the use of various research methods in PPP research. This chapter aims to address this lacuna in two ways. First, it aims to give an overview of the past and current methodological trends in PPP research. Second, it explores a number of research methods that have been – until now – only sparsely used in our studies of PPPs. A closer look into these promising methods helps to determine whether they can contribute to future PPP research and the development of PPP as a research area. More diversity in research methods may enrich our knowledge of PPPs, help to address new research questions, and provide a new perspective to existing topics within PPP research. Note that in this chapter I will use the term 'methods', referring to tools and techniques for research, and not so much the term 'methodology', which refers to the ontological and epistemological positions that underpin a research question (see Haverland and Yanow 2012).

The outline of this chapter is as follows. The next section provides a comprehensive overview of the most commonly used methods in PPP research thus far, addressing four dominant methods in some more detail. Next, the third section focuses on a number of less commonly used methods in PPP research. I briefly discuss what each method entails and present several benefits and drawbacks of the given method. This section also provides examples of studies on PPPs that have already applied these methods. These frontrunners illustrate the potential of these methods for PPP research. Finally, the conclusion aims to identify some lessons on the use of methods in PPP research.

Current use of research methods in public–private partnership studies

To provide an overview of the most commonly used methods in PPP research thus far, one needs to review the existing body of empirical studies on PPPs. This chapter builds upon twelve existing reviews of PPP studies, ranging from traditional reviews and commentaries to systematic literature reviews and bibliographic analysis. Some of these reviews provide a broad overview of the present state of affairs in PPP research (see, for example, Hodge and Greve 2007, Narbaev et al. 2020, Roehrich et al. 2014). Other reviews have a rather specific focus on a particular topic, sector, or discipline (see, for example, Torchia et al. 2015, Wang et al. 2018, and Zhang et al. 2016). Altogether, the reviews paint a clear and consistent picture regarding the use of methods, both in different disciplines and for PPP research in general (see Table 3.1), as almost all reviews highlight the same methods.

Based on the reviews, we can conclude that case study research and survey research are the two dominant methods in primary PPP research. Furthermore, a literature review is a frequently used method. Many other additional reviews and theoretical and conceptual studies on PPPs have been published (for example, Bovaird 2004, Broadbent et al. 2003, Hueskes et al. 2019, Roehrich et al. 2014). However, in this chapter the focus lies on methods designed to collect and analyze empirical data in PPP research. That is, primary PPP research, where the researcher gathers their own data as the basis for their analysis. Finally, the use of mixed methods is also frequently mentioned. In some studies, this entails a combination of qualitative (interviews) and quantitative (questionnaires) data-collection methods, sometimes within a case study design. Combining multiple methods can be very valuable; it offers the possibility of overcoming the drawbacks of using one specific method and dealing with potential issues stemming from common method bias. Nevertheless, the remainder of this chapter addresses each method individually rather than combinations of research methods.

The remainder of this section addresses the most dominant methods in PPP research, namely (a) qualitative case study research and (b) surveys. It also touches upon two common PPP primary research methods: (c) policy analysis and (d) quantitative analysis using secondary data.

Table 3.1   Overview of reviews and their statements on methods in PPP research

Author(s)	Year of publication	Focus	Comments regarding research methods
Hodge and Greve	2007	No specific focus	Little attention on research methods.
Kwak et al.	2009	No specific focus	Little attention on research methods, except the statement that literature reviews, case studies, and interviews are research methods used in studies identifying critical success factors.
Tang et al.	2010	Focus on PPP in construction industry	Case study is the dominant method (N = 57), followed by survey research (N = 43), literature reviews (N = 34), interviews (N = 19), and workshops (N = 2).
Marsilio et al.	2011	No specific focus	Little attention on research methods.
Roehrich et al.	2014	No specific focus	Case study is identified as the dominant method, followed by surveys and conceptual work. Methods focused on longitudinal or process-oriented research are rarely used.
Osei-Kyei and Chan	2015	Focus on critical success factors in PPP	This review identifies case study as the most favored method (41 per cent), followed by surveys (37 per cent) and mixed methods (22 per cent).[1]
Torchia et al.	2015	Focus on PPP in the health sector	Qualitative methods – mainly interviews and case study research – are the dominant research method (44 per cent), followed by conceptual studies (41 per cent) and survey research (15 per cent).
Zhang et al.	2016	Focus on PPP in both Chinese and international journals[2]	This review shows differences in research methods used in international and Chinese studies. The first predominantly uses surveys (28.6 per cent), followed by literature reviews (26.3 per cent) and case studies (19.8 per cent). For the latter, case studies are most popular (28.5 per cent), followed by literature reviews (20 per cent) and modeling (19 per cent).

Author(s)	Year of publication	Focus	Comments regarding research methods
Cui et al.	2018	No specific focus	Little attention on research methods, although the review mentions the use of literature analysis, surveys, result analysis, modeling, and case studies in empirical PPP research.
Wang et al.	2018	Focus on PPP in the public administration discipline	Little attention on research methods. Both qualitative (case studies) and quantitative methods are mentioned being used in PPP research.
Petersen	2019	Focus on cost, quality, and value for money of PPPs	The review shows predominantly qualitative methods, like case studies. It also presents a few quantitative studies and secondary analyses. A lack of more advanced evaluation designs, like quasi-experimental methods, is noted.
Narbaev et al.	2020	No specific focus	The review presents methods used in PPP research, including case studies, surveys, comparative analysis, content analysis, expert judgement, factor and regression analysis, simulation, and scenario analysis.

Notes: [1]A combination of interviews, case study, and surveys is also considered mixed methods in this review. However, the combination of interviews and case study in particular is not always considered a mixed method. This is often considered as a case study, regardless of how the data is collected. [2]The ratio between studies from these journals is very skewed. In their review the share of articles from Chinese journals is overwhelming, with 615 studies against only 70 studies published in international journals.

The use of case studies in public–private partnership research

Perhaps the most common method in primary PPP research is the use of case studies. As mentioned above, several reviews highlight the case study as a typical or dominant method to study PPPs (see Cui et al. 2018, Narbaev et al. 2020, Osei-Kyei and Chan 2015, Petersen 2019, Roehrich et al. 2014, Tang et al. 2010, Torchia et al. 2015). This is not surprising as the use of case studies is a common research method in many disciplines. The method is both applauded for its attention to detail and context as well as being criticized for its incapability to test hypotheses and generalize findings beyond the set of selected cases (Flyvbjerg 2006). Case studies consist of a detailed examination of one or more examples. As most scholars are familiar with this method, and many handbooks address the design and application of case studies (for example, Blatter and Haverland 2012, Hartley 2004, Yin 2011), this chapter will not go into any depth about the method and the many ways case study research can be designed.

There is much to say about the benefits and drawbacks of this method, despite its common usage. Scholars often use case study research because of its proximity to reality and the 'irreducible quality of good narratives' (Flyvbjerg 2006). Case studies provide rich and in-depth knowledge on a certain phenomenon and can be used to study a variety of topics, including those that do not lend themselves to large-N research (Haverland and Van der Veer 2017, Yin 2011). Finally, this method allows scholars to pay attention to important issues like process, complexity, and the role of time (Haverland and Van der Veer 2017). Despite these advantages, there has also been much critique on the use of case studies, in particular because of its limited ability to test theory and its inability to generalize findings to a broader set of subjects. In particular, case studies that lack an explicit theoretical base do not easily add up, and make it difficult to generalize their findings from a case to the population at large (Haverland and Yanow 2012). Importantly, though, not all scholars agree with these critiques. One of them is Flyvbjerg (2006), who claims that some forms of case study research are in fact engaged in theory-building and theory-testing as well. This applies, for example, to hypotheses generating case studies and confirming or invalidating case studies.[1] However, even in those cases, some scholars point towards the risk of false positives as scholars are focused on patterns and often do not recognize non-patterns. A potential way to take this into account is to test multiple theories within the same case study (Toshkov 2016).

Turning towards the use of case studies in PPP research, there is no shortage of examples of rich, detailed case studies on PPPs. In fact, the number of case studies in the field of PPPs is so vast that Xiong et al. (2019) have used existing case studies for their review on the success and failure of governance in PPP projects. They identify 52 articles with a case study design and use those to identify the governance issues most relevant for PPPs. Some case studies on PPPs focus on developments in a particular country or specific sector (for example, Koppenjan (2005) on PPP in the Netherlands or Smith et al. (2018) on PPP in the Swedish water and sewerage sector). Other scholars use case studies to illustrate how certain theories or frameworks work in PPPs. Garvin and Bosso (2008), for instance, present a case study of several PPP programmes in the US to illustrate the functioning of their equilibrium framework[2] that helps to assess the effectiveness of PPP. The article by Reeves (2008) reflects a similar approach. In his study, Reeves uses case study research to test two different theories – transaction cost economics and socio-legal theory – in PPPs by focusing on transactional and relational contracting in the Irish school sector (Reeves 2008). Finally, case study research on PPPs provides lessons about a wide range of topics, ranging from value for money to governance and management. In the latter category, the work of Edelenbos and Teisman (2008) is illustrative of PPP case study research. They use a single case of a spatial development PPP project to study project and process management. Examples like the study of Ahmadabadi and Heravi (2019) on two PPP highway projects in Iran, and the case study of three Dutch PPPs by Klijn and Teisman (2003), show that case studies are also used to identify success factors and barriers for the use of PPPs.

All in all, case study research provides scholars with detailed knowledge on PPPs and their context, which enhances our understanding of the functioning of PPPs in real-life situations. It can be used to address a variety of topics and study the use of PPP over time or in specific settings. However, as case studies often take into account the individual characteristics of particular projects and include the role of context, it is harder to compare PPPs across sectors and countries, or to generalize findings beyond the case itself.

The use of surveys and questionnaires in public-private partnership research

The use of surveys is a well-known method that allows for a wide range of statistical analyses ranging from simple correlation and regression analysis to more complex multi-level analysis and structural equation modeling. In this method, samples are drawn, respondents are questioned, and data is analyzed in order to extrapolate to a population of interest (Lee et al. 2012). Using a relatively small sample, scholars using surveys are able to assess perceptions, attitudes, and correlations that apply to a larger population (Swidorski 1980). Just like case study research, this is a common method most scholars are familiar with. Survey design and application are again discussed in detail in various handbooks (for example, Nardi 2018, Rossi et al. 2013). Here, we will focus on some of the benefits and drawbacks of this method of which researchers need to be aware.

The use of surveys has become a common research method for various reasons. First, perhaps the most obvious advantage of this method is its capability to generalize the conclusions from a sample to the population of interest (Lee et al. 2012). In contrast to case study research, it is possible to make reliable estimations that apply to a population of interest without studying the majority of the population. Crucial in this respect is the representativeness of the sample, generally referred to as 'external validity' (Lee et al. 2012). With the ability to generalize the findings from a sample to a larger population, the method is also very suitable to test hypotheses and theories (Gerring 2007, Haverland

and Van der Veer 2017). In doing so, the method is not limited to a particular topic, although the study seems to be mainly focused on the individual level, assessing the opinions and perceptions of individuals (Haverland and Van der Veer 2017). This is partially due to one of the drawbacks of the method: its need for a large N (Groeneveld et al. 2015). It is therefore more difficult for survey research to test theories that deal with macro-level phenomena, such as the development of national PPP policies (Haverland and Van der Veer 2017). A second disadvantage is that surveys are often a self-administered instrument. When participants provide information on their own opinion, behavior, or organization, this might lead to a bias. This and other potential sources of error that can bias survey findings are addressed in the total survey error framework. This includes, among others, coverage error (where the sample does not properly reflect the entire population) and nonresponse error (when response rates are low). These errors are likely to affect the outcomes of a study (Fowler 2002, Lee et al. 2012). Although countermeasures to reduce the risk of bias are possible, it is something scholars need to take into account when designing survey research.

Turning to the use of surveys in PPP research, the literature reviews show several examples. One example is the study of Klijn and Koppenjan (2016), who studied the role of contract characteristics on PPP performance. For their study they approached almost the entire population consisting of professionals from PPP projects in the Netherlands. This was necessary to reach a large N and prevented sampling errors. Using the same dataset, Warsen et al. (2018) studied the role of trust and network management and its effect on the performance and cooperation of PPP projects. Taking into account that some respondents worked for the same project, and were thus more likely to give similar answers, they performed a multi-level analysis to correct for the fact that their respondents – on an individual level – were asked questions about topics on a project level. Morallos et al. (2009) approached the same issue slightly differently. In their study on PPP value for money, they questioned transportation agency officials regarding their use of assessments and tools to evaluate PPPs, thus focusing on the (self-reported) behavior of these officials rather than on value for money on a project level. Zhang et al. (2009) explicitly used survey research to test theory. Using a survey among 244 partners in PPPs in healthcare in China, they tested the mediating role of formal and informal contracts in linking cooperation characteristics to cooperation success, using the social exchange theory as their basis.

All in all, survey research in the field of PPPs provides scholars with a good opportunity to test existing theories that might be relevant in PPP research, such as transaction cost economics, social exchange theory, or governance theories. It allows for generalizations, which shows its added value compared to case study research. As the examples above show, the method can be used for a range of PPP-related topics. However, in doing so it mainly uses the opinions or assessments of individuals – such as professionals working in PPP projects – as input, even to formulate conclusions about projects, sectors, or policies. As a consequence, using survey research to study macro-level topics, like the development of PPP as a governance tool, is complicated.

The use of policy analysis in public–private partnership research

Although not identified as frequently as case study or survey research, policy analysis is also a method used in PPP research. Indeed, policy analysis has a long historical pedigree and covers a broad terrain (Parsons 1995). Some of the aforementioned reviews include PPP policy as an emerging topic in PPP research and bring up various studies that have been published in journals with a strong focus on policy analysis, such as the *Journal of Comparative Policy Analysis*, indicating the use of this method (for example, Roehrich et al. 2014, Wang et al. 2018). Policy analysis emerged to better understand and gain knowledge of the policy-making process (Fischer and Miller 2017). It provides insight into the formulation of policies, agenda-setting, and policy reform. It might also elaborate on the role of argumentation, rhetoric, and narratives in the process (Fischer and Miller 2017). Therefore, it can bring to light less visible characteristics of PPPs, such as symbolism in PPP policy, the use of power, and the legitimacy of public or private actions. A second benefit of policy analysis is that this method is able to take into account a time dimension. Its capacity to analyze the development of a particular process or policy over time is something not all methods are equipped to do. Third, it lends itself to an international or comparative approach in which the policy development of countries is compared. Finally, there are various ways to gather data for a policy analysis. This method often uses (policy) documents, but it is also possible to use interviews, questionnaires, media reports, and other sources to gather information as input for the policy analysis. While the use of predominantly written information is suited to studying the development and formulation of policies, it is less equipped to study behavior or observe policy implementation in practice.

Policy analysis in PPP research does not focus on PPPs as individual projects. It rather studies PPP as a policy or a governance tool. To study the development of PPP policy, the work of Koppenjan and de Jong (2017) is a clear example. Using predominantly written policy documents, they analyzed the development of PPP in the Netherlands over time. A more comparative approach is taken by Petersen (2011). He compares the adoption of PPP in Ireland and

Denmark, combining a case study design with policy analysis. In his study he made ample use of policy documents, including policy statements, legislation, and government reports. A more extensive international comparative policy analysis can be found in the work of Van den Hurk et al. (2016). They compare PPP support in nineteen European countries, using both interviews and document analysis for their policy analysis. Recently Greve and Hodge (2020) used policy analysis to study the global diffusion of PPP policy. Besides a focus on the formulation and development of PPP policies, policy analysis can also be used to focus on the role of language and the discourse on PPPs. Several scholars have addressed the question of whether PPP is really a new form of project delivery or whether it should be considered more as a language game (see Klijn 2010, Linder 1999).

The examples above show the varied use of policy analysis to understand the formulation and adoption of PPP in national, international, and comparative settings. It allows scholars to take into account the occurrence of changes over time (for example, Koppenjan and de Jong 2017) or adopt a comparative perspective (for example, Petersen 2011, Van den Hurk et al. 2016). Finally, it might be an interesting method to study PPP from different theoretical perspectives. Rather than the commonly used economic or collaboration-oriented theories, policy analysis allows for the use of framing theory to study PPPs.

The use of quantitative analysis with secondary data in public-private partnership research

This method provides scholars with the opportunity to run analysis with data originally collected, compiled, and analyzed for another purpose (Dale et al. 2008, Johnston 2014). The use of this method has become more popular due to the increase of technological advances and the increasing availability of data through national archives (Dale et al. 2008, Johnston 2014). Nowadays several data sources fitted for secondary analysis are available online, like nationwide surveys, longitudinal datasets that allow for historical comparison over time, and comparative international studies and datasets (Dale et al. 2008). The use of quantitative data analysis using secondary data – or secondary analysis in short – has some clear advantages. First, secondary analysis enables researchers to analyze data that would be difficult or time-consuming to collect. This is both cost-effective and convenient, and opens up a new array of research questions that scholars would otherwise have too little information about to address (Dale et al. 2008, Johnston 2014, Smith 2008). As the data-collection phase is often eliminated in this type of research, this speeds up the research, which can be considered another advantage of secondary analysis (Doolan and Froelicher 2009). The fact that researchers do not perform part of the research process themselves may also hint towards some drawbacks of this method. Since the dataset was not collected with the scholars' research question in mind, the dataset needs to be appropriate to study the research topic in order to provide meaningful answers. A good fit between the research question and the dataset is crucial for the quality of the analysis (Dale et al. 2008, Doolan and Froelicher 2009, Johnston 2014, Smith 2008). To answer a particular research question using secondary analysis, the researcher is dependent on the datasets available and the existence of sufficient, appropriate, and comparable documentation. Furthermore, as the researcher did not participate in the data-collection process, the researcher does not exactly know how the data was conducted, making it harder to identify potential flaws and other issues in the dataset (Johnston 2014).

A good example of PPP research using secondary analysis is the work of Albalate, Bell, and Geddes. In their study into contractual choices, risk, and labor costs in PPPs in the US water industry, they made use of secondary data, stemming from the International Major Projects Survey 2008 from Public Works Financing (Albalate et al. 2013). Another example of researchers using secondary analysis are Irish PPP scholars Reeves, Palcic, and Flannery. In collaboration with other scholars around the globe, they have conducted a series of studies on PPP tendering periods in various countries (see Casady et al. 2019, Palcic et al. 2019, Reeves et al. 2015, Reeves et al. 2017). They constructed a database on PPP tendering periods using data from various available datasets from Her Majesty's Treasury in the UK (Reeves et al. 2017), the Canadian Council for Public-Private Partnerships' P3 Spectrum database in Canada (Casady et al. 2019) and the World Bank's World Governance Indicators database (Palcic et al. 2019).

All in all, secondary analysis might help to provide knowledge on a range of topics in relation to PPPs, although the options are limited by the existence and availability of datasets. When sufficient data is available, the method can allow for international, comparative research. It is possible that this method leans towards the study of topics that can be captured in numbers and figures, such as tender periods (see Palcic et al. 2019) or financial and economic variables (Albalate et al. 2013). Several PPP scholars already make use of secondary data, using both descriptive and uncomplicated inferential statistics to gain new insights into the development and performance of PPPs (for example, Albalate et al. 2013, Palcic et al. 2019, Reeves et al. 2015, Reeves et al. 2017).

Looking to the future: the potential of new methods for public-private partnership research

The previous section provided an overview of commonly used methods for empirical research into PPPs. This current section highlights several methods that are not commonly used in PPP research, namely qualitative comparative analysis (QCA), Q methodology, and experimental research. They might have the potential to address new research questions and enhance the methodological diversity within PPP research.

Qualitative comparative analysis and its potential for public-private partnership research

QCA is a method that is becoming more and more popular in PPP research. This set-theoretic method aims to uncover which combinations of conditions are present in cases that display a certain outcome. Krogslund et al. (2015) explain its heritage, saying: 'as long as social science has been split between scholars employing large-N, quantitative methods and those employing small-N, qualitative methods, enterprising methodologists have sought to create new analytical techniques that might span this epistemological divide' (Krogslund et al. 2015: 21). QCA is one of these methods and aims to combine the in-depth case knowledge from qualitative studies while addressing comparison issues of small-N studies.

Here we will briefly address the main rules of thought one needs to grasp to understand the functioning of QCA. For a more detailed discussion of the underlying principles and functioning of QCA, we refer to various handbooks (for example, Rihoux and Ragin 2009, Schneider and Wagemann 2012). The first principle is that of conjunctural causation. This means that 'the effect of a single condition unfolds only in combinations with other conditions' (Schneider and Wagemann 2012: 78). The second is the idea of equifinality, which assumes that different configurations can produce a similar outcome. Just as there are multiple ways to Rome, there can be multiple explanations of a particular outcome. The third principle is that of causal asymmetry, which implies that the set of conditions leading towards an outcome can be different from those leading to the non-outcome (Ragin 2008). Terms one will find often in QCA studies to describe the importance of the tested conditions are 'necessity' and 'sufficiency'. A condition is considered necessary if the outcome could not be achieved without the presence of that condition. Regarding sufficiency, the outcome may occur without the condition being present, but the presence of sufficient conditions always means the outcome is present as well (Schneider and Wagemann 2012).

As with any other method, QCA has its benefits and drawbacks. Proponents highlight its ability to combine a focus on rich, in-depth knowledge while allowing for studying causal patterns across cases. Whereas most methods display one of these features, QCA tries to include both. A second advantage of QCA is that it embraces complexity. Whereas most methods try to remove complexity, QCA allows for complexity, because of its assumption that different configurations can lead towards a similar outcome and that the effect of a condition only unfolds in combination with other conditions (Gerrits and Verweij 2018). Finally, QCA can be used to address descriptive, explanatory, and evaluative research questions (see, for example, Pattyn et al. 2019). It allows for the creation of typologies, evaluation of existing hypotheses, study of the causes of a given effect, and development of new theories (Thomann and Magetti 2020). On the other hand, there are also drawbacks. First, QCA might run the risk of Type I errors, where the study presents causal relationships that do not exist in the data used for the study. The outcome could be the result of chance (see, for example, Braumoeller 2015). Underlying this critique is a debate about the main purpose of QCA. If QCA should aim to make causal claims, a correct QCA solution should only contain causally relevant factors[3] (see, for example, Baumgartner and Thiem 2017). If the purpose is 'to find meaningful super- and/or subsets of the phenomenon to be explained' (Schneider 2016: 2) a QCA solution should be both plausible and free from logical contradictions (see, for example, Thomann and Magetti 2020). However, both approaches agree that a set relation alone is not enough to postulate a cause (Schneider 2018, Thiem and Baumgartner 2016). New alternatives are designed to deal with the issues that might occur in QCA. One of these alternatives is coincidence analysis, which is closely related to QCA but focuses on analyzing causal structures with multiple outcomes (Baumgartner and Ambühl 2020). The second criticism indicates that the case sensitivity of QCA poses challenges to the external validity of the study. To clarify the external validity of QCA results, scholars should provide a transparent justification of the assumptions that are made about logical remainders and the remainders' implications (Schneider and Wagemann 2012, Thomann and Magetti 2020). Third, the matter of measurement errors needs to be addressed. The QCA approach aims to tackle validity issues through a strong case orientation, using purposively selected cases (external validity) and in-depth knowledge to ensure internal validity (Rihoux and Ragin 2009). However, Hug (2013: 252) states that 'scholars employing QCA rarely reflect on the possibility that the data they have gathered and used in their analysis might be error-prone and thus affect their conclusions'. QCA does not offer a direct way to incorporate the error term, which might affect the validity of a QCA analysis.

QCA is increasingly being used in PPP research (for example, Casady 2020, Soecipto and Verhoest 2018, Verweij 2015, Warsen et al. 2019). Most of these studies either focus on the performance of PPP projects or address the management and governance of these partnerships. The dissertation of Verweij, for example, includes several studies on PPPs that use QCA to analyze the management of implementation processes in PPP projects and the success of these partnerships (Verweij 2015). Warsen et al. (2019) use fuzzy-set QCA to test which combinations of contractual and relational governance mechanisms are present in successful PPP projects. The existing studies of PPP using QCA show that this method is able to compare more cases than traditional case studies. Warsen et al. (2019), for example, included 25 Dutch and Flemish PPP projects, whereas Casady (2020) studied the institutional settings of 48 PPP markets across the globe. The growing popularity of QCA in PPP research might be due to its potential to marry quantitative and qualitative research data, to compare cases in a more systematic way, or because of its appealing logic of multiple paths to outcomes. However, QCA is particularly suited to study PPPs because of its ability to embrace complexity. PPP projects are often rather complex due to the involvement of many actors with different interests and goals, challenges regarding the scope and construction of the project, and the environment that forms a dynamic and sometimes unpredictable context in which the projects take place (see, for example, Gerrits and Verweij 2018, Warsen 2021). To properly study complex projects, we need methods that take this complexity into account (Gerrits and Verweij 2018). QCA could be one of these methods.

All in all, QCA could be an interesting method as it embraces the complexity of PPPs. It might be used to address descriptive, explanatory, and evaluative research questions, as long as these questions allow for the combined effect of multiple conditions. QCA thus helps scholars to study the relevance of combinations of conditions, rather than individual relationships. QCA is particularly suited to a study of medium-N cases – whether these cases are PPP projects, PPP markets, or countries with a PPP policy.

Q methodology and its potential for public-private partnership research

A rarely used method in PPP research is Q methodology. Q methodology was developed around 1935 by William Stephenson and had its origin in psychology. Over the years it has been widely applied in multiple disciplines

(Molenveld and Nederhand 2020, Watts and Stenner 2012). The method is designed to study the perceptions and viewpoints of individuals, and allows scholars to identify different discourses and reveal the significant differences and similarities in these discourses (Brown 1980, Molenveld and Minkman 2020). Even though the method allows for theory-building and the study of how theoretical concepts resonate in practice, it is often not considered suitable to test predefined categories from the literature (Molenveld and Nederhand 2020, Watts and Stenner 2012).

A Q-method study should focus on questions regarding subjectivity. By studying the discourse regarding a particular topic, statements are drafted. These statements are presented to a relatively small number of participants; about 30 is considered sufficient. As Q methodology assumes subjectivity, there is no representative sample from the population – as would be the case in quantitative research. However, respondents must be selected in a purposeful manner, meaning that they need to be relevant both theoretically and empirically for the research question at hand (see Brown 1980, Watts and Stenner 2012). The respondents sort the statements, usually resulting in a normal distribution. The statements on both edges of the distribution represent those the respondents agree with most and least (Brown 1980). A factor analysis shows the different perspectives that exist among the respondents regarding the topic at hand. This section only explains the functioning of Q methodology in a nutshell. Further information on the application of Q methodology can be found, for example, in the work of Brown (1980) or the handbook of Watts and Stenner (2012), who provide a clear overview on how to conduct this method.

As with any method, Q methodology has its benefits and drawbacks. First, it can be considered a powerful method to identify people's shared viewpoints regarding a particular topic (Brown 1980, McKeown and Thomas 2013). In doing so, it shows both the dominant and minor viewpoints regarding a particular topic. The method allows for both depth (a characteristic of qualitative studies) and significance (a characteristic of quantitative studies). Finally, relatively few respondents are needed to perform a solid analysis, which makes this method also suitable for research on topics or questions where large-N is not available (Molenveld and Minkman 2020). A drawback of the method is that it often remains descriptive. It does not offer explanations for the different perspectives in a discourse, nor explain why some respondents have a different viewpoint than others (McKeown and Thomas 2013). Explanatory research requires additional research methods. Second, although the statistical analysis behind this method is easy to perform, scholars need time to understand the interpretation of the findings properly and immerse themselves in the different perspectives in the discourse (Molenveld and Minkman 2020).

One of the few examples using Q methodology in PPP research is the work of Warsen et al. (2020). Including respondents working for both public and private partners in PPPs from three different countries (Canada, Denmark and the Netherlands), the study identified four different perspectives among PPP professionals regarding the governance of PPPs. As the work of Warsen et al. (2020) shows, Q methodology can contribute to our knowledge on PPP by answering descriptive research questions and studying the perceptions of individuals regarding particular topics. However, Q methodology also allows for more evaluative studies (for example, Van der Steen et al. 2018). Focusing on the discourse that exists among professionals on important PPP-related topics, such as innovation, risk allocation, or governance, would be a relatively new approach to PPP research. It would imply an increased focus on humans' behavior and the role their subjectivity might play in their behavior. The focus on the micro level, by studying the perceptions of individuals, is an interesting contribution to PPP research, which is still mainly focused on the project or policy level. It provides the opportunity to study how elements from theoretical constructs are valued and combined by professionals working with PPP (Molenveld and Nederhand 2020). Furthermore, the Q methodology also allows for a comparative design (see, for example, Durose et al. 2016, Warsen et al. 2020). Although the method is not designed to ascertain how culture or country affects the viewpoints of professions, it is able to show which elements in the discourse are more prominent than others in one country (Molenveld and Nederhand 2020).

Experiments and their potential for public-private partnership research

Research on PPPs does not have a history of experimentation – a feature this field of study has in common with the field of public administration. Instead, it is by and large dominated by qualitative and survey research. Nevertheless, experimental research can be very useful as it has the potential to answer causal questions and contribute to theory development (Bouwman and Grimmelikhuijsen 2015). In an experiment, scholars deliberately manipulate one potential variable that could cause an effect in another variable. Various forms of experiments differ in their degree of experimenter control and context. The first refers to the extent to which the researcher has control over what participants are exposed to, while the latter refers to the nature of the subject pool, the information that they bring to the task, the task itself, and the environment in which subjects operate (Bouwman and Grimmelikhuijsen 2015, Harrison and List 2004). Ranging from high control to low control and from low context to high context, five different types of experiments can be considered: laboratory experiment, artifactual field experiment, survey experiment, framed field experiment, and natural (field) experiment.

The use of experimental research has a few distinct advantages compared to the research methods often used in PPP research. First, experimental design is very well designed to deal with endogeneity. It helps to control for the presence of an uncontrolled confounding variable, which influences both the dependent and independent variables of a model (Morton and Williams 2010). Experiments are particularly rigorous as they allow for random assignment and control of the experimental setting (Haverland and Van der Veer 2017). It is therefore one of the most suitable methods for studying causality and test theory. However, the need to control the information the participants get, and the need to manipulate only one variable while keeping all other variables equal, also pose some challenges and lead to criticism regarding the use of experiments. Some critics point out that experiments often rely on the use of convenience samples, like student samples. There is a debate on whether students are representative for other populations, because of their high education level. This might lead them to react differently to manipulations (Bouwman and Grimmelikhuijsen 2015, Charness and Kuhn 2011). Others claim that students and other groups react similarly to stimuli (Anderson and Edwards 2015, Bouwman and Grimmelikhuijsen 2015) and that the homogeneous group of students is even an advantage, because a true effect in a homogeneous sample is harder to detect than in a heterogeneous sample (Bouwman and Grimmelikhuijsen 2015). Another issue is the limited generalizability of experiments and their alleged lack of external validity (see, for example, Bouwman and Grimmelikhuijsen 2015 for a reply to this). For scholars that are not used to work with experimental research, the situation participants are presented with might feel somewhat artificial and distant from real life, as scholars need to gain enough control over the situation to rule out the effects of extraneous variables. Finally, just like survey research, experiments do need a large N to do robust testing. This means that not all questions are suitable for experimental research, and that this is particularly focused on the individual level and more particularly their behavior (Haverland and Van der Veer 2017).

Examples of experimental research in PPP research are rare. One of the few exceptions is the article by Hoppe et al. (2013). They ran an experiment on procurement where they compared PPP with traditional procurement. Four hundred students from the University of Cologne were presented with a situation in which a government agency wanted public infrastructure to be built and managed. In different treatments, focusing on different procurement methods, the party in charge of the building could decide how much they wanted to invest during the construction stage. More recent experimental research was done by Weißmüller, who wrote her dissertation on the role of risk in PPP, and made ample use of experimental research. In one study, an experiment regarding the behavioral mechanisms of building and eroding trust in partnering across sectors at the micro level of interaction between public and private partners is presented (Weißmüller and Vogel 2020). The strictly controlled experimental design allowed for the systematic manipulation of context parameters in order to isolate singular causal mechanisms (Walker et al. 2017).

The examples presented above show that experiments enable the studying of individual behavior. In the context of PPP research, this would mean that experiments can help us to understand the behavior of PPP professionals, and how they act in, for instance, negotiation, collaboration, or risk-allocation situations. Besides insight into the behavior of individuals in PPPs, experiments also offer an opportunity to rigorously test theory and answer causal questions, something that other methods, such as case study research and Q methodology, are less equipped to deal with. Experiments enable PPP researchers to test the findings earlier case studies have presented to us in this respect.

Longitudinal research and its potential for public-private partnership research

Finally, we make a plea for the use of methods that are particularly focused on capturing the long-term nature of PPP projects. Some of the previously discussed methods are able to take into account the long-term nature of PPPs, but there are methods designed to conduct long-term research, such as process-tracing methods. The long-term nature of PPPs is one of the core characteristics of any type of PPP, but rarely takes center stage in PPP research. There is only limited evidence of publications adopting a longitudinal perspective. Important whole-life-cycle management issues, such as staff turnover and relationship management and their effect on the process of designing, building, and maintaining PPPs are not frequently studied. These constitute fruitful research avenues (Roehrich et al. 2014). Therefore, the use of research methods focused on the long-term nature of PPP in particular, such as process-tracing methods, might prove useful in this respect.

Conclusion: stepping up our methodological game in public-private partnership research

The previous section provided an overview of some 'new' and 'innovative' methods in PPP research. Together with the methods that are already common practice in PPP research, these form a broad palette of research methods that we can use to advance our knowledge on PPPs. All could be regarded as valid potential methods as long as researchers fully understand the bases on which their chosen research method operates. Each research method – if properly used – may contribute new knowledge on PPPs. Nevertheless, there are significant differences between the various research methods in the knowledge they might provide. The overview in Table 3.2 shows how each method is suited for different types of research questions, and studying PPP on different levels of analysis.

This chapter illustrates that PPP research allows for both qualitative (case) studies and quantitative (survey) research. Scholars might collect their own data or build upon existing data; for example, for policy analysis or quantitative secondary analysis. Existing research on PPP has given us insight into the concept and the development of PPPs, PPP policy, and the performance of many PPP projects in various countries. There are, however, also questions harder to answer with the currently used research methods. For example, several studies have addressed critical success factors of PPPs, but little is yet known about how these factors interact. Several studies have addressed the policy developments regarding PPP in different countries. However, little is yet known about how professionals react to these developments. Several studies have addressed the various forms of PPP and their performance, but little is yet known about how professionals behave and make decisions within these partnerships. The adoption of other research methods, such as QCA, Q methodology, and experiments, might help to address new research questions, explore different research avenues, and expand our knowledge on PPPs. The inclusion of new research methods should not mean that existing research methods are superfluous. It is precisely the diversity of methods that can help us research PPPs. After all, it is our job as scientists to gather as many clues from as many sources as possible, and put these together. We always need several avenues on which to investigate a phenomenon, so that we can better understand how the world works, and why. When we base ourselves on one or just a few research methods, we leave room for doubt.

This chapter not only provides an overview of existing and possible future methods in PPP research, but it is also primarily a plea for a more diverse use

Table 3.2   Overview of common and 'new' methods in PPP research

Method	What does it entail?	Sample size	Level of analysis	Type of research question
Case study	Detailed examination of one or more examples	Small N	Meso-level: projects, although studies of countries are also possible	Explorative, descriptive, explanatory, evaluative
Survey	Data from a sample is analyzed to extrapolate to a population of interest. Assesses perceptions, attitudes, of individuals	Large N	Micro-level: individuals, although the perceptions can be used to study larger units of analysis, like projects	Descriptive, explanatory, theory-testing
Policy analysis	Emerged to better understand and gain knowledge of the policy-making process	Small, medium, and large N possible	Often macro-level: policy of sectors or countries	Descriptive, evaluative
Secondary analysis	Run analysis with data originally collected, compiled, and analyzed for another purpose	Large N (in case of quantitative analysis)	Different levels possible; allows for both individual, project-level and cross-country studies	Descriptive, evaluative
QCA	Set-theoretic method designed to systematically compare cases, and test combinations of conditions using minimization and Boolean algebra	Preferably medium N	Different levels possible; allows for the analysis of individuals (micro), projects (meso), and countries (macro)	Descriptive, explorative, theory-testing, evaluative

Method	What does it entail?	Sample size	Level of analysis	Type of research question
Q methodology	Systematic analysis of the viewpoints of individuals; based on subjectivity	Medium N	Micro-level: study of individuals and their perceptions	Descriptive, explorative, evaluative
Experiments	Study in which scholars deliberately manipulate one potential variable that could cause an effect in another variable, often used to study behavior of individuals	Large N	Micro-level: study of individuals and their behavior	Explanatory, theory-testing

of methods in PPP research. The methods presented in this chapter are just a few examples that can help generate new insights either at a different level or tap into new types of knowledge. For example, a QCA can help to compare cases in a more systematic way, while Q methodology and experiments help scholars to acquire knowledge at an individual level (professionals) rather than at project or policy level. Methodological diversity can help our research field further. New methods confirm our existing knowledge, deepen it, and offer the opportunity to discover new avenues of research.

Notes

1. There are different forms of case study research. Although there are multiple typologies, here we make use of the work of Lijphart (1971) and Eckstein (1975).
2. The Garvin and Bosso (2008) equilibrium framework notes that beneficial PPP outcomes and the long-term success of a PPP program depends heavily on establishing a balance between the interests of the state, society, industry, and market.
3. Important in this debate is the role of redundancy-free models. Only one of three possible ways to display the results of the analysis of sufficiency – that is, to show which combinations of conditions are sufficient for the outcome – is able to eliminate all causally irrelevant (redundant) factors. This critique is addressed more elaborately in the work of Baumgartner and Thiem (for example, Baumgartner 2015, Baumgartner and Thiem 2017, Thiem and Baumgartner, 2016). The work of Thomann and Magetti (2020) provides a good overview of the main critiques and responses.

References

Ahmadabadi, A.A., and Heravi, G. (2019) The effect of critical success factors on project success in public-private partnership projects: A case study of highway projects in Iran. *Transport Policy*, 73: 152–161. https://doi.org/10.1016/j.tranpol.2018.07.004.

Albalate, D., Bel, G., and Geddes, R.R. (2013) Recovery risk and labor costs in public–private partnerships: Contractual choice in the US water industry. *Local Government Studies*, 39 (3): 332–351. https://doi.org/10.1080/03003930.2013.778831.

Alinaitwe, H., and Ayesiga, R. (2013) Success factors for the implementation of public–private partnerships in the construction industry in Uganda. *Journal of Construction in Developing Countries*, 18 (2): 1–14.

Anderson, D.M., and Edwards, B.C. (2015) Unfulfilled promise: Laboratory experiments in public management research. *Public Management Review*, 17 (10): 1518–1542. https://doi.org/10.1080/14719037.2014.943272.

Baumgartner, M. (2015) Parsimony and causality. *Quality and Quantity*, 49: 839–56. https://doi.org/10.1007/s11135-014-0026-7.

Baumgartner, M., and Ambühl, M. (2020) Causal modeling with multi-value and fuzzy-set coincidence analysis. *Political Science Research and Methods*, 8 (3): 526–542. https://doi.org/10.1017/psrm.2018.45.

Baumgartner, M., and Thiem, A. (2017) Model ambiguities in configurational comparative research. *Sociological Methods and Research*, 46: 954–87. https://doi.org/10.1177/0049124115610351.

Baumgartner, M., and Thiem, A. (2020) Often trusted but never (properly) tested: Evaluating qualitative comparative analysis. *Sociological Methods and Research*, 49: 279–311. https://doi.org/10.1177/0049124117701487.

Benitez-Avila, C., Hartmann, A., Dewulf, G., and Henseler, J. (2018) Interplay of relational and contractual governance in public-private partnerships: The mediating role of relational norms, trust and partners' contribution. *International Journal of Project Management*, 36 (3): 429–443. https://doi.org/10.1016/j.ijproman.2017.12.005.

Blatter, J., and Haverland, M. (2012) *Designing Case Studies: Explanatory Approaches in Small-N Research*. London: Palgrave Macmillan.

Bouwman, R., and Grimmelikhuijsen, S. (2015) Experimental public administration from 1992 to 2014: A systematic literature review and ways forward. *International Journal of Public Sector Management*, 29 (2): 110–131. https://doi.org/10.1108/IJPSM-07-2015-0129.

Bovaird, T. (2004) Public–private partnerships: From contested concepts to prevalent practice. *International Review of Administrative Sciences*, 70 (2): 199–215. https://doi.org/10.1177/0020852304044250.

Braumoeller, B.F. (2015) Guarding against false positives in qualitative comparative analysis. *Political Analysis*, 23: 471–87. https://doi.org/10.1177/0049124117729700.

Broadbent, J., Gill, J., and Laughlin, R. (2003) Evaluating the Private Finance Initiative in the National Health Service in the UK. *Accounting, Auditing and Accountability Journal*, 16 (3): 422–445. https://doi.org/10.1108/09513570310482309.

Brown, S.R. (1980) *Political Subjectivity: Applications of Q Methodology in Political Science*. New Haven, CT: Yale University Press.

Casady, C.B. (2020) Examining the institutional drivers of public-private partnership (PPP) market performance: A fuzzy set qualitative comparative analysis (fsQCA).

Public Management Review. Online first. https://doi.org/10.1080/14719037.2019.1708439.

Casady, C.B., Flannary, D., Geddes, R.R., Palcic, D., and Reeves, E. (2019) Understanding PPP tendering periods in Canada: A duration analysis. *Public Performance and Management Review*, 42 (6): 1259–1278. https://doi.org/10.1080/15309576.2019.1597739.

Charness, G., and Kuhn, P.J. (2011) *Lab Labor: What Can Labor Economists Learn from the Lab?* National Bureau of Economic Research Working Paper Series, No. 15913. https://doi.org/10.3386/w15913.

Cui, C., Liu, Y., Hope, A., and Wang, J. (2018) Review of studies on the public-private partnerships (PPP) for infrastructure projects. *International Journal of Project Management*, 36 (5): 773–794. https://doi.org/10.1016/j.ijproman.2018.03.004.

Dale, A., Wathan, J., and Higgins, V. (2008) Secondary Analysis of Quantitative Data Sources, in *The SAGE Handbook of Social Research Methods*, edited by P. Alasuutari, L. Bickman, and J. Brannen. London, UK: SAGE.

Doolan, D.M., and Froelicher, E.S. (2009) Using an existing data set to answer new research questions: A methodological review. *Research and Theory for Nursing Practice*, 23 (3): 203–215. https://doi.org/10.1891/1541-6577.23.3.203.

Durose, C., Van Hulst, M., Jeffares, S., Escobar, O., Agger, A., and De Graaf, L. (2016) Five ways to make a difference: Perceptions of practitioners working in urban neighborhoods. *Public Administration Review*, 76 (4): 576–586. https://doi.org/10.1111/puar.12502.

Eckstein, H. (1975) Case Studies and Theory in Political Science, in *Handbook of Political Science*, edited by F.I. Greenstein and N.W. Polsby. Reading, MA: Addison-Wesley.

Edelenbos, J., and Klijn, E.-H. (2009) Project versus process management in public-private partnership: Relation between management style and outcomes. *International Public Management Journal*, 12 (3): 310–331. https://doi.org/10.1080/10967490903094350.

Edelenbos, J., and Teisman, G.R. (2008) Public-private partnership on the edge of project and process management: Insights from Dutch practice – The Sijtwende spatial development project. *Environment and Planning C: Government and Policy*, 26: 614–626.

European Commission (n.d.) PPP. https://ec.europa.eu/inea/en/ten-t/ten-t-projects/projects-by-transport-mode/ppp.

Fischer, F., and Miller, G.J. (2017) *Handbook of Public Policy Analysis: Theory, Politics, and Methods.* New York, NY: Routledge.

Flyvbjerg, B. (2006) Five misunderstandings about case-study research. *Qualitative Inquiry*, 12 (2): 219–245. https://doi.org/10.1177/1077800405284363.

Fowler, F.J. (2002) *Survey Research Methods*, 3rd ed. Thousand Oaks, CA: SAGE.

Garvin, M.J., and Bosso, D. (2008) Assessing the effectiveness of infrastructure public-private partnership programs and projects. *Public Works Management and Policy*, 13 (2): 162–178. https://doi.org/10.1177/1087724X08323845.

Gerring, J. (2007) *Case Study Research: Principles and Practices.* Cambridge: Cambridge University Press.

Gerrits, L., and Verweij, S. (2018) *The Evaluation of Complex Infrastructure Projects.* Cheltenham, UK and Northampton, MA, USA: Edward Elgar Publishing.

Ghobadian, A., Gallear, D., O'Regan, N., and Viney, H. (2004) *Public-Private Partnerships: Policy and Experience.* Houndmills: Palgrave Macmillan.

Greve, C., and Hodge, G.A. (2020) Global diffusion of P3 policy: Learning perspectives for social infrastructure. *Public Works Management and Policy*, 25 (3): 312–332. https://doi.org/10.1177/1087724X20927714.

Groeneveld, S., Tummers, L., Bronkhorst, B., Ashikali, T., and Van Thiel, S. (2015) Quantitative methods in public administration: Their use and development through time. *International Public Management Journal*, 18 (1): 61–86. https://doi.org/10.1080/10967494.2014.972484.

Harrison, G.W.G., and List, J.A.J. (2004) Field experiments. *Journal of Economic Literature*, 42 (4): 1009–1055. https://doi.org/10.1257/0022051043004577.

Hartley, J. (2004) Case Study Research, in *Essential Guide to Qualitative Methods in Organizational Research*, edited by C. Cassell and G. Symon. London: SAGE.

Haverland, M., and Van der Veer, R. (2017) The Case of Case Study Research in Europe: Practice and Potential, in *The Palgrave Handbook of Public Administration and Management in Europe*, edited by S. Van Thiel and E. Ongaro. London: Palgrave Macmillan.

Haverland, M., and Yanow, D. (2012) A hitchhiker's guide to the public administration research universe: Surviving conversations on methodologies and methods. *Public Administration Review*, 72 (3): 401–408. https://doi.org/10.1111/j.1540-6210.2011.02524.x.

Helmy, R., Khourshed, N., Wahba, M., and Bary, A.A.E. (2020) Exploring critical success factors for public private partnership case study: The educational sector in Egypt. *Journal of Open Innovation: Technology, Market, and Complexity*, 6 (4): 142. https://doi.org/10.3390/joitmc6040142.

Hodge, G.A., and Greve, C. (2007) Public–private partnerships: An international performance review. *Public Administration Review*, 67 (3): 545–558. https://doi.org/10.1111/j.1540-6210.2007.00736.x.

Hodge, G.A., and Greve, C. (2013) Public–Private Partnership in Turbulent Times, in *Rethinking Public–Private Partnerships: Strategic Approaches for Turbulent Times*, edited by C. Greve and G.A. Hodge, G.A. Oxford: Routledge.

Hodge, G.A., and Greve, C. (2017) On public–private performance: A contemporary review. *Public Works Management and Policy*, 22 (1): 55–78. https://doi.org/10.1177/1087724X16657830.

Hoppe, E.I., Kusterer, D.J., and Schmitz, P.W. (2013) Public–private partnerships versus traditional procurement: An experimental investigation. *Journal of Economic Behavior and Organization*, 89: 145–166. https://doi.org/10.1016/j.jebo.2011.05.001.

Hueskes, M., Koppenjan, J.F.M., and Verweij, S. (2019) Public-private partnerships for infrastructure: Lessons learned from Dutch and Flemish PhD theses, *European Journal of Transport and Infrastructure Research*, 19 (3): 160–176. https://doi.org/10.18757/ejtir.2019.19.3.4383.

Hug, S. (2013) Qualitative comparative analysis: How inductive use and measurement error lead to problematic inference. *Political Analysis*, 21 (2): 252–265. https://doi.org/10.1093/pan/mps061.

Jamali, D. (2004) A public-private partnership in the Lebanese telecommunications industry: Critical success factors and policy lessons. *Public Works Management and Policy*, 9 (2): 103–119. https://doi.org/10.1177/1087724X04268365.

Johnston, M.P. (2014) Secondary data analysis: A method of which the time has come. *Qualitative and Quantitative Methods in Libraries*, 3 (3): 619–626.

Klijn, E.-H. (2010) Public Private Partnerships: Deciphering Meaning, Message and Phenomenon, in *International Handbook of Public–Private Partnerships*, edited by

G.A. Hodge, C. Greve, and A.E. Boardman. Cheltenham, UK and Northampton, MA, USA: Edward Elgar Publishing.

Klijn, E.-H., and Koppenjan, J.F.M. (2016) The impact of contract characteristics on the performance of public–private partnerships (PPPs). *Public Money and Management*, 36 (6): 455–462. https://doi.org/10.1080/09540962.2016.1206756.

Klijn, E.-H., and Teisman, G. (2003) Institutional and strategic barriers to public–private partnership: An analysis of Dutch cases. *Public Money and Management*, 23 (3): 137–146. https://doi.org/10.1111/1467-9302.00361.

Koppenjan, J.F.M. (2005) The formation of public-private partnerships: Lessons from nine infrastructure projects in the Netherlands. *Public Administration*, 83 (1): 135–157. https://doi.org/10.1111/j.0033-3298.2005.00441.x.

Koppenjan, J.F.M., and de Jong, M. (2017) The introduction of public-private partnerships in the Netherlands as a case of institutional bricolage: The evolution of an Anglo-Saxon transplant in a Rhineland context. *Public Administration*, 96 (1): 171–184. https://doi.org/10.1111/padm.12360.

Krogslund, C., Choi, D.D., and Poertner, M. (2015) Fuzzy sets on shaky ground: Parameter sensitivity and confirmation bias in FsQCA. *Political Analysis*, 23 (1): 21–41. https://doi.org/10.7910/DVN/27100.

Kwak, Y.H., Chih, Y.Y., and Ibs, C.W. (2009) Towards a comprehensive understanding of public private partnerships for infrastructure development. *California Management Review*, 51 (2): 51–78.

Lee, G., Benoit-Bryan, J., and Johnson, T.P. (2012) Survey research in public administration: Assessing mainstream journals with a total survey error framework. *Public Administration Review*, 72 (1): 87–97. https://doi.org/10.1111/j.1540-6210.2011.02482.x.

Lijphart, A. (1971) Comparative politics and the comparative method. *American Political Science Review*, 65 (3): 682–693. https://doi.org/10.2307/1955513.

Linder, S. (1999) Coming to terms with the public-private partnership: A grammar of multiple meanings. *American Behavioral Scientist*, 43 (1): 35–51. https://doi.org/10.1177/00027649921955146.

Marsilio, M., Cappellaro, G., and Cuccurullo, C. (2011) The intellectual structure of research into PPPs, *Public Management Review*, 13 (6): 763–782, https://doi.org/10.1080/14719037.2010.539112.

McKeown, B.B., and Thomas, D. (2013) *Q Methodology*. Thousand Oaks, CA: SAGE.

Molenveld, A., and Minkman, E. (2020) *Q-methodologie als methode om beleid te beschrijven, te ontwikkelen of te evalueren*. Beleidsonderzoek Online. https://doi.org/10.5553/BO/221335502020000001001.

Molenveld, A., and Nederhand, J. (2020) Q-Methodology: State of the art in public administration research, in *Encyclopedia of Public Administration*, edited by B.G. Peters and I. Thynne. Oxford: Oxford University Press.

Morallos, D., Amekudzi, A., Ross, C., and Meyer, M. (2009) Value for money analysis in U.S. transportation public–private partnerships. *Transportation Research Record*, 2115 (1): 27–36. https://doi.org/10.3141/2115-04.

Morton, R.B., and Williams, K.C. (2010) *Experimental Political Science and the Study of Causality*. New York, NY: Cambridge University Press.

Narbaev, T., De Marco, A., and Orazalin, N. (2020) A multidisciplinary meta-review of the public–private partnerships research. *Construction Management and Economics*, 38 (2): 109–125, https://doi.org/10.1080/01446193.2019.1643033.

Nardi, P.M. (2018) *Doing Survey Research: A Guide to Quantitative Methods*. New York, NY: Routledge.

Osei-Kyei, R., and Chan, A.P.C. (2015) Review of studies on the critical success factors for public-private partnership (PPP) projects from 1990 to 2013. *International Journal of Project Management*, 33: 1335–1346. https://doi.org/10.1016/j.ijproman.2015.02.008.

Palcic, D., Reeves, E., Flannery, D., and Geddes, R.R. (2019) Public-private partnership tendering periods: An international comparative analysis. *Journal of Economic Policy Reform*. 1–17. Online first. https://doi.org/10.1080/17487870.2019.1657016.

Parsons, W. (1995) *Public Policy: An Introduction to the Theory and Practice of Policy Analysis*. Aldershot, UK and Brookfield, VT, USA: Edward Elgar Publishing.

Pattyn, V., Molenveld, A., and Befani, B. (2019). Qualitative comparative analysis as an evaluation tool: Lessons from an application in development cooperation. *American Journal of Evaluation*, 40 (1): 55–74.

Petersen, O.H. (2011) Public-private partnerships as converging or diverging trends in public management? A comparative analysis of PPP policy and regulation in Denmark and Ireland. *International Public Management Review*, 12 (2): 1–37.

Petersen, O.H. (2019) Evaluating the costs, quality, and value for money of infrastructure public-private partnerships: A systematic literature review. *Annals of Public and Cooperative Economics*, 90 (2): 227–244.

Ragin, C.C. (2008) *Redesigning Social Inquiry: Fuzzy Sets and Beyond*. Chicago, IL: University of Chicago Press.

Reeves, E. (2008) The practice of contracting in public private partnerships: Transaction costs and relational contracting in the Irish schools sector. *Public Administration*, 86 (4): 969–986. https://doi.org/10.1111/j.1467-9299.2008.00743.x.

Reeves, E., Palcic, D., and Flannery, D. (2015) PPP Procurement in Ireland: An analysis of tendering periods. *Local Government Studies*, 41 (3): 379–400. https://doi.org/10.1080/03003930.2014.982108.

Reeves, E., Palcic, D., Flannery, D., and Geddes, R.R. (2017) The determinants of tendering periods for PPP procurement in the UK: An empirical analysis. *Applied Economics*, 49 (11): 1071–1082. https://doi.org/10.1080/00036846.2016.1210779.

Rihoux, B., and Ragin, C.C. (2009) *Configurational Comparative Methods: Qualitative Comparative Analysis (QCA) and Related Techniques*. Thousand Oaks, CA: SAGE.

Roehrich, J.K., Lewis, M.A., and George, G. (2014) Are public-private partnerships a healthy option? A systematic literature review. *Social Science and Medicine*, 113: 110–119. https://doi.org/10.1016/j.socscimed.2014.03.037.

Rossi, P.H., Wright, J.D., and Anderson, A.B. (2013) *Handbook of Survey Research*. New York, NY: Academic Press.

Schneider, C.Q. (2016) Real differences and overlooked similarities: Set-methods in comparative perspective. *Comparative Political Studies*, 49: 781–792. https://doi.org/10.1177/0010414015626454.

Schneider, C.Q. (2018) Realists and idealists in QCA. *Political Analysis*, 26 (2): 246–254. https://doi.org/10.1017/pan.2017.45.

Schneider, C.Q., and Wagemann, C. (2012) *Set-Theoretic Methods for the Social Sciences: A Guide to Qualitative Comparative Analysis*. New York, NY: Cambridge University Press.

Smith, E. (2008) Pitfalls and promises: The use of secondary data analysis in educational research. *British Journal of Educational Studies*, 56 (3): 323–339. https://doi.org/10.1111/j.1467-8527.2008.00405.x.

Smith, E., Umans, T., and Thomasson, A. (2018) Stages of PPP and principal–agent conflicts: The Swedish water and sewerage sector. *Public Performance and Management Review*, 41 (1): 100–129. https://doi.org/10.1080/15309576.2017.1368399.

Soecipto, R.M., and Verhoest, K. (2018) Contract stability in European road infrastructure PPPs: How does governmental PPP support contribute to preventing contract renegotiation? *Public Management Review*, 20 (8): 1145–1165. https://doi.org/10.1080/14719037.2018.1428414.

Swidorski, C. (1980) Sample surveys: Help for the 'out-of-house' evaluator. *Public Administration Review*, 40 (1), 67–71. https://doi.org/10.2307/976110.

Tang, L., Shen, Q., and Cheng, E.W.L. (2010) A review of studies on public–private partnership projects in the construction industry. *International Journal of Project Management*, 28: 683–694. https://doi.org/10.1016/j.ijproman.2009.11.009.

Thiem, A., and Baumgartner, M. (2016) Back to square one: A reply to Munck, Paine, and Schneider. *Comparative Political Studies*, 49 (6): 801–806. https://doi.org/10.1177/0010414015626455.

Thomann, E., and Magetti, M. (2020) Designing research with qualitative comparative analysis (QCA): Approaches, challenges, and tools. *Sociological Methods and Research*, 49 (2): 356–386. https://doi.org/10.1177/0049124117729700.

Torchia, M., Calabrò, A., and Morner, M. (2015) Public–Private Partnerships in the Health Care Sector: A systematic review of the literature. *Public Management Review*, 17 (2): 236–261. https://doi.org/10.1080/14719037.2013.792380.

Toshkov, D. (2016) *Research Design in Political Science*. Basingstoke: Palgrave Macmillan.

Van den Hurk, M., Brogaard, L., Lember, V., Petersen, O.H., and Witz, P. (2016) National varieties of public–private partnerships (PPPs): A comparative analysis of PPP-supporting units in 19 European countries. *Journal of Comparative Policy Analysis: Research and Practice*, 18 (1): 1–20. https://doi.org/10.1080/13876988.2015.1006814.

Van der Steen, M., Van Twist, M.J.W., and Bressers, D. (2018) The sedimentation of public values: How a variety of governance perspectives guide the practical actions of civil servants. *Review of Public Personnel Administration*, 38 (4): 387–414. https://doi.org/10.1177/0734371X16671369.

Verweij, S. (2015) *Once the Shovel Hits the Ground*. PhD dissertation. Rotterdam: OGC.

Walker, R.M., James, O., and Brewer, G.A. (2017) Replication, experiments and knowledge in public management research. *Public Management Review*, 19 (9): 1221–1234. https://doi.org/10.1080/14719037.2017.1282003.

Wang, H., Xiong, W., Wu, G., and Zhu, D. (2018) Public–private partnership in public administration discipline: A literature review. *Public Administration*, 20 (2): 293–316. https://doi.org/10.1080/14719037.2017.1313445.

Warsen, R. (2021) *Putting the Pieces Together: Combining Contractual and Relational Governance for Successful Public-Private Partnerships*. PhD dissertation. Rotterdam: OGC.

Warsen, R., Greve, C., Klijn, E.-H., Koppenjan, J.F.M., and Siemiatycki, M. (2020) How do professionals perceive the governance of public–private partnerships? Evidence from Canada, the Netherlands and Denmark. *Public Administration*, 98 (1): 124–139. https://doi.org/10.1111/padm.12626.

Warsen, R., Klijn, E.-H., and Koppenjan, J.F.M. (2019) Mix and match: How contractual and relational conditions are combined in successful public–private partnerships. *Journal of Public Administration Research and Theory*, 29 (3): 375–393. https://doi.org/10.1093/jopart/muy082.

Warsen, R., Nederhand, J., Klijn, E.-H., Grotenbreg, S., and Koppenjan, J.F.M. (2018) What makes public-private partnerships work? Survey research into the outcomes and the quality of cooperation in PPPs. *Public Management Review*, 20 (8): 1165–1185. https://doi.org/10.1080/14719037.2018.1428415.

Watts, S., and Stenner, P. (2012) *Doing Q Methodological Research: Theory, Method and Interpretation*. London: SAGE.

Weißmüller, K.S., and Vogel, R. (2020) Sector-specific associations, trust, and survival of PPPs: A behavioral experiment based on the Centipede Game. *Journal of Public Administration and Theory*. Online first. https://doi.org/10.1093/jopart/muaa050.

Wettenhall, R. (2008) Public-private mixes and partnerships: A search for understanding. *Asia Pacific Journal of Public Administration*, 30 (2): 119–138. https://doi.org/10.1080/23276665.2008.10779347.

World Bank (2018) *Procuring Infrastructure Public-Private Partnerships*. Washington, DC: World Bank.

Xiong, W., Chen, B., Wang, H., and Zhu, D. (2019) Governing public–private partnerships: A systematic review of case study literature. *Australian Journal of Public Administration*, 78 (1): 95–112. https://doi.org/10.1111/1467-8500.12343.

Yin, R.K. (2011) *Applications of Case Study Research*. Thousand Oaks, CA: SAGE.

Zhang, S., Chan, A.P.C., Feng, Y., Duan, H., and Ke, Y. (2016) Critical review on PPP research: A search from the Chinese and international journals. *International Journal of Project Management*, 34: 597–612. https://doi.org/10.1016/j.ijproman.2016.02.008.

Zhang, Z., Wan, D., Jia, M., and Gu, L. (2009) Prior ties, shared values and cooperation in public-private partnerships. *Management and Organization Review*, 5 (3): 353–374. https://doi.org/10.1111/j.1740-8784.2009.00154.x.

PART II

New frontiers in a contested world

4 Public–private partnerships in an economist's eye: a gleam or a beam?[1]

Dmitri Vinogradov and Elena Shadrina

Introduction

Several disciplines claim interest in the subject of public–private partnerships (PPPs) – including medicine, healthcare, public administration, management, economics, urban studies, accounting, law and others, in no particular order. Academic texts that use 'public–private partnership' and simultaneously one of the above discipline names (as a proxy for a subject inclination of the text) grow exponentially and roughly at the same pace across all subjects; see Figure 4.1(a). The interest in this topic among major publishing houses that print academic journals also seems to be roughly equal (Emerald being the only exception) – Figure 4.1(b) shows that the percentage of papers that mention 'public–private partnership' steadily grows from the 1980s onwards. All this might give a happy and glamorous picture of a sustained growth in interdisciplinary research on the topic, uniformly covering a variety of perspectives and critical angles.

Reality is far less glamorous if we look at the top journals in respective subjects. We took the journal ranking of the Chartered Association of Business Schools (UK) and selected the top-ranked journals in the disciplines of accounting, economics, finance, management, social sciences and public administration.[2] For each of them we searched for articles that contain 'public–private partnership'. Our search returned four results in the *Quarterly Journal of Economics* and in *Accounting, Organizations and Society*; three in the *Strategic Management Journal*, the *Academy of Management Journal*, the *Academy of Management Review*, and the *Administrative Science Quarterly*; two in the *Journal of Management* and the *Journal of Accounting and Economics*; and one in the *Review of Economic Studies*, the *Review of Financial Studies*, and the *Journal of Financial Economics*. Full stop. Other top journals return the disappointing 'No results found'. This refers to all years and issues, and all mentions

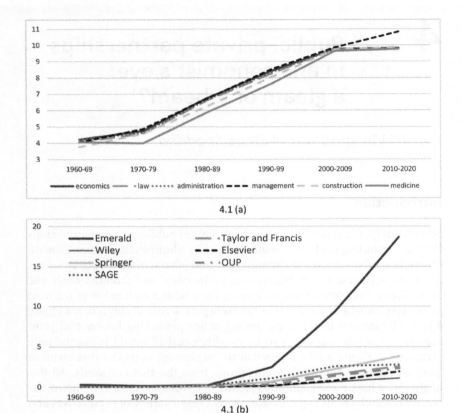

4.1 (a)

4.1 (b)

Notes: 4.1(a) Frequency of documents (vertical axis, in log) in English that simultaneously contain 'public-private partnership' and one of the terms 'economics', 'law', 'administration', 'management', 'construction', 'medicine', by decades (horizontal axis) since 1960. Data from Google Scholar, manual search. 4.1(b) Percentage of articles (vertical axis) containing 'public-private partnership' in the total number of articles published by leading academic publishers by decade (horizontal axis). Data from publishers' web search engines, manual search

Figure 4.1   Academic interest in public-private partnerships

of PPPs. The top field *Journal of Public Economics* returns 13 papers in all issues ever. At the same time, *Public Administration Review* has 76 papers on the topic, and the *Journal of Public Administration Research and Theory* lists 93 of them, each of these two journals having at least twice as many publications on the topic as top accounting, finance, management and economics journals altogether. Why such a disproportion? Do economists ignore PPPs as something not worth studying, or did they just overlook them so far and now show the first sparks of interest? Is there anything an economics perspective can add to the understanding of PPPs in the neighbouring field of public administration? These are the questions we wish to address in this chapter.

Public–private partnerships versus other forms of public good provision[3]

As the name suggests, a public–private partnership is a form of public good provision jointly by the public sector and private businesses. Key elements here are '*a* form' (there exist other forms, ways and approaches to provide public goods), 'public good' (something of a value for the society, that many could use; involvement of the public party in the partnership implies there should be public interest in it, hence public good), 'jointly' (which implies cooperation/collaboration) and 'partnership' (apparently something beyond mere collaboration, otherwise how does it differ from other forms?). 'Partnership' is admittedly a rather elusive term, interpretations of which are numerous, 'ranging from informal, oral understandings to formal agreements' (Ehrhardt and Brigham 2006, p. 4), often encompassing agreement on values and objectives (Brinkerhoff 2002) and good relationships between partners, typically stronger than may be achieved through a purely contractual collaboration. In what follows, we outline an economics argument that helps formalize this distinction between a PPP and other approaches to produce public goods.

Provision of public goods without and with partnership

Public goods may be produced by the public sector itself (public provision), by cooperating with the private sector through outsourcing (contracting out, whereby some tasks are commissioned from the private sector) or by moving their provision to the private sector completely, as happens in privatization (Stiglitz 2002, Joha and Janssen 2010). Public goods are non-excludable in consumption (everybody can consume the good or service) and non-rivalrous (nobody is worse off if an additional member of society begins consuming it). These two properties generate the free-rider problem (if nobody can be excluded from consumption, why pay for it?), leading to a market failure (nobody wants to finance the public good provision). For private goods with positive externalities (typical examples would include street lights, greening or gentrification) a common outcome in a competitive environment is under-provision (the amount provided is lower than socially desirable). This brief account of the well-established core of public economics (see, for example,

Laffont 1988) justifies delegating the provision of public goods to the state and financing them through taxes. (See, however, a note on complete and incomplete contracts below.)

A public enterprise is socially oriented, solves the problem of negative externalities but usually exhibits low efficiency compared to profit-oriented private businesses, especially in a competitive environment (Boardman and Vining 1989, Vining and Boardman 1992) typically due to a lack of incentives for managers either to reduce production costs (Bos 1991) or to properly monitor the efficiency of the use of human and other resources, in particular because the objectives of public enterprises often lack precision and are frequently changing (Alchian and Demsetz 1972). A review of literature on advantages of private businesses as compared to public ones is in Megginson and Netter (2001); in a later work, Bartel and Harrison (2005) explicitly show that in comparable conditions performance of public sector enterprises is below that of their private sector peers.

The state can exploit the efficiency benefits of private businesses by outsourcing the provision of public goods. This differs from the private provision of public goods in that the public body decides on the quantity, thus solving the underprovision problem. Allowing for more collaboration between the public and the private parties, we may introduce a consolidated public–private enterprise, which assumes provision of resources by all parties and the coordination of the parties' actions when implementing the project. Consolidation is justified when parties have comparative advantages in the provision of various resources, where each party should supply the resource that it can provide at a lower cost. Contributions of the public and of the private parties do not need to be limited to labour, capital and materials; additionally, the private party provides valuable managerial skills ensuring efficiency. The most common resources supplied by the public partner include land, access to funding, and human capital that brings in specialized knowledge and expertise (Besley and Ghatak 2001) as well as administrative experience and skills (Mahalingam et al. 2011), particularly with respect to reducing compliance and red-tape costs (Vinogradov et al. 2014).

Does it matter who owns the enterprise that provides the public good? In a world where everything may be specified in a clear and comprehensive contract (*complete* contract), and all contributions of parties involved may be guaranteed in full and on time, ownership makes no difference (Hart 2003): the government can commission the required public good from the private provider and get exactly the same result as if that good is produced within the private sector at a state-owned enterprise, or by a joint venture between the government and the private business. The difference only arises when contracts are *incomplete*; that is, when not all contributions can be specified, not all situations can be foreseen by the contract or enforcement does not work. In a world with incomplete contracts, state ownership or co-ownership of enterprises producing public goods is justified by the ability of the government 'to keep things under control', because, strictly speaking, the owner has the residual property rights. For projects that fully depend only on the private sector contribution, having a complete contract, although not always possible, is more likely than for projects that involve several parties. In many cases, the public sector also has an input; as projects become increasingly collaborative, the incompleteness of contracts becomes even more relevant. A good review of PPP-relevant literature elaborating complete and incomplete contracts can be found in de Bettignies and Ross (2010).

We have thus far covered the 'form', 'public good' and 'jointly' components of our definition; the remaining component is the 'partnership'. The partnership principle assumes partners mutually agree on their objectives and rationally decide how to achieve them (Brinkerhoff 2002). Hodge and Greve (2007) note that the interdependence and equality in decision-making, as well as equal benefits to parties, constitute an important aspect of partnerships. From an economics perspective, if contracts are incomplete, objectives of parties may diverge, which helps justify partnerships due to their ability to 'increase efficiency by aligning the incentives of the parties' (Grout 2003, Vinogradov et al. 2014, Vinogradov and Shadrina 2018a).

Contractual relationships and feasibility of collaborative projects

The core of the collaborative projects approach is contracting under asymmetric information (Roels et al. 2010; Kim and Netessine 2013). A project is characterized by inputs (contributions) of the two parties and by the sensitivity[4] of the project to the parties' inputs. As an illustration, using lower-quality building materials would require more frequent repair, and result in a higher maintenance cost of a road or other infrastructure objects, thus lowering their social value; these projects may be referred to as sensitive to the private party input. In addition, they are also sensitive to the input of the public party, which usually contributes at the planning and design stage. For the sake of exposition, we understand sensitivity in a very intuitive sense, as in 'the project's success to 40 per cent depends on the public input, and to 60 per cent – on the private input'. If the sum of sensitivities (to both inputs) cannot exceed 100 per cent, any project can be depicted as a point in the space of sensitivities, within the triangle constrained by conditions that sensitivities cannot be negative and cannot exceed 100 per cent in sum, as in figures 4.2(a) and 4.2(b). Within this project space, we wish to discriminate between (a) projects that can be implemented by having some type of a contractual agreement between the parties, and (b) projects for which even an optimal contract cannot guarantee sufficient profitability of the private partner (infeasible projects), and (c) infeasible projects that can be implemented under a partnership principle; that is, when some benefits of cooperation exist but are not contractable.

Under asymmetric information, parties do not freely observe each other's inputs. To give an example, a commissioning authority may be unaware of the exact number of workers employed or of the amount of materials used to construct a bridge, yet can obtain this information at some cost; for instance, through monitoring. If a party provides less input than contractually agreed, it is subject to penalties. Penalties can be monetary or non-pecuniary, associated with the loss of reputation and forgone future profit opportunities. For the private partner the penalty may include the value of their physical assets (bankruptcy value). The harshest penalty that can be imposed on a public partner is the exhaustion of their reserves and the dismissal of the relevant public managers.[5]

A contract between the public and the private party specifies their respective inputs, the remuneration to the private partner, the liabilities of the parties (in particular, penalties), and, in the framework used here, the type of reporting on costs and contributions (input verification). Three types of contracts are conceivable: those where only public input or private input is verified respectively, or where no input verification is done. The verification of both parties' inputs is unnecessary because knowing the outcome of the project and the credibly verified input of one party should suffice to establish whether the other party underprovides.[6]

The public partner designs the contract with an objective to maximize the project's social value, minus the costs of its provision and the related verification costs. A contract with the verification of the private party's input will specify that the private partner is only paid once inputs are confirmed; we refer to it as an *input-contingent* contract (IC contract). An alternative arrangement is when the private partner is paid only if the project is successfully completed. In this case, there may be a need to verify the contribution of the public partner. If the exact contribution of the private partner cannot be credibly established, the success of the project (achieving the target value) implies agreed resources were delivered in full, and hence payment is due. If the project fails, and it is established that the public partner delivered in line with the agreement, this implies that the private partner failed to meet the terms of the contract, and penalties are imposed. Alternatively, if the public party failed to deliver, it is accordingly penalized in favour of the private party. This type of contract is referred to as *output-contingent* (OC contract).

Instead of verifying the inputs, a third type of contract creates incentives for the private partner to properly contribute to the project. This can be achieved by making the remuneration dependent on the value that the project generates. Theoretically, contracts of this sort (*performance-based*, PB contracts) are justified in microeconomics (for example, Bhattacharyya and Lafontaine 1995; Kim and Wang 1998) for the cases where each party has an incentive to minimise their inputs and let their counterpart bear the costs. Practically, this corresponds to the concession approach often used in PPP: the private party operates an infrastructure object and derives profit from payments by the end users or by the government, proportional to the actual usage of that object (see, for example, Iossa 2015 for a detailed description and examples of concessions and revenue-generation mechanisms in the design, construction, maintenance and operation of the transport infrastructure).

A project is feasible if both parties agree to implement it by entering one of the above contractual agreements. The optimal contract is chosen by maximizing the total surplus generated by the project under different contractual provisions. In the input- and output-contingent contracts input verification raises the effective cost of resources. One has therefore to compare the cost of the project with and without verification. An important parameter for this comparison is the verification cost relative to the provision cost; that is, by how much more expensive (in per cent) in total would be a particular resource if one has to monitor its provision. This is what we understand under the verification cost. For example, a complex bridge incurs higher costs of resources (per unit) than a road because a bridge would involve unique solutions, while constructing a road involves a repetition of more standard techniques at each segment of the road. At the same time, it is easier to verify the quality of the bridge and the resources used by parties, as it is a localized object, while it is more expensive to monitor the actual provision of resources for each mile of a road. For these reasons, the verification cost (relative to the provision cost) is expected to be lower for the bridge and higher for the road. Even if resources of both parties have identical provision and verification costs, different contracts imply different *effective* cost. In the OC contract it is the public input that is verified and therefore becomes more costly than the private input. In the IC contract (private input verified) the private input will be more expensive when verification costs are considered. The sensitivity of the project to inputs determines then the type of the optimal contract: the OC contract (public input verified) is preferred to the IC contract (private input verified) if the project is less sensitive to the public input than to the private input, and vice versa. This is because choosing a contract that incurs verification cost for the input of the public party (OC contract) reduces the optimal amount of this input (due to its higher overall cost compared to the contract with no verification of this input), which does affect the final value of the project, yet this impact is smaller if the project has lower sensitivity to this resource. In Figure 4.2, OC contracts are optimal for projects with low sensitivity to public input and high sensitivity to private input (vice versa for IC contracts).

Unlike IC and OC contracts, verification does not take place in the PB contract. There is a trade-off between paying for information verification but achieving maximum value out of the project and saving on the verification cost but reducing the project's value (incentives without verification are weaker, hence the contribution of the parties within a PB contract is lower than in the first-best case). If verification costs are high, a PB contract would be preferable to both IC and OC. However, this would only hold true if the sensitivity of the project to the inputs is rather low, otherwise even a small reduction in the input due to weaker incentives would lead to a severe loss of the value for the project. For this reason, PB contracts cannot outperform IC and OC contracts at higher values of sensitivities. In Figure 4.2, therefore, PB contracts are shown as optimal only for projects with rather low sensitivity to inputs.

Not all projects are feasible even if contracts are optimally designed. One reason for this is costly verification. Projects with high sensitivity to both inputs and with relatively high verification costs are likely to be impractical because they become too costly with IC and OC contracts and generate a too low value with a PB contract. Additionally, projects may be infeasible due to the remuneration of the private partner, for whom there exists a participation threshold: even if the required input is small, a private partner would not be interested in taking part in the project if the payoff is below their acceptable threshold. The value of the project may be insufficient to justify high payoffs to the private partner, thus making the project infeasible. Note that these projects despite not being financially viable may still be socially desirable.

Partnership vs contractual relationships

The partnership principle either brings extra benefits to the private partner, for which reason it can lower the participation threshold, or improves productivity of resources due to a deeper cooperation and thus saves on the production cost. A reduction in the information and production cost may come through close cooperation and aligned objectives. The partnership element also facilitates co-production through improved communication and knowledge spillovers. These benefits are unlikely to be contractually binding, stressing the incomplete contracts point in the justification of PPPs.

Reduced participation thresholds and lower information and production costs enable the implementation of projects that would be infeasible under standard contract conditions considered above. This aspect of PPP is demonstrated in Figure 4.2: infeasible projects here are those that cannot be implemented even through a PPP, while the areas denoted as 'PPP projects' correspond to those that would have been infeasible if relationships between the parties were limited to 'working to contract'. Note that the set of contracts that can be used to form a PPP is the same as the one used for contracting out: IC contracts are optimal for projects with higher sensitivity to the public input, OC contracts for projects with higher sensitivity to private input and PB contracts outperform the two for projects with low sensitivity to both inputs. In Figure 4.2(a), verification costs and the participation threshold are small, for which reason the benefits from a PPP are rather small: establishing a PPP would enable implementation of a small number of specific projects that were not otherwise feasible. When, however, information costs and participation thresholds are high, establishing a PPP can be highly beneficial for a large number of otherwise infeasible projects, as in Figure 4.2(b).

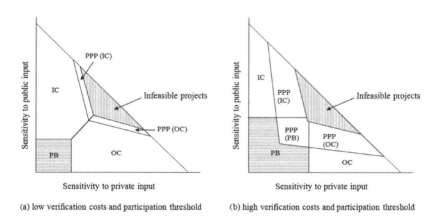

(a) low verification costs and participation threshold   (b) high verification costs and participation threshold

Figure 4.2   Joint public–private projects (IC, OC and PB contracts) versus PPPs

A PPP is thus a better option than outsourcing only if the verification cost and the participation threshold are relatively high. Moreover, a PPP is optimal only for projects with relatively high sensitivity to inputs of either or both parties.

This is because when the sensitivity of the project to inputs is small, parties can employ fewer resources that are too costly to verify, without a significant impact on the project value. In contrast, projects with relatively high sensitivity to both inputs incur high verification costs, and can become infeasible, which is where a PPP can help.

In this section, we have outlined, in a non-technical way,[7] a model that formalizes and justifies public–private partnerships from an economics perspective. Extending the informal definition from the beginning of this section, the model defines a public–private partnership as a consolidated (joint) enterprise that enables a reduction in the information and transaction costs (through a strong relationship, trust, and a lower administrative burden) to improve the contractual feasibility of otherwise non-contractible public projects. Clearly, developing strong relationships is costly per se and cannot be done on a large-scale basis. Fortunately, not all projects would fall in the subclass of those that need to be run through a PPP: all other subclasses should fall under standard public procurement contracts if they cannot be efficiently delivered by the public sector on its own.

Towards the economics of PPPs

The economic analysis of PPPs widely uses the mechanism design and contract theory approach, exemplified above. A significant strand of literature investigates, for example, whether some or all tasks within one, typically infrastructure, project should be delegated to a single private partner (Hart 2003, Bennett and Iossa 2006, Martimort and Pouyet 2008, Maskin and Tirole 2008, Chen and Chiu 2010). 'Bundling' consecutive tasks creates incentives for the private partner to perform well during the earlier stages of the project as this influences the outcomes at later stages, affecting the same private partner and creating incentives as in the PB contract above. At the same time, this approach 'unbundles' contributions of the public partner from the project, and ignores benefits potentially arising through close collaboration, covered in the previous section.

An aspect we only slightly articulated in the previous section is uncertainty. Some uncertainty, relating to the efforts exercised by the parties, can be resolved by obtaining information at a cost. There is therefore a trade-off between the level of trust parties show towards each other and the cost they wish to bear to verify each other's inputs. A different type of uncertainty refers to productivity shocks. Idiosyncratic shocks having an impact on the

PPP project can range from natural catastrophes to miscalculations or unexpected findings (such as an ancient Roman mosaic underground, requiring application of special heritage-preserving regulation). Lewis and Bajari (2014) investigate moral hazard in public procurement and the efficiency of penalties in preventing it. In their analysis, if unanticipated production shocks distort the initial schedule of road construction works, project managers exert efforts to adjust the construction plan in such a way as to remain on schedule. Moral hazard manifests when managers do nothing or very little, if penalties are not high, which is especially true for very large and costly projects. Reducing moral hazard through penalties is an approach known since Becker (1968): the theoretically optimal punishment should be as high as possible. But the upper limit of the fine is different for different people. Moreover, having fines too high may deter potential contractors, especially if they overestimate the likelihood of being punished (Vinogradov and Shadrina 2018b); more generally, 'the fine should fit the crime'.[8] The result of Lewis and Bajari (2014) thus has a practical dimension of finding the efficient penalty rule for specific contracts; this result naturally extends to the public–private partnership context, since public procurement and PPPs function under the same contractual arrangements. Unobservable efforts can have a different angle: if implementing new projects requires innovative solutions, how should innovation be rewarded? The problems here are similar to those above: efforts of contractors and their research cost are not directly observable. Weyl and Tirole (2012) justify the PB-type contracts in PPPs by the consideration of offering a sufficient reward for innovation.

As for the contribution of the public partner, a large strand of literature in economics and finance deals with state-owned enterprises and their efficiency. A particular source of inefficiency is political influence, as suggested by Shleifer and Vishny (1994). Maskin and Tirole (2008) derive optimal regulatory provisions to tackle the potential political bias in choosing the private partner for a PPP. Recently, Alok and Ayyagari (2020) empirically document that projects run by state-owned enterprises, especially in infrastructure, have more capital expenditure in election years, and in particular in districts with close elections and high-ranking politicians. If the inefficiency created by this political cycle is transferred to a PPP (for example, by deterring public resources from a PPP project in favour of another politically motivated investment), what implications would this have on the private partner? The problem would be especially relevant for longer-term projects spanning over a few political cycles.

The collaborative model we outlined depicts the economics view of PPP by focusing on social objectives to be achieved, contributions of parties and contractual arrangements to combine them. Economists study why various forms of public good provision (should) exist and in what sense they may contribute to social welfare. Economics offers insights into the type of contract that is suitable for a PPP project and into optimal methods to select the private partner for the collaborative project. Economics is also helpful for getting insights into the frictions (information, uncertainty) that impede project implementation.

Some important areas remain underinvestigated. There is so far no research on optimal funding schemes for a PPP, and this is where economics and finance could contribute: if choosing between debt and equity finance matters for corporations, what are the implications for ventures with public participation – should the private partner issue shares, or bonds, or apply for a bank loan?[9] Or, maybe emerging fintech solutions, ranging from crowdfunding to blockchain-based tokens and initial coin offerings, are more suitable? We touched somewhat upon a 'strong relationship' and possible knowledge transfer within a PPP – this form of collaboration may have an indirect effect on the private sector, by transferring practices (for example, sustainable procurement) the government wishes to promote. No research on changes in behaviour and performance of private partners after their cooperation with the government exists to date. Finally, given public procurement often aims at supporting small businesses, how does the PPP practice fit into this same objective? These are some of the issues yet unanswered with respect to PPPs, at least from an economics perspective.

A suitable parallel may be drawn between economics of PPP and that of financial institutions. Economic models of banks as institutions that improve the allocation of resources in the economy were first developed in the 1980–1990s, when the banking industry had already existed for ages. The modern economics of financial institutions covers their *raison d'être*, including why they co-exist with financial markets, the type and nature of contracts between all parties involved, risks arising from asymmetric information between parties and from exogenous sources, the role the industry structure (monopolistic or competitive) plays for banks' performance and stability, the role banks play for the economy as a whole, and relevant regulation to protect consumers and prevent banking crises. If PPPs earn attention as institutions that serve some purpose differently from and better than other existing arrangements (public provision of public goods or public procurement to outsource this provision), we may expect the economics of PPP to develop in a similar fashion. Some economic analysis of the nature and rationale of PPPs, as well as the analysis of contracts (to be) used in PPPs, already exists. A comprehensive theory of PPP would need to complement this research with the economic analysis of risks, performance, effect on the economy, possible dangers arising from using PPPs and regulation to prevent them. Solid steps in this direction have already been made through books by Grimsey and Lewis (2005), de Vries and Yehoue (2013), Engel et al. (2014) and Saussier and de Brux (2018) – with a difference of just under 15 years, the former begins by saying that the literature at that time was relatively new, while the latter opens up with a remark that the economics of PPP is 'largely perceived as too difficult to understand by stakeholders outside of academia and/or the field of economics … [T]his is an incredibly extensive, heterogeneous, somewhat fragmented, and often very complex literature' (p.vi). They cover many of the topics we outlined above, including the nature of PPP, efficiency gains from it, incentives and contracts, as well as issues in governance and financing of PPPs, mainly with applications to infrastructure projects. We call for a generalization of this view on PPPs; there is still much to understand about them and the improvements they bring about, and not only in the infrastructure. Is there interest in these topics in the public administration research of PPP?

The economics of PPP and the public administration research

A review by Wang et al. (2018), using 186 articles in 56 journals listed under the subject area 'public administration' in the ISI Web of Science database, identifies four key themes arising in papers devoted to PPPs: types of PPP, performance (efficiency), risk (types of risk and risk-sharing) and drivers of PPP (factors of adoption of the PPP format). Cui et al. (2018) searched through 754 articles on PPP in infrastructure projects, among which 234 were in construction, 81 in public administration, 35 in urban studies and 28 in economics, identifying a set of research topics that partially overlaps with the above set of research topics: nature and rationale for PPPs, merit and worth, decisions to undertake PPPs, regulation and guidance, *ex post* evaluations of PPP. By combining merit and worth with *ex post* evaluation, we come close to the performance (efficiency) topic in Wang et al. (2018). While Cui et al. (2018) omit the risk discussion (which may partly fall under merit and worth, and partly under decisions to undertake), they come up with an additional topic of regulation. To complement both analyses, we focused on three journals only – the *Journal of Public Administration Research and Theory*, *Public Administration Review* and *Public Management Review* – yet we extended the search to all papers that contain the phrase 'public–private partnership' in any field, the same as we did in the introduction for other journals, and did not restrict it to infrastructure only. On top of the above topics, our search highlighted the discussion of the impact of politicians and the society on adoption and performance of PPPs (Ghere 1996, Boyer et al. 2016, Guo and Ho 2019), which some might place within 'drivers' and 'performance', and the discussion of the management of the overall project, its human resources and relationships between the partners (Lippi et al. 2008, Koppenjan and Enserink 2009, Waring et al. 2013, Vangen et al. 2015), which does not straightforwardly fall under any of the above. We therefore end up with seven main themes around PPP in public administration literature: (1) nature and rationale, (2) performance and efficiency, (3) risks and uncertainty, (4) drivers of adoption, (5) regulation, (6) management and relations, and (7) politicians and society. How do they fit in the economics perspective?

As we highlighted above, topic (1) – nature and rationale – is a key element of having a comprehensive economic theory of PPP. The contract analysis, widely undertaken in economics, adds to our theoretical understanding of optimal design to ensure performance and efficiency, signifying a contribution from economics to topic (2). Simultaneously, as illustrated in the collaborative model in the second section, contract theory highlights the importance of relationships and their management, topic (6), yet more needs to be done in this direction. Topic (3) – risks and uncertainty in PPP – has been poorly analyzed so far from an economics perspective: extant economics research mainly deals with counterparty risks within the asymmetric information approach, while other types of risks, provisions against them and their assessment are not yet covered with respect to PPP. An important issue within the risk and uncertainty topic, from an economics perspective, is different degrees of aversion both to risks (those that can be measured with probabilities) and ambiguity (description of possible development of events where a unique probability measure cannot be conceived). The political dimension – topic (7) has received some attention in the context of state-owned enterprises, as well as in studies of corruption in public procurement. An economic judgement on drivers of PPP adoption and success (topic 4) requires a thorough workhorse model of a PPP, which to date does not exist. Similarly, an established workhorse model is needed to precisely pinpoint the deficiencies in the PPP arrangements that need addressing from the regulatory perspective (topic 5), and to distinguish them from those stemming from poor assessment of risks, suboptimal usage of contracts, and so on.

As the field is growing, and the public administration literature emphasizes the need for further analysis, economics will hopefully respond. The key problem, as of now, appears to be the heterogeneity of views on PPP and the rather loose terminology used within public administration, across subjects and across countries.[10] This lack of consensus impedes the perception of PPPs as distinct institutions. For example, Weyl and Tirole (2012) see PPP as an arrangement in which 'the builder of the new infrastructure derives substantial revenue from its later operations' (p. 1995), effectively synonymizing the institution (PPP) with a particular type of contract (concession). Engel et al. (2013) use effectively the same definition (although they acknowledge other definitions are in use, too), echoing Hart (2003). As a result, there is too little novelty associated with PPPs from the perspective of the cutting-edge economics research: if it is a type of a contract – there is a large literature on contracts, where PPP would serve yet another example; if it is outsourcing – there is literature on public good provision by private sector, where PPP is again just an example; if it is a corruption scheme – there is literature on that, too, so why focus on PPPs specifically?

Conclusion

Public–private partnerships are institutional arrangements in which the public and the private sector jointly provide public services, under 'special relations' that govern their cooperation. The economics approach justifies 'special relations' by considering the world with and without them, and by concluding whether the former is any better than the latter, in terms of the benefits for the society. Modelling a PPP as a collaborative project allows identifying in what situations and how 'special relations' may help deliver public goods when other arrangements fail; that is, when the public sector neither on its own, nor by contracting some tasks out to the private sector through traditional public procurement, can efficiently deliver a project of social value. This view neither confines PPPs to be 'long-term' or 'infrastructure' projects only, nor imposes any conditions on 'risk-sharing', nor restricts attention to a specific type of contract. Rather, it highlights the distinctive feature of PPPs in general, which makes them stand out among various forms of public good provision.

Economic analysis of PPP is currently spread over social welfare (with respect to identifying the need in and the benefits of the public good provision), mechanism design (applied specifically to the optimal provision of public goods by private businesses jointly or on behalf of the public sector) and political economy (in what relates to politicians' objectives and their impact on public sector projects). Extant mechanism design research focuses on types of contracts, information frictions (such as moral hazard) and optimal contract provisions (penalties and rewards) to overcome them and resulting implications for bundling or unbundling of tasks within one project. The political economy view suggests public projects are likely to be affected by political cycles, yet implications for PPPs are not well established. Some other questions gaining attention in economics and finance but not yet well investigated with respect to PPPs, include, for example, optimal funding schemes for PPPs, including alternative finance and fintech solutions; optimal PPP governance and political connections; implications of uncertainty for PPP, including unquantifiable, Knightian uncertainty; and related notions of pessimism and optimism of decision-makers, among others.

A comprehensive economic theory of PPP, with workhorse models suitable for welfare, policy and regulation analysis, is desirable. The wide interest towards PPPs in the public administration literature centres around the topics such a theory would cover. A necessary step towards that is finding a consensus on the nature of PPP interdisciplinarily, which would enable a spillover of the broad range of observations from public administration research to economics, and reciprocally of conceptual ideas from economics to public administration. Economists keep an eye on PPPs, and there is a gleam in that eye: more comprehensive research is ready to come once public–private partnerships are seen as a distinct large class of institutions, not many 'classes of their own'.

Notes

1. The authors acknowledge support through the Russian Foundation of Basic Research (RFBR) grant 18-010-01166.
2. Admittedly, ranking methodologies differ, yet there is some consensus with respect to top journals.
3. Parts of this section are based on Vinogradov and Shadrina (2018a).
4. Sensitivity describes by how much the generated social value changes in response to a variation in the input of either party. In microeconomics, a traditional measure of sensitivity would be the factor elasticity of the output.
5. See Vinogradov and Shadrina (2018a) for examples.
6. This emphasises that mistrust between the parties, which makes them believe that there is a need to monitor actions of each other, leads to a suboptimal outcome, as in an equilibrium less resources will be provided in total, yielding a lower value of the project. For this reason, the benefits from a partnership in the framework employed in this paper would only become larger, as it is assumed that improved communication in a partnership contributes to developing more trust between the partners.
7. An interested reader can find the formal model and analysis in Vinogradov and Shadrina (2016).
8. 'Optimal fines should rise with the severity of the infraction, that is, the penalty should "fit the crime."' (Andreoni 1991, p. 385).
9. Maskin and Tirole (2008) show the role of financiers in the PPP context may differ from that in traditional corporate finance, in particular, monitoring from an external financing body may mitigate inefficiencies arising due to political biases in partner selection.

10. The heterogeneity of definitions and approaches in the public administration research has been highlighted, for example, by Wang et al. (2018).

References

Alchian, A. A., and Demsetz, H. (1972) Production, information costs, and economic organization. *American Economic Review*, *62*: 777–795.

Alok, S., and Ayyagari, M. (2020) Politics, state ownership, and corporate investments. *Review of Financial Studies*, *33*(7): 3031–3087.

Andreoni, J. (1991) Reasonable doubt and the optimal magnitude of fines: Should the penalty fit the crime? *RAND Journal of Economics*, *22*(3): 385–395.

Bartel, A., and Harrison, A. (2005) Ownership versus environment: Disentangling the sources of public-sector inefficiency. *Review of Economics and Statistics*, *87*(1): 135–147.

Becker, G. S. (1968) Crime and punishment: An economic approach, in *The Economic Dimensions of Crime*, edited by N. G. Fielding, A. Clarke and R. R. Witt. London: Palgrave Macmillan, pp. 13–68. https://doi.org/10.1007/978-1-349-62853-7_2.

Bennett, J., and Iossa E. (2006) Building and managing facilities for public services. *Journal of Public Economics*, *90*: 2143–2160.

Besley, T. J., and Ghatak, M. (2001) Government versus private ownership of public goods. *Quarterly Journal of Economics*, *116*(4): 1343–1372.

Bhattacharyya, S., and Lafontaine, F. (1995) Double-sided moral hazard and the nature of share contracts. *RAND Journal of Economics*, *26*(4): 761–781.

Boardman, A. E., and Vining, A. R. (1989) Ownership and performance in competitive environments: A comparison of the performance of private, mixed, and state-owned enterprises. *Journal of Law and Economics*, *32*(1): 1–33.

Bos, D. (1991) *Privatization: A Theoretical Treatment*. Oxford: Oxford University Press.

Boyer, E. J., Van Slyke, D. M., and Rogers, J. D. (2016) An empirical examination of public involvement in public-private partnerships: Qualifying the benefits of public involvement in PPPs. *Journal of Public Administration Research and Theory*, *26*(1): 45–61.

Brinkerhoff, J. M. (2002) Assessing and improving partnership relations and outcomes: A proposed framework. *Journal of Evaluation and Program Planning*, *25*(3): 215–231.

CEDR (2009) Public Private Partnerships. Conference of European Directors of Roads, May 2009. www.cedr.fr/home/fileadmin/user_upload/Publications/2009/e_Public _private_partnerships_(PPP).pdf.

Chen, B. R., and Chiu Y. S. (2010) Public-private partnerships: Task interdependence and contractibility. *International Journal of Industrial Organization*, *28*(6): 591–603.

Cui, C., Liu, Y., Hope, A., and Wang, J. (2018) Review of studies on the public–private partnerships (PPP) for infrastructure projects. *International Journal of Project Management*, *36*(5): 773–794.

De Bettignies, J. E., and Ross, T. W. (2010) The economics of public–private partnerships: some theoretical contributions, in *International Handbook on Public–Private Partnerships*, edited by G. A. Hodge, C. Greve and A. E. Boardman. Cheltenham, UK and Northampton, MA, USA: Edward Elgar Publishing, pp. 132–158.

De Vries, P., and Yehoue, E. B. (Eds.) (2013) *The Routledge Companion to Public-Private Partnerships*. Abingdon: Routledge.

Ehrhardt, M., and Brigham, E. F. (2006) *Corporate Finance: A Focused Approach*, 2nd edition. Mason, OH: Thomson South-Western.

Engel, E., Fischer, R., and Galetovic, A. (2013) The basic public finance of public–private partnerships. *Journal of the European Economic Association, 11*(1): 83–111.

Engel, E., Fischer, R. D., and Galetovic, A. (2014) *The Economics of Public-Private Partnerships: A Basic Guide*. New York, NY: Cambridge University Press.

European Commission (2003) *Guidelines for Successful Public-Private Partnerships*. Brussels: Directorate General Regional Policy.

Ghere, R. K. (1996) Aligning the ethics of public-private partnership: The issue of local economic development. *Journal of Public Administration Research and Theory, 6*(4): 599–621.

Grimsey, D., and Lewis, M. K. (2005) *The Economics of Public Private Partnerships*. Cheltenham, UK and Northampton, MA, USA: Edward Elgar Publishing.

Grout, P. A. (2003) Public and private sector discount rates in public–private partnerships. *Economic Journal, 113*(486): C62–C68.

Guo, H., and Ho, A. T. K. (2019) Support for contracting-out and public-private partnership: Exploring citizens' perspectives. *Public Management Review, 21*(5): 629–649.

Hart, O. (2003) Incomplete contracts and public ownership: Remarks and an application to public-private partnerships. *Economic Journal, 113*(486): C69–C76.

Hodge, G. A., and Greve C. (2007) Public-private partnerships: An international performance review. *Public Administration Review, 67*(3): 545–558.

Iossa, E. (2015) Contract and procurement design for PPPs in highways: The road ahead. *Journal of Industrial and Business Economics (Economia e Politica Industriale), 42*: 245–276.

Joha, A., and Janssen, M. (2010) Public-private partnerships, outsourcing or shared service centres? Motives and intents for selecting sourcing configurations. *Transforming Government: People, Process and Policy, 4*(3): 232–248.

Kim, S. H., and Netessine, S. (2013) Collaborative cost reduction and component procurement under information asymmetry. *Management Science, 59*(1): 189–206.

Kim, S. K., and Wang, S. (1998) Linear contracts and the double moral-hazard. *Journal of Economic Theory, 82*(2): 342–378.

Koppenjan, J., and Enserink B. (2009) Public-private partnerships in urban infrastructures: Reconciling private sector participation and sustainability. *Public Administration Review, 69*(2): 284–296.

Laffont, J.-J. (1988) *Fundamentals of Public Economics*. Cambridge, MA: MIT Press.

Lewis, G., and Bajari, P. (2014) Moral hazard, incentive contracts, and risk: Evidence from procurement. *Review of Economic Studies, 81*(3): 1201–1228.

Lippi, A., Giannelli, N., Profeti, S., and Citroni, G. (2008) Adapting public–private governance to the local context: The case of water and sanitation services in Italy. *Public Management Review, 10*(5): 619–640.

Mahalingam, A., Devkar, G. A., and Kalidindi, S. N. (2011) A comparative analysis of public-private partnership (PPP) coordination agencies in India: What works and what doesn't. *Public Works Management and Policy, 16*(4): 341–372.

Martimort, D., and Pouyet, J. (2008) To build or not to build: Normative and positive theories of public–private partnerships. *International Journal of Industrial Organization, 26*(2): 393–411.

Maskin, E., and Tirole, J. (2008) Public–private partnerships and government spending limits. *International Journal of Industrial Organization*, *26*(2): 412–420.

Megginson, W., and Netter, J. (2001) From state to market: A survey of empirical studies on privatization. *Journal of Economic Literature*, *39*(June): 321–389.

OECD (2010) *Dedicated Public-Private Partnership Units: A Survey of Institutional and Governance Structures*. Paris: OECD Publishing.

Roels, G., Karmarkar, U. S., and Carr, S. (2010) Contracting for collaborative services. *Management Science*, *56*(5): 849–863.

Saussier, S., and de Brux, J. (2018) *The Economics of Public-Private Partnerships*. Cham: Springer.

Shleifer, A., and Vishny, R. W. (1994) Politicians and firms. *Quarterly Journal of Economics*, *109*(4): 995–1025.

Stiglitz, J. E. (2002) New perspectives on public finance: Recent achievements and future challenges. *Journal of Public Economics*, *86*: 341–360.

Vangen, S., Hayes, J. P., and Cornforth, C. (2015) Governing cross-sector, inter-organizational collaborations. *Public Management Review*, *17*(9): 1237–1260.

Vining, A. R., and Boardman, A. E. (1992) Ownership versus competition: Efficiency in public enterprise. *Public Choice*, *73*(2): 205–239.

Vinogradov, D., and Shadrina, E. (2016) *Public-Private Partnerships as Collaborative Projects: Testing the Theory on Cases from EU and Russia* (February 5, 2016). Essex Finance Centre Working Paper No 6: 02-2016, Essex Business School, University of Essex. Available at SSRN: https://ssrn.com/abstract=2728197 or http://dx.doi.org/10.2139/ssrn.2728197.

Vinogradov, D., and Shadrina, E. (2018a) Public-private partnerships as collaborative projects: Testing the theory on cases from EU and Russia. *International Journal of Public Administration*, *41*(5–6): 446–459.

Vinogradov, D. V., and Shadrina, E. V. (2018b) *Discouragement through Incentives*. WP 2018-05. Working Paper, Adam Smith Business School, University of Glasgow.

Vinogradov, D., Shadrina, E., and Kokareva, L. (2014) Public procurement mechanisms for public-private partnerships. *Journal of Public Procurement*, *14*(4): 538–566.

Wang, H., Xiong, W., Wu, G., and Zhu, D. (2018) Public–private partnership in public administration discipline: A literature review. *Public Management Review*, *20*(2): 293–316.

Waring, J., Currie, G., and Bishop, S. (2013) A contingent approach to the organization and management of public–private partnerships: An empirical study of English health care. *Public Administration Review*, *73*(2): 313–326.

Weyl, E. G., and Tirole, J. (2012) Market power screens willingness-to-pay. *Quarterly Journal of Economics*, *127*(4): 1971–2003.

5   New frontiers in the politics of public–private partnerships

Anthony M. Bertelli and Eleanor F. Woodhouse

Introduction

While a variety of scholars have considered the politics behind certain aspects of public–private partnerships (PPPs) (Flinders 2005, Hellowell 2010, Boardman and Hellowell 2017), this work has not yet come together to form a systematic research agenda. Much of this attention to PPPs has been motivated, rightly, by a desire to understand whether or not these contractual arrangements offered value for money when compared with full public provision and management of public goods and services. However, this has come at the cost of an established, comparative understanding of what PPPs mean in a politicized environment.

In this chapter, we build on a research agenda that we have been undertaking to advance the frontiers of a political conception of PPPs. We do so by accomplishing four things. First, we provide an analytic definition of the concept of a PPP that clarifies its political relevance and potential. Second, we examine the strategic importance of PPPs so defined for electoral representatives. Third, we consider the way in which PPPs as institutions are viewed by voters. Finally, we elaborate a research agenda that addresses questions of electoral accountability and representation in both domestic and comparative contexts. This chapter focuses on a research agenda addressing both advanced and transitional economies and using comparative, systematic, and quantitative analytical methods, an approach that differs from the case studies often adopted when analyzing the politics of PPPs.

Our chapter responds to calls for more research that aims to understand why PPPs have remained so popular among governments despite their mixed performance record (Hodge and Greve 2010). Only in this way, we argue, will it be possible to understand how PPPs 'contribute politically, and develop stronger analytical frameworks to analyze [PPPs] as a governing mechanism with political payoffs' (Hodge and Greve 2017a, p. 69). These are questions that are important and of urgency for both the academic and policy-making communities. Without a better understanding of why PPPs are adopted by governments, the current suboptimal situation wherein PPPs often seem to offer greater value to private sector actors than to the taxpayer may persist without due scrutiny for many years to come (Hodge and Greve 2017b).

PPPs and distributive benefits

We believe that at the core of the politics of PPPs is an understanding that they are a mechanism for delivering distributive benefits to citizens. When providing public goods, such as water treatment facilities or cellular towers, that benefit citizens, Bertelli (2019) contends that the following features make merely entering into a PPP an attractive proposition and something for which politicians seek credit from voters. PPPs are contracts that promise to provide public goods with benefits that are geographically concentrated (the cellular towers have a limited service area) and costs that are spread across a much broader area (taxpayer contributions and development funds that match private investment could have been used elsewhere). Because the private part-ners' efforts are secured by contract, PPPs are more credible than the claims politicians make to funding through budget projects that are subject to change or the use of funds through international organizations. Moreover, because PPPs are by definition not short-term endeavors, the promises to provide the public goods they encapsulate increase in value when government continues to support them politically and financially; that is, once the cellular towers are in operation. Finally, after the goods are provided, it is difficult for politicians to redeploy them in another jurisdiction or put them in the service of a different constituency. These elements place PPPs at the center of a Laswellian politics— of who gets what, when, how.

We claim that understanding this politics is served through a nascent research agenda that examines two broad questions. How do politicians make use of the PPP as a mechanism to distribute goods and services to important constitu-encies? How do citizens react to the use of private partners in delivering these goods and services? The broadly comparative research agenda that we and our colleagues have pursued thus far places these questions at the center of a dis-tributive politics, which has crucial implications for electoral accountability and for representation.

The incentives of politicians

PPPs are complicated agreements, but at their political essence they are a contract between a state actor and a private consortium for the purpose of providing public goods or services. In this way, they are an alternative to full public management, and that is precisely why they are a part of the legacy of New Public Management. Like full public management, they involve a delegation of authority to make decisions about how to make public goods or services operational, and that authority is granted to private entities instead of a state administrative organ. We maintain that the frontiers of researching the politics of PPPs cannot be reached by simply thinking of the 'democratic deficit' involved in such delegations—such delegations are commonplace in modern governance worldwide—but by considering the different ways in which PPPs structure those delegations when compared to, say, the contracting out of public services.

One helpful way forward is to consider the incentives politicians face to use PPPs as a 'mega-credit card' to deliver public goods or services (Hodge 2002). The potential abuses of such a device are immediately apparent. As Hodge (2004, 174) puts it, such arrangements are appealing for '[a] government that wants to both deliver immediate policy solutions to a voting public and demonstrate physical achievements and success before the next election. No prizes also for figuring out who pays for this folly if the price is higher than it need be after the deal is signed.' PPPs, then, represent a doubly attractive opportunity for governments in that they offer a way to finance a public good, but they push back the cost implications to a later stage when the government may be able to shirk responsibility—either because the instigating politicians are no longer in office or because they can pass the buck to the private partners involved in the project. Beyond the temporal inconsistency of preferences, PPPs seen in this light allow politicians to bypass the normal budgetary process and to consider the costs differently.

Yet a key difference from full public management is that PPPs vary in the *ex ante* commitments they make to deliver goods or services that are public in nature. PPP contracts for providing public infrastructure, for instance, grant rights to own and operate assets across three stages: building, operating, and a post-contractual stage (Bertelli 2019). For example, a build-lease-transfer agreement leaves ownership with the government and leases it to the private consortium for operation, while in a build-operate-transfer agreement, the consortium owns the asset during the operating stage. In both cases, when the agreement is done, the asset is public. After the contract, politicians are not bound to operate the asset, and they can write another contract with the same consortium or a different one. Thus, the credit-claiming described above is for probabilistic benefits because the value to citizens is yet to be seen. The control rights granted in different forms of contract can increase or decrease the 'publicness' of the project (Bozeman 1987). Claiming credit for a public good that will not be as public, as in the build-operate-transfer agreement, is a different matter conceptually.

Analyzing more than 4,300 PPP agreements for new construction of infrastructure in 83 developing economies, Bertelli (2019) finds that build-operate-transfer agreements, with their long-term private control rights, are less popular among party governments that are long-serving, but also when key political offices, or what Tsebelis (2011) calls 'veto players,' are more frequently replaced. That is, competitive elections make the 'credit card' attractive, but even more so when an incumbent party has an expectation to control at least one key institutional veto player—for instance, the executive or legislature. In addition, Bertelli, Woodhouse, Castiglioni and Belardinelli (2021) find in a large-scale study discussed in more depth momentarily that a residual public claim, as with a build-operate-transfer, is associated with higher-quality project teams.

The type of PPP politicians adopt depends on the electoral pressures imposed on them. What is more, political institutions influence the adoption of those partnerships. In one example, studying 116 countries between 1984 and 2012, Bertelli, Mele and Woodhouse (2021) find that public sector corruption has no impact on the number of partnerships adopted in democracies, but more partnerships emerge in non-democracies precisely as corruption in the bureaucracy worsens. Without electoral pressures present in functioning democracies, politicians have little incentive to monitor corruption, and private benefits (for example, bribes and favorable contract terms) may well be responsible for making partnerships more appealing. In another example, Bertelli, Mele and Whitford (2020) employ a mixed-method research design to show two intriguing things. First, while the cancellation of contracts is a rare event, it is a valid measure of the failure of a PPP that provides public goods. Second, across 89 developing countries and more than 4,000 agreements to build infrastructure via PPP, these deals are less likely to fail when domestic political institutions offer more veto players to check politicians from unilaterally meddling with the implementation of public policies. The nature of political institutions present in a given context affects how PPPs are used and implemented by political elites, and there is much work to be done in understanding the mechanisms underlying this influence.

Additional evidence suggests that politicians' interest in shoring up support in different areas of the electoral map is reflected in the geographic distribution of PPP agreements within nations. Woodhouse (2019) analyzes whether or not PPPs follow nonprogrammatic distributive patterns and explores how a project's features affect its distributive use. Studying a dataset linking public infrastructure PPPs to subnational electoral districts in 13 low- and middle-income countries over 24 years, she shows that PPPs are used to target government-aligned swing districts, thus providing evidence in favor of politicians' interest in using partnerships to garner greater support in specific, electorally strategic areas. She also finds that when projects are less directly attributable to the government this targeting pattern disappears, suggesting that other political logics are at work when governments cannot convincingly claim credit for projects. In this, Woodhouse (2019) shows how politicians use PPPs to their strategic advantage, targeting key areas of the electoral map and claiming credit for projects over the course of their negotiation and implementation—well before the public goods themselves are delivered.

Scholars have thus started to establish systematic quantitative evidence that shows that politicians use PPPs strategically, for electoral ends, and according to the credit-claiming potential of partnership agreements. However, much remains to be done if we wish to better understand which types of PPPs represent the most effective credit-claiming opportunities in order to disentangle those delivery choices that represent strategic political maneuvers and those that represent reasoned policy choices motivated by a concern for public welfare.

One additional analytic concern for understanding the politics of PPPs regards the nature of the partners with which politicians engage. In *Partnership Communities: Political Accountability and the Success of Infrastructure Development around the World* (Bertelli et al., 2021), we study over 32,000 infrastructure PPPs from across the globe to better understand the constellations of private partners that collaborate with governments in PPPs. We define 'partnership communities' as networked communities of private firms and consortia that enter into long-term contractual arrangements with governments. After initial partnerships create a demand for firms to collaborate with a specific national government and local talent advantages are exploited, we argue with evidence that partnership communities congeal to provide the private investment necessary to unlock the efficiency and political benefits of PPPs, while mitigating risk that individual firms face when contracting in a specific national institutional environment. What results is not a competitive market for partners, but a limited number of communities, dominated by individual firms, that act as repeat agents for delivering infrastructure projects for a government. We show that in our worldwide sample between 1985 and 2020, the number of partnership communities increases with government project announcements (or government demand) to a point, but then falls as announcements continue. Strikingly, the point of diminishing community development comes at a level of project announcements that almost 77 percent of country-year observations reach in our sample. The consolidation of partnership communities is the rule, not the exception, and what efficiency is coming from PPPs seems clearly not to be because of market-style competition among partners.

We draw attention to these findings because they represent a first step towards building a comprehensive picture of which private partners are involved in PPPs worldwide, the extent to which they dominate national PPP environments, and how their success correlates with political institutions. We believe that the concept and measure of partnership communities that we propose represent powerful tools with which to better understand the delivery of public goods with private involvement from a comparative perspective.

There are many important questions to be explored regarding how to best quantify the influence that certain companies possess over how infrastructure is delivered across countries or precisely how certain political institutions encourage varying levels of market dominance in the delivery of PPPs. Our findings suggest that political and judicial institutions have an important impact on partnership communities (Bertelli et al., 2021). For example, partnership communities suffer when courts routinely accept side payments, but strengthen when bureaucrats have a penchant for doing the same. Moreover, where Laswellian distributive politics is commonplace in infrastructure spending, partnership communities are stronger. Analyzing a novel measure of project quality, we also show, inter alia, that the rule of law is associated with higher- but distributive politics with lower-quality projects (Bertelli et al., 2021). While our findings suggest that political and judicial institutions shape the risk-sharing that partnership communities bring, it will be imperative to delve deeper into such mechanisms if we want to develop a deeper understanding of the political determinants shaping how infrastructure is being delivered with private participation.

The attitudes of voters

We have been considering the PPP as a policy tool with distinct advantages for politicians, and our argument has included the use of this tool as a means of credit-claiming. Yet, for this strategy to be successful in regimes with competitive elections, we must try to understand how PPPs are perceived by voters. PPPs are problematic in that they blur the lines between the public and private and, thus, can give governments room to shirk stewardship responsibilities in governance (Hodge 2004) as they are not the sole party responsible for the delivery of the public good. This blurring occurs because the private actors involved in PPPs bear a significant part of the risk involved in the construction and management of infrastructure, giving them strong incentives to act in a profitable way (Engel, Fischer and Galetovic 2013).

However, there is very little work to date (but see Boyer and Van Slyke 2019) that systematically investigates how voters perceive PPPs and relate them to politics. An exception is Woodhouse, Belardinelli and Bertelli (2022), which conducts a survey experiment on over a thousand Americans, to assess how the allocation of public goods shapes voters' preferences over incumbent politicians. The authors find that voters prefer a mixture of public–private financing and management when it comes to the delivery of infrastructure. However, once performance information is available, the mode of infrastructure delivery no longer influences electoral outcomes. Subgroup analysis shows that the preference for a mixture of public and private involvement in public service delivery is driven by citizens with high political knowledge. These high-political-knowledge individuals seem to be more skeptical of private involvement in the delivery of public goods, suggesting that they are attuned to the risks that come with the involvement of the private sector in the delivery of public infrastructure, such as cost overruns, delays, renegotiations, and difficulty in enforcing payment or delivery of services in the case of bankruptcy claims. Voters in the study are indeed sensitive to the way in which their public goods are delivered. But this is one experiment in a single country and—as we laid out in the first section of this essay—comparative work and replication will be essential in establishing whether this is a generalized phenomenon or specific to certain national, institutional contexts.

Further evidence that voters are responsive to how their public services are delivered comes from Colombia, where Angulo Amaya, Bertelli and Woodhouse (2020) analyze 109 Colombian PPP projects between 1998 and 2014, and over 8,700 individual survey responses, to show that vote intention for the incumbent executive or her party decreases as experience with more PPPs in respondents' districts grows. These results suggest that negative experiences with PPPs—which are very salient in Colombia, where several high-profile disasters have occurred involving PPPs, such as the Hidroituango hydroelectric dam or the Ruta del Sol highway—introduce a sociotropic (meaning that voters look beyond their own interests) turn in individual voting whereby bad experience crowds out the possibility that promising a new project will improve a voter's own welfare. These findings add further nuance to our understanding of how voters perceive PPPs in that they demonstrate that simply providing infrastructure is not sufficient to win over voters; they respond to failures in delivery, and this is reflected in their voting intentions.

The beginnings of a research agenda into voters' perceptions of PPPs and their political responses are thus emerging. It will be essential for future work to drill down, continuing to explore the microfoundations of individuals' preferences for certain forms of public service delivery. Moreover, such an understanding will be shaped by national context; it will be important for us to understand how such preferences change according to varying experiences with private involvement in the public sector. Do citizens from countries with a strong history of public management of infrastructure or services react differently to private involvement than those from countries where private involvement in public goods provision is well established? Does the proximity of the public partner to the voter (local versus national government) affect voter attitudes? Such questions are crucial to understanding the political payoffs that come with PPPs. By deepening our understanding of how voters react to PPPs, we will get to the heart of one of the questions that hangs over the use of PPPs: namely, whether they undermine the democratic process. If voters do indeed feel disenfranchised or alienated by private involvement or less able to understand whether politicians are responsible for the performance of public goods and services, then PPPs can be argued to come with a non-ignorable cost for democracy. One possible way to think about reconciling potential democracy-eroding qualities of PPPs is to involve citizens more in the processes through which governments enter into PPPs. By increasing citizen involvement (Boyer, Van Slyke and Rogers 2016), PPPs may be able to better achieve the goals of representative democracy by weakening the incentives for politicians to shirk responsibility for PPPs or use them as electoral tools.

Conclusions

The research agenda we have reviewed is only the beginning of a systematic, theoretical understanding of the politics of PPPs. Like most scholars, we think that the PPP is a policy tool, but we are convinced that this policy tool must be recast into a political domain at the frontier of any broader agenda for understanding its political relevance. Like a block grant, for example, the PPP is a way of providing goods or services to citizens, and it creates political incentives. That citizens perceive the PPP as a different tool than public management means that these incentives have crucial implications for representatives. Moreover, this policy tool has formal provisions and informal relationships that can lead to its success or failure (see, for example, Delmon 2017).

We have argued that PPPs as mechanisms for providing public goods and services must be examined both from the perspective of politicians and citizens. This has important implications for electoral accountability. We know, of course, that holding politicians to account for specific issues can be very hard in competitive elections, but retrospective evaluation of services can influence the vote (see, for example, Bertelli and Van Ryzin 2020, Bertelli 2021). Does electoral accountability suffer or thrive as a result of PPPs? If the relative publicness of PPPs can influence the way that voters evaluate public goods and services, questions emerge about how electoral accountability can function when the structure of PPP agreements can provide both credit-claiming and blame-avoidance strategies for politicians.

We further claim that partnership communities, rather than a competitive market of firms, are the agents politicians select to provide public goods or services through PPPs. These communities are not merely epistemic, but, rather, groups with a strong interest in eschewing full public management. Who opposes these groups and how does that opposition manifest itself in both domestic and international—when thinking about development banks, aid organizations and supranational authorities such as the European Union—political arenas? This is a question of representation, and it turns on whether constituents' interests can survive the choice of public management versus PPP.

The use of a PPP creates, in political terms, a long-term relationship between citizen-stakeholders and government on a specific issue, and this relationship is likely to survive the individual politicians who put it into place. Beyond understanding that interaction as a positive matter, we think that normative work, which is already voluminous, should sharpen its focus on the foregoing questions of electoral accountability and representation. What is the appropriate mix of formal and informal controls that maintains these crucial concepts in representative government? Our call here is for more focus in an area of great interest to scholars, practitioners and advocates alike. Examples of questions that directly arise from such an agenda include, but are by no means limited to: do voters respond positively or negatively to targeted PPPs? How do politicians approach the decision of whether to deliver a public good through a PPP of full public management? How constrained are they in their choices of how to deliver infrastructure? How do they interact with the bureaucracy to shape the choice sets open to them? How do partnership communities, and the firms that exert the most influence within them, impact each of these lines of inquiry? Equally, greater information about how politicians shape credit-claiming opportunities—in terms of media strategy and relations with the private sector—would contribute to our understanding of the relationship between PPP usage and credit-claiming. As would investigations into which sectors or types of PPPs garner the most attention from the media and the voting public.

There are manifold questions of theoretical and practical importance that this agenda presents and that we encourage researchers to engage with. These questions compel what we hope will be a robust agenda for future research, and one where quite a lot is at stake for the political systems involved. Yet like our own research highlighted above, we believe it should continue to take a comparative perspective if we want to put 'the political governance and regulation of PPPs at the forefront' of our research (Hodge and Greve 2010, S17). To the best of our knowledge, the vast majority of PPP studies involving politics are single-country cases (Hood, Fraser and McGarvey 2006; Cunha Marques and Berg 2011; Reeves 2013; Willems 2014; Reynaers and Grimmelikhuijsen 2015) or are, at least, narrowly defined geographically or theoretical in nature (Stephenson 1991, Peters and Pierre 2010, Jooste and Scott 2012, Iossa and Martimort 2014). While single-country studies can, of course, be highly illuminating in terms of identifying phenomena and looking into the mechanisms behind them, it is comparative work that can tell us whether these phenomena are specific to particular contexts and can help us to unravel which types of conditions or institutions may be conducive to the manifestation of said phenomena.

References

Angulo Amaya, C., Bertelli, A., and Woodhouse, E. (2020) The political cost of public–private partnerships: Theory and evidence from Colombian infrastructure development. *Governance*, 33(4): 771–788.

Bertelli, A. M. (2019) Public goods, private partnerships, and political institutions. *Journal of Public Administration Research and Theory*, 29(1): 67–83.

Bertelli, A. M. (2021) *Democracy Administered: How Public Administration Shapes Representative Government*. New York, NY: Cambridge University Press.

Bertelli, A. M., Mele, V., and Whitford, A. (2020) When New Public Management fails: Infrastructure public–private partnerships and political constraints in developing and transitional economies. *Governance*, 33(3): 477–493.

Bertelli, A. M., Mele, V., and Woodhouse, E. (2021) Corruption, democracy, and privately financed infrastructure. *Administration & Society*, 53(3): 327–352.

Bertelli, A. M., and Van Ryzin, G. G. (2020) Heuristics and political accountability in complex governance: An experimental test. *Research & Politics*, 7(3): 2053168020950080.

Bertelli, A. M., Woodhouse, E., Castiglioni, M., and Belardinelli, P. (2021) *Partnership Communities: Political Accountability and the Success of Infrastructure Development around the World*, Cambridge Elements in Public and Nonprofit Administration. New York, NY: Cambridge University Press.

Boardman, A. E., and Hellowell, M. (2017) A comparative analysis and evaluation of specialist PPP units' methodologies for conducting value for money appraisals. *Journal of Comparative Policy Analysis: Research and Practice*, 19(3): 191–206.

Boyer, E., and Van Slyke, D. (2019) Citizen attitudes towards public–private partnerships. *American Review of Public Administration*, 49(3): 259–274.

Boyer, E., Van Slyke, D., and Rogers, J. (2016) An empirical examination of public involvement in public-private partnerships: Qualifying the benefits of public involvement in PPPs. *Journal of Public Administration Research and Theory*, 26(1): 45–61.

Bozeman, B. (1987) *All Organizations are Public: Bridging Public and Private Organizational Theories*. San Francisco, CA: Jossey-Bass.

Cunha Marques, R., and Berg, S. (2011) Public-private partnership contracts: A tale of two cities with different contractual arrangements. *Public Administration*, 89(4): 1585–1603.

Delmon, J. (2017) *Public-Private Partnership Projects in Infrastructure: An Essential Guide for Policy Makers*. New York, NY: Cambridge University Press.

Engel, E., Fischer, R., and Galetovic, A. (2013) The basic public finance of public–private partnerships. *Journal of the European Economic Association*, 11(1): 83–111.

Flinders, M. (2005) The politics of public–private partnerships. *British Journal of Politics and International Relations*, 7(2): 215–239.

Hellowell, M. (2010) The UK's Private Finance Initiative: History, Evaluation, Prospects, in *International Handbook on Public–Private Partnerships*, edited by G. A. Hodge, C. Greve and A. E. Boardman. Cheltenham, UK and Northampton, MA, USA: Edward Elgar Publishing, pp. 307–332.

Hodge, G. (2002) Who steers the state when governments sign public-private partnerships? *Journal of Contemporary Issues in Business and Government*, 8(1): 5–18.

Hodge, G. (2004) Risks in public-private partnerships: Shifting, sharing or shirking? *Asia Pacific Journal of Public Administration*, 26(2): 157–179.

Hodge, G., and Greve, C. (2010) Public-private partnerships: Governance scheme or language game? *Australian Journal of Public Administration*, 69(1): S8–S22.

Hodge, G., and Greve, C. (2017a) On public–private partnership performance: A contemporary review. *Public Works Management & Policy*, 22(1): 55–78.

Hodge, G., and Greve, C. (2017b) Private Finance: What Problems Does It Solve, and How Well?, in *Oxford Handbook of Mega Project Management*, edited by B. Flyvbjerg. Oxford: Oxford University Press, pp. 362–388.

Hood, J., Fraser, I., and McGarvey, N. (2006) Transparency of risk and reward in UK public–private partnerships. *Public Budgeting & Finance*, 26(4): 40–58.

Iossa, E., and Martimort, D. (2014) Corruption in PPPs, incentives and contract incompleteness. *International Journal of Industrial Organization*, 44(C): 85–100.

Jooste, S., and Scott, R. (2012) The public–private partnership enabling field: Evidence from three cases. *Administration & Society*, 44(2): 149–182.

Peters, B. G., and Pierre, J. (2010) Public-Private Partnerships and the Democratic Deficit: Is Performance-based Legitimacy the Answer?, in *Democracy and*

Public-Private Partnerships in Global Governance, edited by M. Bexell and U. Mörth. London: Palgrave Macmillan, pp. 41–54.

Reeves, E. (2013) Mind the Gap: Accountability and Value for Money, in *Rethinking Public-Private Partnerships: Strategies for Turbulent Times*, edited by C. Greve and G. Hodge. London: Routledge, pp. 78–97.

Reynaers, A.M., and Grimmelikhuijsen, S. (2015) Transparency in public–private partnerships: Not so bad after all? *Public Administration*, 93(3): 609–626.

Stephenson Jr, M. (1991) Whither the public-private partnership: A critical overview. *Urban Affairs Quarterly*, 27(1): 109–127.

Tsebelis, G. (2011) *Veto Players: How Political Institutions Work*. Princeton, NJ: Princeton University Press. (Originally published in 2003.)

Willems, T. (2014) Democratic accountability: The curious case of Flemish school infrastructure. *Public Administration*, 92(2): 340–358.

Woodhouse, E. (2019) *Public-Private Partnerships, Distributive Politics, and Infrastructure Development*, paper presented at the Midwest Political Science Association annual conference, Chicago, April 2018.

Woodhouse, E., Belardinelli, P., and Bertelli, A. (2022) Hybrid governance and the attribution of political responsibility: Experimental evidence from the United States. *Public Administration Research and Theory*, 32(1): 150–165.

6 Psychological and ontological research on PPPs: what is PPP doing to us?

Sophie Sturup

Introduction

This chapter looks at a small but growing set of research about the psychological/ontological behaviour that is generated in public–private partnership (PPP) and how it is manifesting outside PPP, or driving change beyond the PPP itself. This set of research is important because it reminds us that what is important about PPPs is not only that they work better, effectively, or at all, but also what effect they have on governance, and on society. PPP introduces ways of thinking, being and acting, that are extending well beyond any one PPP, or indeed PPPs in general.

Within literature which explicitly identifies itself as being about PPP, what might be termed as a psychological approach has covered a wide variety of phenomena. Philosophically, this group of work accepts that organisations and the governance arrangements they enter into are a function of individual humans, who individually influence those institutions and/or are also conditioned within the arrangements. Thus in that research, personhood and/or a person's psychology are relevant to the question of how PPPs function, as is sociology and indeed ontology.

Concern with the psychological comes from a wide variety of systems of thought concerning the role of individuals or agents in PPPs. But in general, the research follows some variant of structuration theory, which proposes that structures of governance are incomplete in providing explanations for social phenomena and that an understanding of agent behaviour is also necessary (Sarhadi et al. 2021). As Giddens (1984) said: 'action is not a combination of "acts": "acts" are constituted only by a discursive moment of attention to the dureé or lived-through experience. Nor can "action" be discussed in separation from the body, its mediations with the surrounding world and the coherence of an acting self' (p.3). This concern with understanding individual action led to an explosion of research within a wide range of social science disciplines which moved to add the notion of agents and why they did the things they do (in some cases psychological explanations) to their analysis. In PPP literature, examples include the impact of financial governance on behaviour of parties in the PPP (behavioural economics), the benefits and potential disadvantages of distinctly different cultures (public administration), the motivations for and barriers to PPP use (management science), issues that arise in PPP management due to different cultures and what should be done about them (construction/project management), motivating particular behaviours from parties in PPPs (construction management) and stakeholder management (various disciplines, including planning, public administration, management science).

Of course not all of this type of work can be called psychological, because psychology is concerned with human behaviour as it is generated from thought (including thoughts brought on by emotions). Some of this work comes from understandings that human behaviour stems from visceral responses (emotions as they are felt in the body), or from some combination of both visceral and cerebral engagement (which might be called being). To distinguish psychology from ontology at least in the terms used in this chapter, psychology is concerned with the way people think, the structures of how they think and possibly why humans think that way (theories of identity, ego, and so on) – which variously are considered to drive what they subsequently do and/or how they feel. On the other hand, ontology is concerned with the way people (and indeed anything else) is 'being'. Where being is more than just the fact that a person exists, but the way someone is being-in-the-world at any point in time. Thus what/who a person is at a particular time is embedded in the world they are dealing with, and that world includes their thoughts, but extends well beyond them.

These psychological and ontological approaches often identify and discuss very similar phenomena. That is, they tend to focus on what people tend to end up doing and why. Sometimes there is even a similarity in the cause of these actions; for example, conceptions of something referred to as discourses (Hajer 1995). However, the location of what drives this cause as either thoughts (or thoughts about what is said) or something much more complicated is at the heart of the distinction. Psychology posits human thought as the ultimate cause in any matter, whereas ontology deals with the world in all its comings and goings, in its interconnected messiness, and thus logically leads to a position that there is no cause in the matter. In this chapter psychology is understood to be predicated on Descartes' *cogito, ergo sum* (normally translated as 'I think, therefore I am'). Ontology on the contrary is a different worldview which can include human psychology as an element of being. Ontology is predicated on Heidegger's concern with being-in-the-world (Heidegger 2008, original 1927), a complex phenomenon that arises in relationship to: the world as it is, the world as it is in relationship to the one whose being is the concern, and the way the one whose being is the concern is relating to the world. Because of the closeness of the two approaches, at least in the identification and discussion of phenomena, this chapter will traverse both approaches.

Most of the literature on human behaviour in PPPs is focused on producing an outcome aligned with either creating better PPPs or dealing better with one or more of the many observed flaws in the PPP process. Little of this literature is concerned more explicitly with the question of who people become (or how they come to think) as a result of being in a PPP, and what impact that has on society more broadly. Yet the increasing use of PPP across the world, which is bringing more and more people into contact with the psychology/ontologies that PPP generates, suggests that the concern with this question is one that is ripe for further investigation.

Therefore, this chapter focuses on three sections of the much smaller body of work that extends the psychological/ontological inquiry into the sociological domain and circles around the question 'Who do people become when engaging in PPP, and what impact does this have more broadly (as well as within the PPP itself)?' This section of the literature variously approaches the question from a psychological perspective or an ontological one. Some of this research has come out of mega project research thinking about the impact of the sublime of mega projects on the people that work in them (Flyvbjerg et al. 2003, Sturup 2010, Trapenberg Frick 2008). Some have looked at capacities for partnership and what partnership might make available (Christensen 2015, Wettenhall 2010) as well as how it could be used to perhaps harness the private sector to more progressive aims (Wang et al. 2019, Xiong et al. 2020). Finally, there has been some extensive work done on what happens to society under the influence of a fourth P (project) on workers and work–life balance (Cicmil et al. 2016). The next three sections of this chapter discuss each of these arenas in turn: the sublime of mega projects, partnership capacities and 'projectification'.

Mega projects and sublimes

It is probably true to say that mega projects are a particular class of PPP. This is because nearly all mega projects are or involve some kind of infrastructure.

Government capacity when it comes to building, and even operating, public infrastructure has been completely denuded in most countries through the process of contracting, if not through the use of true PPPs.[1] The exception to this could perhaps be fully private projects, although these rarely rise to the scope of what might be defined as mega (these days generally projects costing more than 1 billion USD). Of course this does not mean that everything about mega projects could be applied to all PPPs. Much of the interest in mega projects relates to the fact that they are colossal in size and scope; captivating because of their size, engineering achievements or aesthetic design; costly – and often under-costed; controversial; complex; and they have control issues (Trapenberg Frick 2008, p.239). Many PPPs are not mega. However it is interesting to reflect on how much of the findings relating to mega projects are in fact related to the mega-ness of them and what is in fact a product of PPP. An example might be the complexity issues. Although complexity rises as projects get larger, it also does so as more parties are involved. From the point of view of a local government in China, for example, engaging the private sector in projects increases complexity considerably. There are, for example, an entirely different set of laws pertaining to PPPs. Similarly from the point of view of such local governments, projects which are large enough to attract private finance are in fact much larger than projects which they engage in as business as usual.

One facet of mega project research which appears to relate to the behaviour of persons within the projects and to perhaps leak out to impact on wider arenas is the idea of the mega project sublime. In this set of research, the word 'sublime' refers to the 'the relationship between human beings and those aspects of their world that excite in them particular emotions, powerful enough to evoke transcendence, shock, awe, and terror' (Costelloe 2012, p.2). Those aspects of the world include both natural sites, architectural forms and technological achievements (Nye 1994, quoted in Trapenberg Frick 2008, p.239). Things thus can create the experience of the sublime in humans, but they can also be said to have 'a' sublime, meaning a set of factors that stand to make possible the experience of the sublime.

Without doubt, mega projects often create a sense of the sublime in observers. This can be observed in the enthusiasm engendered in those who work on these projects, and after they are completed, in those who observe them. Research into what generates this sense has identified three different types of sublime in mega projects: the technical (or design) sublime, the political sublime and the project sublime (Sturup 2010, Trapenberg Frick 2008).

The technical (or design) sublime is the kind of awe that is also encountered when people experience the sublime in nature (Cronon 1995). In observing natural phenomenon such as the Grand Canyon, awe is present in part due to the realisation of the incredible forces in play that brought the phenomenon into existence, coming face to face with the extraordinary technological brilliance of the planet. In mega projects the technical sublime relates to both an appreciation of the technological marvel, and the elegance of finding a technological solution. It is the beauty and seduction of something whose form perfectly matches its function. This sublime affects engineers and designers, and those lay persons who have developed an appreciation of engineering and design. It is related at times to the overcoming of nature, to the thrill of big machines which move masses of materials, but it is also seen through the graceful lines built of tonnes of steel and concrete (Trapenberg Frick 2008).

The political sublime of mega projects affects the politicians, but also those who look for something that can be called leadership. It can be seen in the ribbon-cutting opening of these projects, in the 'rock star' appeal of politicians who push through the odds, through the bureaucracy (Hodge et al. 2010), and produce a result, open a bridge, solve a problem (Sturup 2015). The political sublime raises the stakes; it is the source of thinking which says 'this is too big to fail' (Sturup et al. 2015). The political sublime is the source of much of the madness of mega projects; it commits the leaders and even stakes the legitimacy of the government on the success of the deal (Pittman and Day 2020).

The political sublime provides some explanation for the Machiavellian view of mega projects (Flyvbjerg 2005), wherein cost overruns, delays, debts and failure to meet projected revenues, environmental and social impacts are seen to result from the use of the Machiavellian formula for project approval. This formula is one of understated costs and overstated benefits, generated by the belief of some project proponents that their projects will benefit society and that they are justified in lying about the costs and benefits to get projects built (Flyvbjerg 2005). The sublime works to disguise this lying, even to the proponents who are doing it. Power, and the exercise of it, acts to distort people's view of what can be done. It defines what counts as rationality and knowledge and thereby what counts as reality and what gets dealt with (Flyvbjerg 1998).

The final element of mega project sublime is project sublime (Sturup 2010). It is the seduction and awe of the project itself. Project management is about defining your goals, breaking the seemingly insurmountable into fragments, which can be delivered within a budget, and inside a set time. The vast and chaotic coordination effort of a mega project is bracketed, contained, managed. The attraction of mega projects in particular is the edge-of-the-seat management required, the sense of opening your veins, giving everything to something bigger than yourself. As George Bernard Shaw put it so well:

> This is the true joy in life, the being used for a purpose recognized by yourself as a mighty one; the being a force of nature instead of a feverish, selfish little clod of ailments and grievances complaining that the world will not devote itself to making you happy ...
> I want to be thoroughly used up when I die, for the harder I work the more I live. I rejoice in life for its own sake. Life is no "brief candle" for me. It is a sort of splendid torch which I have got hold of for the moment, and I want to make it burn as brightly as possible before handing it on to future generations. (Shaw 1973, p.84)

Part of the definition of a project is that it is an exception to business as usual (Project Management Institute 2000). The description of the project sublime above demonstrates how deeply this definition impacts the way that projects are seen, and the kind of being they call for. Projects create a state of exceptionalism (Cicmil and O'Laocha 2016). The project demands all that can be given and more, and justifies that because it is an exception to normal and thus requires exceptional behaviour. The project is a one-off, and thus will soon be over, meaning that sacrifices made now can be justified on the basis of 'short term pain, long term gain', a way of thinking that is not uncommon to humans that brings with it a raft of problems (Harari 2015, Kahneman 2013).

Taken together and applied in a mega project, these sublimes merge and interact to provide a sense of transcendence and awe in observers and participants to the project. This sense of transcendence and awe combines with ideas of power, the seduction of a technical solution and the exceptionalism of project mentality to create a rationality which might be described as 'the show must go on'. Nearly anything is justifiable in support of the project, which comes by definition to embody the 'greater good'. This is highly seductive, even addictive. Outside observers see careers made, and more vitally, important work completed. In a world where there is rarely clarity on whether one is doing the right thing, the kind of certainty about this being the right thing to do which comes with these projects is very attractive (Sturup 2010). Mega projects thus not only provide scope for a way of being for those within the project, they exemplify or remind others of this way of being. Mega projects embody overcoming the odds, teamwork, leadership and the highest expression of the human spirit, and remind the communities that own them of the possibilities inherent in that way of being.

Partnership

Whether they are defined narrowly, as a contractual relationship between the private sector and public sector that involves risk-sharing and private finance (Eldrup and Schütze 2013), or more loosely, as 'cooperative institutional arrangements between public and private sector actors' (Hodge et al. 2010, p.4), a key element in PPPs is that there are at least two parties and they need to work together. While it is possible for two organisations to create a partnership on paper through some form of agreement and the establishment of governance arrangements, the success of the arrangement will depend on the people who implement it. They will need to work together, which requires an adjustment in their thinking (psychology) and/or way of being.

Successful working together requires particular psychologies or ontologies. Van Ham and Koppenjan (2010) suggest that parties will only really be working together once they both have the creative capacity to envisage the joint activity. This requires the generation of a level of trust, which Stelling (2014) suggests requires a commitment to a future together that allows uncertainty to be ignored in favour of a focus on what will be achieved. As Wettenhall (2007) says, a real partnership allows both parties to pursue benefits and share them. For this to happen, there is a requirement to be willing to see the partnership from the view of the other party, a skill which over the course of the partnership only deepens (Sturup 2017). It is through this process of coming to see the other's point of view that partners start to take on the characteristics of each other. This can be a cause for celebration or a cause for concern. These possible changes in direction for how we think or 'be' deserve serious consideration.

The Chinese government has a stated ambition to use PPPs to variously stimulate more harmonious and moderate behaviour in the private sector, and to bring greater competency to the public sector (Wang et al. 2019). The second part of this is not dissimilar from the longstanding acknowledgement in many national PPP approaches that a core benefit to bringing the private sector into the public sector will shift the focus toward lower costs as a result of the introduction of a profit motive (Koppenjan 2008), and a speeding up of a somewhat moribund and bureaucratic public sector with the energy and innovation of the private sector (Kumaraswamy and Morris 2002). What is less familiar, however, is the suggestion that PPPs could be used as a kind of civilising process in which private sector rapaciousness is moderated and harnessed for a greater good (or even in the pursuit of sustainable urbanisation) (Xiong et al. 2020). It is even more unusual to see an acknowledgement that the process of enculturation in these projects could lead to changes to the way people operate in business more generally. There has been little research done on the success of this ambition.

On the other hand, some research has been conducted into whether partnership is cause for concern. Sturup (2014) questioned whether proposals to 'deepen' partnerships in PPPs ran the risk of either creating quangos out of the private sector or mercantile governments out of the public sector. The initial finding from her two case studies was that at least in some circumstances there is a real risk that the private sector will simply be absorbed into the public sector, leaving many of the supposed benefits of PPPs unavailable.

Other research following the same methodology demonstrates the potential problems that arise from governments becoming too entrepreneurial (Pittman and Day 2020). It seems likely that some of the bizarre behaviour of the Victorian State government around Melbourne's 'East-West Tunnel' project (for further details, see Pittman and Day 2020) can be explained by a public sector which had become overly entrepreneurial in its outlook. In that project, the government was willing to try to guarantee delivery of the contract by adding punitive clauses against any future government should it revoke the contract, even though the contract was signed just days before an election embargo came into force, and it was clear from public statements that the then opposition was promising to revoke the contract should they win the election.

Looking through this lens of the impact of partnership, it can be observed that it is clearly possible for governments to become too attached to the notion that governments should steer rather than row (Osborne and Gaebler 1992) with sometimes dire consequences. The use of private sector contracting has found its way deep into the psychology (possibly into the ontology) of the public sector in Victoria, Australia. The state of Victoria was one of the world's keenest governments in privatising and contracting-out public sector services throughout the 1990s (Hodge 2003, 2004). This initiative, however, has become so embedded in public sector thinking and processes that any other way of getting things done is unthinkable. The implication of this transition was brought to the public's attention recently during an inquiry into breaches of security and an associated Covid-19 outbreak from a quarantine hotel in May 2020. A central question of the inquiry was how it came about that security at the quarantine facilities was given to private contractors rather than to the police or armed services. For several weeks people gave evidence on this matter. It was quite clear that for many public servants, and even for the head of the inquiry, the question itself was difficult to grasp. A possible reason for this confusion would be that the question simply did not occur to those making the arrangements. It was not necessary for someone to decide to contract the service; that is simply what you do, and anything else was literally unthinkable. In other words, from the perspective of those inside today's automated 'contracting-out state', asking who made this vital decision was weird. To these public servant insiders, this was just the way today's state 'was' in its being. There is clearly space for further research into this hypothesis, and into the way the public sector is changing under the influence of PPPs and other engagements with the private sector.

Projectification

A project is defined as a discrete piece of work bounded by time and cost that is outside normal business practice. Many PPPs are envisaged as projects, or at least as something outside business as usual. That is the reason that a partnership (often a new partnership) is necessary. The parties do not have all the skills and resources necessary separately to produce the required outcome. This means that the exceptionalism seen in projects, and as observed above in mega projects, is often present even in smaller PPPs, and in partnerships which are not supposed to be projects.

A huge amount of work has been done in management literature to examine behaviour in projects, much of it with the ambition of improving the way projects are managed, but some of this literature has considered the emotional and psychological impact on workers (Lindgren et al. 2014). For example, Cicmil et al. (2006) have been working for a number of years on the lived experience of projects and project managers.

> [A]ctuality research, as a stream of thought, demonstrates a deep interest in lived experience of project actors, with the aim to understand what is actually going on in the arrangements labelled "project" over time, to give an alternative account of what project managers do in concrete project situations and to explore skills and knowledge that constitute the social and political action in managing projects. Researching the actuality of projects means focusing on social process and how practitioners think in action, in the local situation of a living present. (p.676)

Project management is a powerful tool, and has gained traction in many places as a way of working continuously. A lot of work is now conceived of by managers and workers alike as a series of projects, wherein there is no conception of business as usual. More recently Cicmil's research has turned toward the impact this has on people who work in projects (Cicmil et al. 2016). The research demonstrates that ongoing use of projects creates a vulnerability to decline, decay and exhaustion in organisations and workers, brought about by being in a state of exceptionalism all the time. As described in the section above on mega project sublimes, this exceptionalism requires continued sacrifice by individuals. Cicmil et al. (2016) find that in project workers, resilience is internalised as coping with vulnerability by 'letting some elements of life being destroyed' (Cicmil et al. 2016, p.1). This points to the way that projects have an impact directly on the people who are working on them. But they also have an impact on the lives of people who are associated with people who do projects. There is no doubt that this kind of behaviour is present in at least some PPPs; how much of it might be due to understanding the PPP as a project, and what might be happening as a result of the partnership itself, is an area ripe for further research.

One example of taking this kind of work into questions of partnership can be found in White et al. (2019). This paper documents the experience of people who are working on the front line of partnerships between academic institutions and small to medium enterprises. The study found that workers who were asked to embed themselves in the organisation and act as liaison between the two dealt with periods of frustration and demotivation, often associated with attempting to find a way to be useful to the partner organisation at a time before they had fully understood the other's business and culture. This period was also associated with periods of confusion over the goals of the partnership, and the role and expectations of the people within it (White et al. 2019). Apart from providing some useful information on issues likely to arise in PPPs, this literature also points to the degree to which project thinking is impacting on many facets of work life, even where things are a partnership and not a project.

Project thinking has clearly escaped the confines of projects, and as a discourse has come to inhabit modern workplaces, as well as people's personal lives. A central question for PPPs is not only to consider how 'project' impacts PPPs, but what role PPP has in promulgating the spread of this discourse. Does the use of PPP reflect a further colonisation of project thinking, or does it provide scope for some other discourse? There are PPPs which are about long-term partnerships which it could be said are designed to create ongoing alternations in the practice of business as usual. It is possible therefore that true long-term partnerships (and indeed some forms of PPP) could be seen as a countervailing discourse to 'project'.

Conclusion

This chapter has explored several domains of research which attempt to consider the impact of psychologies or ways of being that might be generated in PPPs, the reasons for them and how those ways of being might be spreading more widely. In the section on mega projects it was suggested that there is scope for further work in untangling which of the findings about mega projects are a function of the fact that they are mega, and what might usefully be applied to PPPs. This section also discussed the three elements of the mega project sublime. Some work has already been completed on how the quest for the technological sublime has driven innovation in American history, and on how the political sublime gets in the way of rational planning. There remains, however, considerable scope for consideration of how the project sublime might be influencing the spread of project discourse. Taken together, these sublimes merge and interact to generate powerful influences on what gets done and what does not. The difficulty of getting things done which are not able to be classified as mega projects is one instance.

The section on partnership demonstrated how PPPs are not only changing the relationship between the public and the private sector, they are also being used in some cases to actively change the private sector (making them more moderate or perhaps socially conscious), and in some cases whether by accident or design are changing the public sector, making them more entrepreneurial. There is an opportunity to consider further the political ecology of PPPs, and what might be the impact of these changes. It is easy to see the separate roles of the private and public sector as something relatively immutable. To do so is to forget that historically both roles have changed and evolved. Perhaps climate change provides a global imperative to civilise and tame the private sector, and maybe PPPs have a role to play in doing that? This is clearly a domain ready for interdisciplinary research.

Finally, the section on projectification raises very important questions about the sociological impact of projects and the projectification of workplaces. Changes to work and life such as discussed in the section have far-reaching consequences. Projects are part of a process of change to work where the worker's personhood becomes relevant and integral to their job. For some this process may have increased job satisfaction by providing a justification for placing work over all other concerns in life, but it may also have something to do with the increases in stress and mental illness observed in many places. There is a clear need for further research on this. For PPPs and especially for those PPPs that are trying to establish long-term partnerships (perhaps as part of the abovementioned change in the relationship of the public and private sector), there is a need to consider how the findings on projects apply to PPPs. Is one of the core reasons for the failure of partnership in PPP actually the result of conceptualising the PPP as a project?

This chapter has demonstrated two clear avenues for future research. The first is to bring into the research on PPP the work that is being done on projects. There is a lot of strong work being done on this fourth P and it should be brought to bear on the general project of PPP research, to improve their chances of success. The second avenue for research is that there is a clear need to extend the consideration of behaviour in PPPs beyond how it can be brought to improve the PPP itself. People are watching PPPs, and learning from them. The ways of being that are promulgated within PPPs leak out into other domains of activity, and importantly to management behaviour. It is useful from time to time to consider what is leaking out, and how it is being picked up. One place where a research agenda in this direction might usefully delve is into the historical relationship between the private and public sector in order to bring to light the potential and peril of different allocations of tasks between the sectors, and indeed of what in the relationship between the two should be maintained in order to maximise benefit to society as a whole.

Note

1. This distinction is only necessary if it is accepted that the proper definition of a PPP is one where the arrangement involves private sector finance (Eldrup and Schütze 2013). Other definitions are of course possible, including what Wettenhall (2010) refers to as 'public–private mixes'.

References

Christensen, L. T. (2015) The return of the hiearchy: SOEs in marketisation. *International Journal of Public Sector Management*, 28: 307–321.

Cicmil, S., Lindgren, M. and Packendorff, J. (2016) The project (management) discourse and its consequences: On vulnerability and unsustainability in project-based work. *New Technology, Work and Employment*, 31: 58–76.

Cicmil, S., and O'Laocha, E. (2016) The logic of projects and the ideal of community development: Social good, participation and the ethics of knowing. *International Journal of Managing Projects in Business*, 9: 546–561.

Cicmil, S., Williams, T., Thomas, J., and Hodgson, D. (2006) Rethinking project management: Researching the actuality of projects. *International Journal of Project Management*, 24: 675–686.

Costelloe, T. M. (2012) The Sublime, in *The Sublime: From Antiquity to the Present*, edited by T. M. Costelloe. Cambridge: Cambridge University Press.

Cronon, W. (1995) *Uncommon Ground: Toward Reinventing Nature.* New York, NY: W. W. Norton & Co.

Eldrup, A., and Schütze, P. (2013) *Organization and Financing of Public Infrastructure Projects: A Path to Economic Growth and Development of the Danish Welfare Model.* Copenhagen: ATP, PFA, PKA, SamPension, PensionDenmark.

Flyvbjerg, B. (1998) *Rationality and Power: Democracy in Practice.* Chicago, IL: University of Chicago Press.

Flyvbjerg, B. (2005) Machiavellian megaprojects. *Antipode*, 37: 18.

Flyvbjerg, B., Bruzelius, N., and Rothengatter, W. (2003) *Megaprojects and Risk: An Anatomy of Ambition.* Cambridge: Cambridge University Press.

Giddens, A. (1984) *The Constitution of Society: Outline of the Theory of Structuration.* Cambridge: Polity Press.

Hajer, M. (1995) Discourse Analysis, in *The Politics of Environmental Discourse: Ecological Modernisation and the Policy Process*, edited by M. A. Hajer. Oxford: Oxford University Press.

Harari, Y. N. (2015) *Sapiens: A Brief History of Humankind.* New York, NY: HarperCollins.

Heidegger, M. (2008[1927]) *Being and Time.* New York, NY: Harper Perennial.

Hodge, G. A. (2003) Privatisation: The Australian Experience, in *International Handbook on Privatisation*, edited by D. Parker and D. Saal. Cheltenham, UK and Northampton, MA, USA: Edward Elgar Publishing.

Hodge, G. A. (2004) Introduction, in *Power Progress: An Audit of Australia's Electricity Reform Experiment*, edited by G. Hodge, V. J. Sands, D. Hayward and D. Scott. Melbourne: Australian Scholarly Publishing.

Hodge, G. A, Greve, C., and Boardman, A. E. (2010) Introduction: The PPP Phenomenon and Its Evaluation, in *International Handbook on Public–Private Partnerships*, edited by G. A. Hodge, C. Greve and A. E. Boardman. Cheltenham, UK and Northampton, MA, USA: Edward Elgar Publishing.

Kahneman, D. (2013) *Thinking Fast and Slow.* New York, NY: Farrar, Straus and Giroux.

Koppenjan, J. (2008) Public-Private Partnership and Mega-Projects, in *Decision-Making on Mega-Projects: Cost-Benefit Analysis, Planning and Innovation*, edited by H. Priemus, B. Flyvbjerg and B. van Wee. Cheltenham, UK and Northampton, MA, USA: Edward Elgar Publishing.

Kumaraswamy, M. M., and Morris, D. A. (2002) Build-operate-transfer type procurement in Asian megaprojects. *Journal of Construction Engineering and Management – ASCE*, 128: 93–102.

Lindgren, M., Packendorff, J., and Sergi, V. (2014) Thrilled by the discourse, suffering through the experience: Emotions in project-based work. *Human Relations*, 67: 1383–1412.

Osborne, D., and Gaebler, T. (1992) *Reinventing Government: How the Entrepreneurial Spirit Is Transforming the Public Sector.* Reading: Addison-Wesley.

Pittman, N., and Day, J. (2020) The problem/solution nexus in mega project planning. *Journal of Mega Infrastructure and Sustainable Development*, 1: 151–170.

Project Management Institute (ed.) (2000) *A Guide to the Project Management Body of Knowledge (PMBOK Guide)*. Newtown Square, PA: Project Management Institute.

Sarhadi, M., Hasanzadeh, S., and Yousefi, S. (2021) Evolving history of sustainable project: Exploring existential meaning at the agency level. *Journal of Legal Affairs and Dispute Resolution in Engineering and Construction*, 13. https://ascelibrary.org/doi/abs/10.1061/%28ASCE%29LA.1943-4170.0000459.

Shaw, G. B. (1973) *Man and Superman*. Baltimore, MD: Penguin.

Stelling, C. (2014) *Public Private Parternships and the Need, Development and Management of Trusting: A Processual and Embedded Exploration*. PhD, Copenhagen Business School.

Sturup, S. (2010) *Managing Mentalities of Mega Projects: The Art of Government of Mega Urban Transport Projects*. PhD, University of Melbourne.

Sturup, S. (2014) Deepening partnership in PPP: How do we know when we are in too deep? *Public-Private Partnership Conference Series CBS-Saunder-Monash*. Melbourne.

Sturup, S. (2015) The Problem/Solution Nexus and its Effect on Public Consultation, in *Instruments of Planning: Tension and Challenges for More Equitable and Sustainable Cities*, edited by R. Leshinsky and C. Legacy. Melbourne: Routledge.

Sturup, S. (2017) Swimming or drowning in the depths of partnership. *Australian Journal of Public Administration*, 76: 288–300.

Sturup, S., Pittman, N., and Day, J. (2015) *Compelling and Perpetuating: How an Unpopular Infrastructure Project Stayed Alive in an Era of Public Consultation*, paper presented to Association of European Schools of Planning Conference. Prague.

Trapenberg Frick, K. (2008) The Cost of the Technological Sublime: Daring Ingenuity and the New San Francisco-Oakland Bay Bridge, in *Decision-Making on Mega-Projects: Cost-Benefit Analysis, Planning and Innovation*, edited by H. Priemus, B. Flyvbjerg and B. van Wee. Cheltenham, UK and Northampton, MA, USA: Edward Elgar Publishing.

Van Ham, H., and Koppenjan, J. (2010) Building public-private partnerships: Assessing and managing risks in port development. *Public Management Review*, 3: 593–616.

Wang, L., Sturup, S., and Cross, A. (2019) *Harmony, Moderation and Public Private Partnerships (PPPs) in the Chinese Context*. 23rd International Research Society on Public Management. Wellington, New Zealand.

Wettenhall, R. (2007) ActewAGL: A genuine public-private partnership? *International Journal of Public Sector Management*, 20: 392–414.

Wettenhall, R. (2010) Mixes and Partnerships Through Time, in *International Handbook on Public–Private Partnerships*, edited by G. A. Hodge, C. Greve and A. E. Boardman. Cheltenham, UK and Northampton, MA, USA: Edward Elgar Publishing.

White, G. R. T., Cicmil, S., Upadhyay, A., Subramanian, N., Kumar, V., and Dwivedi, A. (2019) The soft side of knowledge transfer partnerships between universities and small to medium enterprises: An exploratory study to understand process improvement. *Production Planning and Control*, 30: 907–918.

Xiong, W., Chen, B., Wang, H., and Zhu, D. (2020) Public–private partnerships as a governance response to sustainable urbanization: Lessons from China. *Habitat International*, 95: 102095.

7 What can behavioural science teach us about the policy settings for privately financed public infrastructure?

Sebastian Zwalf

Introduction

The last three decades has seen the emergence of privately financed public infrastructure projects (PFPI) as an increasingly large and common part of the infrastructure programs of governments around the world. However, despite their common acceptance by governments across nearly three decades (Zwalf 2020), PFPI have attracted a substantial degree of academic interest, with much of it being critical (Grimsey and Lewis 2004).

A number of scholars have proposed that PFPI have become a widely used infrastructure delivery mechanism because of the political benefits that accrue to the governments who approve them, or, to be more specific, to those who approve the policy settings in which they are enabled.[1] Boardman and Hellowell (2017) have summarised that:

- Pollitt (2002) identifies that governments are drawn to the perceived efficiency of PFPI;
- Governments see PFPI as representing reduced downside risk (in other words, greater certainty of cost and delivery times);
- Hellowell (2010) identifies that politicians want to 'curry favour' with financiers, consultants and others involved in PFPI consortia;
- Irwin (2012) argues that PFPI have helped governments to circumvent public borrowing constraints; and
- Similarly, governments have been able to defer costs for major infrastructure through leasing it.[2]

Separately, Flinders (2005) argues that PFPI – as the delivery model associated with greater efficiency – have been used by governments to fill a growing 'expectations gap' between what politicians promise to deliver and can practically do so (this argument shares some overlap with the view that PFPI allow for deferred costs), and Moore and Vining (2019) have argued that PFPI may assist governments to obscure their role as enforcing tolls on users under certain conditions. However, while scholars have postulated reasons for governments' assumed preference for the PFPI delivery model, there is a lack of empirical evidence to validate the accuracy of these claims: no scholarly studies have sought the views of politicians with respect to the drivers for PFPI (Zwalf, 2021).

Hodge and Greve (2019) have proposed that behavioural science – which has been increasingly used to explain human decision making – may be one logic stream that sits behind the adoption of the PFPI delivery model by governments. They suggest that governments may have been influenced by a number of factors which are explained by behavioural science, including how framing influences the decisions and choices we make, the mental shortcuts we make in our thinking (and in the process, disregarding other relevant facts) and our intertemporal preferences in which we often show preferences for short-term pay-offs. This introduces a new theoretical lens through which to consider the evolution of public policy which has supported PFPI. Moreover, it may assist scholars to explain why governments have continued to employ PFPI in the face of mounting arguments by critics about their alleged shortcomings. Accordingly, this chapter:

- Establishes the public-policy and social context in which PFPI have emerged, and summarises relevant ongoing debates about their efficacy;
- Explores what behavioural science is, and identifies where it may be relevant to decision making in public policy;
- Identifies where behavioural science overlaps with the public-policy and social context of PFPI and whether it could explain some of the phenomena in PFPI with respect to their policy settings.

Theory and background

The social context of privately financed public infrastructure

> [T]oo much weight is placed upon subjective judgments of risk, which can easily be adjusted to show [the PFPI option] as cheaper. (United Kingdom National Audit Office 2009, 8)

PFPI have become increasingly common in the infrastructure programs of governments around the world. With antecedent policy experiments taking place as early as the 1960s, the early-mid 1990s saw PFPI emerge as a common infrastructure delivery model, and by the late 1990s a common policy model with similar features had been developed to underpin them (Siemietycki 2013, Zwalf 2020). PFPI have been associated with re-embracing markets as a public-policy principle in the 1980s and 1990s, such as through privatisation and outsourcing (Teicher et al. 2007). Zwalf (2020) has argued that governments saw PFPI as a way to be seen to embrace markets and that in at least some jurisdictions, 'third-way' social-democratic governments were particularly keen to be associated with them. Somewhat similarly, and independently, Quiggan (2006) argues that the earliest PFPI were attempts by government to harness the skills and perceived efficiency of the private sector, suggesting a level of dissatisfaction with traditional projects on the part of governments; PFPI may have been a response to policy and political frustrations that emerged with so-called traditional public sector procurement of major infrastructure projects. Flyvberg (as cited in Flyvbjerg et al. 2005) notes that such projects – until recently, mostly managed by government in one form or another – saw substantial overruns in cost and delivery times, potentially causing embarrassment to the governments who commissioned them. PFPI were intended to address such inefficiencies and also to reduce messy litigation associated with large government-managed infrastructure projects (Grimsey and Lewis 2004).

Critics of PFPI have charged that they are more costly to government over the long term (Parks and Terhart 2009), that their success in the government approvals process relies upon overly favourable evaluation processes (UK National Audit Office 2009) and that many PFPI are seen to have 'failed' financially, resulting in projects being returned to public hands or renegotiated on terms favourable to the PFPI provider (Oliveira et al. 2016). While much has been made of these debates, they have remained largely unsettled, with advocates and critics still taking seemingly unreconcilable positions.

Behavioural science

> Behavioural economists, on the other hand, believe that people are susceptible to irrelevant influences from their immediate environment ..., irrelevant emotions, short-sightedness, and other forms of irrationality. (Ariely 2008, 318)

Drawing upon the fields of economics, psychology, sociology and neuroscience, the last two decades have seen the popular emergence of behavioural science which has offered new explanations for human decision making (Ariely 2008, French and Oreopoulos 2017). In doing so it has challenged prevailing orthodoxies of traditional economic thought in which early economists such as Adam Smith (1776), John Stuart Mill (1836) and Vilfredo Pareto (1906), among others, argued that human behaviour could be largely explained by self-interest and rationality (Bauer and Wätjen 2018). While Tversky and Kahneman are credited with challenging these assumptions – perhaps first establishing behavioural science as a discipline in the 1970s – scholars before them provided a platform on which to question neo-classical economic orthodoxies. As early as 1892, Emile Durkheim theorised about the cultural norms that bind us together – social facts. Indeed, entire humanities disciplines have since acknowledged human beings as social creatures whose decisions were influenced by and psychologically subject to the cultural and emotional mores of their peer groups. In 1920, Thorndike first identified the halo effect, making the case that our perceptions can be heavily subjective. Simon (1956) challenged the very notion of rational human thinking, arguing that much of our thinking is based on quasi-rational mental reckoning. In the 1970s Tversky and Kahneman consolidated these ideas and undertook countless experiments of their own, disproving consistent rationality and re-articulating the role of heuristics and framing in human decision making (Chetty 2015). In the period that has followed, the legitimacy of behavioural science has become increasingly accepted and its principles have been adopted in some areas of public management. Several governments have created so-called 'nudge units' of government, dedicated to tackling public policy challenges through the exploration and manipulation of human behaviour.

So, what is it that almost five decades of behavioural science has taught us? It has confirmed the frailties and subjectiveness of human behaviour; that our decision making can be flawed, non-rational and biased. It has challenged the economists' central assertion that human decision making is rational and has done so using the language and concepts of economists. It has given a theoretical basis to the much-vaunted gap between stated and revealed preferences in economics.[3] Increasingly, the emergence of big data and greater understanding of methods for conducting rigorous empirical research has given behavioural economists the opportunity to assess human behaviour in unprecedented ways and to support the long-held views of sociologists that human behaviour is complex and frequently non-rational. The following is just some of what behavioural scientists have confirmed about us.

First, we are far more driven by our social factors than Smith, Mill or Pareto would have you believe. We follow social norms – conforming to societal and behavioural expectations (Elster 1989), and our behaviour can at times be characterised by herding – people being led by the behaviours of others rather than acting on their own information and assessments (Haberl et al. 2018). We observe the actions of others and hate feeling like others might be having rewarding experiences while we are missing out – fear of missing out (Przybylski et al. 2013).

As Tversky and Kahneman first told us, our thinking is heavily influenced by heuristics – cognitive shortcuts to simplify thinking and decision-making processes (Haberl et al. 2018). These include affect heuristics – reliance on feelings that are good or bad in relation to a particular stimulus (Slovic et al. 2002); availability heuristics – making judgements about the likelihood of a particular event or events based on how easily an example comes to mind, often ignoring other relevant facts (Tversky and Kahneman 1973); and take-the-best heuristics – we can be easily swayed between options when one option has a single good feature, despite other options having a sum of positive features that is greater (Gigerenzer and Gaissmaier 2011).

Similarly, our ability to make decisions can be heavily influenced by the way in which options and choices are presented to us, otherwise known as 'choice architecture' (Haberl et al. 2018). Examples of these vulnerabilities in our decision making include anchoring – exposure to an initial but unrelated fact can affect our judgements in unrelated decisions (Haberl et al. 2018); framing – choices can be presented in such a way to be highly determinative to the decisions we make (Kahneman and Tversky 1979, Mulino et al. 2009); and words and phrases to which we might apply a positive or negative connotation can impact our decision making in subsequent, unrelated, events – (conceptual) priming (Tulving et al. 1982).[4]

When faced with choices, our decision-making habits can often let us down. We are known to suffer confirmation bias – the tendency to seek out information that fits with our pre-existing views (Haberl et al. 2018). We can sometimes view people and things in more generous terms than are justified because of unrelated attributes – the halo effect (Nisbett and Wilson 1977). We often find ourselves 'satisficing' – making decisions that are sufficient and satisfactory (Simon 1956) – and perhaps unsurprisingly, we have a tendency to adhere to a natural inertia; the status quo effect (Kahneman et al. 1991).

We are not very good when it comes to counting either. We can often believe that independent events are in fact interrelated – gambler's fallacy. We are not rational when it comes to intertemporal choice – we are biased towards receiving rewards in the present versus the future, even when the future payoff is larger (Lowenstein and Thaler 1989). We have been shown to underestimate the likelihood of negative events – optimism bias (Haberl et al. 2018). We view our losses in disproportionately negative terms when compared to our gains – loss aversion – and we will often stick with particular investments because we feel committed to them – sunk cost fallacy (Haberl et al. 2018).[5] We have an aversion to risk and show a strong preference for the known versus the unknown despite the relative pay-offs – ambiguity aversion (Ellsberg 1961).

So, what is the significance of this? Behavioural science has argued that our decision making is imperfect and that, as humans, we are subject to a range of unconscious influences which cause our decision making to, at times, be non-rational. This chapter is concerned with PFPI and in particular seeks to apply a behavioural science lens to the arguments that governments have developed policy settings which have taken PFPI from being a policy option to a policy preference for infrastructure delivery (Hodge and Greve 2013, Zwalf 2020). How would behavioural scientists explain why governments may have found PFPI to be an attractive policy option? In the next section we look at some of the behavioural science phenomena and apply them to the arguments about the so-called political rationale for PFPI. Before we do this, however, we must consider perspectives on behavioural economics' shortcomings.

Behavioural science: a critical evaluation

It has generally been accepted that behavioural science has established that human decision making can be non-rational. However, this has been subject to qualification, even from its supporters. While it is generally accepted that the explanatory power of behavioural science is strong, several behavioural scientists – Leigh (2015), Chetty (2015), Bauer and Wätjen (2018) among them – have noted that their discipline lacks a general theory that consistently explains its assertions. Indeed, behavioural science has largely been a negative endeavour, disproving prior assertions that human behaviour is rational and self-interested, rather than establishing a positive model of science, psychology or even sociology in its own right, except of course to assert that human decision making can be defined as quite often non-rational. Perhaps of more significance, some of the findings of behavioural science with respect to human behaviour overlap with, and in other cases contradict, other findings. While behavioural science has successfully described a range of phenomena that may be observable in human decision making, its findings are not necessarily consistent in themselves.[6] For example, the behaviour of herding contradicts that of the status quo bias, and optimism bias could easily trump confirmation bias or vice versa. These are just two examples. Indeed, the behavioural science literature often over-simplifies the flaws in human decision making (this chapter included), choosing only to focus on the proportion of respondents in experiments whose behaviour is non-rational and ignoring all others (Bauer and Wätjen 2018).

The public policy context of PFPI

It is commonly accepted that there is a role for behavioural science in public administration, and behavioural science has expanded the tools available to governments to achieve policy outcomes (Chetty 2015). Leigh (2015) and French and Oreopoulos (2017) note its application in fields as varied as encouraging citizens to pay taxes, fees and infringements on time; undertaking additional physical exercise; and saving for retirement. However, with the exception of Hodge and Greve (2019), no scholarly literature appears to exist which connects public-policy debate around PFPI to behavioural science.[7] A search by this author of the *EconLit* online academic database of 550 business and economics scholarly journals identified just three articles which discussed both PFPI and behavioural science (none of which are relevant to this chapter).[8] It appears that Hodge and Greve (2019) alone have made the connection between public policy around PFPI and behavioural science. Therefore, this chapter is timely and fills a space that Hodge and Greve – both prominent PFPI scholars – have identified but have not covered in depth.

So, how would behavioural scientists explain what Boardman and Hellowell (2017) and Flinders (2005) have asserted is a preference for PFPI on the part of governments, especially in the face of scholarly criticisms which has strongly argued their shortcomings? In the next section, we apply behavioural science hypotheses to the decision making behind PFPI.

PFPI and behavioural science

[Governments] may be overly responsive to the irrational concerns of citizens, both because of political sensitivity and because they are prone to the same cognitive biases as other citizens. (Kahneman 2011, 142)

For the purposes of this chapter, it is important to consider the relationship between public administration and behavioural science from two perspectives. First, could it be the case that the decisions our governments make are subject to the same or similar biases and irrationalities we identified in the earlier section? Second, could it also be the case that while governments themselves may not make decisions that are biased or non-rational, they are making decisions that mimic the biases of the citizens they represent, therefore remaining attuned to public opinion? Kahneman (2011) tells us that experienced decision makers too are flawed in their decision making, albeit perhaps slightly less so than the average of the population; 'experts show many of the same biases as the rest of us in attenuated form' (p. 140). He also points to situations where public reactions to issues have led to governments adopting policy positions which are only arrived at as responses to public sentiment – in other words, making decisions which respond to the non-rational thinking of their electorates.[9] This suggests that analysing the motivations of governments with respect to policy settings and what drives their formation are salient areas for inquiry. The next section identifies several behavioural science concepts and explains their potential relationship to the debate around the political drivers for adopting PFPI. In doing so, it draws upon an existing base of scholarly opinion and significant issues with regard to the public administration of PFPI. For the sake of our analysis, it also assumes several other factors that are implicit in the observations made by the likes of Boardman and Hellowell (2017) and Flinders (2005) with respect to the political drivers for PFPI:

1. So-called traditional procurement of large infrastructure projects became problematic for governments due to factors such as cost and time overruns.
2. That governments have, over time, demonstrated a policy preference for PFPI, and in doing so have eschewed so-called traditional procurement of infrastructure (Hodge and Greve 2013, Moore and Vining 2019).
3. The alternative to PFPI is so-called traditional procurement, and governments face a binary choice between PFPI and traditional procurement.[10]
4. Systems of government which are democratic, under which governments are incentivised to remain popular with the citizens they represent.[11]

This analysis is, of course, subjective in its nature given the absence of empirical research on which to draw.

Social factors

Whenever I attend a dinner party, I bring either wine, or chocolates, or both. I do not do this because I fear that without my contribution the host's supplies for the evening will run short; I do this because it is a social norm in the society in which I live. Durkheim (1982[1895]) posited that we bind ourselves to norms – practices that we expect others to abide by and others expect of us – and that our norms are part of our social culture. Elster (1989), drawing upon Tylor (1871), notes that such norms form part of the broader culture of the society in which we live.[12]

One explanation for the preference of governments for PFPI is that governments have been influenced by public policy norms that have seen a shift towards societal preferences for market contestability and for service delivery by private enterprise.[13] In other words, service delivery driven by markets has become a social and public policy norm and this, in turn, has influenced the way in which politicians have developed policy settings that are favourable to PFPI. In a similar vein, Ariely (2008) has written of the phenomenon of herding, in which a decision maker determines their own behaviour simply on observing the actions of others. It may be possible that governments have shown evidence of herding in their behaviour in the way in which they rapidly adopted policy arrangements for the adoption of PFPI, and this may explain why the PFPI policy settings frequently look so similar across jurisdictions, a kind of contagion effect (Siemietycki and Farooqi 2013, Zwalf 2020). Similarly, Przybylski et al. (2013) identify that humans, as social creatures, fear being left out of 'rewarding' experiences (fear of missing out). It is possible that delivering infrastructure in a new, market-focused method was a policy experience that governments did not want to miss out on. Social norms, herding and fear of missing out may help explain the relative enthusiasm for the PFPI model by governments. Hodge and Greve (2019) suggest similar motivations may be at play.

Choice architecture

The comedian Sacha Baron Cohen came to prominence for using his faux-Rastafarian alter-ego, Ali G, to ask inane questions of businessmen and politicians to howls of laughter from delighted audiences around the world. What was his secret? By pretending that Ali G hails from a unique sub-culture, Baron Cohen encourages his victims to adjust their expectations for the discussion, and they then allow the interview to proceed on terms that would otherwise be totally unacceptable to them. This is a case of the anchoring effect at work.

Ariely (2008) and Kahneman (2011) tell us that we can be heavily persuaded to behave in a particular way based on other information that is presented to us, even if that information is seemingly unrelated. This may well apply to the public policy process also, and it seems highly probable that the policy tendencies of governments of the last two decades with respect to PFPI can be at least in part explained by this phenomenon. It seems likely that governments have seen PFPI as a logical alternative to traditional procurement and that this is a case of choice architecture at play. In doing so, they may have come to view traditional government-run projects as increasingly litigious (Grimsey and Lewis 2004) and associated with embarrassing delays and cost blowouts (Flyvbjerg et al. 2005). Therefore, they may have been driven towards the PFPI option as a logical alternative to government-managed large infrastructure projects. A related phenomenon is that of framing. It is possible that the PFPI delivery option – rhetorically associated with private sector efficiency – has appealed to governments, or indeed to electors (or to both), who have shown a preference for service delivery that is associated with the private sector.[14] Thorndike's halo effect may have some explanatory value also (Thorndike 1920, in Leuthesser et al. 1995). Thorndike first identified that we can sometimes view things in more generous terms than are justified because of unrelated attributes. It is possible that because of their strong association with private sector efficiency, PFPI have been pre-judged by governments in favourable terms, relative to the traditional option. The market-led approach to project delivery that a PFPI represents – associated with large well-known companies – is perhaps strongly associated with efficiency and effectiveness causing PFPI to be considered favourably by governments.[15] Indeed, if we assume that governments or society at large has come to believe that the private sector is naturally more efficient and effective at developing large-scale infrastructure, there may be a case to say that governments have shown a preference for PFPI simply as a matter of confirmation bias against traditional procurement. Choice architecture, framing, the halo effect and confirmation bias could all have significant explanatory value for the policy settings for PFPI.

Heuristics

When we drive our car to places with which we are unfamiliar, we tend to pay close attention to avoid hazards and to avoid getting lost. When we travel on routes that we are familiar with, we relax somewhat, assuming that we know the road, its particular hazards and that we will not forget our way. This is the effect of heuristics – mental shortcuts – at work. Tversky and Kahneman (1973) describe how these shortcuts often have the effect of saving us time when making decisions, especially those that we make often.

Two kinds of heuristic decision making may have some explanatory power as regards the perceived preference of governments for PFPI. Tversky and Kahneman (1973) argue that we can find ourselves making judgements about the chance of a particular event or events based on how easily an example comes to mind, often ignoring other relevant facts. This is the availability heuristic. In the context of government's preference for PFPI, this preference may have emerged because government has become overly conscious of government-led infrastructure projects which have been seen to fail (for example, with cost blowouts or delays) and as a result has an overly negative view of government-led infrastructure projects and so has opted to establish the policy settings for PFPI as an alternative. Somewhat similarly, the affect heuristic describes that we will often rely on feelings that are good or bad in relation to a particular question, eschewing more detailed analysis (Slovic et al. 2002). It is quite possible that the behaviour of governments has been influenced by heuristics in making decisions about PFPI – and in so doing, rejecting traditional procurement – by making decisions based on negative experiences associated with traditional procurement.[16]

Intertemporal decision making

In March 2020, when the economic effect of the COVID-19 pandemic was bearing down upon the world, the Australian government gave its citizens the option of making early withdrawals from their retirement savings in order to help get them through the financial impacts of the expected downturn. In doing this, the Australian government was giving its citizens a choice between accessing those funds now or allowing those funds to continue to grow and be drawn upon in future. Behavioural science tells us that we will often be biased towards receiving pay-offs in the present, despite the availability of bigger rewards in the future (Lowenstein and Thaler 1989). Indeed, the Australian government offer was taken up by hundreds of thousands of its citizens. Boardman and Hellowell (2017), among others, argue that governments have found benefit in being able to defer costs for major infrastructure through leasing it, in other words: delivering in the present and paying for it in the future. Similarly, Irwin (2012) argues that governments saw an advantage in being able to use PFPI to avoid self-imposed debt ceilings, taking advantage of the accounting standards on leased infrastructure to commission new infrastructure projects which would not have been permissible if done as traditional procurement.[17] Zwalf (2021) has suggested citizens may similarly find an appeal in benefiting from infrastructure in the short term but deferring its payment to the long term. If we are to believe these claims, they can be explained in behavioural science terms as preferences around intertemporal choice, with governments demonstrating a preference for short-term rewards relative to long-term pay-offs. This bias towards present-day consumption appears to have significant explanatory power in the apparent preference that governments have shown for PFPI; like the people that elect them, they appear to have at least something of a preference for short-term rewards relative to long-term pay-offs.

Our aversion to losses and uncertainty

Each evening at about 6 pm, when it is time for my three-year-old to have her nightly bath, she protests vigorously. Only after much cajoling will she agree to cooperate with our daily bathing routine. About half an hour later, when it is time to finish her bath, the routine begins all over again. But this time our energies are applied to convincing her to leave the bath. My daughter's behaviour can be explained by the endowment effect; that is, that we have a tendency to try to hold onto what we already have, disproportionally valuing losses relative to gains.[18] This too may manifest itself in the public policy arena. Traditional procurement has been associated with cost and budget overruns and litigious contract disputes. These can all be sources of substantial political embarrassment to governments. It could be the case that these governments have been driven to a preference for PFPI because of the losses associated with traditional procurement; lost time, lost funds and loss of face. This could have been driven by particular projects which have been seen very publicly to fail and which governments are therefore keen to avoid repeating. Similarly, Ellsberg (1961) identifies that we have a tendency to favour the known over the unknown; we prefer certainties and eschew risk, which he called 'loss aversion'. This too may explain the appeal of PFPI for governments, with typical PFPI projects guaranteeing a project price and being seen to be more reliable with respect to delivering projects on time. A related theme is status quo bias, whereby we can be shown to irrationally adhere to a 'natural inertia' (Kahneman et al. 1991). In public policy terms, this suggests that once policy has been adopted, we are unlikely to reverse or seek changes to it, a concept known to economists and sociologists as 'path dependency'. If this were to be true, it would explain why the PFPI policy settings have emerged into a global policy consensus (Siemietycki and Farooqi 2013) and why they have remained largely unchanged since then.[19] A still related phenomena is that of sunk cost fallacy, where even in the face of more lucrative alternatives we will often stick with investment decisions because we feel committed to them (Ariely 2008, Kahneman 2011). Thousands of contract renegotiations and adjustments have taken place in PFPI, resulting in governments paying more for contracts that the PFPI provider has been unable to deliver upon (Oliveira et al. 2015, in Oliveira et al. 2016). Our human tendency to double-down on unsuccessful investments could explain the tendency of governments to re-negotiate troubled PFPI with project consortia – instead of terminating the project – in a bid to keep the project going having made an initial commitment to it. Our aversion to losses and uncertainty could have substantial explanatory power for the preference of governments for PFPI.

Discussion

This chapter sets out a series of hypotheses to help explain some of the decision-making behaviour that has given rise to the claim of a preference of governments for the PFPI delivery model. These hypotheses implicitly assume that governments demonstrate non-rational preferences and biases in their decision making, or that they have sought to ape the biases of citizens in order to remain aligned with public opinion. Perhaps both are true. These explanations can be grouped into a series of related arguments and if we are to accept these explanations, we can summarise the behaviours of governments with respect to PFPI as follows:

1. A preference for markets and service delivery by the private sector has become a social norm, in public policy, if not among the community at large;
2. Governments find themselves heavily influenced by policy trends they observe in other jurisdictions;
3. Problems such as delays, cost overruns and contract disputes have negatively affected the perception of traditional procurement, and therefore the decision making of governments with respect to PFPI has become favourable;
4. Governments show a preference for early pay-offs when faced with intertemporal choices;
5. Governments have a preference for certainty in project delivery on questions of cost and timeline; and
6. Governments are averse to outright losses and will therefore provide additional funding to PFPI in order to meet delivery targets.

These arguments provide a new angle to the presumed political benefits of PFPI that Boardman and Hellowell (2017), Flinders (2005), Moore and Vining (2019) and others identify. However, while this chapter provides a series of behavioural science hypotheses for the arguments about the drivers that these authors have made, it is based on assumptions; our assessment remains subjective. It is time for research that surveys public-policy decision makers on their attitudes towards PFPI to ascertain in empirical terms what the drivers have been. It would be possible to conduct studies that test the hypotheses noted in this chapter by surveying those at the most senior levels of government – senior public servants, ministers, ministerial advisers – about their attitudes to PFPI and the decision-making processes that have led to current policy settings for PFPI. Such surveys could be designed to identify biases of decision makers through testing their opinion on a range of PPP and infrastructure questions germane to the hypothesis in this chapter. Should such research demonstrate that governments have indeed been subject to collective cognitive biases in their decision making, it may put pressure on governments to reconsider those policy settings and potentially to develop policy settings that are less responsive to cognitive bias. An example of this is research by Saad and Hegezy (2015) which identifies options for the improvements in the maintenance of public assets in the face of decision-making bias. Such research would also complement emerging fields of study around the so-called political drivers for PFPI (for example, Bertelli and Woodhouse in this book and de la Higuera-Molina et al., 2021) and around the behavioural political economy (the application of behavioural science to political decision making; Berggren 2012).

Lastly, consideration should be given to the suitability of the language of behavioural economics to public administration and to the policy-making process. How illuminating is it to describe the actions of governments as either rational or non-rational? Or, further still, apply these labels to the key decision makers within these governments? While behavioural science puts its own construction of 'rationality' at its centre and defines non-adherents (frequently, most of us) as non-rational, this is unhelpful language when we are considering the actions of governments, especially when governments so often act in ways that are consistent with the values and preferences of their electorates as Kahneman (2011) and Sunstein and Kuran (1999; cited in Kahneman, 2011) suggest. Softer language such as 'deliberative' in place of 'rational', and 'feeling' instead of 'non-rational', would provide more description to human cognitive processes (and indeed to the cognitive processes of government decision makers) and do so in a less pejorative fashion than the discipline's traditional labels. If behavioural scientists seek to idolise 'rational decision making', the first thing they could do is find ways to avoid shaming the bulk of humanity who frequently exhibit so-called 'non-rational' behaviours.

Conclusion

Over the last quarter of a century, PFPI have emerged as an increasingly common delivery mechanism for large-scale public infrastructure projects. They have attracted a large volume of scholarly interest, much of which has pointed to the supposed shortcomings of PFPI, and despite this an apparent enthusiasm by governments to license them as the preferred delivery mechanism for major infrastructure (Hodge and Greve 2013). In turn, it has been argued that PFPI have been preferred because of the benefits that have accrued to the governments who commission them. Drawing upon the arguments of Hodge and Greve (2019), this chapter has considered what explanations behavioural science may give to the way in which governments created the policy settings for PFPI. It develops a series of behavioural science hypotheses that may explain the approach taken by governments with respect to PFPI policy settings. While it sheds new light on prevailing arguments about the possible public policy influences for PFPI, they are arguments built upon assumptions. It is clear that empirical research is needed into the drivers for PFPI, and that such research must survey the practitioners themselves as to their preferences and seek to determine what informs these. This is a promising new research frontier for PFPI.

Notes

1. Necessarily, this applies most strongly to countries with systems of democratic government, which is the focus of this chapter.
2. To be accurate, not all of these drivers remain available. For example, adherence to recent changes in accounting standards means that long-term leases should be re-included as liabilities on government balance sheets.
3. It has often been joked that while economics students are taught that markets are unquestionably efficient, students of business are encouraged to find niches for their products, thus inoculating them from market competition. Business scholars, too, have for a long time shown insights into the frailties of human decision making that appear to have escaped their economist cousins.
4. As Ariely (2008, p. 7) says in relation to framing: 'we are always looking at things around us in relation to others'. Indeed, even this chapter does so – it compares PFPI to government-managed infrastructure projects, even though several, even numerous, varieties of each exist and we do so to simplify our decision making, or in this case, to simplify our comparisons.
5. The observations in this section can strictly speaking be connected as falling under specific themes within behavioural science; most commonly these are seen to be around framing, heuristics, market inefficiencies and hyperbolic discounting (Leigh 2015). For stylistic reasons, the observations above have not been presented in this form.
6. Indeed, Bauer and Wätjen (2018) observe that even linguistics have caused confusion among behavioural science scholars, with several terms being used to describe the same or similar phenomena but describing them differently because of the academic foundations from which respective scholars have visited them.
7. This is a significant gap given the extent to which various scholars have debated the assumed drivers for governments to have embraced PFPI. Indeed, much of that commentary has centred on economic and financial analysis of PFPI, and this

chapter and Hodge and Greve (2019) make the case that PFPI should be considered through a behavioural lens.

8. To be fair, the same database identified 441 articles which discuss both behavioural science and public policy.

9. Sunstein and Kuran (1999) identify massive and substantial public responses on issues leading to public policy responses as being 'availability cascades'.

10. This is, of course, an oversimplification with many models for so-called traditional procurement and a number of variations of PFPI being available to governments.

11. Positive political theory and public choice theory remind us that these are generally safe assumptions to make.

12. Miller et al. (2015) argue that conforming to norms is a behaviour practised not just by people, but also by nation states.

13. Authors such as Demeulenaere (2005), Holborow (2015) and Allsop et al. (2018) – all from other disciplines – argue that the acceptance, if not embrace, of market forces is a social norm.

14. Indeed, the idea that PFPI are rhetorically positioned is not new; it has long been argued that linguistics have been influential in the success of PFPI (Linder 1999; Hodge and Greve 2007).

15. In doing so, however, they may be overlooking that government can engage the private sector to deliver large projects, albeit without the financing and ongoing operation of the PFPI model.

16. It is not the topic of this chapter, but one could easily argue that much of the argument about PFPI from both advocates and detractors may indeed be impacted by affect heuristics with so much of the debate seeming to come down to private-sector-versus-public-sector rhetoric.

17. Changes to international accounting standards in 2005 and 2018 have largely nullified this as an option.

18. Note that this concept has in recent times been challenged by several studies which suggest no loss aversion effect exists, or if it does, it can be isolated to a small number of decisions (Yechiam 2015).

19. Having said this, it does not on its own explain why traditional procurement became less commonly employed when it did.

References

Allsop, B., Briggs, J., and Kitney, B. (2018) Market values and youth political engagement in the UK: Towards an agenda for exploring the psychological impacts of neo-liberalism. *Societies*, 8 (4): 95. https://doi.org/10.3390/soc8040095.

Ariely, D. (2008) *Predictably Irrational*. New York City, NY: HarperCollins.

Bauer, F., and Wätjen, M. (2018) A Positive Typology of Irrational Decision Strategies, in *Behavioural Economics Guide*, edited by A. Samson, www.behavioraleconomics.com, pp. 110–119.

Berggren, N. (2012) Time for behavioral political economy? An analysis of articles in behavioral economics. *Review of Austrian Economics*, 25: 199–221.

Boardman, A., and Hellowell, M. (2017) A comparative analysis and evaluation of specialist PFPI units' methodologies for conducting value for money appraisals. *Journal of Comparative Policy Analysis: Research and Practice*, 19 (3): 191–206. https://doi.org/10.1080/13876988.2016.1190083.

Chetty, R. (2015) Behavioural science and public policy: A pragmatic perspective. *American Economic Review: Papers and Proceedings*, 105 (5): 1–33.

De la Higuera-Molina, E.J., Esteve, M., Plata-Díaz, A.M., and Zafra-Gómez, J.L. (2021) The political hourglass: Opportunistic behavior in local government policy decisions. *International Public Management Journal*. www.tandfonline.com/doi/pdf/10.1080/10967494.2021.1905117?needAccess=true.

Demeulenaere, P. (2005) Economic behaviour and the norms of capitalism. *International Social Science Journal*, 57 (185): 421–431.

Durkheim, E. (1982[1895]) *The Rules of the Sociological Method*, edited by S. Lukes, trans. by W.D. Halls. New York, NY: Free Press.

Ellsberg, D. (1961) Risk, ambiguity, and the Savage axioms. *Quarterly Journal of Science*, 75 (4): 643–669.

Elster, J. (1989) Social norms and economic theory. *Journal of Economic Perspectives*, 3 (4): 99–117.

Flinders, M. (2005) The politics of privately financed public infrastructure. *British Journal of Politics and International Relations*, 7: 215–239.

Flyvbjerg, B., Skamris Holm, M., and Buhl, S. (2005) Underestimating costs in public works projects: Error or lie. *Journal of the American Planning Association*, 68 (3): 279–296.

French, R., and Oreopoulos, P. (2017) Applying behavioural science to public policy in Canada. *Canadian Journal of Science*, 50 (3): 600–635.

Gigerenzer, G., and Gaissmaier, W. (2011) Heuristic decision making. *Annual Review of Psychology*, 62 (1): 451–482.

Grimsey, D., and Lewis, M. (2004) *Privately Financed Public Infrastructure: The Worldwide Revolution in Infrastructure Provision and Project Finance*. Cheltenham, UK and Northampton, MA, USA: Edward Elgar Publishing.

Haberl, A., Hulse, C., and Mills, R. (2018) Selected behavioural science concepts, in *Behavioural Economics Guide*, edited by A. Samson, www.behavioraleconomics.com, pp. 121–163.

Hellowell, M. (2010) The UK's Private Finance Initiative: History, evaluation, prospects, in *International Handbook in Public–Private Partnerships*, edited by G.A. Hodge, C. Greve, and A.E. Boardman. Cheltenham, UK and Northampton, MA, USA: Edward Elgar Publishing, pp. 132–158.

Hodge, G., and Greve, C. (2007) Public–private partnerships: An international performance review. *Public Administration Review*, 67 (3): 545–558.

Hodge, G., and Greve, C. (2013) Introduction: Privately financed public infrastructure in turbulent times, in *Rethinking Privately Financed Public Infrastructure*, edited by G.A. Hodge and C. Greve. Abingdon: Routledge, pp. 1–32.

Hodge, G., and Greve, C. (2019) *The Logic of Public–Private Partnerships: The Enduring Interdependency of Politics and Markets*. Cheltenham, UK and Northampton, MA, USA: Edward Elgar Publishing.

Holborow, M. (2015) *Language and Neoliberalism*. London: Routledge.

Irwin, T. (2012) *Accounting Devices and Fiscal Illusions*. IMF Staff Discussion Note, 28 March. Washington, DC: International Monetary Fund. https://doi.org/10.5089/9781475502640.006.

Kahneman, D. (2011) *Thinking Fast and Slow*. New York, NY: Farrar, Straus and Giroux.

Kahneman, D., Knetsch, J.L., and Thaler, R.H. (1991) The endowment effect, loss aversion, and status quo bias. *Journal of Economic Perspectives*, 5 (1): 193–206.

Kahneman, D., and Tversky, A. (1979) Prospect theory: An analysis of decision under risk. *Econometrica*, 47: 263–291.

Leigh, A. (2015) How behavioural science does and can shape public policy. *Economic and Labour Relations Review*, 26 (2): 339–346.

Leuthesser, L., Kohli, C.S., and Katrin, R.H. (1995) Brand equity: The halo effect measure. *European Journal of Marketing*, 29 (4): 57–66.

Linder, S.H. (1999) Coming to terms with public-private partnership: A grammar of multiple meanings. *American Behavioural Scientist*, 43: 35–51.

Lowenstein, G., and Thaler, R. (1989) Anomalies: Intertemporal choice. *Journal of Economic Perspectives*, 3 (4): 181–193.

Mill, J.S. (1836) Civilisation. *London & Westminster Review*. April 1–28.

Miller, J.L., Cramer, J., Volgy, T.J., Bezerra, P., Hauser, M., and Sciabarra, C. (2015) Norms, behavioral compliance, and status attribution in international politics. *International Interactions*, 41 (5): 779–804.

Moore, M., and Vining, A. (2019) Privately financed public infrastructure: A principal-agent View. Draft paper. www.cpsa-acsp.ca/documents/conference/2019/816.Moore-Vining.pdf.

Mulino, D., Scheelings, R., Brooks, R., and Faff, R.R. (2009) Does risk aversion vary with decision-frame? An empirical test using recent game show data. *Review of Behavioural Finance*, 1 (1): 44–61.

National Audit Office (2009) *Private Finance Projects: A Report to the House of Lords Economic Affairs Committee*. London: Stationery Office.

Nisbett, R.E., and Wilson, T.D. (1977) The halo effect: Evidence for unconscious alteration of judgments. *Journal of Personality and Social Psychology*, 35 (4): 250–256.

Oliveira, M., Ribeiro, J., and Macario, R. (2016) Are we planning investments to fail? Consequences of traffic forecast effects on PFPI contracts: Portuguese and Brazilian cases. *Research in Transportation Economics*, 59 (2016): 167–174.

Pareto, V. (1906) *Manual of Political Economy*. Milan: Milano Societa Editrice.

Parks, R., and Terhart, R. (2009) *Evaluation of Privately Financed Public Infrastructure*. Ottawa: Blair, Mackay, Mynett Valuations, Inc./Canadian Union of Public Employees.

Pollitt, M. (2002) The declining role of the state in infrastructure investments in the UK, in *Private Initiatives in Infrastructure: Priorities, Incentives, and Performance*, edited by S.V. Berg, M.G. Pollitt and M. Tsuji. Cheltenham, UK and Northampton, MA, USA: Edward Elgar Publishing, pp. 142–177.

Przybylski, A.K., Murayama, K., DeHaan, C.R., and Gladwell, V. (2013) Motivational, emotional, and behavioral correlates of fear of missing out. *Computers in Human Behavior*, 29 (4): 1841–1848.

Quiggan, J. (2006) Privately financed public infrastructure: Options for improved risk allocation. *UNSW Law Journal*, 29 (3): 289–293.

Saad, D., and Hegezy, T. (2015) Behavioral economic concepts for funding infrastructure rehabilitation. *Journal of Management in Engineering*, 31 (5). https://doi.org/10.1061/(ASCE)ME.1943-5479.0000332.

Siemiatycki, M. (2013) The global production of transportation privately financed public infrastructure. *International Journal of Urban and Regional Research*, 37 (4): 1254–72.

Siemiatycki, M., and Farooqi, N. (2013) Value for money and risk in privately financed public infrastructure. *Journal of the American Planning Association*, 79 (3): 286–299.

Simon, H.A. (1956) Rational choice and the structure of the environment. *Psychological Review*, 63 (2): 129–138.

Slovic, P., Finucane, M., Peters, E., and MacGregor, D.G. (2002) Rational actors or rational fools: Implications of the affect heuristic for behavioural science. *Journal of Socio-Science*, 31: 329–342.

Smith, A. (1776) *An Inquiry into the Nature and Causes of the Wealth of Nations*. London: Strahan and Cadell.

Teicher, J., Alam, Q., and Van Gramberg, B. (2007) Managing trust and relationships in PFPI: Some Australian experiences. *International Review of Administrative Sciences*, 72 (1): 85–100.

Tulving, E., Schacter, D.L., and Stark, H.A. (1982) Priming effects in word fragment completion are independent of recognition memory. *Journal of Experimental Psychology: Learning, Memory and Cognition*, 8(4): 336–342.

Tversky, A., and Kahneman, D. (1973) Availability: A heuristic for judging frequency and probability. *Cognitive Psychology*, 5: 207–232.

Tylor, E. (1871) *Primitive Culture*. New York, NY: J.P. Putnam's Sons.

Yechiam, E. (2015) The psychology of gains and losses: More complicated than previously thought. *Psychological Science Agenda*, January. www.apa.org/science/about/psa/2015/01/gains-losses.

Zwalf, S. (2020) From turnpikes to toll-roads: A short history of privately financed public infrastructure in Australia. *Journal of Economic Policy Reform*. https://doi.org/10.1080/17487870.2020.1716754.

Zwalf, S. (2021) Managing goal conflict. The case of agency theory in the policy settings for public–private partnerships; A perspective on citizen and government interests. *Annals of Public and Cooperative Economics*.

8 A public turn in the governance of infrastructure

Lene Tolstrup Christensen and Carsten Greve

Introduction

> The governance of infrastructure [can be understood as] the planning, financing, contracting and building of the public physical infrastructure essential for economic and social activities […] Without the financial, regulatory and coordinating role of governments, infrastructure investment would simply not happen. (Wegrich, Hammerschmid and Kostka 2017, 2)

This chapter argues that the public administration literature on public–private partnerships (PPPs) and infrastructure governance is currently witnessing 'a public turn' with more explicit government involvement and less reliance on pure market forces. This is reinforced by the recent focus on a renewed role for the state. Alasdair Roberts (2019) has argued for the relevance of the 'strategies for governing' that states take on. As a counterweight to the trend in Public Administration and Management for micro-studies and use of methods from behavioural sciences, Roberts suggests the state can once more be seen as a legitimate object for research. The renewed role of state power has been amplified by governments' response to Covid-19 across the world. Roberts (2020) has also argued that this latest crisis comes on top of others like the financial crisis and the climate crisis, and that we should see turbulence as the new norm – and states' strategies as a key part of the response to these crises. A similar call for public action in the wake of Covid-19 comes from Janine O'Flynn (2020), who argues that a stronger emphasis on public responsibility in Public Administration and Management research will be a likely outcome of the Covid-19 crisis.

Over recent decades, the policy and scholarly debate on the governance of infrastructure has been dominated by a focus on the potential and problems of involving private actors under headings such as 'contracting out' (Kettl 2015), 'privatization' (Parker 2009, 2012), 'public–private partnership' (Hodge et al. 2010, 2017) and 'regulation' (Levi-Faur and Jordana 2004, 2011). After years in this direction, the assumption that infrastructure governance per se should

149

include private sector actors led to what could be called 'the inevitable theses on ever increasing private actor involvement' when it comes to infrastructure delivery and solving the acclaimed infrastructure gap (Wegrich, Kostka and Hammerschmid 2017).

The research questions asked in this chapter are: how did the transition from a PPP model to a broader infrastructure governance model occur? Is there a new model of infrastructure governance, and if there is, what does it look like?

First, we outline the argument for the public turn academically by focusing on the reinforced role of the state and how this is operationalized in the literature on public administration when it comes to organizational responses to the infrastructure challenge. Second, we illustrate the public turn empirically with the example of the Organisation for Economic Co-operation and Development's (OECD's) policy development on infrastructure. Finally, we discuss and conclude on the implications for such a public turn from a public administration perspective.

A public turn in the public administration literature

Many scholars have pointed to the swings or turns between the preference for state control and market control in the area of infrastructure (Dobbin 1994, Lodge 2002, Perrow 2002, Roberts 2010) and thus to an historical and contextualized understanding of infrastructure governance. Alasdair Roberts' observation in his 2010 Logic of Discipline book, for example, emphasized that after the Second World War, governments around the world had been progressively 'disciplined' to stay out of the way of global capital (Roberts 2010). Contrasting this, however, his most recent analysis of international events and numerous crises pointed to a renewed interest in strategies for governing by states. Our argument for a new public turn in this chapter is based on at least three interlinked developments. First, the financial crises in 2007–2009 showed the limitations in uncontrolled markets and in the area of infrastructure that led to the exposure of the risks with privatized models. PPP models and concessions failed and had to be bailed out by the state (Hodge and Greve 2013). The financial markets dried out and thus the attractiveness for the privatized models imploded. Second, some decades into the upswing of privatized policies and models, the performance of the privatized alternatives still shows mixed results (Hood and Dixon 2015). Her Majesty's Treasury in the UK does not use the Private Finance Initiative and Private Finance 2 (PF2) anymore (Infrastructure and Projects Authority 2018). In non-Anglo-Saxon countries, the literature has shown that the New Public Management (NPM) reforms are out there and alive, but often the reform elements are combined and layered with other ways of governance (Greve et al. 2016, Polzer et al. 2016). Third, academically there has recently started to be an interest in the already existing more-public models of state-owned enterprises (SOEs) and agencies as an alternative to privatization (Bernier et al. 2020, Bernier and Reeves 2018, Christensen and Greve 2018, Grossi et al. 2015). One might suspect in retrospect that academia and the policy institutions were blinded by the attractions of privatization and did not sufficiently acknowledge the existing governance structures that were there all along and did not disappear in the heydays of privatization (Florio and Fecher 2011). This is what we call upon in a research agenda on the public turn in the governance of infrastructure. In relation to the governance of infrastructure, at least two streams of literature within the realm of public administration have been seminal in their contributions to analyzing and better understanding the governance of infrastructure: the regulation literature and the public governance literature.

Regulation literature: from privatization focus to re-centering of the state and SOEs

When it comes to the regulation literature on infrastructure, the last few decades have witnessed a focus on how to understand and create regulation as the backdrop of privatization of infrastructure (Levi-Faur and Jordana 2011), including a substantial focus on the creation of independent market regulators (Baldwin et al. 2012). This 'regulatory state' idea highlights that state authority is dispersed over more governmental levels as well as transnationally. It also highlights that regulation is more than legal acts from the national government, but also involves international and private regulation (Levi-Faur and Jordana 2004, 2011). In the area of infrastructure there is, however, an acknowledgement of the central role for the national state (Wegrich, Kostka and Hammerschmid 2017). Examples here include establishing a national plan for infrastructure and the introduction of independent infrastructure advisory boards. The adjacent utility regulation literature, which itself has a long history, reminds us that infrastructure is basically networks where each sector faces different governance challenges when it comes to competition and market regulation (Florio 2017). The literature primarily focuses on market dynamics in privatization with a rational choice approach and the applied ambition to secure economic and legal optimization. There has long been a normative focus towards more privatization, but more recently there has been a move to revisit this bias and reflect on state ownership as a legitimate way of infrastructure delivery (Bernier et al. 2020, Bernier and Reeves 2018,

Florio 2013, Florio and Fecher 2011). The public turn in the regulation of infrastructure, we argue, can be seen as a move from a one-eyed focus on the potential and pitfalls of privatization to the re-acknowledgement of the role of the state and public alternatives in infrastructure governance such as SOEs against the backdrop of the financial crises.

Public governance: from NPM reforms to mixed reforms and more models

The second strand of literature is the literature on public governance that focuses on the steering aspects and the inter-organizational relations with the state as an actor among others (Osborne 2010b) when analyzing infrastructure governance. What is key is that the state has many other tasks than that of a regulator (Torfing et al. 2020). The state is responsible for the policy formulation and legal framework and later the execution via agencies (Verhoest et al. 2012), the state is the purchaser and later contractor of services (Hodge et al. 2017, Kettl 2015) and the state is also the facilitator of networks of organizations involved in the delivery (Klijn and Koopenjan 2015). In this strand of literature, there has also been a bias towards focusing, exploring and explaining the introduction of market mechanisms in the infrastructure delivery like PPPs (Hodge et al. 2010) and privatization (Kettl 2015; Parker 2009, 2012). However, in this literature the public turn can be identified through the way our attention has turned from only focusing on NPM reforms to a contextualized and normative exploration and explanation of concepts such as New Public Governance (Osborne 2010a) and the Neo-Weberian state (Greve et al. 2016, Pollitt and Bouckaert 2017). Here the different reforms have been analyzed as co-existing as hybrid governance arrangements including paradigms of traditional public administration (Christensen and Lægreid 2011, Polzer et al. 2016). On an organizational level, there has recently been a call to once again focus on the state as owner (Bruton et al. 2015, Christensen 2016, Grossi et al. 2015), which is especially important in the area of infrastructure and service delivery where ownership is a widespread practice (OECD 2014). This has also led to a re-orientation towards local companies (Andrews et al. 2019), agencies (Hermann and Verhoest 2012) and joint service delivery (Voorn et al. 2019). To acknowledge this public turn and thus understand and explain infrastructure governance and the broader public policy implications of infrastructure as a part of public service, we suggest paying closer attention to arguments of institutionalization and institutional change (Conran and Thelen 2016, Pierson 2004, Streeck and Thelen 2005) as the move from PPPs only to more state-oriented solutions becomes evident.

Empirical illustration of the public turn: the case of the OECD policy on infrastructure

The OECD (2020) has recently published an official *Recommendation on the Governance of Infrastructure*. This marks a shift from earlier, when the OECD (2012) published recommendation on principles for public governance of PPPs. The focus in public administration is now on infrastructure governance in broad terms and less on the specific model of PPPs, and even includes explicit recognition of SOEs as a part of the governance. The OECD recommendation indicates that we are entering a new period where a more prominent role for the state seems to be more accepted again when it comes to solving complex societal challenges like the infrastructure gap. It can also be seen as a greater acceptance of public–private (mixed) provision of infrastructure, where private finance and private provision is countered more by state-led engagement.

The OECD has gone through a change in its approach to PPP. The OECD began its work on PPPs with the establishment of the meetings of the Network for Senior Budget and PPP Officials. The network first produced a report on the standard issues of a PPP. This first report was entitled *Public-Private Partnerships: In Search of Risk Sharing and Value for Money* (OECD 2008). These were the two key items in the initial PPP debate. Risk-sharing is of course a crucial part of the PPP debate. Value for money was one of the preferred official arguments for establishing PPP projects in many countries. Later on, the OECD examined the institutional framework and made a report on 'dedicated PPP units' (OECD 2010). One of the recommendations was that each country should have a PPP unit for PPPs to get going. After more meetings in the policy officials' network, the OECD (2012) came up with the Recommendations for Public Governance of PPPs. The 12 recommendations reflect the OECD's position on the essential requirements that governments must attend to when developing a PPP policy. The OECD helped the Association of Southeast Asian Nations (ASEAN) countries develop their recommendations, which amounted to 14 (more on transparency was added) (ASEAN 2014). In the mid-2010s the OECD used its own framework to review the PPP policy of several nations, including the UK (OECD 2015a) and Kazakhstan (OECD 2019). Sub-national experiences with PPPs in cities and regions were also examined (OECD 2018). These were thorough reviews that examined the PPP policy of those nations very carefully and made assessments of whether the PPP policy was sound. In the course of the late 2010s, the OECD had gathered much information about PPPs.

Little by little, member countries began to present information on infrastructure projects that was not exclusively on PPPs. Within the OECD itself, there were other types of working groups or offices, which also were working on infrastructure. There was a group on public investments. And connected to the OECD policy community, there was a group within the International Transport Forum (ITF) working on private finance and transport infrastructure, but with a wider brief than just looking at PPPs (ITF 2018). The ITF report compared the PPP model with the regulated asset base model (RAB) of providing public infrastructure. The emerging availability and acknowledgement that PPPs were not the only show in town anymore became clear with the publication *Towards a Framework for Infrastructure Governance* (OECD 2015b) that led to an OECD report that in 2017 emerged as *The Governance of Infrastructure* and an accompanying policy recommendation paper, *Getting Infrastructure Right* (OECD 2017). In this report, the OECD focused on infrastructure governance as the main concept while the 'delivery models' of PPP, SOE and RAB were listed on an equal basis. In the final version of the report, the focus on the 'delivery models' was placed in the appendix and did not even feature in the main parts of the report. In 2020, ten new recommendations on the governance of infrastructure were published by the OECD (see Box 8.1).

Box 8.1   The OECD's (2020) 'Recommendations on the governance of infrastructure'

1. Develop a long-term strategic vision for infrastructure.
2. Guard fiscal sustainability, affordability and value for money.
3. Ensure efficient procurement of infrastructure projects.
4. Ensure transparent, systematic and effective stakeholder participation.
5. Co-ordinate infrastructure policy across levels of government.
6. Promote a coherent, predictable and efficient regulatory framework.
7. Implement a whole-of-government approach to manage threats to integrity.
8. Promote evidence-informed decision making.
9. Make sure the asset performs throughout its life.
10. Strengthen critical infrastructure resilience.

It is not just about the PPP organizational form anymore, but about a broader agenda on resilient infrastructure governance. A public turn had occurred in the OECD.

The establishment of new international centers for collecting, processing and assessing information on infrastructure governance can also be seen as a further gradual change to institutions advising on how to regulate and govern infrastructure. Developments in other international organizations seem to confirm this change. In 2014 the G20 Global Infrastructure Hub was established. The Hub provides a sort of a clearing house for information on infrastructure governance, and it has got ample resources from the G20 countries. It employs a number of experts in its office in Sydney, Australia. They consider PPP projects, but also other type of infrastructure projects.

After several decades where the individual countries have evaluated PPP projects in their own countries, there is now a shared commitment to learn from the knowledge assembled globally. The World Bank together with many other international organizations established the PPP Knowledge Lab in 2015. While this center is focused on PPPs, it is also considering infrastructure projects more broadly.

Overall, we have illustrated how the OECD as one of the leading policy centers on PPPs globally has gradually changed its focus from stressing models for infrastructure that include private sector actors to a broader governance focus. This new governance perspective has an emphasis on the role of the state, including SOEs as legitimate organizational and financial models for infrastructure.

Towards a new research agenda that acknowledges the public turn in infrastructure governance

These observations on the public turn in how we as academics think and how the bureaucrats and politicians act in the infrastructure governance domain have implications for our future research agenda. We suggest that the research agenda on PPP moves to a focus on infrastructure governance that explores and acknowledges the reinforced role of the state and considers the diverse organizational expressions of this role such as SOEs, RAB and other hybrid arrangements. This breaks with the recent trend towards performance studies of the most optimal PPP model.

The role of the state and the politics of infrastructure governance should be of most interest. When studying PPPs as models for a specific project, the traditional view of politics is seen as a matter of pork barrel politics (Wegrich and Hammerschmid 2017). However, this could be expanded to consider the relation between bureaucracy and politicians when choosing a certain mode of delivery for a given project. This will bring attention to the more gradual institutional changes in the study of infrastructure governance (Conran and Thelen 2016, Mahoney and Thelen 2010, Streeck and Thelen 2005). The role of SOEs (Bernier et al. 2020, Bernier and Reeves 2018, Christensen 2020, Grossi et al. 2015) and local and municipality corporations (Andrews et al. 2019) are expanding research fields in relation to infrastructure provision. This also points to the importance of the long-term perspective of infrastructure governance. Most infrastructure projects require high investments and maintenance costs to support the assets, which are there for decades and are unchangeable. This leads to the question of accountability and especially the future generation perspective (Jordana 2017), which in turn concerns the role of the state.

The move towards a situation where the state (again) plays a bigger role in infrastructure governance potentially changes the conditions for doing research. Whereas the PPP phenomenon was introduced in an increasingly globalized economy where countries were eager to share best practices of how to develop the partnerships, the return to a more state-oriented approach may indicate that states are likely to guard their own solutions and keep their cards closer to their chests. The geo-political implications of a new competition between the U.S., China and Russia may even mean that sharing knowledge on the technicalities of how to design and fund PPP projects may give way to more strategic and guarded approaches to governments in how they construct infrastructure projects. This is already evident in the case of cyber-defense matters where the sharing of knowledge is not straightforward. At this point in time, the argument above is more speculative, and a more pragmatic approach to infrastructure governance may prove the argument wrong, but the geo-political stakes of what is guarded by the state and what is not is worth looking at in the future.

References

Andrews, R., Ferry, L., Skelcher, C., and Wegorowski, P. (2019) Corporatization in the public sector: Explaining the growth of local government companies. *Public Administration Review*, 80(3): 482–493. https://doi.org/10.1111/puar.13052.

ASEAN (2014) ASEAN Principles for PPP frameworks [Press release].

Baldwin, R., Cave, M., and Lodge, M. (2012) *Understanding Regulation: Theory, Strategy, and Practice*. Oxford: Oxford University Press.

Bernier, L., Florio, M., and Bance, P. (2020) *The Routledge Handbook of State-Owned Enterprises*. New York, NY: Routledge.

Bernier, L., and Reeves, E. (2018) The continuing importance of state-owned enterprises in the twenty-first century: challenges for public policy. *Annals of Public and Cooperative Economics*, 89(3): 453–458.

Bruton, D. G., Peng, M. W., Ahlstrom, D., Stan, C., and Xu, K. (2015) State-owned enterprises around the world as hybrid organizations. *Academy of Management Perspectives*, 29(1): 92–114.

Christensen, L. T. (2016) *State-owned Enterprises as Institutional Market Actors in the Marketization of Public Service Provision: A Comparative Case Study of Danish and Swedish Passenger Rail 1990–2015*. PhD Dissertation, Copenhagen Business School, Frederiksberg. Retrieved from http://openarchive.cbs.dk/.

Christensen, L. T. (2020) State-owned Enterprises as Institutional Market Actors: A Gradual Institutional Change Perspective on Domestic SOEs in the Marketization of Public Services, in *The Routledge Handbook of State-owned Enterprises*, edited by L. Bernier, M. Florio and P. Bance. Abingdon: Routledge, pp. 239–255.

Christensen, L. T., and Greve, C. (2018) Choosing state owned enterprises over public-private partnerships for infrastructure governance. *International Public Management Review*, 18(2): 137–161.

Christensen, T., and Lægreid, P. (2011) Complexity and hybrid public administration: theoretical and empirical challenges. *Public Organization Review*, 11: 407–423.

Conran, J., and Thelen, K. (2016) Institutional Change, in *The Oxford Handbook of Historical Institutionalism*, edited by O. Fioretos, T. G. Falleti and A. Sheingate. Oxford: Oxford University Press, pp. 71–88.

Dobbin, F. (1994) *Forging Industrial Policy: The United States, Britain, and France in the Railway Age*. Cambridge: Cambridge University Press.

Florio, M. (ed.) (2013) Public enterprises and quality institutions: Alternatives to privatisation. *International Review of Applied Economics*, Special Issue, 27(2): 135–296.

Florio, M. (ed.) (2017) *The Reform of Network Industries: Evaluating Privatisation, Regulation and Liberalisation in the EU*. Cheltenham, UK and Northampton, MA, USA: Edward Elgar Publishing.

Florio, M., and Fecher, F. (2011) The future of public enterprises: Contributions to a new discourse. *Annals of Public and Cooperative Economics*, 82(4): 361–373.

Greve, C., Lægreid, P., and Rykkja, L. (eds) (2016) *Nordic Administrative Reforms: Lessons for Public Management*. London: Palgrave Macmillan.

Grossi, G., Papenfuß, U., and Tremblay, M.-S. (2015) Corporate governance and accountability of state-owned enterprises. *International Journal of Public Sector Management*, Guest editorial, 28(4/5): 274–285.

Hermann, C., and Verhoest, K. (2012) The Process of Liberalisation, Privatisation and Marketisation, in *Privatization of Public Services: Impacts for Employment, Working Conditions, and Service Quality in Europe*, edited by C. Hermann and J. Flecker. Abingdon: Routledge, pp. 6–32.

Hodge, G., and Greve, C. (2013) Introduction: Public–Private Partnerships in Turbulent Times, in *Rethinking Public–Private Partnerships: Strategies for Turbulent Times*, edited by C. Greve and G. Hodge. London: Routledge, pp. 1–32.

Hodge, G., Greve, C., and Boardman, A. E. (2017) Public-private partnerships: The way they were and what they can become. *Australian Journal of Public Administration*, 76(3): 273–282.

Hodge, G. A., Greve, C., and Boardman, A. E. (eds) (2010) *International Handbook on Public–Private Partnerships*. Cheltenham, UK and Northampton, MA, USA: Edward Elgar Publishing.

Hood, C., and Dixon, R. (2015) *A Government that Worked Better and Cost Less? Evaluating Three Decades of Reform and Change in UK Central Government*. Oxford: Oxford University Press.

Infrastructure and Projects Authority (2018) Budget 2018: Private Finance Initiative (PFI) and Private Finance 2. www.gov.uk/government/publications/private-finance -initiative-pfi-and-private-finance-2-pf2-budget-2018-brief.

ITF (2018) *Private Investment in Transport Infrastructure: Dealing with Uncertainty in Contracts*. www.itf-oecd.org/private-investment-transport-infrastructure-uncertainty.

Jordana, J. (2017) Accountability Challenges in the Governance of Infrastructure, in *The Governance of Infrastructure*, edited by K. Wegrich, G. Kostka and G. Hammerschmid. Oxford: Oxford University Press, pp. 43–62. https://doi.org/10 .1093/acprof:oso/9780198787310.003.0003.

Kettl, D. F. (2015) The job of government: Interweaving public functions and private hands. *Public Administration Review*, 75(2): 219–229.

Klijn, E.-H., and Koopenjan, J. F. M. (2015) *Governance Networks in the Public Sector*. London: Routledge.

Levi-Faur, D., and Jordana, J. (2004) *The Politics of Regulation: Institutions and Regulatory Reforms for the Age of Governance*. Cheltenham, UK and Northampton, MA, USA: Edward Elgar Publishing.

Levi-Faur, D., and Jordana, J. (eds) (2011) *Handbook on the Politics of Regulation*. Cheltenham, UK and Northampton, MA, USA: Edward Elgar Publishing.

Lodge, M. (2002) *On Different Tracks: Designing Railway Regulation in Britain and Germany*. Westport, CT: Praeger Publishers.

Mahoney, J., and Thelen, K. (eds) (2010) *Explaining Institutional Change: Ambiguity, Agency, and Power*. Cambridge: Cambridge University Press.

OECD (2008) *Public-Private Partnerships: In Pursuit of Risk Sharing and Value for Money*. Paris: OECD.

OECD (2010) *Dedicated Public-Private Partnership Units: A Survey of Governance and Institutional Structures*. Paris: OECD.

OECD (2012) *Recommendations of the Council on Principles for Public Governance of Public-Private Partnerships*. Paris: OECD.

OECD (2014) The Size and Sectoral Distribution of SOEs in OECD and Partner Countries. Paris: OECD Retrieved from http://dx.doi.org/10.1787/9789264215610 -e.

OECD (2015a) *OECD Review of Public Governance of Public-Private Partnerships in the United Kingdom*. Paris: OECD.

OECD (2015b) *Towards a Framework for the Governance of Infrastructure*. Paris: OECD. www.oecd.org/gov/budgeting/Towards-a-Framework-for-the-Governance -of-Infrastructure.pdf.

OECD (2017) *Getting Infrastructure Right: A Framework for Better Governance*. Paris: OECD.

OECD (2018) *Sub-National Public-Private Partnerships: Meeting Infrastructure Challenges*. Paris: OECD.

OECD (2019) Public-private partnerships: review of Kazakhstan. *OECD Journal of Budgeting*, 19(2). https://doi.org/10.1787/f7696c94-en.

OECD (2020) *Recommendation on the Governance of Infrastructure*. Paris: OECD.

O'Flynn, J. (2020) Confronting the big challenges of our time: Making a difference during and after Covid-19. *Public Management Review*, 23(7): 961–980. https://doi .org/080/14719037.2020.1820273.

Osborne, S. P. (2010a) Conclusions: Public Governance and Public Service Delivery – A Research Agenda for the Future, in *The New Public Governance? Emerging Perspectives on the Theory and Practice of Public Governance*, edited by S. P. Osborne. London: Routledge, pp. 413–428.

Osborne, S. P. (ed.) (2010b) *The New Public Governance? Emerging Perspectives on the Theory and Practice of Public Governance.* London: Routledge.

Parker, D. (2009) *The Official History of Privatization, Vol. 1: The Formative Years 1970–1987.* London: Routledge.

Parker, D. (2012) *The Official History of Privatization, Vol. 2: Popular Capitalism 1987–1997.* London: Routledge.

Perrow, C. (2002) *Organizing America: Wealth, Power, and the Origins of Corporate Capitalism.* Princeton, NJ: University presses of California, Columbia and Princeton.

Pierson, P. (2004) *Politics in Time.* Princeton, NJ: Princeton University Press.

Pollitt, C., and Bouckaert, G. (2017) *Public Management Reform: A Comparative Analysis – Into the Age of Austerity* (4th edition). Oxford: Oxford University Press.

Polzer, T., Meyer, R. E., Höllerer, M. A., and Seiwald, J. (2016) Institutional hybridity in public sector reform: Replacement, blending, or layering of administrative paradigms – how institutions matter! *Research in the Sociology of Organizations,* 48B: 69–99.

Roberts, A. (2010) *The Logic of Disicipline: Global Capitalism and the Architecture of Government.* New York, NY: Oxford University Press.

Roberts, A. (2019) *Strategies for Governing: Reinventing Public Administration for a Dangerous Century.* Ithaca, NY: Cornell University Press.

Roberts, A. (2020) The third and fatal shock: How pandemic killed the millennial paradigm. *Public Administration Review,* 80(4): 603–609.

Streeck, W., and Thelen, K. (eds) (2005) *Beyond Continuity: Institutional Change in Advanced Political Economies.* Oxford: Oxford University Press.

Torfing, J., Andersen, L. B., Greve, C., and Klausen, K. K. (2020) *Public Governance Paradigms.* Cheltenham, UK and Northampton, MA, USA: Edward Elgar Publishing.

Verhoest, K., Van Thiel, S., Bouckaert, G., and Lægreid, P. (eds) (2012) *Government Agencies: Practices and Lessons from 30 Countries.* Basingstoke: Palgrave Macmillan.

Voorn, B., Van Genugten, M., and Van Thiel, S. (2019) Multiple principals, multiple problems: Implications for effective governance and a research agenda for joint service delivery. *Public Administration,* 97(3): 1–15. https://doi.org/10.1111/padm.12587.

Wegrich, K., and Hammerschmid, G. (2017) Infrastructure Governance as Political Choice, in *The Governance of Infrastructure,* edited by K. Wegrich, G. Kostka and G. Hammerschmid. Oxford: Oxford University Press, pp. 21–42.

Wegrich, K., Hammerschmid, G., and Kostka, G. (2017) The Challenges of Infrastructure: Complexity, (Ir)rationalities, and the Search for Better Governance, in *The Governance of Infrastructure,* edited by K. Wegrich, G. Kostka and G. Hammerschmid. Oxford: Oxford University Press, pp. 1–18.

Wegrich, K., Kostka, G., and Hammerschmid, G. (eds) (2017) *The Governance of Infrastructure.* Oxford: Oxford University Press.

9 New frontiers in planning: city building through public–private partnerships?

Matti Siemiatycki

Introduction

A school is a road, is a subway, is a hospital. That, in a nutshell, is the way that much of the scholarly research treats the study of infrastructure public–private partnerships (PPPs). The PPP itself is the object of interest and of study, regardless of the type of infrastructure. Over the past three decades, Hodge and Greve have documented the most pressing questions asked by PPP scholars (see the Introduction of this book). Are PPPs privatization by another name? What is value for money (VfM) in a PPP relative to a traditionally procured project, and how is VfM calculated? Do PPPs deliver better on-time and on-budget results than alternative delivery models? For long periods of time, PPPs were studied 'through a set of technical, formal and utilitarian objectives' (Hodge and Greve 2019). More recently, the lens for analyzing PPPs has widened further, with scholars from a broad array of academic disciplines examining questions about the formal and informal governance of PPPs, the presence of international PPP markets and industry actors, the financialization of infrastructure, and the politics, ideologies and pressures on governments to choose PPPs (Whitefield and Smyth 2019, Warsen et al. 2020, Whiteside 2020).

One area that has received comparatively less focus in the PPP-specific literature are detailed evaluations of the spatial, social and environmental outcomes of PPPs as major pieces of civil or social infrastructure that exist and impact on communities. This is not entirely surprising, as it mirrors the PPP industry, which treats PPPs as financial instruments, project-delivery tools, legal contracts and complex engineering challenges (Omega Centre 2011, 114). In most countries, the government PPP agencies that have been formed to promote and deliver PPPs are primarily staffed with financial, accounting, legal and engineering experts. Likewise, the major firms and professions that dominate the private sector PPP industry are global investors, financial advisors, legal advisors, and engineering and construction management giants (Siemiatycki 2012). As Van den Hurk and Siemiatycki (2018) note, architects and planners play a subservient and secondary role in the PPP arrangements, both on the public and private sector sides of major infrastructure PPP deals.

Yet for students of cities – primarily from the disciplines of urban planning and geography – PPPs have posed a very different set of questions. PPPs have a long history in city-building practice of delivering the infrastructure that underpins the functioning of a modern city, including the highways, bridges, transit lines, water and waste facilities, energy grids, schools, affordable housing, courthouses, libraries, parks and recreation centres. What is the impact of the way that a project is delivered on the planning process, the actors involved and its material outcomes in the communities in which it is built? Do PPPs lead to better public services or more unequal access to key infrastructure? Can PPPs drive greater environmental sustainability and livability? Do PPPs deliver innovation, architecture and design excellence or mediocrity? How do PPPs perform over a long-term operating contract in an urban environment where there can be immense uncertainty and policy change? The answers to these fundamental questions are embedded in an extensive and ever-growing body of past scholarship on urban infrastructure, and will guide the future research agenda on PPPs in cities.

Foundations for a new research agenda

The literature on infrastructure PPPs in cities in the geography and planning disciplines has generally (though not exclusively) been quite critical of the ways in which PPPs drive social inequality and put private profit ahead of public benefit (see Kayden 2000, Miraftab 2004, Sagalyn 2007, Fainstein 2008, Sclar 2015). The unbundling of infrastructure from an integrated network into a series of discrete financial assets has given global investors greater power in the statecraft of cities and has led to increasingly splintered patterns of urbanism (Graham and Marvin 2001, Ashton et al. 2016, O'Neil 2019, Pike et al. 2019a, O'Brien et al. 2019). PPPs typically deliver average architecture and design, rather than the exceptional architecture and design that becomes the cornerstone of great cities, as PPP processes are optimized to deliver the lowest lifecycle cost infrastructure (Van den Hurk and Siemiatycki 2018). For similar reasons, innovation realized through PPPs has tended to be evolutionary rather than realizing wholesale transformations in the way that public services are provided (Himmel and Siemiatycki 2017). Infrastructure PPPs with long-term operating contracts, especially those that transfer demand risk to the private sector, have tended to create policy lock-ins and are inflexible to changing urban conditions, leaving the public worse off (Cruz and Marques 2013, Ross and Yan 2015). It is not uncommon for tensions to arise between the public and private sector partners in a PPP, or for projects to experience significant contract renegotiations and even defaults (Siemiatycki 2010).

After two decades of long-term design-build-finance-operate-maintain (DBFOM)-style PPPs being the global state of the art for delivering large-scale urban infrastructure projects, favour is waning. There is now a growing international step back in the popularity of long-term infrastructure-contract-style PPPs for municipal infrastructure in many developed countries, including Canada, the United States, the United Kingdom and Israel (see Siemiatycki 2015b, Bel et al. 2018, Razin et al. 2020). To be certain, PPPs are still widely used in cities around the world. But particularly in developed countries, the triumphant view from the early days of PPPs when they were a powerful brand and politically presented as the 'only show in town' has given way to a more hard-headed assessment of the pros and cons of using a PPP approach on a project-by-project basis (Bentley 2020). Additionally, in many contexts the PPP models that are used are increasingly resembling traditional procurements, with less long-term private capital in the deals, shorter operating periods and fewer risks transferred to the private sector (Heald 2002, Siemiatycki 2015b).

While the PPP brand may be damaged, there remains a strong political impetus to provide and govern infrastructure through partnerships between the public, private and non-profit sectors – to tap into shared resources, spread risk and bring forward new ideas. In place of the one-size-fits-all Private Finance Initiative (PFI)/DBFOM-style PPP has emerged a blossoming of a wider range of partnership approaches, designed to achieve a broader set of goals than narrowly defined VfM. The financialization of infrastructure proceeds apace, bringing a new set of rationales, players and power dynamics into urban infrastructure partnerships (O'Brien and Pike 2017). The rise of smart cities has brought a new breed of tech entrepreneurs to the forefront of city-building partnerships with the promise of bringing about radical urban transformations (Zukin 2020). The fledgling practice of social impact bonds introduces companies, non-profits and philanthropists into the provision of key social programs, governed through pay-for-performance mechanisms (Warner 2013). Global institutional investors are also becoming more prominent as the owners and operators of major public use infrastructure. At the same time, as Van Montfort and Michels (2020) identify, innovative forms of partnerships in the housing, energy, transportation and social services sectors are increasingly being explored to realize more livable cities.

New frontiers in urban PPP research

There are now new frontiers of PPPs taking place in cities, and along with them new frontiers for urban research on infrastructure delivered through partnerships. The sections below identify key areas for research on urban PPPs, which grapple with the evolving practice of partnerships in cities.

New rationales for urban PPPs

The rationales for PPPs vary by jurisdiction and have evolved over time. As Siemiatycki (2015b) documents, early PPPs were motivated by political desires to tap into private capital to pay for critical public infrastructure, off-balance-sheet accounting to avoid debt limits, and in some cases, challenges to the power of organized labour and a view that the private sector was more efficient than government. Early PPPs in cities were thus wrapped up in heated ideological debates about the role of the state, privatization and the balance of power between capital and labour, debates that are captured in the scholarly literature (Savas 2000, Sclar 2001, Loxley and Loxley 2010). In the second wave of PPPs, VfM and risk transfer have come to be the dominant drivers of urban infrastructure PPPs. In this conceptualization, private finance is the glue that binds together the partners, incentivizing firms with risk capital at stake to deliver on their contractual obligations. This is a more technocratic terrain that still embodies deeply political questions about the appropriate returns for private investors in infrastructure and the role of the private sector in implementing public policy.

Today, in what may be described as a third wave of PPPs, innovation, capacity and political legitimacy are more important than ever as rationales for urban PPPs. There is a growing recognition that the complex challenges that cities face – homelessness, unaffordable housing, concentrated poverty, drug addiction, traffic congestion, pollution and climate change, to name a few – will not be solved by any sector on their own. Rather, multi-party, intersectoral collaborations are more important than ever. Deep, meaningful partnerships beyond the classic, transactional DBFOM-style PPP are being created between public, private and non-profit organizations to achieve what Huxham and Vangen (2005, 5) call a collaborative advantage. Achieving a collaborative advantage is commonly based on access to resources from multiple organizations, shared risk, enhanced efficiency, improved coordination and mutual learning that supports innovation. With organizations from all sectors promoting collaboration, however, there is the risk that partnerships again become part of a language game to reframe more polarizing practices of asset sales, privatization and contracting out (Hodge and Greve 2010).

New types of partnership

In the urban sphere, the contemporary rationales for using PPPs have led to a flourishing of a wide variety of PPP models. The term 'public–private partnership' is in fact a blanket concept that describes a wide variety of relationships between the public and private sectors. Hodge and Greve (2010, s9) insightfully identify five families of partnership: long-term infrastructure contracts, institutional alliances and cooperation, public policy networks, community development partnerships, and urban renewal and revitalization partnerships. Much of the PPP literature has focused on the United Kingdom-style PFI, a long-term infrastructure contract model of partnership that has spread around the world.

Yet as Klijn and Teisman (2000) note, the PFI-style PPP is more akin to a public–private contract than a true partnership. It is a carefully choreographed contractual relationship to manage incentives and risk with little interdependence between the partners outside of the project agreement. As the rationales for delivering PPPs in cities have evolved towards achieving collaborative advantages through interorganizational alliances, the scholarly literature is catching up by digging deeper into alternate forms of urban partnership.

New PPP models seek to encourage greater innovation and efficiency by broadening the role of the private sector and providing firms with greater responsibility for designing and implementing public services. The old mantra that governments steer by setting the policy direction while the private sector and non-profits row by producing urban services is giving way to an expanded private sector role in policymaking. In the social impact bond model, for instance, the private sector service provider moves beyond a contractor of pre-defined public services, and instead takes the lead in designing programs to address key social issues such as prisoner reoffending or long-term unemployment. The service provider, often a non-profit backed by a philanthropist or social impact investor, only recoups their investment with payments from the state if the program achieves pre-determined levels of performance such as reduced recidivism for criminal offenders or stable employment for workers who may require retraining and support in finding a job (McHugh et al. 2013, Warner 2013).

Another emerging form of urban development partnership is the creative mixed-use building. In this model, the siloed approach to infrastructure planning where each piece of infrastructure is considered on its own is replaced by the co-location of public, private and non-profit uses in the same building. It is becoming more common for schools, libraries, daycares, fire stations, theatres, long-term care homes and recreation centres to be integrated into buildings with social services, affordable housing, apartments, offices and shops. Innovative examples of creative mixed-use buildings include a YMCA recreation centre co-located with a student residence in the same building, a large public high school in the podium of a building with two condominium towers up above, and a fire station in Vancouver with affordable rental housing located up above. Each occupant in these mixed-use buildings is the owner of their own space, deepening the interdependencies and relationship management that is required (Lau et al. 2005, Siemiatycki 2015b).

Partnerships to implement smart city initiatives position private firms even further into the spheres of urban policymaking, regulation and governance, seen as the catalyst to enable boundary-pushing innovations in areas like mobility as a service, new building techniques and renewable energy (Morgan and Webb 2020, Zukin 2020). Lee et al. (2014) find that sustainable smart cities result from open innovation platforms that are based on coordinated activities between public and private sector parties. Companies also play a bigger role in collecting and sharing the urban data from the ubiquitous sensors that power smart city technologies.

But this comes at a significant cost in terms of loss of public control, citizen participation, privacy and intellectual property. A common critique is that smart city public–private partnerships are overly technocratic, and driven by market-oriented solutions to urban challenges rather than those grounded in deep meaningful community engagement and the public interest (Cardullo and Kitchin 2019, Morgan and Webb 2020). Smart city advances tend to conceive of technology solutions to complex urban challenges that may be more deeply rooted in political disenfranchisement and structural inequalities.

A new set of PPP actors

The key players involved in the production of urban PPPs, both the people and institutions, have long been an area of scholarly interest. In particular, scholars have focused on connecting how the up-front production of urban infrastructure impacts on the outcomes of infrastructure projects – especially the role of the private sector, and the unequal spatial, economic, racial and gendered outcomes of mega-projects (O'Brien et al. 2019). Infrastructure PPPs in cities around the world are produced by a relatively small global network of elite firms and special-purpose government agencies. The PPP industry is also largely male-dominated, and masculinity is deeply interwoven into the production of PPP projects (Siemiatycki et al. 2019).

For Shaoul et al. (2007), the repeated use of a handful of financial consultants that advise both the public and private sectors on PPP policy has created a powerful promoter of this model of project delivery. Similarly, the creation of special-purpose PPP units like Infrastructure Ontario and Partnerships BC provides expertise and thought leadership that embed PPPs as the model of choice to deliver complex infrastructure projects (Rachwalski and Ross 2010). As Whiteside (2020) argues, the ideas and models promoted by the major international accounting firms, Macquarie Bank, the World Bank's Public-Private Infrastructure Advisory Facility (PPIAF) and others were essential in the global spread of PPPs around the world.

International networks of investors also influence where PPP projects are developed. Torrance (2008) shows that international institutional investors based in a relatively small number of cities – London, Toronto, New York, Sydney and Amsterdam, to name a few – play a significant role in identifying the places where PPP projects are financially bankable. These investors create risk maps of the world that exclude large areas of the Global South. Additionally, institutional investors tend to favour premium networks and user-fee-supported infrastructure, prioritizing infrastructure in wealthier parts of cities where customers have the ability to pay (Graham and Marvin 2001). Only in recent years have South–South investment patterns, regional investing blocks and the rise of China as a major infrastructure investor created new sources of capital to invest in emerging markets that have traditionally been deemed high-risk (Mohan and Tan-Mullins 2018).

The new types of PPP rationales and partnership models are giving rise to an influx of a new set of people and institutions participating in urban PPPs. Smart city PPPs have brought a new breed of actors into urban development projects. Urban tech entrepreneurs and venture capital investors now scour the world's cities looking for living labs to pilot and scale up their innovative technologies in areas like mobility, property tech, construction methods, green building, asset management, clean energy and smart city management. Working for both small plucky start-ups and well-capitalized corporate siblings of tech giants like Google and Amazon, the new cadre of urban tech entrepreneurs are more used to operating in the 'move fast and break things' ethos of the internet, rather than the deeply political and negotiated realm of city building. This can create culture clashes when trying to foster collaborative advantages through partnerships (Goodman and Powles 2019).

For many urban tech companies, Uber's original strategy of principled confrontation, which entailed the sidestepping of existing rules to build large user bases to force regulators to respond, was the playbook to enter new markets. Having seen the limitations of this strategy, as the confrontations can ultimately lead to shutdowns and backlashes, urban tech firms are now more likely to seek collaborations and partnerships with governments when launching their products and services. For example, in the case of Sidewalk Labs, the Google sibling company successfully bid to develop an ambitious smart city 'from the internet up' on Toronto's waterfront in collaboration with a local government agency. Yet Sidewalk Labs and Waterfront Toronto were consistently at loggerheads over who controlled the vision for the project, data privacy and intellectual property from innovations developed in the project (Morgan and Webb 2020). Ultimately the project floundered and Sidewalk Labs pulled out in the spring of 2020.

PPPs for a livable city have also brought in a new set of non-profit actors. Non-profit arts, culture, childcare, affordable housing and religious institutions are increasingly participating in partnerships with government and industry to directly deliver critical public infrastructure or undertake major mixed-use building projects. For example, in Toronto a new homeless shelter for women and families operated by a non-profit organization is co-located into the side of an upscale private condominium building (Siemiatycki 2017). Social impact bonds are also bringing major philanthropists, foundations and social impact investors into urban partnerships. Indeed, a cohort of large, sophisticated, well-financed non-profits and philanthropists are emerging to participate in more complex urban city-building partnerships (Warner 2013). Additionally, government departments that may not have been partner-facing in the past for capital projects, like libraries, fire and paramedic emergency services, and shelter and social services, are now more actively exploring opportunities to enter into increasingly complex, mixed-use, long-term collaborations with the private and non-profit sectors. This is contributing to a new ethos to balance managerial and entrepreneurial governance approaches, as well as the need for non-profits to be increasingly partnership-ready. While the mantra of partnerships predominates, scholars continue to examine the underpinnings of these partnerships, the uneven power dynamics between partners, and the risk that market forces are replacing the public interest tests as the drivers of collaboration (Joseph et al. 2019).

Are urban PPPs better than the alternatives?

Does urban infrastructure delivered through PPPs produce better city-building outcomes than traditional procurement alternatives? This should be a straightforward question, and one that is especially urgent as trillions of dollars are being spent on infrastructure annually. After decades of research on the topic, however, the uncomfortable answer is that we still do not know definitively. As noted above, the literature on urban infrastructure PPPs in planning and geography is often highly critical of the high costs and unequal impacts of PPPs.

Yet many of the significant studies of the impacts of urban infrastructure PPPs focus exclusively on PPP projects without a rigorous comparison of the outcomes from alternative project-delivery models (Hodge 2010). For instance, Miraftab's (2004) study of PPPs as 'The Trojan Horse of Neoliberal Development?' has been important in defining equity concerns with PPPs. Sagalyn's (2007) study in the leading *Journal of the American Planning Association* synthesizes the literature on public/private development projects to provide planners with lessons on planning, deal-making and project outcomes. Similarly, Fainstein (2008) draws on three case studies of PPP property mega-projects in New York, London and Amsterdam to show how the level of government commitment to public benefits is critical in determining the equity of PPP project outcomes. Siemiatycki's research on planning concerns with PPPs like transparency and loss of long-term policy flexibility has not provided direct comparisons of the strengths and shortcomings of other procurement alternatives (Siemiatycki 2007, 2010, 2015b). Van Montfort and Michels (2020) have edited an entire collection of chapters on innovative approaches to partnerships for a livable city.

Why after all these years of intensive research has the urban planning literature on PPPs focused so singularly on the outcomes of partnerships and PPPs and not studied them more systematically in direct comparison to other alternatives? The answers are likely both technical and instrumental. Data is a major shortcoming. In jurisdictions where PPPs have become the main method of delivering large infrastructure projects, there may be a lack of directly comparable projects for analysis. While collecting data on PPP performance can be difficult due to commercial confidentiality, Siemiatycki (2007) concludes that it is often more difficult to obtain the same data on traditionally procured projects that have not faced the same public demands for greater transparency as PPPs. There can also be rivalries between the special-purpose PPP agencies and the government departments that develop traditional infrastructure. The result is a wariness to share information or participate in studies that would enable appropriate empirical comparisons of PPPs and traditionally procured project outcomes that may prove organizationally embarrassing. Urban PPPs are also highly particular to their urban context. It can be exceedingly difficult methodologically to tease out the impacts of the procurement model on project outcomes relative to the many other financial, policy and environmental conditions that impact on project outcomes (Omega Centre 2011). In some cases, projects are considered to be sufficiently unique that comparison is neither valid nor warranted.

Finally, for scholars, PPPs are an exciting area of research in their own right, theoretically and societally. Deep analytical studies of PPPs provide scholars with a window into a variety of timely ideological and political debates related to neoliberalism, financialization, the role of the state and a key policy approach that is transforming cities worldwide. In this context there may be less impetus to undertake detailed comparative studies of the outcomes of PPPs relative to other alternatives.

Shifting terrain of contestation

PPPs are both a governance approach for providing large infrastructure projects, and a political tool and language game that reshapes the role of government (Hodge and Greve 2010). Scholars continue to examine urban PPPs along these two tracks. During the early wave of scholarship, the discourse was shaped by widely polarized accounts of the merits of PPPs in cities (see Savas 2000, Sclar 2001). Now the terrain is shifting under a body of scholarship where there have long been flares of contestation.

PPP scholars continue to unpick the evolving models, merits and critical success factors of PPPs to deliver urban infrastructure in ever more detail. Recently, studies of PPPs as a governance approach have branched out beyond the PFI/DBFOM-style PPPs. They now explore a wider range of partnerships, including creative mixed-use buildings, public–private–community development partnerships (Schaller 2018), social impact bonds (Vecchi and Casalini 2018) and smart city developments. In this research a main point of contestation is evaluating whether PPPs are an appropriate and optimal model of project delivery and community development. Or, put differently, do they deliver VfM and societal benefit? Scholars and PPP practitioners tend to debate the criteria for judging a successful project, data quality, analytical methods and the interpretation of the results.

At the same time, a burst of urban scholarship is focusing on the deeply contested, political and ideological aspects of infrastructure PPPs and the power structures that have supported their global proliferation in cities. The primary concern of this research is to undertake a political economic analysis of the actors involved, the logics of partnership and the transformation of the state to accommodate increasingly entrepreneurial, market-oriented solutions to urban challenges (Pike et al. 2019b, Whiteside 2020). A key area of intense interest is the implications of the treatment of urban infrastructure as an asset class that is increasingly financialized, and the new types of investors that are entering the market. Thus far, the literature in urban geography and planning is overwhelmingly, though not exclusively, critical of the ways that the financialization of infrastructure shapes the urban landscape in terms of the environmental sustainability of mega-projects, the fiscal health of cities, equality of access to critical facilities and risks to democratic accountability (Clark et al. 2012, Theurillat and Crevoisier 2012, Tricarico and Sol 2016, Beswick and Penny 2018). The critical focus of this urban infrastructure scholarship is often underpinned by an analytical framework that aims to 'follow the money' to understand how various actors refashion the state and infrastructure into profitable financial assets (Pike et al., 2019b, 794), and stands in contrast to the more favourable scholarship that sees the positive dawn of a 'new era of infrastructure investing' (Clark et al. 2012, 103). In the face of deep critiques of infrastructure financialization, the responses and resistance to the financialization of urban infrastructure are another area of significant research focus (McManus and Haughton 2021).

Conclusions: a research agenda

For urban scholars, a school is not a road, is not a subway, is not a hospital. PPPs are not evaluated narrowly as financial instruments or project management tools. Rather, each type of infrastructure, and in fact each project itself, is vastly different in its role and impact on the communities in which it is developed. The arrival of new players in the urban infrastructure space, particularly major global investors, tech firms, non-profits and philanthropists, has the potential to considerably reshape the political logics of urban PPPs. PPPs are seen as part of a larger political ideology where financialization is restructuring the governance of cities.

The dividing lines are increasingly drawn at the frontiers of urban scholarship on PPPs. First, are there PPP approaches that work as governance tools to deliver urban infrastructure that advances equity, sustainability, resilience, inclusive prosperity and democratic inclusion? While the PFI/DBFOM models have struggled to live up to their expectations in many cases, more research is needed to assess their outcomes relative to other project-delivery alternatives. Further examination is also needed of the emerging models of partnership that move beyond being a narrow contractual relationship to form deeper connections where a collaborative advantage can thrive.

Second, financialization appears to be trending in the academic literature as a key lens through which to explore PPPs and the provision of urban infrastructure. For financialization to retain its analytical power, scholars will need to carefully continue applying it rigorously as a framework to assess the partnership models, industry participants, power dynamics and restructuring of the state that is taking place under this regime. Moreover, focus is needed on the connections that exist between the emerging networks of actors and institutions involved in PPPs in the financialized city, and project outcomes (O'Brien et al. 2019).

Third, if not PPPs and financialization as a way of delivering positive infrastructure outcomes, then what? A future research agenda is needed that both uncovers the flawed logics and negative outcomes of the current practice of PPPs, and also points to alternative ways of providing infrastructure that will achieve results that are more equitable, sustainable and just. While the PPP brand may be damaged, reinvigorating the place of meaningful partnerships and collaboration in city building is as important as ever to tackle the most pressing urban challenges.

References

Ashton, P., Doussard, M., and Weber, R. (2016) Reconstituting the state: City powers and exposures in Chicago's infrastructure leases. *Urban Studies*, 53 (7): 1384–1400.

Bel, G., Hebdon, R., and Warner, M. (2018) Beyond privatization and cost savings: Alternatives for local government reform. *Local Government Studies*, 44 (2): 173–182.

Bentley, Z. (2020) How 'PFI or bust' went bust. *Infrastructure Investor*. www.infrastructureinvestor.com/how-pfi-or-bust-went-bust/.

Beswick, J., and Penny, J. (2018) Demolishing the present to sell off the future? The emergence of 'financialized municipal entrepreneurialism' in London. *International Journal of Urban and Regional Research*, 42 (4): 612–632.

Cardullo, P., and Kitchin, R. (2018) Smart urbanism and smart citizenship: The neoliberal logic of 'citizen-focused' smart cities. *Environment and Planning C*, 37 (5): 813–830.

Clark, G.L. Monk, A.H. Orr, R., and Scott, W. (2012) The new era of infrastructure investing. *Pensions*, 17: 103–111.

Cruz, C.O., and Marques, R.C. (2013) Flexible contracts to cope with uncertainty in public–private partnerships. *International Journal of Project Management*, 31 (3): 473–483.

Fainstein, S. (2008) Mega-projects in New York, London and Amsterdam. *International Journal of Urban and Regional Research*, 32 (4): 768–785.

Goodman, E., and Powles, J. (2019) Urbanism under Google: Lessons from Sidewalk Toronto. *Fordham Law Review*, 88 (2): 457–498.

Graham, S., and Marvin, S. (2001) *Splintering Urbanism*. New York, NY: Routledge.

Heald, D. (2002) Value for money tests and accounting treatment in PFI schemes. *Accounting, Auditing & Accountability Journal*, 16 (3): 342–371.

Himmel, M., and Siemiatycki, M. (2017) Infrastructure public–private partnerships as drivers of innovation. *Environment and Planning C*, 35 (5): 746–764.

Hodge, G., and Greve, C. (2010) Public–private partnerships: Governance scheme or language game? *Australian Journal of Public Administration*, 69 (Suppl. 1): S8–S22.

Hodge, G.A. (2010) Reviewing public–private partnerships: Some thoughts on evaluation, in *International Handbook in Public–Private Partnerships*, edited by G.A. Hodge, C. Greve and A.E. Boardman. Cheltenham, UK and Northampton, MA, USA: Edward Elgar Publishing, pp. 81–112.

Hodge, G.A., and Greve, C. (2019) *The Logic of Public–Private Partnerships: The Enduring Interdependency of Politics and Markets*. Cheltenham, UK and Northampton, MA, USA: Edward Elgar Publishing.

Huxham, C., and Vangen, S. (2005) *Managing to Collaborate*. New York, NY: Routledge.

Joseph, M.L., Chaskin, R.J., Khare, A.T., and Kim, J.-E. (2019) The organizational challenges of mixed-income development: Privatizing public housing through cross-sector collaboration. *Urban Research & Practice*, 12 (1): 1–23.

Kayden, J.S. (2000) *Privately Owned Public Spaces*. New York, NY: Wiley.

Klijn, E.-H., and Teisman, T.R. (2000) Governing public-private partnerships, in *Public-Private Partnerships: Theory and Practice in International Perspective*, edited by S.P. Osborne. London: Routledge, pp. 84–102.

Lau, S.S.Y., Giridharan, R., and Ganesan, S. (2005) Multiple and intensive land use: Case studies in Hong Kong. *Habitat International*, 29 (3): 527–546.

Lee, J.H., Hancock, M.G., and Hu, M-C. (2014) Towards an effective framework for building smart cities: Lessons from Seoul and San Francisco. *Technological Forecasting and Social Change*, 89 (C): 80–99.

Loxley, J., and Loxley, S. (2010) *Public Service, Private Profits*. Winnipeg: Fernwood Publishing.

McHugh, N., Sinclair, S., Roy, M., Huckfield, L., and Donaldson, C. (2013) Social impact bonds: A wolf in sheep's clothing? *Journal of Poverty and Social Justice*, 21 (3): 247–257.

McManus, P., and Haughton, G. (2021) Fighting to undo a deal: Identifying and resisting the financialization of the WestConnex motorway, Sydney, Australia. *Environment and Planning A*, 53 (1): 131–149.

Miraftab, F. (2004) Public-private partnerships: The Trojan Horse of neoliberal development? *Journal of Planning Education and Research*, 24 (1): 89–101.

Mohan, G., and Tan-Mullins, M. (2018) The geopolitics of South–South infrastructure development: Chinese-financed energy projects in the global South. *Urban Studies*, 56 (7): 1368–1385.

Morgan, K., and Webb, B. (2020): Googling the City: In search of the public interest on Toronto's 'smart' waterfront. *Urban Planning*, 5 (1): 84–95.

O'Brien, P., O'Neil, P., and Pike, A. (2019) Funding, financing and governing urban infrastructures. *Urban Studies*, 56 (7): 1291–1303.

O'Brien, P., and Pike, A. (2017) The financialization and governance of infrastructure, in *Handbook on the Geographies of Money and Finance*, edited by R. Martin and J. Pollard. Cheltenham, UK and Northampton, MA, USA: Edward Elgar Publishing, pp. 223–254.

Omega Centre (2011) *Mega Projects and Mega Risks: Lessons for Decision-Makers through a Comparative Analysis of Selected Large-Scale Transport Infrastructure*

Projects in Europe, USA and Asia Pacific, Volume 5. www.omegacentre.bartlett.ucl
.ac.uk/open/OMEGA-2-Final-Report-Vol-5.pdf.

O'Neil, P. (2019). The financialisation of urban infrastructure: A framework of analysis. *Urban Studies*, 56 (7): 1304–1325.

Pike, A., O'Brien, P., Strickland, T., Thrower, G., and Tomany, J. (2019a) *Financialising City Statecraft and Infrastructure*. Cheltenham, UK and Northampton, MA, USA: Edward Elgar Publishing.

Pike, A., O'Brien, P., Strickland, T., Thrower, G., and Tomany, J. (2019b) *Financialising City Statecraft and Infrastructure*: A reader's guide. *Environment and Planning A*, 52 (4): 791–795.

Rachwalski, M., and Ross, T.W. (2010) Running a government's P3 program: Special purpose agency or line departments? *Journal of Comparative Policy Analysis*, 12 (3): 275–298.

Razin, E., Hazan, A., and Elron, O. (2020) The rise and fall (?) of public-private partnerships in Israel's local government. *Local Government Studies*. https://doi.org/10.1080/03003930.2020.1832892.

Ross, T.W., and Yan, J. (2015) Comparing public–private partnerships and traditional procurement: Efficiency vs. flexibility. *Journal of Comparative Policy Analysis*, 17 (5): 448–466.

Sagalyn, L.B. (2007) Public/private development. *Journal of the American Planning Association*, 73 (1): 7–22.

Savas, E.S. (2000) *Privatization and Public-Private Partnerships*. New York, NY: Seven Bridges Press.

Schaller, S. (2018) Public–private synergies: Reconceiving urban redevelopment in Tübingen, Germany. *Journal of Urban Affairs*, 43 (2): 288–307. https://doi.org/10.1080/07352166.2018.1465345.

Sclar, E. (2015) The political economics of investment Utopia: Public–private partnerships for urban infrastructure finance. *Journal of Economic Policy Reform*, 18 (1): 1–15.

Sclar, E. (2001) *You Don't Always Get What You Pay For: The Economics of Privatization*. New York, NY: Century Foundation.

Shaoul, J., Stafford, A., and Stapleton, P. (2007) Partnerships and the role of financial advisors: Private control over public policy? *Policy & Politics*, 35 (3): 479–495.

Siemiatycki, M. (2010) Delivering transportation infrastructure through public-private partnerships: Planning concerns. *Journal of the American Planning Association*, 76: 43–58.

Siemiatycki, M. (2017) Developing homeless shelters through public–private partnerships: The case of the Red Door Family Shelter in Toronto. *Journal of Urban Affairs*, 43 (2): 236–250.

Siemiatycki, M. (2015a) Mixing public and private uses in the same building: Opportunities and barriers. *Journal of Urban Design*, 20 (2): 230–250.

Siemiatycki, M. (2015b) Reflections on twenty years of public-private partnerships in Canada. *Canadian Public Administration*, 58 (3): 343–362.

Siemiatycki, M. (2012) The global production of transportation public–private partnerships. *International Journal of Urban and Regional Research*, 37 (4): 1254–1272.

Siemiatycki, M. (2007) What's the secret? The application of confidentiality in the planning of infrastructure using private-public partnerships. *Journal of the American Planning Association*, 73 (4): 388–403.

Siemiatycki, M., Enright, T., and Valverde, M. (2019) The gendered production of infrastructure. *Progress in Human Geography*, 44 (2): 297–314. https://doi.org/10.1177/0309132519828458.

Theurillat, T., and Crevoisier, O. (2012) The sustainability of a financialized urban megaproject: The case of Sihlcity in Zurich. *International Journal of Urban and Regional Research*, 37 (6): 2052–2073.

Torrance, M.I. (2008) Forging glocal governance? Urban infrastructures as networked financial products. *International Journal of Urban and Regional Research*, 32: 1–21.

Tricarico, A., and Sol. X. (2016) Re-building the world: The structural adjustment through mega-infrastructures in the era of financialization. *Development*, 59: 53–58.

Van den Hurk, M., and Siemiatycki, M. (2018) Public–private partnerships and the design process: Consequences for architects and city building. *International Journal of Urban and Regional Research*, 42 (4): 704–722.

Van Montfort, C., and Michels, A. (2020) *Partnerships for Livable Cities*. Cham: Palgrave Macmillan.

Vecchi, V., and Casalini, F. (2018) Is a social empowerment of PPP for infrastructure delivery possible: Lessons from social impact bonds. *Annals of Public and Cooperative Economics*, 90 (2): 353–369.

Warner, M. (2013) Private finance for public goods: Social impact bonds. *Journal of Economic Policy Reform*, 16 (4): 303–319.

Warsen, R. Greve, C. Klijn, E.-H., Koppenian, F.M., and Siemiatycki, M. (2020) How do professionals perceive the governance of public–private partnerships? Evidence from Canada, the Netherlands and Denmark. *Public Administration*, 98 (1): 124–139.

Whitefield, D., and Smyth, S. (2019) Infrastructure investment: The emergent PPP equity market. *Annals of Public and Cooperative Economics*, 90 (2): 291–309.

Whiteside, H. (2020) Public-private partnerships: Market development through management reform. *Review of International Political Economy*, 27 (4): 880–902.

Zukin, S. (2020) Seeing like a city: How tech became urban. *Theory and Society*, 49: 941–964.

10 New frontiers of PPP law

Christina D. Tvarnø and Sarah Maria Denta

1. Introduction to the legal framework for public–private partnerships

The purpose of this chapter is to present the existing legal frontiers of public–private partnerships (PPPs) and to also discuss the future challenges and possibilities for PPPs in regard to the green transition.

Twenty years ago, PPP arrangements were mainly driven by a general limitation in public funds to cover investment needs in the public sector. The purpose of PPPs has since developed, and PPPs are now also driven by the interests of increasing the quality and efficiency of public services in general (Tvarnø et al. 2019). In many countries, PPPs are a significant tool for solving infrastructure needs (Greve et. al. 2021) and are a cost-efficient (lower life-cycle cost) alternative that creates benefits for both the public and private sector, as well as developing growth and innovation (Tvarnø 2012). Furthermore, PPPs are used as a tool for developing more efficient ways of providing local services, such as schools, hospitals, prisons, climate-resilient infrastructure, and so on. Future PPPs may even develop to include climate change, sustainability and environmental interests. The green transition and the challenge of transforming society from a linear to a circular economy require investment. These investments can be boosted through PPPs. Innovation, the redesigning of products and the recycling of waste could be addressed, and investments and risks could be shared in a PPP project.

The aims of PPPs are to meet the needs of the national or local society and to utilize resources from the private sector (Osborne 2000) through private financing and collaboration (Huxham and Vangen 1996). The new legal frontiers of PPP law would have to include green innovation and climate change, as well as providing a legal framework for supporting the green transition. The European Union (EU) has considered PPPs as a significant tool for the green transition, and the EU strategy for public private collaboration on climate change is defined in the 'Paris Protocol: A Blueprint for Tackling Global Climate Change Beyond 2020'.[1] Furthermore, Preamble 11 of the proposal for the EU Climate Law Regulation COM (2020)80 states that the goal of a climate-neutral EU by 2050 requires significant public–private investments. However, the EU has not yet provided sufficient PPP legislation that promotes the use of climate PPPs. Hence, it is the national legislation in the EU Member States and the EU public procurement law in general that govern PPPs in the EU.

This chapter concerns the legal aspects of PPPs. There is no worldwide legal definition of a PPP, but the general legal understanding of a PPP is that it is a collaboration between a public and a private party through a public contract. In this chapter, the legal understanding of a PPP will be as follows: a PPP is a long-term contract between a private sector company that provides a public asset or service and a public party. A PPP is procured under the public procurement law in general or under a specific PPP Act.[2] All countries define and govern PPPs in their own way through different legal structures and different PPP regulations. Hence, a common legal analysis of PPP law is not possible.

This chapter presents different types of regulation for PPPs in Section 2 based upon their common law and civil law tradition. Section 3 analyses the need for regulating PPPs in the future with the green transition in mind. Section 4 presents a climate perspective on new types of PPPs that have not been regulated yet. Section 5 compares common law and civil law, as well as discussing the potential for creating new legal frontiers for climate PPPs. Section 6 presents concluding remarks on the present and future PPP legal regime. Consequently, this chapter covers matters concerning existing PPP legal frameworks and points to some new directions for PPPs as a tool for the climate change transition.

2.   Regulating PPPs

This section will present a general overview of the different types of legal PPP instruments, focusing on the EU and some selected countries outside of the EU, as well as different PPP regulations on a specific level. In general, civil law countries (including the EU) have a strict procurement regime, and common law countries, such as Ireland, Canada and Australia, have a principle-based public law regime. This chapter differentiates civil law and common law countries in order to comment on whether the structure of each legal system is likely to promote or restrict the use of green PPPs in the future. This will be discussed further below as well as in Section 5.

The establishment of a strong PPP sector requires a solid public and private business case regarding, for example, infrastructure projects. By adopting a PPP Act, it is possible to ensure a coherent approach to PPPs in the public sector, given the complexity and long-term scope that PPPs offer for public services. The Organisation for Economic Co-operation and Development (OECD) recommends that governments establish a 'clear, predictable and legitimate institutional framework supported by competent and well-resourced authorities' (OECD 2012, p. 4). Furthermore, the OECD emphasizes the need for awareness of the relative costs, benefits and risks; active consultation; and engagement with stakeholders (and end-users) by ensuring that all significant regulation that affects the operation of PPPs is clear, transparent and enforced (OECD 2012).

Several of the countries above have PPP regulation and explicitly define PPP projects in their national law. Only few of the countries have legislation promoting the use of PPPs through economic initiatives. Governmental non-legally-binding PPP guidelines are used in several countries to supervise the public sector and the private industry in procuring, bidding on and contracting a PPP project. Many countries have prioritized establishing a central PPP unit to support the use of PPPs, to procure the PPP projects and, in some cases, to run those projects.

Furthermore, common law and civil law have different legal approaches to PPPs. The continental EU Member States have a legal tradition based on civil law, which means that the law derives from a set of written rules or a civil code. The public law provides the legal framework within which PPP contracts must be procured, quite the opposite to a private contract, which is subject to the legal principle of freedom of contract. In the United Kingdom, common law is defined as a legal tradition based on case law and precedents, and thus commercial transactions and competition. Here, the legal approach to a PPP contract is based upon the legal tradition of private contracts. PPPs differ significantly from traditional procurements, but under EU law, PPPs are governed by the same rules as traditional procurement projects.

As illustrated in Table 10.1, Canada and Australia are jurisdictions which are subject to the common law tradition and do not have public procurement legislation nor PPP Acts. Conversely, France—a civil law country—has a specific PPP Act, PPP guidelines and a central PPP agency. Ireland represents a mixture of legal tradition; on the one hand, being a common law country, and, on the other hand, adopting a PPP Act, PPP guidelines and a central PPP agency. Hence, the four countries represent different legal regimes in regard

Table 10.1   Overview of legal PPP instruments

Country	PPP acts/orders	PPP guidelines	PPP units
*Australia[1]	-	+	+
Austria	-	+	-
Belgium	+	-	+
Bulgaria	+	-	-
*Canada[2]	-	+	+
Croatia	+	-	+
Cyprus	-	+	-
Czech Republic	-	-	+
Denmark	-	+	-
Estonia	-	-	-
Finland	-	-	-
France	+	+	+
Germany	-	+	+
Greece	+	-	+
Hungary	-	+	-
*Ireland	+	+	+
Italy	+	+	+
Latvia	+	-	-
Lithuania	-	+	-
Luxembourg	-	-	-
*Malta	-	-	+
Netherlands	-	+	+
Poland	+	-	+
Portugal	+	-	-
Romania	+	+	+
Slovakia	-	-	+
Slovenia	+	+	+
Spain	+	-	-

Country	PPP acts/orders	PPP guidelines	PPP units
Sweden	-	-	-
*United Kingdom³	-	+	+

Notes: * Common law countries. The remaining countries (without a *) are civil law countries. The data in the table derives from the following sources: EPEC (2019), Tvarnø (2016), World Bank (2020, 2021b). ¹ In some regions. ² In some regions. ³ Scotland and Northern Ireland in regard to PPP unit

to PPPs. The following subsections will briefly present the PPP law of France, Ireland, Canada and Australia, and in the EU.

Regulating PPPs in France

By tradition, France is a civil law country. Furthermore, France was the first Member State to introduce a PPP Act; the *Ordonnance sur les contrats de par-tenariat*, in 2004,³ amended in 2008.⁴ The PPP Act defines a PPP contract and thus includes an explicit legal PPP definition (Vaissier et al. 2015).⁵ The PPP contract is an administrative contract, under which a public entity entrusts to a private party the comprehensive project relating to the design, the construction or conversion, the maintenance, operation or management of works, equipment or intangible assets necessary to the public service, as well as to the total or partial financing of the latter. The PPP prevails for a period set according to the amortization of investment or agreed financing terms. The public authority will pay a monthly rent to the private partner in exchange for the performance of the project (Vaissier et al. 2015). Consequently, PPP contracts are defined as administrative contracts under French law. Furthermore, the specific use of PPP contracts is strictly regulated in the 2004 PPP Act.

According to Article 19, the government and its public institutions, local authorities and local public institutions may all enter into partnership contracts if the PPP project is related to the construction, maintenance, operation or management of work necessary for public service. PPPs may only be entered into, however, if the public authority demonstrates an element of complexity, emergency or economic efficiency (Vaissier et al. 2015). Article 3 demands transparency and equal treatment in the evaluation of a PPP project. The procurement procedures are regulated in Article 5, and Article 8 defines the concept of total cost as follows: 'Total cost of the offer means the sum, in current value, generated by the design, financing, construction or conversion, upkeep, maintenance, operation or management of structures, facilities, or intangible assets, and the provision of services planned for the term of the contract.'⁶

Under French law, it is required that a PPP contract defines the duration of the PPP contract, the conditions for sharing risks between the public authority and its co-contracting party, the performance objectives assigned to the co-contracting party, the payment terms and the consequences of termination of the contract all in accordance with Article 1, Article 11 and Article 12 in the PPP Act (Vaissier et al. 2015).

Additionally, France has established a central PPP unit: the Mission d'appui aux partenariats public-privé,[7] which assists public authorities in implementing PPP contracts. The Mission is placed at the Treasury Department of the Ministry of Economy, Finance and Industry, and it is responsible for the validation of the preliminary evaluations, prepared by procuring authorities before launching a tender, and for preparing and negotiating the PPP contract (Vaissier et al. 2015). State procuring authorities (for example, ministries and public institutions) and local authorities[8] are obliged to submit their preliminary evaluations to the Mission for its validation (Vaissier et al. 2015).

Regulating PPPs in Ireland

Irish law is based upon the common law tradition but in 2002 Ireland adopted the State Authorities (Public Private Partnership) Act,[9] and in 2006 the National Development Finance Agency presented a 'template PPP project agreement' followed by a PPP guideline providing a clause-by-clause commentary on the template project agreement.[10] The template PPP project agreement concerns 25- to 30-year design-build-finance-operate or design-build-finance-maintain PPP contracts. Hence, Ireland is an example of a common law country with specific PPP legislation and a template agreement which is uncommon compared to common law countries in general.

The Irish PPP Act explicitly defines PPP projects as having a minimum duration of five years without any upper limit on the length of the PPP contract, involving a monthly payment by the authorities to the PPP company and to be based on the whole-life costs of designing, constructing, operating, maintaining and financing the project alongside an agreed profit for the project company (Dunne 2015).

In Ireland, the National Development Finance Agency 2002 Act[11] places the procurement of all PPP projects over €30 million at the National Development Finance Agency, except for PPP projects regarding transport and water, which are procured and carried out by the National Roads Authority and the Railway Procurement Agency. The National Development Finance Agency holds the power to enter into PPPs and later transfer the PPP project to the relevant state authority, or to act as agents for state authorities for PPP procurement.

PPPs in common law countries: Canada and Australia

The national framework for PPPs in Canada and Australia—both common law countries—will be explained to give an overall picture of PPPs in these countries.[12] However, the development of PPPs in Canada and Australia was, and still is, led by the countries' provinces and states with limited federal government involvement. In both countries, the federal government only became involved, and only to a limited extent, after PPPs were well established at the provincial/state level (Griffiths and Carney 2021, Shkordoff et al. 2015).

Canada is a bijural[13] country, where the common law and civil law coexist. Therefore, Canada's legal system is based on a combination of common law and civil law.[14] All provinces and territories within Canada, excluding Québec, follow the common law legal tradition (Campbell and Cotter 2018). Québec is the only province with a civil code[15] based on the French Code Napoléon.[16] Matters of private law in Québec are governed by the civil law. Federal bills and regulations must respect both types of systems, and the legal concepts within these laws must be expressed in both English and French (Government of Canada 2015).

Canada has a federal level and a regional level of government, the latter being the provinces.[17] The Treasury Board of Canada Secretariat[18] defines a PPP as a

> Long-term contractual relationship between a public authority and the private sector that involves the following: provision of goods or services to meet a defined output specification (i.e., defining what is required, rather than how it is to be done); Integration of multiple project phases (e.g., design, construction, operations); Transfer of risk to the private sector, which is anchored with private sector capital at risk; and a performance-based payment mechanism. (Government of Canada 2021a, Section 9.60)

At both federal and provincial level, a central PPP unit or agency has been introduced. The PPP unit is responsible, for example, for implementing PPP guidelines, procuring the PPP project and managing the process and evaluation of the PPP. The provincial, legislative and regulatory frameworks are governing the procurement of PPP projects in a municipality. However, there is no uniform legislation to cover such procurement, and thus the rules can vary between sectors and asset classes. Even though the public legislation is often flexible, it does also have constraints and requirements that can have an impact on a PPP procedure (Government of Canada 2021a, Regimbald 2011).

It is also a local decision to set up a PPP procurement procedure at the municipal level. However, such a procedure must consider the provincial legislative/regulatory aspect, as well as policies (if there are any), before proceeding with a PPP. Furthermore, the procedure must ensure that the government has approved a formal alternative procurement or PPP policy, which includes an evaluation, approval and prioritization, and that the bids are consistent with provincial regulations and laws (Government of Canada 2021b).

Australia and its states and territories[19] follow the common law legal system, and Australia's common law is enforced uniformly across the states and territories. The two main sources of law are either case law or common law, and legislation is made by parliaments.[20] The Australian Constitution of 1901 established a federal system of government in Australia. Under a federal system, powers are distributed between a central government and regional governments.[21] Much like Canada, Australia has two levels of government division: the federal government and the states and territories. These are self-administered regions with local legislation, police force and certain civil authorities, which also are represented in the Parliament.[22]

Australia has limited legislative or regulatory constraints on the use of PPP contracts in the country. A government agency that is procuring a PPP must have statutory power to do so and must comply with any applicable legislative requirements, such as planning legislation (Griffiths et al. 2019). For PPPs, Australian state governments use policies and guidelines to set out rules for the use of PPPs. The most important guidelines can be found in the National Public Private Partnerships, Policy Framework (Australian Government 2015), which has been endorsed by all Australian state and territory governments, as well as the Commonwealth Government. It applies to all PPPs that are released to the market in relation to the procurement of infrastructure via PPPs (Australian Government 2015). National PPPs do not apply to the local government sector, but the guidelines say: 'local government entities may consider the benefits of using this National Policy when developing any PPP project' (Australian Government 2015, p. 7).

According to the national guidelines, the aim of a PPP is 'to deliver improved services and better value for money, primarily through appropriate risk transfer, encouraging innovation, greater asset utilisation and integrated whole-of-life management, underpinned by private financing' (Australian Government, 2015, p. 3).

The Australian state and territory governments are committed to public infrastructure being well planned and effectively delivered, and Australia sees

PPPs as a cooperation between the public and the private parties that, under appropriate circumstances, can make the best use of resources for both parties (Australian Government 2015). According to the National Public Private Partnerships Guidelines, it is required by policy (not the law) to consider PPP procurement if a project has a total capital value exceeding $50 million. Projects with a value of less than $50 million may also be suitable for a PPP delivery if they exhibit sufficient value for money (Australian Government 2015). In New South Wales, Victoria and Queensland, the National Public Private Partnerships are supplemented by state-specific PPP guidelines (New South Wales Treasury 2017, Queensland Government 2015, Victorian Government 2016), which set out state-specific requirements of PPPs.[23]

Regulation of PPPs in the EU

The EU public procurement law is founded on a civil law tradition. The European Commission describes PPPs as public projects providing additional capital, alternative management and implementation skills, added value to the consumer and the public at large, better identification of needs and an optimal use of resources (European Commission 2003). Consequently, PPPs differ significantly from traditional procurement (Tvarnø 2010), but the European Commission has not presented legislation that takes this difference into consideration. As a result, PPPs are governed by the same rules as traditional procurement projects under the EU law. The Public Procurement Directive[24] concerns all types of public contracts works, supplies or services, due to Article 1(2) under the thresholds in accordance with Article 1(1) of the Directive. The directive does not address that PPPs are more complex long-term contracts compared to the average public contracts. Fourteen per cent of the public budget in the EU is used on public contracts. Hence, the Procurement Directive concerns the majority of public contracts, but not specifically PPPs. The EU law does not define PPPs in the EU Public Procurement Directive. This leaves procurements of PPPs in a legal vacuum, and EU law does not regulate nor embrace the specific dynamics, collaborations, investment incentives, and green and innovative potentials found in PPPs.

In order to comply with the Paris Agreement, the EU has adopted the European Climate Law Regulation.[25] Section 7 in the regulation presents that a mobilization of public–private climate finance can be transformed through large-scale shifts in the investment patterns to meet the objectives of the EU Paris Protocol.[26] Hence, the public sector climate finance might play an important role in mobilizing resources after 2020, yet the private sector is still needed for upscaling climate finance. Consequently, PPPs might play a prominent role in the green transition in the EU (Tvarnø 2020). The prospect for green

PPPs is comprehensive in the EU. The EU climate law is aimed at covering all sectors of the economy, which is why the private sector is going to be involved in meeting the climate law goals concerning the limiting of the temperature rise to 1.5°C, net-zero CO_2 emissions at a global level by 2050.[27]

The 2014/24/EU Directive introduces the most economically advantageous tender criteria and the notion of life-cycle cost. According to the directive, the EU legal definition of the life-cycle cost is all costs over the life-cycle of works, supplies or services, including research, development, production, transport, use, maintenance and end-of-life disposal cost and pollution. The introduction of procurement with a best-life-cycle-cost perspective underpins decision making for PPP projects, and it assists in achieving the economically most advantageous criterion, which is a necessary requirement for PPP procurement.

On the one hand, the EU procurement law does not prevent PPPs, but on the other hand, it does not promote PPPs through legislation. The Public Procurement Directive[28] aims to increase the efficiency of the public procurement system and open up the EU's public procurement market in order to prevent national protectionist policies from the Member States. Hence, the EU has adopted a strict legal instrument to ensure legal efficiency, simplification, innovation and compliance of public tendering in the EU without any specific PPP legal measures nor with any consideration for the green transition.

The lack of PPP regulation in the EU results in various differences in PPP legislation at the level of Member States, as can be seen between France and Ireland, for example.

3.   Demand for future PPP regulation

As mentioned above, PPPs are regulated through the EU public procurement law. The question is then whether this is enough to support PPPs in the EU. France and Ireland have both chosen to adopt specific PPP regulations. Since 2004—when the European Commission presented the PPP Green Paper[29]— PPPs have not been on the EU agenda. Both political research and economic research have shown the economic and political advantages of PPPs without any legal impact at EU level.

The World Bank

The World Bank sees PPPs as a tool for getting a higher quality of infrastructure for more people. According to the World Bank, PPPs can 'when designed well and implemented in a balanced regulatory environment bring greater efficiency and sustainability to the provision of public services such as energy, transport, telecommunications, water, healthcare and education. PPPs can also allow for better allocation of risk between public and private entities' (World Bank 2021a, p. 1).

Among other things, the World Bank helps governments make informed decisions in relation to PPPs as a delivery option. The World Bank is working on supporting strong institutions, strengthening data, building capacity, developing and testing tools, promoting transparency and encouraging engagement with all stakeholders. All of this contributes to helping countries become able to create effective PPPs (World Bank 2021a). In 2016, the World Bank developed the PPP Knowledge Lab,[30] an online knowledge resource on PPPs.

PPP Knowledge Lab

The PPP Knowledge Lab has made a Reference Guide (World Bank 2017) to help decision makers and PPP practitioners. The current third edition of this guide is particularly interested in the development of efficient and institutional frameworks that help governments identify and select PPP projects. The Reference Guide is divided into three modules. Module 2 explains the PPP legal framework, which refers to all laws and regulations that govern the PPP project cycle. It is not only PPP-specific legislation and regulations that affect the PPP project, but also all legislation in general.

Naturally, the legal framework will depend on the legal tradition of the country in which the PPP project is contracted, as well as on that country's legal system. The Reference Guide says that PPPs can be implemented without a specific legal and institutional framework, but it also says that most countries with successful PPP programs rely on a sound PPP framework (World Bank 2017).

The PPP Knowledge Lab states that PPP-specific legislation can strengthen the profile of PPP and demonstrate political commitment to PPP programs. However, they also emphasize that a special consideration for avoiding conflicts with existing relevant laws is needed and that '[a] well-designed PPP law typically sets out principles, which may be supported by more detailed regulations—with a view to avoiding rigidity and enabling the PPP programs to adapt over time' (World Bank 2017, p. 67).

The OECD

The establishment of a strong PPP sector does not just occur out of the blue. It requires more than just a political strategy to ensure a solid public and private business case regarding infrastructure projects, for example. The OECD argues that PPPs operate best in a legal and regulatory environment that is based upon transparency, with clarity about the legal framework, and where the terms in the PPP contract are enforced. Furthermore, the OECD argues that before regulating PPPs, a national central PPP unit should be established to ensure efficient and proper knowledge of the PPP market (OECD 2008).

The OECD defines a PPP as

> an agreement between the government and one or more private partners (which may include the operators and the financers) according to which the private partners deliver the service in such manner that the service delivery objectives of the government are aligned with the profit objectives of the private partners and where effectiveness of the alignment depends on a sufficient transfer of risk to the private partners. (OECD 2008, p. 17)

We noted previously that the OECD recommended clear, predictable and legitimate institutional frameworks be established by governments, along with well-resourced and competent authorities. Perhaps this is easier said than done! But there is little doubt that the OECD's policy guidance work over decades has strengthened the awareness of the relative costs, benefits and risks with PPPs, as well as emphasizing the need for active consultations, and engagements with stakeholders (and end-users). Its work and policy guidance has been a positive force for improved PPP decision making. The different types of PPP measures within the EU Member States, nonetheless, also suggest that different legal measures can provide either a strong or a weak PPP sector. Consequently, the recommendations from the OECD point in a regulatory direction for the future of PPPs.

4.   PPPs and climate change

Since climate change is on the agenda, PPP projects with a climate aim could be (or maybe should be) a common solution for the future. The Paris Agreement was adopted in 2015,[31] and with this agreement the world committed to undertake ambitious efforts in order to combat climate change. One of the Paris Agreement's central aims is to limit the rise in global temperatures, and, additionally, the agreement aims to strengthen countries' ability to deal with the impacts of climate change. Some would say that the world needs private companies to invest, innovate and invent climate change solutions, which is the exact reason why PPPs came into the picture in the first place: to strengthen innovation and invention. Private investments through the PPP route can offer an innovative mechanism for meeting the goals of, for instance, infrastructure development and climate change mitigation. However, the private parties in PPPs often focus exclusively on the project economics, even though they have the potential to provide innovative technical, financial and managerial solutions (Tharun and Laishram 2017).

The following section therefore presents some examples of PPPs from a climate change perspective. PPPs indeed may provide an interesting contemporary role in furthering effective climate change policies.

Climate change and PPPs in the future

The World Bank has introduced the concept of Climate-Smart Infrastructure PPPs as one solution to climate change, carbon emissions and carbon resilience. According to the World Bank, climate-smart infrastructure solutions must be developed and implemented to achieve the goals of the Paris Agreement. As public finance is limited, private investments and expertise through PPP models are necessary.

> The majority of greenhouse gas (GHG) emissions today is associated with carbon-intense infrastructure construction and operation, particularly in the energy, public transport, water supply and sanitation sectors. At the same time, it is expected that economies will need to make significant investments over the next 10–15 years to build new or to rehabilitate ageing infrastructure to meet the global demand with emerging economies and developing countries accounting for roughly two thirds of global infrastructure investment. (World Bank 2020, p. 1)

Climate-Smart Infrastructure PPPs are a public instrument to ensure private investments in climate change adaptation, disaster risk management and low-carbon infrastructure (World Bank 2020), through, for example, low-carbon-emission 'green' buildings and improved life-cycle performance. Consequently, the public sector must present a PPP contract, including requirements to the private sector's climate responsibility in a way that respects the allocation of risks, the level of bargaining power (Buso and Stenger 2018) and incentives for climate innovation (Denta 2021). Climate-Smart Infrastructure PPPs can play a significant role in the development of climate-resilient infrastructure if the public sector introduces a mitigation of greenhouse gas emissions, resilience of infrastructure assets to future climate change and, in general, an anticipation of climate change challenges and innovation in the procurement of PPPs.

Climate change can be a game-changer regarding PPP projects. Long-term projects like PPPs call for solutions for innovation, uncertainty and climate change. Climate change is a relevant risk factor for both the public party and the private party. Hence, climate change will be a part of future PPP contracts. However, Climate-Smart Infrastructure PPPs can be a relevant tool for reducing global warming and the emission of greenhouse gases. The World Bank has described relevant climate change issues in regard to PPPs, such as ensuring that a PPP project is 'planned, designed, built and operated in a way that anticipates, prepares for and adapts to uncertain and potentially permanent effects of climate change'. Furthermore, it must be ensured that the PPP project provides climate resilience and thus 'does not harm and delivers related benefits to wider systems, communities, households and individuals (e.g., sea barriers, flood protection)' (World Bank 2020).

The World Bank recommends that climate change considerations can be used as a parameter when conducting a value-for-money analysis[32] or life-cycle-cost analysis during the project development phase. The United States has introduced some guidelines (Columbia Law School 2021) for assessing the impact on climate change in PPP projects. The guidelines provide an instruction for governments on how to evaluate the climate risk. This should be conducted in the context of an environmental impact assessment.[33] The guidelines facilitate the assessment of how climate change may impact a project and its surrounding environment, how climate change implicates the environmental consequences of the project, and how the appropriate adaptation and resilience measures to address climate-related risks can be selected. The EU has adapted a similar assessment in Directive 2014/52/EU. The directive introduces an assessment of the effects of certain public and private projects concerning environmental issues, such as an assessment of the impact of projects on the climate (for example, greenhouse gas emissions) and their vulnerability to climate change. In a global perspective, a PPP will be awarded as a public contract under the procurement regime and Climate-Smart Infrastructure PPPs must include distinct climate incentives in their procurement documents. Furthermore, both the climate and the procurement law should support Climate-Smart Infrastructure PPPs.

Private collaboration as an alternative PPP solution

Waste pollution, especially plastic waste, is one of the most troublesome and complicated environmental and sustainable development challenges on national, regional and global levels. According to Siam Commercial Bank's Economic Intelligence Center,[34] Thailand is the world's sixth biggest contributor of ocean waste pollution. In 2018 Thailand generated 1.03 million tons of plastic waste, with over 3 percent of that finding its way into the ocean.

In June 2018, the Thailand Public-Private Partnership for Plastic and Waste Management (PPP Plastic) was established. PPP Plastic was established by the Plastic Industry Club and the Federation of Thai Industries in partnership with the Thailand Business Council for Sustainable Development, multiple organizations from the public and private sectors, and members of society. Funding for PPP Plastic came from Dow[35] and other leading companies in Thailand. Initially, 15 organizations joined the PPP Plastic program. By 2019, the membership had more than doubled to 33 organizations, and PPP Plastic is now cooperating with many different parties in the market. All parties decided to join the partnership as they recognized the significance of the plastic waste problem and were interested in resolving this problem together. PPP Plastic aims to reduce marine plastic debris by at least 50 percent by 2027. The plan is to achieve this through solutions such as sustainable waste management and the circular economy, and by reducing, reusing and recycling (Denta 2021).

PPP Plastic is relying on collaboration rather than coercion. In January 2020, some of the leading department stores in Thailand stopped handing out single-use plastic bags, and since the launch of the campaign Everyday Say No to Plastic Bag in 2019, Thailand has managed to reduce the consumption of single-use plastic bags by more than 2 billion bags (Denta 2021).

PPP Plastic is not a PPP as defined in this chapter but is rather an example of a broader category of PPPs, which may become more common in the future. It would be hard, probably impossible, to make a legal frame for PPPs like PPP Plastic, but this kind of PPP will make it easier for governments to subsequently make regulations and rules within the PPP project area—in this case regarding regulations for plastic pollution.

The EU and climate change: PPPs as an investment tool

In 2015, the European Commission presented a strategy (Communication 2015)[36] for the future climate challenges in the EU from 2020 and forward. In accordance with the Paris Agreement,[37] the EU is obliged to secure ambitious reductions of greenhouse gas emissions by 'specifying that the long-term goal should be to reduce global emissions by at least 60 percent below 2010 levels by 2050; in that context setting out clear, specific, ambitious and fair legally binding mitigation commitments that put the world on track towards achieving the below 2°C objective'.[38]

One way to comply with the Paris Agreement and the EU strategy is by proposing to include the finance from the private sector. As stated by the European Commission in the Paris Protocol climate strategy:

> encourage climate-resilient sustainable development by promoting international cooperation and supporting policies that decrease vulnerability and improve countries' capacity to adapt to the impacts of climate change; and promote efficient and effective implementation and cooperation by encouraging policies that mobilise substantial, transparent and predictable public and private sector investment in low-emission climate-resilient development.[39]

Hence, a collaboration between the public and private sectors is a key element in future climate-resilient development. It can be argued that EU regulation needs to include specific PPP legislation to support the demanded private finance of future climate initiatives and innovation, since the current public procurement law does not provide sufficient legal support for PPP projects (Tvarnø 2020). Therefore, this chapter calls for more research that is related to climate PPPs, and the possibilities for regulations or specific guidelines.

5.   Common law versus civil law in a PPP climate perspective

As mentioned in Section 2, common law and civil law are based upon different legal traditions, which create different potentials for PPPs. Civil law is based upon a substantive written legislation, and common law is found in past decisions and has thus evolved into a system of rules based on precedents (Zweigert and Kötz 1998), which guides judges in making later decisions in similar cases. Compared to civil law, common law is flexible and adapts to changing circumstances due to the tradition of announcing new legal doctrines or changing old ones.

Common law is based upon the Westminster system of responsible government and the nature of ministerial power and accountability (Russel and Serban 2020). Common law combined with the size and nature of PPP programs in Canada and Australia, the flexibility of the PPP policy and legal structure supports the PPP development in these countries.

Conversely to common law, civil law does not adapt to changing circumstances. Hence, civil law is based upon civil codes and general principles. Civil law requires specific regulation to support or change the PPP development. The French PPP Act is an example of a civil law country regulating the field of PPP in order to support and promote the establishment of PPP projects. In regard to common law, this chapter has presented the PPP law of Canada and Australia. Canadian provinces and Australian states have broad infrastructure and service delivery functions, restricted only by the limited functions reserved to their national governments. Furthermore, it should be noted that it is not possible to compare the Canadian and Australian PPP law with the EU public procurement law, as there are simply too many differences between the EU and Canada and Australia. The EU has, firstly, a different constitutional structure; secondly, a strict civil law tradition; and, thirdly, a different economic structure. Fourthly, most Canadian provinces and Australian states have a significantly larger land mass area and less population in these areas than all (or most) of the EU Member States.

Public procurement law is defined by the EU and applies in the EU Member States (such as Ireland and France). Consequently, Ireland, as the only common law EU country included in this chapter, has adopted PPP legislation to support PPPs, and the Irish PPP legislation supports the superior EU public procurement law.

The EU has not adopted PPP legislation to support PPP projects, but regulates PPPs as traditional public contracts without acknowledging the significant difference between the two types of contracts. EU law does not have the flexibility afforded by the more policy-based PPP frameworks, as seen in jurisdictions such as the Canadian provinces and Australian states. Consequently, the lack of PPP regulation in the EU might result in a loss of adaptive climate measures from the private sector in the EU.

Common law ensures that Canada and Australia continually innovate and refine their approaches to PPPs through, for example, different tender processes and bid evaluation methodologies. A potential EU PPP regulation could consider some of these legal principles to promote climate PPPs.

As discussed further above, France, Ireland, Canada and Australia present different approaches to PPP legal frameworks that all have the aim of enabling long-term contracts to be properly structured for effective implementation. Furthermore, this chapter has presented the future relevance for PPPs in a climate perspective. Regarding the future transition to a climate-neutral society, PPP is a relevant tool for ensuring support from private investments in order to reach the climate goals in the Paris Agreement. The need for legal support, regulation and innovation is essential and calls for the EU to adapt a PPP legislative framework to support these goals.

6.   Concluding remarks

PPPs offer an alternative contract and financial structure to public contracting, and efficient PPP projects can be promoted by effective rules. Furthermore, PPPs are relevant in innovative sectors, such as green transition and climate change, for example. Legal rules for climate PPPs might become more relevant in the future, as more of these partnerships will start to show up.

In the EU, the Public Procurement Directive governs PPPs. The directive does not define PPPs, and it does not take into consideration that PPPs are more long-term contracts compared to average public contracts, nor does it consider the green transition that is presented in the European Climate Law Regulation. EU law does not prevent PPPs, but it does not promote PPPs through legislation either. Some Member States have local legislation, and some have guidelines and PPP units.

Common law and civil law provide different PPP approaches. In civil law jurisdictions, the law is interpreted through authoritative codifications in a constitution or statute passed by legislature to amend a code. In common law systems, the law is defined through the decisions in cases ruled by judges. Ireland is an example of a combination of the traditional common law and the EU civil law, and it thus represents an alternative to PPP law which may in fact become a new legal frontier in regard to PPPs.

The World Bank and the OECD both recommend some kind of PPP framework. Furthermore, the PPP Reference Guide from the PPP Knowledge Lab states that PPPs are mostly successful in countries with a specified PPP framework. From this perspective, the EU should consider regulating PPPs in the future, similar to either the French civil law solution or the Irish combination of civil law and common law. It might be a fruitful way to promote PPPs generally in the EU, as well as a solution to help in handling climate issues. A pure common law solution for PPPs in the EU would move too far away from the civil law traditions of the EU.

In this chapter, it is recommended that the new legal frontiers of PPPs should promote different ways for PPPs to be used, as well as promoting how PPPs can support reaching the climate goals of the Paris Agreement.

Notes

1. European Commission, 'The Paris Protocol: A blueprint for tackling global climate change beyond 2020' (Communication 2015) COM/2015/081.
2. There is a significant distinction between PPPs and concessions in a legal context. This chapter defines concessions and PPPs under EU law. Thus, concessions are defined as end-user-pays projects, and PPPs are defined as government-pays projects. Under EU law, end-user-paid concession projects are regulated by the Concession Directive (Directive 2014/23/EU of the European Parliament and of the Council of 26 February 2014 on the award of concession contracts, OJ L 94, 28.3.2014, pp. 1–64). PPPs as government-pays projects are regulated by the Public Procurement Directive (Directive 2014/24/EU of the European Parliament and of the Council of 26 February 2014 on public procurement and repealing Directive 2004/18/EC, OJ L 94, 28.3.2014, pp. 65–242). The analyses in this chapter regard government-pays PPP projects and not end-user-pays concessions projects.
3. Ordonnance n° 2004-559 du 17 juin 2004, Version consolidée 04 avril 2016.
4. LOI n° 2008-735 du 28 juillet 2008 relative aux contrats de partenariat, version consolidée au 04 avril 2016d.
5. In France, there is a specific legal difference between concessions and the legal basis for PPP projects. France regards a concession as an end-user payment project in which all powers delegated to a private party with all associated risks and perils and PPP projects are regarded as a new phenomenon on the basis of which no project has yet been designed where risks and finances are shared.
6. LOI n° 2008-735 du 28 juillet 2008 relative aux contrats de partenariat (1), NOR: ECEX0774541L, Version consolidée au 31 mars 2016 (Order No. 2004-559 of 17 June 2004 on partnership contracts).
7. Order No. 2004-1119 of 19 October 2004.
8. Furthermore, in accordance with the 2008 PPP Act, in Article 9, last paragraph, PPP contracts must be communicated to the Mission d'appui aux partenariats public-privé after their signature due to statistical reporting requirements and necessary economic analyses. Furthermore, the procurement of a PPP follows specific French PPP public procurement rules implicating the principles from the EU public procurement law. This aspect is not covered in this chapter.
9. State Authorities (Public Private Partnership Arrangements) Act, Number 1 of 2002.
10. Irish National Development Finance Agency (NDFA), www.ndfa.ie/Publications/stdDocumentation.htm (last visited September 4, 2020).
11. National Development Finance Agency Act, Number 29 of 2002.
12. See Section 5 for a discussion of common law versus civil law in a PPP climate perspective.
13. 'Bijuralism' can be approached from several angles: the simple co-existence of two legal traditions, the interaction between two traditions, the formal integration

of two traditions within a given context (for example, in an agreement or a legal text) or, on a more general level, the recognition of and respect for the cultures and identities of two legal traditions. However, beyond the factual situation that it presupposes with respect to the co-existence of traditions, bijuralism raises the issue of the interaction or relationship between different legal traditions (Allard 2015).

14. Canada's legal system is based on the English and French systems. Explorers and colonists brought these systems to Canada in the 17th and 18th centuries. After the Battle of Québec in 1759, the country fell under English common law, except for Québec, which follows civil law (Government of Canada 2015).

15. Civil Code of Québec.

16. Code Napoléon, officially the Code civil des Français, is the French civil code established under the French Consulate in 1804 and still in force, although frequently amended.

17. For a mapping in regard to federal, regional and local perspective in Canada, see Conteh (2013).

18. The Treasury Board is a Cabinet committee of the Queen's Privy Council of Canada. It was established in 1867 and given statutory powers in 1869 and is responsible for accountability and ethics, financial, personnel and administrative management, comptrollership, approving regulations and most Regulations-in-Council (Government of Canada 2021b).

19. Australia consists of six states (New South Wales, Queensland, South Australia, Tasmania, Victoria and Western Australia) and three self-governing territories: Australian Capital Territory, Northern Territory and Norfolk Island.

20. Including those to whom Parliament has delegated authority.

21. In Australia, that distribution is between the Commonwealth and the six states. The Constitution defines the boundaries of law-making powers between the Commonwealth and the states/territories (Australian Government 2010).

22. Territories rely on federal legislation and additional financial contributions to operate, which means that they have less representation in the Senate.

23. The National PPP Guidelines Volume 6 have state/territory-specific PPP guidelines for Western Australia and the Australian Capital Territory, and there are jurisdictional requirements for the remaining states and the Northern Territory (Australian Government 2014).

24. Directive 2014/24/EU of the European Parliament and of the Council of 26 February 2014 on public procurement and repealing Directive 2004/18/EC, OJ L 94, 28.3.2014.

25. European Commission, 'Proposal for a Regulation of the European Parliament and of the Council establishing the framework for achieving climate neutral economy' (Communication 2018) COM (2018) 773.

26. European Commission, 'The Paris Protocol: A blueprint for tackling global climate change beyond 2020' (Communication 2015) COM/2015/081.

27. European Commission, 'A clean planet for all: A European strategic long-term vision for a prosperous, modern, competitive and climate neutrality and amending Regulation (EU) 2018/1999 (European Climate Law) COM(2020)80'.

28. Directive 2014/24/EU of the European Parliament and of the Council of 26 February 2014 on public procurement and repealing Directive 2004/18/EC, OJ L 94, 28.3.2014.

29. COM(2004) 327, Green Paper on Public-Private Partnerships and community law on public contracts and concessions, Brussels, 30.4.2004.

30. The PPP Knowledge Lab was created with funding from the Public-Private Infrastructure Advisory Facility (PPIAF) and is a collaboration between the African Development Bank, Asian Development Bank, European Bank for Reconstruction and Development, Inter-American Development Bank, Islamic Development Bank and the World Bank Group.
31. The Paris Agreement is a legally binding international treaty on climate change. It was adopted by 196 Parties at the COP21 in Paris on 12 December 2015. The EU formally ratified the Agreement on 5 October 2016, thus enabling its entry into force on 4 November 2016.
32. Value for money is not a legal principle in the EU. Directive 2014/24/EU introduced the economically most advantageous tender in Article 67.
33. Environmental Impact Assessments (EIAs) are a part of a feasibility study developed at Columbia Law School and are typically used to identify and assess climate change impacts of a project as well as potential mitigation and adaptation measures. The findings can then be used as a basis for adjusting existing modalities for project design, approval and implementation to avoid and/or minimize harm and to improve environmentally sustainable outcomes (Columbia Law School 2021 and World Bank 2020).
34. The Economic Intelligence Center (EIC), a unit of Siam Commercial Bank, provides business executives with valuable insights for effective decision making. It evaluates market situations and business implications through forward-looking risk factors and potential consequences (SCB EIC 2021).
35. Dow Thailand Group is the leading science group of companies in Thailand and is the largest manufacturing base of Dow in the Asia-Pacific region.
36. European Commission, 'The Paris Protocol: A blueprint for tackling global climate change beyond 2020' (Communication 2015) COM/2015/081.
37. United Nations (2015).
38. European Commission, 'The Paris Protocol: A blueprint for tackling global climate change beyond 2020' (Communication 2015) COM/2015/081, Section 2.
39. European Commission, 'The Paris Protocol: A blueprint for tackling global climate change beyond 2020' (Communication 2015) COM/2015/081, Section 2.

References

Allard, F. (2015) *The Supreme Court of Canada and Its Impact on the Expression of Bijuralism*, General Counsel, Department of Justice, Ottawa.

Australian Government (2010) *Australia's Constitution With Overview and Notes by the Australian Government Solicitor*, Parliamentary Education Office and Australian Government Solicitor, Canberra.

Australian Government (2014) *National Public Private Partnership Guidelines, Volume 6: Jurisdictional Requirements*, Department of Infrastructure and Regional Development, Canberra.

Australian Government (2015) *National Public Private Partnerships, Policy Framework*, Department of Infrastructure and Regional Development, Canberra.

Buso, M., and Stenger, A. (2018) Public-private partnerships as a policy response to climate change. *Energy Policy*, 119 (2018): 487–494.

Campbell, D., and Cotter, S. (2018) *Comparative Law Yearbook*, Kluwer Law International, Alphen aan den Rijn.

Canadian Council for Public-Private Partnerships (2011) *Public Private Partnership: A Guide for Municipalities*, Canadian Council for Public-Private Partnerships, Toronto.

Columbia Law School (2021) EIA Guidelines for Assessing the Impact of a Project on Climate Change. https://climate.law.columbia.edu/content/eia-guidelines-assessing -impact-project-climate-change.

Conteh, C. (2013) Changing trends in regional economic development policy governance: The case of Northern Ontario, Canada. *International Journal of Urban and Regional Research*, 37 (4): 1419–1437.

Denta, S. M. (2021) Public-private partnership for the climate: From a plastic pollution perspective. *EPPPL* 16 (4): 318–328.

Dunne, M. (2015) Ireland, in *The Public Private Partnership Law Review*, edited by B. Werneck and M. Saadi, Law Business Research, London.

EPEC (2015) *PPP Motivations and Challenges for the Public Sector*, European PPP Expertise Centre, Luxembourg.

EPEC (2019) *Review of the European PPP Market in 2019*, European PPP Expertise Centre, Luxembourg.

European Commission (2003) *Guidelines for Successful Public-Private Partnerships*, Directorate-General, Regional Policy, Brussels.

Government of Canada (2015) *Canada's System of Justice*, Department of Justice, Ottawa.

Government of Canada (2021a) *Supply Manual*, Strategic Policy Sector, Public Works and Government Services Canada, Ottawa.

Government of Canada (2021b) Treasury Board of Canada Secretariat. www.tbs-sct.gc .ca.

Greve, C., Christensen, L. T., Tvarnø, C., Nielsen, S. N., and Denta, S. M. (2021) Public-private partnerships in the healthcare sector: Limited policy guidelines, but active project development in Denmark. *Journal of Economic Policy Reform*. https:// doi.org/10.1080/17487870.2020.1855174.

Griffiths, A., and Carney, N. (2021) In review: Governing rules and procedures for PPP projects in Australia. Lexology. www.lexology.com/library/detail.aspx?g=0a0b47b2 -4206-4c45-ad24-1218fbc47c4d.

Griffiths, A., Wei, L., and Carney, N. (2019) An introduction to public-private partnerships in Australia. Lexology. www.lexology.com/library/detail.aspx?g=ddf2fe7f-6cc2 -4107-80af-1bafd44cb89e.

Huxham, C., and Vangen, S. (1996) Working together: Key themes in the management of relationships between public and non-profit organizations. *International Journal of Public Sector Management*, 9 (7): 5–17.

New South Wales Treasury (2017) *Public Private Partnerships, Guidelines, Preparations, Procurement and Contract Management*, Infrastructure and Structured Finance Unit, Sydney.

OECD (2008) *Public-Private Partnership: In Pursuit of Risk Sharing and Value for Money*, OECD, Paris.

OECD (2012) *Recommendation of the Council on Principles for Public Governance of Public-Private Partnerships*, OECD, Paris.

Osborne, S. P. (Ed.) (2000) *Public-Private Partnerships: Theory and Practice in International Perspective*, Routledge, London.

Queensland Government (2015) *Project Assessment Framework, Queensland PPP Supporting Guidelines*, Queensland Government, Brisbane.

Regimbald, G. (2011) *Canadian Administrative Law*, LexisNexis Canada, Toronto.

Russel, M., and Serban, R. (2020) The muddle of the 'Westminster Model': A concept stretched beyond repair. *Government and Opposition*, 56 (4): 744–764.

Shkordoff, N., Johannsen, H., and Barlow, T. (2015) Canada, in *The Public-Private Partnership Law Review*, edited by B. Werneck and M. Saadi, Law Business Research, London.

Siam Commercial Bank Economic Intelligence Center (2021) Home page. www.scbeic .com.

Tharun, D., and Laishram, B. (2017) Public private partnerships for climate change mitigation: An Indian case. Paper presented at International Conference on Advances in Sustainable Construction Materials and Civil Engineering Systems (ASCMCES-17), University of Sharjah, April.

Tvarnø, C. (2010) Law and Regulatory Aspects of Public–Private Partnerships: Contract Law and Public Procurement Law, in *International Handbook on Public–Private Partnerships*, edited by G. A. Hodge, C. Greve and A. E. Boardman, Edward Elgar Publishing, Cheltenham, UK and Northampton, MA, USA.

Tvarnø, C. (2012) Why the EU Public Procurement Law Should Contain Rules that Allow Negotiation for Public Private Partnerships: Innovation Calls for Negotiating Opportunities, in *EU Public Procurement, Modernisation, Growth and Innovation: Discussions on the 2011 Proposals for Procurement Directives*, edited by G. S. Ølykke, C. Risvig Hansen and C. Tvarnø, Djøf Forlag, København.

Tvarnø, C. (2016) Optimizing Public Private Partnership Through Legal and Governmental Initiatives, in *Liber Amicorum Peter Møgelvang-Hansen*, edited by B. Dahl, T. Riis and J. Trzaskowski, Ex Tuto, København.

Tvarnø, C. (2020) Climate Public Private Partnerships in the EU: A climate law and economic perspective, *EPPPL*, 15 (3): 200–208.

Tvarnø, C., Greve, C., and Denta, S. M. (2019) *Offentlige-Private Partnerskaber: I juridisk og politisk perspektiv*, Karnov Group, Stockholm.

United Nations (2015) Paris Agreement, FCCC/CP/2015/10/Add.1.

Vaissier, V., Martin-Sisteron, H., and Seniuta, A. (2015) France, in *The Public-Private Partnership Law Review*, edited by B. Werneck and M. Saadi, Law Business Research, London.

Victorian Government (2016) *Partnerships: Victoria Requirements*, Secretary Department of Treasury and Finance, Melbourne.

World Bank (2017) *Public-Private Partnership: Reference Guide Version 3*, World Bank Group, Washington, DC.

World Bank (2020) PPP units around the world. https://ppp.worldbank.org/public -private-partnership/overview/international-ppp-units.

World Bank (2021a) Climate-smart PPPs. https://ppp.worldbank.org/public-private -partnership/climate-smart/climate-smart-ppps.

World Bank (2021b) Legal framework/enabling environment assessment for PPPs. https://ppp.worldbank.org/public-private-partnership/legislation-regulation/ framework-assessment.

Zweigert, K., and Kötz, H. (1998) *Introduction to Comparative Law*, 3rd ed., Clarendon Press, Oxford.

PART III

Contemporary and continuing themes in a contested world

11 Financialization: the next stage in PPP development

Anne Stafford, Stewart Smyth and Marta Almeida

Introduction

Financialization is often broadly defined as the growing influence of the capital market and related intermediaries and processes in economic, social and political life (Pike and Pollard 2010). Identified by Christophers (2015), among others, as the third development alongside globalization and neoliberalization which characterizes contemporary capitalism, the term 'financialization' is increasingly being used to capture a range of structural transformations and processes that have become more evident since the Global Financial Crisis (GFC) of 2007/08 (Iaonnou and Wójcik 2019).

Financialization as a concept has seen extensive proliferation in academic literature since the GFC, but this has been an 'uneven, negotiated and messy process' (O'Brien and Pike 2017), with a number of different versions emerging. In this chapter we do not seek to cover all aspects of financialization, instead focusing our attention on two foundational versions identified by Christophers (2015) that are relevant to the development of public–private partnerships (PPPs) as an important form of global infrastructure. The first relates to global macro-economic changes of profit generation and capital accumulation (Arrighi 1994, Krippner 2005, Stockhammer 2004). It is characterized by the proliferation of financial markets and the emergence of secondary markets in infrastructure funds. The second relates to changes at the micro level of corporate motives and corporate governance, specifically referencing the shareholder value revolution (Cooper 2015, Froud et al. 2000). We explore both of these versions of financialization through case examples later in the chapter.

The relationships between the many versions of financialization and the development of PPPs have been under-studied to date, but are important due to the all-pervading nature of financialization. This chapter aims to address what financialization means for the future of PPP development through the following four questions: why and how is the emergence of financialization as a phenomenon important in understanding the role of private finance in PPP development? How has financialization been examined in the PPP literature to date? How has financialization shaped the operation of PPPs at different economic levels? Why is financialization still an enduring trend for the future of PPPs?

Although rarely explicitly recognized, we argue that financialization has been an implicit underlying concept in the development and growth of PPPs in Western democracies (O'Brien and Pike 2017). Further, we argue that the experience of PPP financialization illustrates it is the content (of financial logics) rather than the form of debt or equity finance that is important. Finally, we posit that while an assessment of the overall impact of financialization on PPPs requires considerably more research, there is substantial evidence from the UK that excessive profit extraction for private finance providers has been a key outcome of financialization.

The turn to neoliberalism (Harvey 2005) saw a reduction in the state making public money available upfront to finance infrastructure projects. Instead, there was increasing dependency by the public sector on the use of private, or market, capital for the provision of public infrastructure and related service delivery. Early on, policy makers recognized that projects had to be attractive in profit-making terms to ensure private sector investment; this was especially the case in the UK market economy (Froud 2003, Shaoul et al. 2007). Therefore, it was crucial that the policy gave opportunities for private sector partners to manage their exposure to risk and returns on their financial investment, which could take the form of both debt financing and equity investment.

For early PPP projects, the financier was often a bank which, as well as being involved in the debt financing, would also take a small equity stake in the project, due to the capital-intensive nature of PPPs and the other parties' limited experience of such projects. The conditions imposed by banks to participate in the equity of PPPs gave them greater security and control over their investment, as compared to a simple financier role. Typically consortia, usually made up of a construction company, an operations company, and a financier such as a bank, set up a limited liability company, known as a special purpose vehicle (SPV),[1] financed mainly by debt, with a small amount of equity. Such a structure has two relevant consequences. First, there is the opportunity for leveraging significant returns from the small equity positions. Second, as these projects deliver a long-term return on both debt and equity positions through the receipt of regular income, either from the state or through direct user charges, they lead to the creation of long-term financial assets in the SPVs.

Such assets typically deliver low risk and stable returns. For example, a hospital design-build-finance-maintain project is state-funded, therefore low risk, and offers stable returns, as demand for healthcare in Western democracies is forecast to continue rising.

As a result, capital markets now include an infrastructure asset class, of interest to institutional investors, such as pension funds (see the next chapter) and insurance funds, and private equity funds interested in investing for the long term. In addition, many global infrastructure companies operate specialist subsidiaries which invest in infrastructure projects from inception. Some take an active role in the management of the projects. This development is supported by the long-run stable returns which projects offer, and the potential need of their fellow construction shareholders to disinvest from the PPP projects when construction is completed (Demirag et al. 2010).[2]

More recently, the trend has been towards the development of new secondary markets where investment and pension funds can acquire positions in infrastructure projects (Burke and Demirag 2019). Examining the growth in infrastructure investment funds shows the impact of financialization. For example, BlackRock (2015) report a rise in aggregate funds under management from $1.1 bn in 2004 to $317.5 bn in 2014, with Reuters reporting a total above $80 trillion by 2017 (Kelly 2017). However, the need for investment in global infrastructure is immense. While recent estimates vary according to the methodology used, McKinsey (2017) notes that investment of $3.7 trillion a year to 2035 is needed, with a potential further $1 trillion per year to meet the United Nations' Sustainable Development Goals (SDGs), and the G20-funded Global Infrastructure Hub (2017) estimates that, as new investment is unlikely to meet these targets, there will be a global infrastructure financing gap of up to $15 trillion by 2040. One outcome of financialization is that growth in infrastructure investment is increasingly being driven by secondary market transactions; that is, the trading of existing infrastructure assets. Figure 11.1 shows how, although the amount of private infrastructure investment has risen over the past decade, investment via primary markets has fallen in comparison to investment via secondary markets, falling to only 25 per cent of total private infrastructure investment by 2019.

This introduction has shown that financialization is a wide-ranging term that has grown in significance over the past 20 years. It is meaningful in helping us to understand how PPP policy has developed in Western economies. It can also contribute to explaining typical PPP project structures and their investors. Our chapter addresses our four questions as follows. First, we review and define what financialization is, in broad terms, to demonstrate the importance

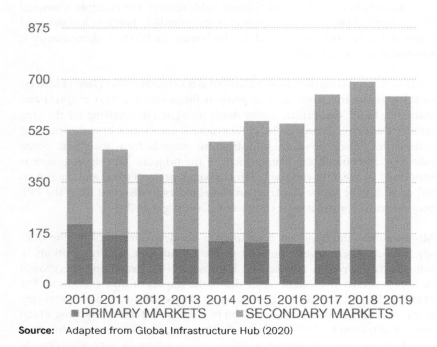

Source: Adapted from Global Infrastructure Hub (2020)

Figure 11.1 Total private infrastructure investment (USD bn)

of its emergence as a phenomenon in understanding the role of private finance in PPP development. We then show how financialization has been reviewed in the literature to date. Next, we identify suitable research approaches in this (so far) under-studied field. We identify a number of areas, including some case examples, where continuing research can be prioritized, including discussion of how financialization shapes the operation of PPPs at different economic levels, and offer some new areas for study. We conclude by explaining why financialization remains an enduring trend for the future of PPPs.

Definitions of financialization

Iaonnou and Wójcik (2019) highlight the interdisciplinary nature of the academic work on financialization over the past couple of decades, leading to a variety of definitions and characterizations of the concept. We note that while the work is often cross-disciplinary, articles tend to cluster within heterodox journals, within individual disciplines.[3] However, there are some commonalities across this work that allow us to set out the understanding of financialization that we utilize in this chapter. First, we follow Bayliss et al. (2017, 358) and 'define financialisation, as the intensive and extensive accumulation of interest-bearing capital to such an extent that there are qualitative and quantitative transformations in both economic and social reproduction'.

In this definition 'intensive' refers to the proliferation of financial markets, while 'extensive' refers to the increased penetration of financial logics into ever more areas of social reproduction – for example, social housing, social care, the water industry. This definition is consistent with the work of Ben Fine, who argues that the 'current era of financialization is precisely one in which there has been not only a disproportionate expansion of capital in exchange, through extensive and intensive proliferation of financial derivatives but also the extension of finance into ever more areas of economic and social reproduction' (Fine 2010, 112).

From this it should be clear that one of the characteristics of financialization is the increase in interest-bearing capital (that is, investment in the form of debt financing) in the UK and global economies (Andersson et al. 2014). For example, McKinsey found that, rather than decreasing, in the decade after the GFC the total global-debt-to-gross-domestic-product ratio grew by 30 points to 236 per cent (McKinsey 2018). Yet, the process of financialization is not limited only to the growth in finance capital. Following Cooper (2015) we can draw on four key characteristics of financialization which are relevant to the PPP arena: the globalization of the financial markets, the increase in income from financial investment, the shareholder value revolution and the intrusion of finance into commercial relations. This last characteristic is exemplified by the increasing use of commercial, financial and/or market logics by both the private and public sector partners in PPPs and other hybrid projects (see, for example, Reay and Hinings 2009, Skelcher and Smith 2015).

Cooper (2015) also recognizes the post-GFC period is one where there is an over-accumulation of capital – characterized by some as a wall of money – looking for investment opportunities. Too often in the period before the GFC, such capital found its way through the financial system to high-return, but apparently low-risk, investments such as collateral debt obligations and other innovative financial products. When this insight is coupled with the emphasis on maximizing shareholder value, this has led to the promotion of investment in PPPs as a safe place with a secure return often over the long term. The global accounting firm PwC is a particularly pertinent example of how such promotion has permeated global neoliberal thought, with its global capital projects and infrastructure section producing numerous publications promoting opportunities to 'secure the best returns' (PwC n.d., 3). The author is Richard Abadie, who left PwC to become head of PFI (Public Finance Initiative) policy at the UK Treasury, then head of Partnerships UK (Shaoul et al. 2007) before returning to PwC and rising to become global leader of PwC's capital projects and infrastructure section. He thus demonstrates in microcosm how financial logics, intrinsically part of the process of financialization, have been brought from the private sector to the public, embedded in the rhetoric and then exported to the world.

Understanding the output to date on financialization and PPPs

This chapter approaches financialization not with the view of trying to identify its nature but as an analytical framing to help us understand the nature of PPPs. We employ Ioannou and Wójcik's (2019) Analytical Spectrum of Financialization, shown in Figure 11.2, to help organize our engagement with the PPP literature.

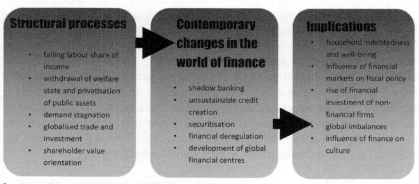

Source: Ioannou and Wójcik (2019, p. 265)

Figure 11.2   The Analytical Spectrum of Financialization

Ioannou and Wójcik's (2019) spectrum starts on the left-hand side by identifying the structural processes that are most associated with neoliberal capitalism, before setting out the contemporary (since *c*.1980) changes in the world of finance. On the right-hand side, they identify a series of implications that follow from the previous two boxes. The examples they give in each box are illustrative and do not constitute a comprehensive list of all the possible contents of that box.

We use their spectrum first to analyze existing literature on financialization and PPPs, and then to identify existing and future areas ripe for further study.

First, in the *Structural processes* box the withdrawal of the welfare state and privatization of assets is a key tenet of PPP, as noted by Hodge's (2002, 11) description of PPPs as the 'latest chapter' in the privatization storybook. There has been widespread neoliberal reform with the introduction of not just private finance but also private sector management techniques that are brought in to transform public infrastructure and services (Newberry 2004, Newberry and Pallot 2003), as part of wider New Public Management (NPM) reform (Lapsley and Miller 2019). The reforms included private sector influence spreading through to permeate PPP policy and practice (Asenova and Beck 2010, Shaoul et al. 2007), with Broadbent and Laughlin (2004) describing PPPs as the latest form of NPM. Academic literature became saturated with studies (see Andon 2012) which critiqued the supposedly impartiality of financial techniques such as value for money, instead identifying the bias towards favouring market investment and legitimizing NPM agendas (Froud 2003, Cooper and Taylor 2005, Shaoul 2005). While this early financial literature on PPP policy growth and development does not refer overtly to the term 'financialization', it indicates how the role of the financial markets, financial logics and their requirements for investment returns became embedded in public sector policy. For the UK, Shaoul et al. (2007) argue that the policy agenda became privatized early on, and thus the importance of financialization became embedded within the UK Treasury at the heart of government. UK policy on PPPs, embodied in the PFI, can therefore be seen as a deliberate move on the part of the British government to create a market for private investors and financiers (Asenova and Beck 2010; Shaoul et al. 2007, 2012).

The debate over the privatization of assets has led to discussion around the legitimacy of extracting profit from infrastructure which can usually be regarded as a social good, such as transport, healthcare and utilities. While the literature may not reference financialization directly, a number of studies examine aspects related to the returns generated by the private sector, and find evidence from early UK PFI projects and related equity sales to support the notion that many of these could be regarded as excessive (Edwards et al. 2004; Hellowell and Vecchi 2012; NAO, 2012, 2018; Shaoul 2005; Smyth and Whitfield 2017; Toms et al. 2011). Such returns are consistent with a maximizing shareholder value orientation.

More recent literature has referred overtly to the role of financialization in public sector reform. A recent case study by Peda and Vinnari (2020) critically discusses the legitimation of profit extraction from an Estonian water company, concluding that the moral case has not been made to a satisfactory level. Also examining the legitimation of profit extraction, Edgar et al. (2018) in their study of three UK companies show how these companies use their annual reports to support public policy and legitimize their involvement in PPP policy.

Second, relating to the *Contemporary changes* box, we argue that PPPs are designed, and in practice work, to maximize shareholder value and rely upon the globalized investment market. Drawing on the work of Hilferding (1981), Aaronovitch (1961) and Glasberg (1987) in relation to the development of financial capital control, Asenova and Beck (2010) conclude that PPP project uptake is completely dependent on whether the financial markets view the project as being able to meet the necessary risk-return criteria. That is, the markets have considerable power in negotiating with government in determining whether or not PPP projects will go ahead.

Over time, financial deregulation and the emergence of infrastructure investment funds as the main participants has led to power shifting away from senior debt financiers, such as banks, whose main concern was to minimize the risk of debt. Instead, the institutional investors, including private equity, and the equity markets have gained in significance (Weber et al. 2016, Whitfield and Smyth 2019). Many large pension and insurance funds have started to invest in the infrastructure asset class in equity markets, where there is the opportunity to gain low-risk but stable returns. However, because these funds place a greater emphasis on risk and profits than on providing a social good (Siemiatycki 2015), one consequence of financialization is that it may not deliver the best projects from the public perspective.

The third box on Ioannou and Wójcik's (2019) spectrum covering the 'Implications' of the previous two – structural processes and contemporary changes – is what we turn to in the next section. We focus on how financialization has shaped the development and operation of PPPs across three levels: macro, meso and micro.

Continuing research on financialization and PPPs

Studying the processes of financialization in relation to PPPs requires an understanding of the international political economy within which global PPP markets, policies and related management reform have first developed and then become entrenched (Whiteside 2020). Such a perspective enables understanding of the neoliberalist mindset and how it led to the transformation of public infrastructure through the use of private finance into financial assets delivering returns to investors. The use of the term 'neoliberalism' as a reference point indicates that much research on financialization therefore falls naturally into what can be classed as critical research (Chiapello 2017). However, Ioannou and Wójcik (2019) helpfully note that financialization is not driven by any specific theory, and instead show that their diagram can be used to contrast alternative theories in terms of their reach and depth across the three boxes.

As well as being open to analysis from many different theoretical perspectives, the field of financialization is open to study at many different levels: macro – for example, at market level (across national/international funds); meso level, by studying at the fund level – for example, through interviews; and also at micro level (individual project/group of projects). At the broad level of neoliberal public sector reform, Chiapello (2017) calls for more detailed critical research into the impact of processes like financialization on practical economic life, and Steccolini et al. (2020) call for more interdisciplinary work between accounting and public administration scholars. Suitable research methods can include conceptual articles; case studies incorporating documentary analysis, interviews and surveys; the use of large-scale datasets; and the many other research methods emphasized in Chapter 3 of this book.

Ioannou and Wójcik's (2019) third box identifies a number of implications arising out of the structural processes and contemporary changes stated in the two left-hand boxes. Within this broad spectrum we next identify some of the implications relating to financialization and PPPs through four short case studies. In the following, our illustrative cases start at the macro level with an examination of asset-backed securitization processes and the growth of markets/secondary markets. This first case illustrates how financialization of PPP projects emerges and continues in a dynamic manner. The second and third cases explore the meso-level impacts of financialization on two PPP road projects in Portugal, setting out the contradictory nature of financialization in practice. Case 4 concerns a micro-level analysis highlighting the preferential role of a financial shareholder in the delivery of a health PPP project in England.

Case 1: macro level – developing secondary markets

In the UK context, the PFI policy idea was driven by the 'desire to privatize elements of the public sector that were not readily amenable for direct sale (such as public infrastructure in sensitive or potentially unprofitable areas) on the heels of selling all that could be easily shed in the 1980s' (Whiteside 2020, 888–889). In the process a primary market was established in public infrastructure projects with a series of related markets in consultancy and advice regarding finance, legal contracts and managing the new PFI arrangements.

The past three decades have seen a growth in financial markets' deregulation and globalization (see *Contemporary changes* in Ioannou and Wójcik's (2019) analytical spectrum). These processes have set the conditions to allow the financialization of PPPs to gather pace. Two examples illustrate these financialization processes in the broad arena of PPPs. First, in the classic UK form of PPP projects to deliver public infrastructure (such as schools, hospitals, and so on), a secondary market in equity transactions has emerged, growing from the first transactions in the late 1990s (Smyth and Whitfield 2017, Whitfield and Smyth 2019).

Initially these secondary market transactions represented capital recycling by, and among, the primary private sector partners, but since 2008 there has been a substantial growth of infrastructure investment funds in this market (Whitfield and Smyth 2019). It is estimated that there were a total 'of 462 transactions between 1998 and 2016 … an estimate of the total value of this market is £10.6 billion' (Whitfield and Smyth 2019, 299). However, by 2012 Whitfield (2012) was able to report that 75 per cent of the transactions in this market involved infrastructure investment funds.

It should be noted that such funds do not bring additional resource to the PPP projects; they simply seek long-term stable profits from an already established and operating project.

Second, a similar process is now evident in the renewable energy industry. The development of this industry does not employ the formalized PPP model such as is evident with the secondary equity market. However, it does fall within the broader view of public–private working where the government plays a central role in stimulating the private sector to invest in renewable energy projects. Such projects will ultimately deliver power for commercial and private home use, and are key to achieving carbon emission reductions and climate change targets.

Finance capital is continuing to find its way to investment funds, in this case for renewable energy, searching out profitable returns.

> For example, in 2019 Aquila Capital acquired two onshore wind parks in Finland with 53 MW capacity; a 400 MW wind farm in Norway, one of Europe's largest wind farms; a portfolio of rights to 400 MW onshore wind projects and 300 MW of solar projects in Spain; and ended the year with a strategic partnership with Daiwa Energy and Infrastructure (Daiwa Securities Group Inc). (Whitfield 2020, 15)

These examples highlight the increased role of finance capital, operating through investment funds, seeking out returns through investment in different PPP forms – equity sales and renewable energy projects. On a macro level these funds are an expression of the 'wall of money' concept where there is an over-accumulation of capital seeking investment opportunities, in the global capitalist system. The next chapter, on pension funds and PPPs, highlights an aspect related to the growth of infrastructure investment funds.

At this stage, there are two noteworthy points – first, the above examples highlight that financialization is not just expressed in the form of debt ('interest-bearing capital' as Bayliss et al. (2017) state). The growth of the PPP equity market highlights that financialization is more than just the form of the financial instrument. Second, with the continued growth of imbalances in the global economic system (Ioannou and Wójcik 2019) the future is likely to see more and larger infrastructure investment funds seeking out projects. This activity will continue to be encouraged by governments but if the UK's path continues to set the precedent, there will be a move away from the classic PPP-style partnership relations to an outright reliance on the private sector to deliver, maintain and manage public infrastructure.

It should be clear that, unless there are strong and committed policies adopted by government to the contrary, financialization of PPP projects will continue for the foreseeable future.

Case 2: meso level – mediating finance providers

This case shows how financialization has permeated PPPs, not only through secondary market transactions, but also through investment funds' direct investment in SPVs from the start of the PPP project. The investment funds' goal is to maximize the rate of return they can extract from the project. The case draws on wider research (Almeida 2019) to compare two private consortia (named Consortium A and Consortium B) set up to deliver Portuguese road PPP projects. The two consortia are comparable except for the shareholder structure. For both consortia, shareholders include construction companies and an operator. In addition, Consortium A has a financial shareholder, an infrastructure investment fund specializing in road PPPs, which is a subsidiary of a global infrastructure company. Its strategy is to acquire an active investor position at the beginning of the projects, assuming the risks associated with the earlier years of the investment, giving it a medium-term horizon on its investments. Unlike all the other shareholders, the financial shareholder is not a service provider to the SPV.

The case focuses on the period of renegotiation of the PPP contract, after Portugal's 2011 bailout.[4] The renegotiations aimed to reduce costs through the scope of the contract, investment and the shareholders' internal rate of return (IRR), this last point being of key interest to our aim of understanding how financialization has penetrated to the PPP project level. The period of renegotiation enabled researchers to study how the two consortia each responded to the proposed contract changes.

Consortium A's response to the renegotiation was led by the financial shareholder focus on the financial sustainability of the SPV as a whole. While financial sustainability was also important in Consortium B, the construction shareholders came together in a dominant position with the main goal of preserving the financial sustainability of the construction work. However, their focus on the short term meant they were willing to sacrifice their long-term returns during the renegotiation. This later led to the PPP contract's termination, due to its financial unsustainability.

The comparison highlights the key role of the financial shareholder in driving the long-term financial perspective, as its main goal is the financial return. The position of the financier in the SPV, with its focus on maximizing the return of the SPV, brings in a balance between the competing positions of the constructor and operator which are also subcontractors of the SPV. As subcontractors, the construction and operating shareholders' desire for profit maximization means that they might favour taking their profit as subcontractors, rather than taking profit in the SPV (where they would share the profit with the remaining shareholders). As such, the financial shareholders tend to play an important mediating role in the management of the SPV and its different shareholders. They are likely to try to prevent and resolve conflicts of interest between and opportunistic behaviour by the construction and operator shareholders. In this example the financial shareholder of Consortium A focused on maximizing the financial returns of the project, through managing the SPV in order to ensure that the returns from the project are kept within the SPV and do not pass through to the service providers in the SPV. This might contribute to a better long-term financial performance of the SPV.

Case 3: meso level – capital recycling

To highlight the link between the development of a secondary market in PPP equity transactions and the role of financial partners in operating projects, this case examines a further set of events in our Portuguese example. Despite the interest from construction shareholders of Consortium B in holding a long-term position in the PPP project due to its potential stable returns, they faced external pressures from the financing banks to disinvest in the PPP projects. This pressure came after Portugal asked for financial assistance from the EU in 2011, and the financing banks started forcing construction companies to divest high-debt projects, such as PPPs, in order to reduce their debt ratio. The fragile financial situation of the construction companies was aggravated by their overseas investments in countries such as Angola, Algeria and Venezuela, which were themselves facing political and economic crisis. In addition, the increased presence of investment and pension funds in the secondary market of Portuguese PPPs brought additional pressures for construction companies to disinvest. The quote below from an administrator exemplifies these various pressures faced by construction companies in Consortium B:

> The goal is the construction – it is not to be concessionaires. What happened in the past is that most of these construction companies had the prospect of turning into concessionaires, but at this point this may not be possible because they have issued debt. And banks, especially in the Portuguese system, want companies to reduce financing as much as possible. So they want construction companies to sell, at any price, and that is the other negative part, because there are concessionaires that have an attractive profitability, even for construction companies who could cope with it. But the banks do not want them to. What they want at the moment is to reduce liabilities, regardless of whether this is a big loss for the company in the future. This is a little irrelevant to them. They have a short-term objective. I understand what is happening with the Portuguese banks at the moment. They have to meet the ratios otherwise they have penalties.

This case exemplifies how external pressures (financing banks' risk management) add to the existing urge from institutional investors to facilitate the growth of the PPP secondary market and capital recycling.

Case 4: micro level – local health PPPs in England

Our final example relates to the impact of financialization on public policy via the privileging of the equity financier in small local health PPPs. These projects have been set up, particularly in deprived socio-economic areas, as joint ventures between local and national health and government organizations and private sector partners to deliver a range of small-scale primary health care facilities. In one example studied (Agyenim-Boateng et al. 2017, 2020), the private partner, owning 60 per cent of the equity, is a wholly owned subsidiary of a holding company, itself a multinational organization, which is in turn owned by a large international construction company and a major bank, both big players in their respective business sectors. The construction company has a history in the construction of large public projects that can be traced back over 150 years. The wholly owned bank subsidiary specialises in infrastructure investments. Of the remaining 40 per cent of equity, 20 per cent is owned by the national organization Community Health Partnerships and the remaining 20 per cent shared between three local health trusts and three local government bodies.

The following three points demonstrate how a focus on the concept of financialization can play out in this project setting. First, government policy (via the UK Department of Health) was set up to privilege the financial capital invested in the project. The private partner had the dominant voting power and therefore controlled the joint venture board working practice. One public sector director commented: 'The power dynamic from the Board really comes from the private partners … I do not consider this as an equal relationship.' The multinational corporate culture that fed down to the private sector directors on the joint venture board led to a feeling of domination and mistrust. One public sector director described the relationship as 'anti-partnership' and 'very commercially focused'.

Second, the Shareholder Agreement makes it clear that the joint venture vehicle is to be managed in a way which will deliver sustainable profits for the shareholders. Institutional investors are thus privileged over the wider range of stakeholders who may benefit from this public health initiative.

Third, the joint venture is required to take the form of a limited liability company, thus legitimating a company structure that must behave as an equity capital-driven entity for economic stewardship purposes. A public sector director explained that these joint ventures were established as companies limited by shares precisely so that they *could* behave as companies limited by shares. As the private partner has control, the private partner directors can control decision-making and monitoring when the project has become operational. In this example, they also use the limited company status of the joint venture to reduce scrutiny and to restrict interactions to their shareholders (the multinational holdings company and its owners) only, and not the public.

Overall, the evidence shows how in this example the policy was deliberately implemented in a way that ensured decision-making and control would be dominated by the financier. The importance of protecting the profit-making capability of the joint venture is assured through the organization structure and the use of the limited liability vehicle.

Discussion and summary

Where Broadbent and Laughlin (2004) could describe PPPs as the latest expression of NPM, nearly 20 years later it is another long-term structural process, financialization, that is increasingly exerting influence on the nature and operation of PPPs. Financialization, as noted by Christophers (2015), is part of the same political and cultural shift in contemporary capitalism as neo-liberalization, but it has remained below the level of visibility in the PPP literature for many years. Yet, almost implicitly, the PPP literature contains various elements of a financialization framing; in this chapter we have sought to bring these elements together using the financialization spectrum of Ioannou and Wójcik (2019) as an organizing mechanism. In the process we address the question, set out at the start of the chapter, of financialization's examination to date in the PPP literature.

In response to our first question at the start of this chapter, we have shown how financialization, in the form of finance logics, was embedded in PFI (and later PPP) from the policy's very inception. Further, financialization, as a concept that captures the changing nature of the global economy, has helped us highlight the growth of infrastructure investment funds and the development of a market in renewable energy and a secondary market in PPP equity.

A financialization lens applied at a meso level has helped us highlight and understand how macro-changes in the global economy can manifest themselves within countries and their PPP projects. These meso-level cases also highlight the contradictory impacts of financialization processes. For example, the growth of a secondary PPP equity market has been welcomed by some authorities as it allows primary private sector partners to disinvest from projects and recycle their capital stakes (Smyth and Whitfield 2017).

This activity creates short-term incentives for primary partners to maximize their short-term returns and then exit the project. In contrast, Case 2 illustrates that where the financial partner is a subsidiary of a large global infrastructure company, it may then have an interest in long-term stable returns such that it acts to mediate the instability created by the other primary partners' financialized activity.

Yet on the other hand, the actions of a different part of the finance system are illustrated in Case 3, where financial institutions are exerting their power to pressure primary partners into deleveraging. One of the easiest ways to do this is by construction firms disposing of their equity stake in PPP projects through the secondary market.

Finally, our last case highlights the impact of financialization at a micro level, where from the initiation of the project concept through to its operation the finance provider has been preferred – from government policy requirements to the shareholders' agreement to the use of the limited liability company form. The four cases illustrate the various ways in which financialization has impacted the operation of PPP projects at different economic levels, and in the process address our third research question.

Based on the above discussion and drawing further on ideas about financialization from earlier, we conclude this chapter by addressing our final initial question and outlining a research agenda that could be pursued on the financialization of PPP projects; part of this agenda illustrates why financialization is an enduring trend for the future of PPP operation and research.

Given the global infrastructure financing gap of an estimated $15 trillion by 2040 (Global Infrastructure Hub 2017) referred to earlier, there is a significant need to understand where that additional private capital may come from. Case 1 provided some evidence both about how the secondary market is working in the UK and how infrastructure investment funds are seeking out projects. There is scope for further research into the role of secondary markets and the impact of capital recycling – what is the extent of recycling that is taking place; what are the motivations for equity disposals; and, in light of Hodge and Greve's (2019, 108) comment in relation to Australian PPPs, 'we simply do not know what the average rate of return is for private investments', is excessive profit-taking occurring (NAO 2012, Smyth and Whitfield 2017)?

Relatedly, financialization is leading to an increased number of PPP projects being majority or wholly owned/controlled by infrastructure investment funds. The implication of this tendency needs to be explored and researched – what are the implications for ongoing performance of projects; how active are the investment funds in managing the PPP operations; what are the likely impacts once the PPP projects' terms start to come to an end? Renewable energy is a developing area where infrastructure investment funds are increasingly being used. As yet we have little understanding of the breadth and depth of private sector involvement in this global industry where public grants have been widely available for private sector use.

At the same time, we are now reaching the point where early PPP projects are maturing – for example, the Australian M4 Motorway (Chung 2016) – or being bought out; for example, the UK's Hexham hospital (Hellowell 2015). There is scope to carry out full project life-cycle studies, examining total returns over the project life and also investigating how capital investment is then recycled.

The growth of secondary markets and capital recycling does not necessarily or directly lead to extra finance being available to fill the global infrastructure funding gap, as they are transactions based on existing and established projects. Given that governments increasingly seek private finance to meet the infrastructure finance gap, regulation is another area of increasing relevance. Evidence to date highlights that this has been done through largely unregulated markets, but the UN SDGs call for improved regulation of the global financial markets and institutions (UN SDG 10, Reduced Inequalities – target 5). This leads us to ask more broadly whether the UN SDGs will reduce or intensify financialization processes.

There is increasing focus on responsible investing with environmental, social and governance (ESG) factors now becoming part of many large investment funds' requirements for investment. How are ESG factors being combined into financialized requirements for PPPs? PPPs, by their very nature of delivering the public goods and services needed for everyday public life, incorporate many ESG aspects. How are these measured and reported in practice? How are conflicts of interest, for example, in relation to legitimation of profit extraction, negotiated?

A related area of research is the use of corporate bonds. Two recent studies of UK social housing highlighted the impact of the shift from public sector funding to private sector financing via the bond market (Smyth et al. 2020, Wainwright and Manville 2017). They showed how key players in the field internalized global capital market requirements, thus deepening the processes of financialization in social housing provision. These housing providers are hybrid organizations – socially hearted, commercially minded. Will engaging in the bond markets, and all the related requirements (for example, securing credit ratings), inevitably accentuate the commercial mind, leading to the social mission being eclipsed? If the answer to this question is affirmative, what implications does that have for the people who live in social housing and the housing system more generally?

The processes of financialization are dynamic and are pushing policy makers to innovate ways to fund public service delivery. A recent example is the growth of social impact bonds (SIBs) in the UK (Cooper et al. 2016, Edmiston and Nicholls 2018, Fraser et al. 2018). They originated with a group of socially motivated financiers in the City of London who sought to apply their skills and knowledge of financial logics to addressing social problems, such as rough sleeping, homelessness and recidivism in the justice system. Strictly speaking, SIBs in the UK context are a form of payment by results (PbR), rather than a financial bond. However, SIBs are premised on the same financial logics that drive financialization when financial capital is involved.

Advocates of the SIB policy claim benefits including innovation in service delivery, improved social outcomes and future cost savings. However, as the policy is at such an early stage (the first SIB in the UK started in 2011), there is 'very little definitive evidence to suggest that services funded through such a mechanism lead to any relative improvement in social outcomes compared to more conventional PbR commissioning models' (Edmiston and Nicholls 2018, 73). Further, in a conclusion very familiar to PPP scholars, Fraser et al. (2018, 16) state: 'There is a need for careful ex ante consideration of the complex balance of risks, drawbacks and benefits in each case, and far more empirical studies ex post.'

The Covid-19 pandemic has seen huge disruption to public life, with a disproportionate impact on different sectors of infrastructure; for example, airports compared to hospitals. How are the changes in revenue streams and costs, mediated by financialization, affecting the various stakeholders, and what are the likely long-term outcomes? Will there be renegotiation of existing contracts, potentially offering greater flexibility, and to whose benefit? Will there be an impact on how demand and volume risk will be taken account of in new projects, further than that already taken account of in cases such as the UK's PF2, where the government takes more risk in return for some equity share (Hellowell 2013)?

Financialization, as we have indicated, provides the opportunity for governments to lead us further down the path to full provision of both infrastructure and related services by the private sector. Is there evidence of the examples already seen in some healthcare provision (Acerete et al. 2012) extending to more countries and to more areas of healthcare? Updates on the impact of marketization and financialization shown by studies such as Newberry and Brennan (2013) on Australian childcare provision and Burns et al. (2016) on UK residential care homes are needed to provide evidence on trends in these and similar areas of public service provision.

Hodge and Greve (2018) report on the emphasis that supra-national bodies (the Organisation for Economic Co-operation and Development, Association of Southeast Asian Nations, International Monetary Fund and World Bank) are placing on PPPs as the mechanism to deliver public infrastructure across the globe, in both developing and developed economies. A global analytical perspective on PPPs will also be enhanced by a financialization lens; as we have shown earlier, it is the deregulation and globalization of financial markets that has aided the development of infrastructure investment funds.

Moving beyond global public infrastructure needs there is another (maybe even, the final) frontier that PPPs have started to operate in: space. Where previously space travel and exploration was carried out almost exclusively by governmental agencies, the emergence of SpaceX over the past two decades has enabled a broad PPP to develop. To the start of 2021 SpaceX has flown 21 resupply journeys to the International Space Station. SpaceX is also in the process of building (potentially) key public infrastructure through its Starlink satellite-based internet network.

In 2020, SpaceX raised $2 bn in funding with a further $750 m raised in February 2021. It is difficult to tell the source of these funds as SpaceX remains in private ownership. However, two smaller satellite-launching companies, Rocket Lab and Astra, both went public in 2021. A financialization lens on PPPs allows us to ask: what are the implications of finance capital driving space exploration? What are the motivations/expectations for space investment and how do they differ from those investing in public infrastructure on the planet? Does there need to be greater regulation of space-based activities (it is estimated that 38,000 satellites will be built and launched in the next decade)? And, if such finance is available, at a time when there is a yawning gap in funding infrastructure on the planet, is this the most appropriate or ethical use of the money?

Conclusion

Through this chapter we have argued that a financialization lens can help us understand the nature and evolution of PPP as a macro-policy and a micro-practice. We argued that financial logics were embedded in PPPs from the origination of the policy, and the de-regulation and globalization of the financial markets has enabled the growth of infrastructure investment funds. These funds are now major investors in already established and operating PPP projects.

We also think it noteworthy that the study of PPP projects and public infrastructure investment can contribute to a better understanding of how financialization processes operate in practice. Understanding financialization as (in part) a process of embedding financial logics, the form that this takes can be multiple. For example, our insight that financialization is not dependent upon the form of financial instrument (that is, interest-bearing capital) but can also embody the equity form in the form of investment fund activity. In this respect, public infrastructure is not just an investment for finance capital but also a destination for speculative – fictitious (Cooper, 2015) – equity capital.

Finally, unless there is a sudden, dramatic change in global infrastructure procurement policy, both PPPs as a delivery mechanism and the financialization of the policy/mechanism are going to continue for the foreseeable future. This makes their study an ongoing and evolving priority for a range of multidisciplinary scholars.

Notes

1.   Often this is a shell company with no employees, which minimizes its risk through a complex web of sub-contracting (Edwards et al. 2004).
2.   The external pressure to disinvest tends to vary inversely with the state of the construction market.
3.   For example, *Economy and Society*; *Competition & Change*; the *International Journal of Political Economy*; *New Political Economy*; *Review of International Political Economy*; the *Accounting, Auditing & Accountability Journal*; *Critical Perspectives on Accounting*.
4.   In 2011, in order to cope with the impact of the Global Financial Crisis, Portugal received a three-year bailout of €78 billion from the European Commission, European Central Bank and International Monetary Fund.

References

Aaronovitch, S. (1961) *The Ruling Class: A Study of British Finance Capital*. London: Camelot Press.
Acerete, B., Stafford, A., and Stapleton, P. (2012) New development: new global health care PPP developments – a critique of the success story. *Public Money & Management*, 32 (4): 311–314.
Agyenim-Boateng, C., Stafford, A., and Stapleton, P. (2017) The role of structure in manipulating PPP accountability. *Accounting, Auditing & Accountability Journal*, 30 (1): 119–144.

Agyenim-Boateng, C., Stafford, A., and Stapleton, P. (2020) Does the United Kingdom's Local Improvement Finance Trust (LIFT) scheme for primary health care enhance partnership working? *Public Works Management & Policy, 25* (3): 231–243.

Almeida, M. (2019) *Examining Portuguese Road Public Private Partnerships through the Lenses of Institutional Logics and Trust*, unpublished PhD thesis, University of Manchester.

Andersson, T., Lee, E., Theodosopoulos, G., Yin, Y.P., and Haslam, C. (2014) Accounting for the financialized UK and US national business model. *Critical Perspectives on Accounting, 25* (1): 78–91.

Andon, P. (2012) Accounting-related research in PPPs/PFIs: present contributions and future opportunities. *Accounting, Auditing & Accountability Journal, 25* (5): 876–924.

Arrighi, G. (1994) *The Long Twentieth Century: Money, Power, and the Origins of Our Times*. London: Verso.

Asenova, D., and Beck, M. (2010) Crucial silences: when accountability met PFI and finance capital. *Critical Perspectives on Accounting, 21* (1): 1–13.

Bayliss, K., Fine, B., and Robertson, M. (2017) Introduction to special issue on the material cultures of financialisation. *New Political Economy, 22* (4): 355–370.

BlackRock (2015) Infrastructure rising: an asset class takes shape. www.laforum.co.uk/download-manager/download-white-paper/220/ (accessed: 12 March 2021).

Broadbent, J., and Laughlin, R. (2004) PPPs: nature, development and unanswered questions. *Australian Accounting Review, 14* (2): 4–10.

Burke, R., and Demirag, I. (2019) Risk management by SPV partners in toll road public private partnerships. *Public Management Review, 21* (5): 711–731.

Burns, D., Cowie, L., Earle, J., Folkman, P., Froud, J., Hyde, P., Johal, S., Jones, I.R., Killett, A., and Williams, K. (2016) Where does the money go? Financialised chains and the crisis in residential care. CRESC Public Interest Report.

Chiapello, E. (2017) Critical accounting research and neoliberalism. *Critical Perspectives on Accounting, 43* (C): 47–64.

Christophers, B. (2015) The limits to financialization. *Dialogues in Human Geography, 5* (2): 183–200.

Chung, D. (2016) Risks, challenges and value for money of public–private partnerships. *Financial Accountability & Management, 32* (4): 448–468.

Cooper, C. (2015) Accounting for the fictitious: a Marxist contribution to understanding accounting's role in the financial crisis. *Critical Perspectives on Accounting, 30* (2015): 63–82.

Cooper, C., Graham, C., and Himick, D. (2016) Social impact bonds: the securitization of the homeless. *Accounting Organizations and Society, 55* (C): 63–82.

Cooper, C., and Taylor, P. (2005) Independently verified reductionism: prison privatization in Scotland. *Human Relations, 58* (4): 497–522.

Demirag, I., Khadaroo, I., Stapleton, P., and Stevenson, C. (2010) *Public Private Partnership Financiers' Perceptions of Risks*. Edinburgh: Institute of Chartered Accountants of Scotland.

Edgar, V.C., Beck, M., and Brennan, N.M. (2018) Impression management in annual report narratives: the case of the UK Private Finance Initiative. *Accounting, Auditing & Accountability Journal, 31* (6): 1566–1592.

Edmiston, D., and Nicholls, A. (2018) Social impact bonds: the role of private capital in outcome-based commissioning. *Journal of Social Policy, 47* (1): 57–76.

Edwards, P., Shaoul, J., Stafford, A., and Arblaster, L. (2004) *Evaluating the Operation of PFI in Road and Hospital Projects* (ACCA Research Report No. 84). Association

of Chartered Certified Accountants (ACCA). http://image.guardian.co.uk/sys-files/
Society/documents/2004/11/24/PFI.pdf (accessed: 12 March 2021).

Fine, B. (2010) Locating financialisation. *Historical Materialism*, *18* (2): 97–116.

Fraser, A., Tan, S., Lagarde, M., and Mays, N. (2018) Narratives of promise, narratives of caution: a review of the literature on social impact bonds. *Social Policy & Administration*, *52* (1): 4–28.

Froud, J. (2003) The Private Finance Initiative: risk, uncertainty and the state. *Accounting, Organizations and Society*, *28* (6): 567–589.

Froud, J., Haslam, C., Johal, S., and Williams, K. (2000) Shareholder value and financialization: consultancy promises, management moves. *Economy and Society*, *29* (1): 80–110.

Glasberg, D. (1987) Finance capital markets and corporate decision-making process: the case of W.T. Grant Company bankruptcy, *Sociological Forum*, *2* (2): 305–330.

Global Infrastructure Hub (2017) Global Infrastructure Outlook. https://cdn.gihub.org/umbraco/media/1529/global-infrastructure-outlook-24-july-2017.pdf (accessed: 14 March 2021).

Global Infrastructure Hub (2020) Infrastructure Monitor 2020: Data-Driven Insights Into Selected G20 Infrastructure Priorities. https://cdn.gihub.org/umbraco/media/3241/gih_monitorreport_final.pdf.

Harvey, D. (2005) *A Brief History of Neoliberalism*. Oxford: Oxford University Press.

Hellowell, M. (2013) PFI redux? Assessing a new model for financing hospitals. *Health Policy*, *113* (1–2): 77–85.

Hellowell, M. (2015) Borrowing to save: can NHS bodies ease financial pressures by terminating PFI contracts? *British Medical Journal*, August, *351*: h4030. https://doi.org/10.1136/bmj.h4030.

Hellowell, M., and Vecchi, V. (2012) An evaluation of the projected returns to investors on 10 PFI projects commissioned by the National Health Service. *Financial Accountability & Management*, *28* (1): 77–100.

Hilferding, R. (1981) *Finance Capital: A Study of the Latest Phase of Capitalist Development*. London: Routledge and Kegan Paul [First published in 1910 as *Das Finanzkapital* in Vienna].

Hodge, G., and Greve, C. (2018) Contemporary public–private partnership: towards a global research agenda. *Financial Accountability & Management*, *34* (1): 3–16.

Hodge, G., and Greve, C. (2019) *The Logic of Public–Private Partnerships: The Enduring Interdependency of Politics and Markets*. Cheltenham, UK and Northampton, MA, USA: Edward Elgar Publishing.

Hodge, G.A. (2002) Who steers the state when governments sign public-private partnerships? *Journal of Contemporary Issues in Business and Government*, *8* (1): 5–18.

Ioannou, S., and Wójcik, D. (2019) On financialization and its future. *Environment and Planning A: Economy and Space*, *51* (1): 263–271.

Kelly, J. (2017) Global assets under management hit all-time high above $80 trillion. Reuters. www.reuters.com/article/us-global-funds-aum-idUSKBN1CZ11B (accessed: 1 June 2021).

Krippner, G. (2005) The financialization of the American economy. *Socio-Economic Review*, *3* (2): 173–208.

Lapsley, I., and Miller, P. (2019) Transforming the public sector: 1998–2018. *Accounting, Auditing & Accountability Journal*, *32* (8): 2211–2252.

McKinsey Global Institute (2017) Bridging infrastructure gaps: has the world made progress? www.mckinsey.com/business-functions/operations/our-insights/bridging-infrastructure-gaps-has-the-world-made-progress (accessed: 1 June 2021).

McKinsey Global Institute (2018) *A Decade After The Global Financial Crisis: What Has (And Hasn't) Changed?* www.mckinsey.com/~/media/mckinsey/industries/financial%20services/our%20insights/a%20decade%20after%20the%20global%20financial%20crisis%20what%20has%20and%20hasnt%20changed/mgi-briefing-a-decade-after-the-global-financial-crisis-what-has-and-hasnt-changed.pdf? (accessed: 18 March 2021).

NAO (National Audit Office) (2012) *Equity Investment in Privately Financed Projects: HC 1792 Session 2010-2012.* London: Stationery Office.

NAO (National Audit Office) (2018) *PFI and PF2: HC 718 Session 2017-2019.* London: Stationery Office.

Newberry, S. (2004) Trade in services: wider implications for accounting standard-setters and accountants. *Australian Accounting Review, 14* (33): 11–21.

Newberry, S., and Brennan, D. (2013) The marketisation of early childhood education and care (ECEC) in Australia: a structured response. *Financial Accountability & Management, 29* (3): 227–245.

Newberry, S., and Pallot, J. (2003) Fiscal (ir)responsibility: privileging PPPs in New Zealand. *Accounting, Auditing & Accountability Journal, 16* (3): 467–492.

O'Brien, P., and Pike, A. (2017) The financialization and governance of infrastructure, in *Handbook on the Geographies of Money and Finance,* edited by R. Martin and J. Pollard. Cheltenham, UK and Northampton, MA, USA: Edward Elgar Publishing.

Peda, P., and Vinnari, E. (2020) The discursive legitimation of profit in public-private service delivery. *Critical Perspectives on Accounting, 69*: 102088.

Pike, A., and Pollard, J. (2010) Economic geographies of financialization. *Economic Geography, 86* (1): 29–51.

PwC (n.d.) *Capital Project and Infrastructure Spending: Outlook to 2025.* www.pwc.com/my/en/assets/publications/cpi-spending-outlook-to-2025.pdf (accessed: 12 March 2021).

Reay, T., and Hinings, C.R. (2009) Managing the rivalry of competing institutional logics. *Organization Studies, 30* (6): 629–652.

Shaoul, J. (2005) A critical financial analysis of the Private Finance Initiative: selecting a financing method or allocating economic wealth? *Critical Perspectives on Accounting, 16* (4): 441–471.

Shaoul, J., Stafford, A., and Stapleton, P. (2007) Partnerships and the role of financial advisors: private control over public policy? *Policy and Politics, 35* (3): 479–495.

Shaoul, J., Stafford, A., and Stapleton, P. (2012) The fantasy world of private finance for transport via public private partnerships. International Transport Forum Discussion Paper.

Siemiatycki, M. (2015) Canadian pension fund investors in transport infrastructure: a case study. *Case Studies on Transport Policy, 3* (2): 166–175.

Skelcher, C., and Smith, S.R. (2015) Theorizing hybridity: institutional logics, complex organizations, and actor identities – the case of nonprofits. *Public Administration, 93* (2): 433–448.

Smyth, S., Cole, I., and Fields, D. (2020) From gatekeepers to gateway constructors: credit rating agencies and the financialisation of housing associations. *Critical Perspectives on Accounting, 71*: 102093.

Smyth, S., and Whitfield, D. (2017) Maintaining market principles: government auditors, PPP equity sales and hegemony. *Accounting Forum, 41* (1): 44–56.

Steccolini, I., Saliterer, I., and Guthrie, J. (2020) The role(s) of accounting and performance measurement systems in contemporary public administration. *Public Administration, 98* (1): 3–13.

Stockhammer, E. (2004) Financialisation and the slowdown of accumulation. *Cambridge Journal of Economics, 28* (5): 719–741.

Toms, S., Beck, M., and Asenova, D. (2011) Accounting, regulation and profitability: the case of PFI hospital refinancing. *Critical Perspectives on Accounting, 22* (7): 668–681.

Wainwright, T., and Manville, G. (2017) Financialization and the third sector: innovation in social housing bond markets. *Environment and Planning A, 49* (4): 819–838.

Weber, B., Staub-Bisang, M., and Alfen, H.W. (2016) *Infrastructure as an Asset Class: Investment Strategy, Sustainability, Project Finance and PPP.* Chichester: Wiley.

Whiteside, H. (2020) Public-private partnerships: market development through management reform. *Review of International Political Economy, 27* (4): 880–902.

Whitfield, D. (2012) *PPP Wealth Machine: UK and Global Trends in Trading Project Ownership.* European Services Strategy Unit Research Report No. 6. www.european-services-strategy.org.uk/wp-content/uploads/2012/11/PPP-Equity-Report-Final-full-4.pdf (accessed: 18 March 2021).

Whitfield, D. (2020) *Equitable Recovery Strategies.* European Services Strategy Unit Research Report No.11. www.european-services-strategy.org.uk/wp-content/uploads/2020/07/Equitable-Recovery-Strategies.pdf (accessed: 18 March 2021).

Whitfield, D., and Smyth, S. (2019) Infrastructure Investment: the emergent PPP equity market. *Annals of Public and Cooperative Economics, 90* (2): 291–309.

12 Great expectations for pension funds: a tale of two cities[1]

Richard Foster and Graeme A. Hodge

Introduction

Insurance companies, pension funds, sovereign wealth funds, endowments and foundations all have the ability to make long-term and intergenerational investments (Clark et al. *c*.2011). They are an important source of long-term capital, and global pension funds stood at around USD 50.9 trillion in 2019 (OECD 2020, 7). At the same time, governments have increasingly been subject to greater constraints in their ability to increase their own public borrowing to finance public infrastructure works such as roads, hospitals and schools. In this context, there has long been a general interest in encouraging institutional investors such as pension funds to play a greater active role in the provision of public infrastructure.

Such calls have come from several quarters. Many governments, for example, have expressed a desire for pension funds to increase their role in supporting public infrastructure. Australia's Treasurer, the Hon Josh Frydenberg, was quoted as saying recently that superannuation (as pensions are commonly known in Australia) was a 'massive pool in savings that should be harnessed more for domestic investment'. Moreover, his view was 'I don't care if they are industry funds or retail funds, I would like to see them both put to work on domestic infrastructure assets more than they have been' (Duke 2020). Interestingly, this statement from the current Morrison Liberal/National coalition government was an echo of a statement made almost a decade previously by the then Labor government's Minister for Infrastructure the Hon Anthony Albanese, when he said:

> there is a natural fit in terms of the long-term nature of those superannuation investments and the long-term nature of infrastructure investment ... Super funds themselves are telling us that when they talk to their superannuants ... they are very

keen to see their funds invested here in nation-building, rather than overseas, or perhaps in equity markets.

Media commentators such as Hilton (2012) argued similarly that to solve the UK's pension problem, funds ought to be both amalgamated and invested in infrastructure. He commented that:

> pension funds have billions of pounds earning next to nothing in government bonds – actually, after inflation, most of it is losing money. Meanwhile, the Treasury estimates that Britain needs [£]30 billion a year of new infrastructure investment for the next 20 years. The answer is obvious: mobilise the pension fund money.

Pension fund industry leaders have also called for an expanded role for pension funds. Dunn (2019), for instance, reports Garry Weaven, founder and former chairman of IFM Investors, and widely considered one of the architects of Australia's superannuation system, as saying that 'there is definitely a role for super funds in nation-building'. Furthermore, Weaven commented that 'Australia should be able to "mutualise" its infrastructure needs, by more directly linking our world class super system to our need for nation-building infrastructure – economic, social and environmental.' In other words, he saw nation-building projects as a huge opportunity for Australian governments and companies to collaborate with the superannuation industry to invest in Australia, 'not only to generate strong investment returns, but to achieve sustainable social, environmental and industry policy objectives' (Dunn 2019).

To date, however, there has only been limited success in mobilising growing pools of pension funds to meet increasing infrastructure needs. This chapter investigates the relationship between pension funds and public–private partnerships (PPPs). It articulates the various regulatory and policy frameworks influencing both and examines both barriers preventing closer ties and incentives encouraging increased investments from this source. Empirical case studies are then presented from different democracies to illustrate the contemporary roles played by pension fund investments in PPPs. The argument made in this chapter is that, while significant pension fund investment in PPPs is already taking place, the evidence is unclear on whether there are strong barriers to greater pension fund investment in PPPs and whether, in any case, encouraging increased infrastructure investments by pension funds is a desirable public policy outcome for citizens. If the case can be made that reforms to promote greater pension fund investment in PPPs are desirable, these reforms may be oriented towards pension funds (to loosen regulatory mechanisms and enable wider investment possibilities, or else increase the capacity of pension institutions to make such investment decisions), or towards PPP policy reforms (in order to attract pension fund investments in public infrastructure). Potential viable options encompass a significant breadth of reform and several layers of complexity, however. These complex interacting frameworks constrain pension fund investment in PPPs and are jurisdictionally contingent, thus making the identification of generalised reform-oriented solutions difficult. In this context, several avenues for future research are recommended.

The next section of this chapter provides some primary conceptual foundations for our argument. It defines both pension funds and PPPs, articulates why pension funds and PPPs may be attracted to each other, and highlights that pension funds finance infrastructure but do not fund it. The section following this then outlines the expectations of governments, of pension funds themselves and of those calling for reforms. We then focus more on the policy and regulatory frameworks influencing pension fund investments, and draw on case studies from three countries to illustrate these. Last, future research directions are posited.

So, what are pension funds and why might there be a mutual attraction between them and PPPs?

Conceptual foundations

Pension funds

A pension fund provides a regular fixed sum payment (that is, a pension) to a person following their retirement or as compensation for a wage earner's death (Penguin English Dictionary 2004, 1029). There are a wide variety of pension fund arrangements throughout the Organisation for Economic Co-operation and Development (OECD). They can be mandatory or voluntary, linked to an occupation or employment (an occupational pension), or a contract with a private pension provider (personal pension plan). Additionally, pensions are most often achieved through either defined contribution or defined benefit arrangements[2] (OECD 2019, 10). The main type of pension arrangement in most OECD countries is an occupation or employer-based arrangement. These pensions are mostly funded through pension funds, although some exceptions exist, including 'countries such as Denmark, Norway and Sweden where pension insurance contracts play a larger role and Germany where book reserves are the main type of financing vehicle' (OECD 2011, 44).

The geographic spread of pension funds throughout the OECD is revealing, with US pension funds dwarfing those of most other countries around the world. Indeed, the United States holds some 65.4 per cent of the world's pension assets, vastly overshadowing the United Kingdom at 7.3 per cent, Canada at 5.7 per cent and Australia at 3.8 per cent. Figure 12.1 shows the size of pension funds around the OECD in absolute terms.

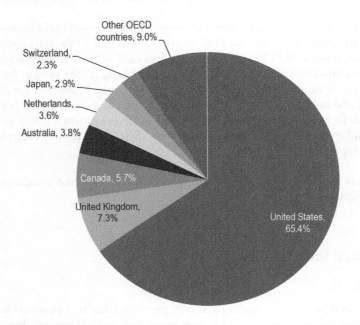

Source: OECD (2020)

Figure 12.1   Geographical distribution of pension assets in the OECD area as at 2019, as a percentage of total pension assets

Aside from absolute wealth measures, another important characteristic is the relative size of a country's pension fund compared to its gross domestic product (GDP). Many countries' pension funds are massive compared to their GDP, as shown in Figure 12.2.

It is evident that several countries hold pension assets larger than their GDP, with countries such as Denmark topping the list at 220 per cent; Canada is at 160 per cent, Australia 138 per cent and the United Kingdom 123 per cent. Figure 12.2 indicates a weighted OECD average pension size in 2019 of 92 per

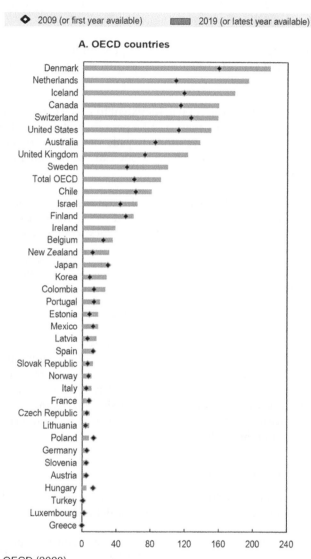

Source: OECD (2020)

Figure 12.2 Total assets in funded and private pension arrangements, in 2009 (or first year available) and 2019 (or latest year available) as a percentage of GDP

cent of GDP.[3] There is clearly a large variation in the relative sizes of pension funds across countries.

Another interesting aspect of OECD country pension funds is the wide variation in the types of assets in which funds are invested. Figure 12.3 indicates this asset spread.

Figure 12.3 shows the huge variation in the extent to which pension funds hold equities (with Poland at one extreme on 82.4 per cent and the Czech Republic at the other, with 1.0 per cent.) A similarly wide variation is found with the holding of bills and bonds (with Mexico at one extreme on 78.7 per cent and Poland at the other, with 8.3 per cent).

Over the past several decades, our public policy interest in pension funds has increased. Pension systems have long combined two components; one public and one private. The OECD (2011, 43) describes these components as follows:

> Public pensions were mandatory, financed on a pay-as-you-go (PAYG) basis, and managed by public sector institutions. Private pensions, on the other hand, were voluntary, employment-based (occupational) pension plans, or individual retirement arrangements (personal pension plans) based on the principle of asset accumulation (funding) or book reserve financing.

The contemporary evolution of pension funds has seen governments increasingly focusing on the capacity for pension schemes to fund themselves through, for example, the establishment of public pension reserve funds to support pay-as-you-go schemes. Governments have also increasingly introduced mandated private pension schemes to assist citizens to save for retirement and to reduce longer-term societal dependence on social security benefits coming directly from the public purse.

Public–private partnerships

We conceptualise a PPP in this chapter as a long-term contract for the provision of public infrastructure. A PPP can then be defined as

> an arrangement between a public authority and a private partner designed to deliver a public infrastructure project and service under a long-term contract. Under this contract, the private partner bears significant risks and management responsibilities. The public authority makes performance payments ... or grants the private partner the right to generate revenues [from] the provision of the service ... Private finance is usually involved in a PPP. (European PPP Expertise Center, quoted in Hodge and Greve 2019, 13)[4]

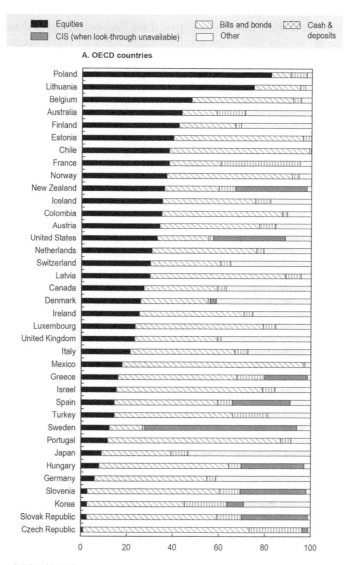

Source: OECD (2020)

Figure 12.3   Allocation of assets in funded and private pension plans in selected asset classes and investment vehicles, 2019 (or latest year available), as a percentage of total investment

The amounts invested in PPPs around the world have been immense. The United Kingdom alone has, over the past three decades, completed some 715 PPP projects[5] with a total capital value of £59.1 billion (HM Treasury and Infrastructure and Projects Authority 2018). In 2017, Canada had 267 PPPs with a total value of CAD 123 billion (Romoff 2017). Australia, too, has been a keen adopter of PPPs, with the state of Victoria, for example, completing 32 partnerships to date at a value of around AUD 30.1 billion.

Clearly, the total size of global pension funds is huge – as are the appetites for private infrastructure investments exhibited by governments in the United Kingdom and Australia. So, why would PPPs be attracted to pension funds and vice versa?

The mutual attraction of PPPs and pension funds

The global infrastructure needs of all countries up to the year 2030 was estimated in an early report (OECD 2011, 15) as around USD 50 trillion. The report also said that a similar additional amount would be needed to adapt to and mitigate the effects of climate change over the next 40 years. In the OECD's words, 'such levels of investment cannot be financed by traditional sources of public finance alone' and there is now 'a widespread recognition of a significant infrastructure gap and the need for greater recourse to private sector finance' (OECD 2011, 15). The implementation of Basel III banking regulations has, at the same time, restrained the availability of credit through the traditional sources of private capital such as banks. As a consequence, 'institutional investors – pension funds, insurance companies and mutual funds – have been called to play a more active role in bridging the infrastructure gap … Institutional investors could be key sources of capital, financing long-term, productive activities that support sustainable growth, such as green energy and infrastructure projects' (OECD 2011, 15).

On the other side of the coin, infrastructure investments are attractive to pension funds for several reasons. Summarising the insights of Orr (2009) and the OECD (2011), Foster (2012a) articulated these claimed advantages as follows:

- Infrastructure investments have long terms that can match the long duration of pension fund liabilities
- Infrastructure investments often have returns linked to inflation, and hence can hedge pension fund liabilities that are sensitive to inflation
- Infrastructure investments can generate attractive investment yields in excess of those available in the fixed income market, but with potentially higher volatility

- Infrastructure investments provide portfolio diversification, due to their low correlation with traditional asset classes. (Foster 2012a, 5)

Prima facie, then, it seems that there is a 'potentially good match of interests', as the OECD (2011, 16) puts it, between pension funds and PPPs. The characteristics of this mutual interest and the pension–PPP relationship itself are both worthwhile investigating further. Many actors in both governments seeking the provision of public infrastructure and pension funds have strong views that reforms are needed to encourage these mutual interests to be consummated. Such advocates also have high expectations of change. So, what are the expectations of governments when calling for greater pension involvement, and vice versa?

Great expectations from government and pension funds

The introduction to this chapter demonstrated the high expectations of ministers as well as the high expectations of other advocates for change. Actors pushing for reforms to increase pension fund investment in PPPs include representatives of:

- Government (Duke 2020)
- Investment banks, such as Investec Bank (Colquhoun 2011)
- Industry associations, such as Australia's peak infrastructure organisation (Infrastructure Partnerships Australia, or IPA), the Confederation of British Industry (Shaikh 2012) and the Association for Consultancy and Engineering (Association for Consultancy and Engineering 2012)
- Infrastructure investment managers, such as Industry Funds Management, which invests on behalf of Australian pension funds (Dunn 2019, Weaven 2012).

Advocates for reform commonly emphasise arguments such as 'the infrastructure deficit continues to grow' (IPA c.2010, 11), 'the need for additional infrastructure is well established' (IPA c.2010, 9) and 'it is clear that the solution to the national infrastructure investment shortfall will require that policy makers develop and implement frameworks that efficiently harness additional private sector capital and expertise in the development of infrastructure assets' (IPA *c.*2010, 11). Accompanied by claims of PPP superiority,[6] the overall position is put plainly for all to understand:

> The symmetry between Australia's infrastructure investment task and our national retirement savings are obvious. Superannuation seeks the type of long-run, stable and strong returns which infrastructure assets provide. Yet to date, finding the structure to reconcile this match has eluded Australia's policy makers. (IPA *c.*2010, 8)

A fascinating but less visible aspect of this policy debate are the less strident voices from opposing industry insiders and stakeholders. Multiple commentators have correctly argued that the slippery emphasis on the need for increased private investment by the political arena and the finance sector has been misplaced. EY and the Financial Services Council (FSC) (2014, 3) put it simply, saying: 'Superannuation funds finance infrastructure they do not fund it. Continued delivery of vital infrastructure largely depends on governments identifying and allocating additional funding sources, not on improving the efficiency of current financing techniques.'[7] Moreover, these voices also dismiss outright the idea that there is a major failure in the market for financing infrastructure and that this needs to be overcome. 'The superannuation industry has an overwhelming view that there are no overarching material failures in the infrastructure investment market' was the clear way that EY and the FSC (2014, 8) put it. On top of this, too, was the observation offered by Industry Super Australia (2018, 4) when it answered the question 'should superannuation funds do more direct lending'? Its observation was that it was the 'large corporates' that were 'calling for greater superannuation fund market participation' and, importantly, it noted explicitly that 'whether this is in the best interest of super fund members from a fiduciary perspective, is questionable'.

Governments, too, have clearly been expecting much from change. PPPs have long provided a means of accessing private finance to fill the infrastructure 'gap', as the OECD noted (OECD 2011). The authors of this chapter have long acknowledged the short-term advantages of adopting private finance to deliver public infrastructure when severe public finance constraints exist. Hellowell (2010) and Hodge and Greve (2019) have also identified political advantages for governments in strengthening their relationship with the private finance industry. There are also other advantages for governments. Australia's Treasurer Josh Frydenberg was quoted as saying recently that he 'wanted funds to invest more heavily into nation-building projects' (Myer 2020) and that 'the [superannuation] sector was in a strong position to invest and support the economy' (Duke 2020). Playing the 'nation building' card is a new tactic, and one holding a deep appeal. Indeed, enabling domestic pension funds to invest more strongly in domestic projects has become a common feature of many calls for reform. So, Colquhoun (2011) and Weaven (2012) argue that we ought to be enabling Australian pension funds to invest in Australian projects, and the Association for Consultancy and Engineering (2012) argues that the UK government ought to enable UK pension funds to invest in UK projects. At issue here is the absence of any real debate on the merits of promoting domestic investment rather than encouraging cross-border pension fund investment and the place of government in appealing to a nationalistic policy preference rather than continued globalisation.

In direct alignment with this debate is the matter of the degree to which pension funds should or should not take matters of social policy and responsibility into account when making investment decisions. This matter has a longer history than any recent call for infrastructure investment reform. Pension funds have long wrestled with calls, for example, to invest more ethically, to invest with greater social responsibility or to disinvest in companies that exacerbate climate change. The Canadian pension fund CDPQ (Caisse de dépôt et placement du Québec) holds some CAD 310 billion of assets and has a history of orienting its investments towards meeting its greenhouse targets (CDPQ 2018). More recently, Toscano (2020, 1) reported that 'Australia's second largest superannuation fund is preparing to dump its shares in companies that derive more than 10% of their revenue from thermal coal mining as it embarks on the most aggressive immediate climate change push of any large local investor.' He said that this 'First State Super' pension fund 'holds AUD 130 billion in retirement savings'.

But as industry commentator Alex Dunnin says, 'the term "nation-building" is a bit nebulous – it's motherhood, who couldn't agree with "building the nation"' (Dunn 2019). Public policy analysts would recognise the 'magic' of this phrase[8] and its immediate attractiveness to all citizens. But as Dunnin reminds us,

> when it comes to "environmental and social development goals", it's less clear … These are increasing challenges, and they'll be magnified … As scale increases, and member activism increases, member demand from groups to have a say, or to be informed about, where the investments are placed; this whole question of social development goals, and who decides those; that's a massive issue. (Dunn 2019)

Added to these calls for reforms have been some analyses with a lower degree of self-interest. The work of Frederic Blanc-Brude from the EDHEC Risk Institute-Asia, for instance, has considered the nature of risk and value for money in social infrastructure PPPs and how this affects pension fund appetites to invest in these projects (Blanc-Brude 2012). He proposes changes to the PPP model to attract pension fund investment.

So, what can be learned overall here? It is clear that PPPs provide a means of accessing private finance and that this appears to fill the infrastructure 'gap'. What is equally clear, however, is that there is usually a large dollop of self-interest in the various calls for reform. Many advocates of reform focus on how PPP models can be changed to suit the appetites of pension funds. Philosophically, perhaps pension funds could be better aligned with national infrastructure investment priorities. But for whose benefit would reforms be undertaken? Table 12.1 shows the multiple goals desired by each of the proponents and relevant groups involved in this policy debate. The interests of these groups are conflicted and there are sizeable tensions pulling against the interests of the primary beneficiaries of pension funds: the pension holders themselves. A balance is required here. It is to this matter that we now turn.

PPPs provide one of the sources of private finance opportunities in which pension funds can invest. Other sources include regulated infrastructure assets, such as some privately owned gas transmission and electricity distribution networks, and other assets of a similar nature.

Pension fund regulatory space

Pension funds exist to provide retirement incomes for pension holders. This desired public policy outcome is pursued in the context of law and regulation. The investment decisions of pension funds are therefore influenced heavily by the jurisdiction's applicable legal and regulatory frameworks as well as other parameters, including the country's historical, cultural, social and political context. It is helpful to map out such primary influences on behaviour. Regulatory scholars refer to this conceptual mapping as 'regulatory space'. The regulatory space for pension fund investments includes three major policy and regulatory frameworks,[9] as shown in Figure 12.4:

*   The applicable PPP framework regulates the PPP contract
*   The financial instruments issued by the PPP contractor are regulated by investment and financial market frameworks, and
*   The pension funds themselves are regulated by the applicable pension fund framework.

Table 12.1   Goals of infrastructure stakeholders

Group	Goal	Criteria	Beneficiary	Benefits
Government leaders/ ministers	• More cranes on the skyline • Infrastructure delivery	Maximise	Political party/ politician	Votes
Finance industry Pension fund leaders/ bankers	• Increased deal flow • Increased investment funds under management	Maximise	Finance industry	Employment Salaries
Pension holders	• Increased rate of returns on pension assets • Social goals (?)	Maximise returns Minimise costs and fees extracted	Pension holders	Retirement incomes
Construction industry	• Increased construction activity	Maximise number of projects delivered (regardless of source of finance)	Industry sector	Employment Salaries
PPP developers/ infrastructure managers	• Increased deal flow • Increased infrastructure provision	Maximise number of PPP projects delivered	Industry sector	Employment Salaries
Citizens/ taxpayers	• Economically efficient provision of essential services • Social and economic goals met	Maximise number of projects delivered under democratic constraints Minimise user charges/taxes Maximise project benefits	Citizens/ taxpayers	Public services
Infrastructure users	• Infrastructure service provision	Minimum price Minimum user charges/taxes	Infrastructure users	Services

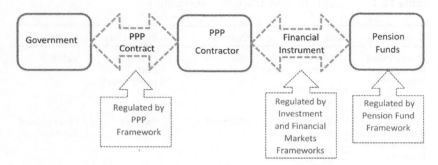

Figure 12.4   Key regulatory frameworks relevant to pension fund investment in PPPs

Governments seeking to encourage pension fund investment in PPPs typically aim to modify each of these frameworks. As noted by Foster (2012a), the PPP framework, for example, can be modified to enable PPP contractors to offer acceptable risk/reward propositions to investors. Existing investment and financial market frameworks can be modified to enable PPP contractors to issue appropriate financial instruments to investors or to create vehicles such as infrastructure investment funds to intermediate between PPP contractors and potential investors. And third, pension fund frameworks can be modified to broaden the ability of pension funds to invest in PPPs. The potential actions undertaken by government depend to an extent on the barriers noted by industry. Fourteen barriers were noted by the OECD (2011) and Foster (2012a) across these three arenas as affecting the ability of pension funds to invest in infrastructure projects. These include those listed in Table 12.2.

Eight barriers were noted as affecting the PPP framework (some of which also affected other frameworks), seven were noted as affecting investment/finance market operation and eight as affecting pension fund frameworks. In light of these barriers, the OECD (2011) also put forward three general policy actions which governments could take to promote pension fund investment in infrastructure. These were:

• Creating policy frameworks supportive of long-term investment,
• Providing a transparent environment for infrastructure investment, and
• Reforming the regulatory framework for long-term investment.

Each of these recommendations deserves discussion, but suffice to say at present that the actions warranted in any country are likely to be quite different and contingent upon that country's present context. All three regulatory

Table 12.2   Barriers to pension fund investment in infrastructure projects

PPP framework	Investment and financial market framework	Pension fund framework
Lack of political commitment		
Regulatory instability		
Fragmentation of the market among different levels of government		Lack of scale of pension funds
No clarity of investment opportunities		Lack of expertise within pension funds
High bidding costs in the procurement process		Short-termism of investors
Investment opportunities are perceived as being too risky		Regulatory barriers
Lack of transparency of the infrastructure sector		
Shortage of data on infrastructure project performance		
	Misalignment of interest between infrastructure funds and pension funds	
	Negative perception of value	

frameworks are also likely to differ from country to country. Take the legislated pension framework, for example. Pension funds tend to be heavily regulated due to their fiduciary responsibility, and this is the primary influence on pension fund investment strategies (Foster 2012a, OECD 2011). As we noted earlier in this chapter (see Figure 12.3), asset allocations of pension funds vary widely, and this is primarily a reflection of the legislated investment restrictions placed upon pension funds. In general terms, such restrictions can cover limits on pension fund investment in selected assets, and limits on foreign assets as well as other quantitative regulations (OECD 2011).

These restrictions represent the balance achieved at the present time by governments weighing the benefits of removing barriers to investment (including investment in PPPs) against the fiduciary and prudential protections required in a pension fund system. As well as aiming to maximise the growth of pension funds, funds also need to continuously match their assets to their liabilities and ensure that sufficient funds are available for retirees at any time. Or, in the famous words of Charles Dickens:

> Annual income twenty pounds, annual expenditure nineteen nineteen and six, result happiness. Annual income twenty pounds, annual expenditure twenty pounds ought and six, result misery. (Dickens 1850, 204)

Together these legal and regulatory frameworks establish the jurisdiction's policy and regulatory environment for that country's pension funds. So how do some of these differences between countries play out in practice, and how are PPP investments affected? The following section illustrates examples from Canada, Australia and New Zealand.

Case study illustrations

Australia

In Australia, domestic and international pension funds (and fund managers on their behalf) are common participants in PPPs. They act both as the initial providers of debt and equity, and also as secondary market investors, purchasing equity stakes in existing PPPs and participating in refinancing. Table 12.3 identifies selected examples from PPPs in the state of Victoria.

Pension funds not only participate in financing projects tendered by governments and in the secondary market, they also proactively seek investment opportunities by submitting unsolicited proposals to governments. In June 2016, Civic Nexus, the private partner in the Southern Cross Station PPP in Melbourne, provided an unsolicited proposal to the government to increase the capacity, amenity and function of the station precinct and to address the expected impacts of future patronage growth. Civic Nexus is owned by IFM Investors, which manages funds on behalf of superannuation funds. In April 2019, the Victoria State government announced that it would not proceed with the proposal (Department of Treasury and Finance, n.d.). IFM Investors and Civic Nexus were also members of a consortium that proposed a new, dedicated premium rail line from Southern Cross Station to Melbourne Airport (AirRail 2019). A decision not to proceed with this proposal was also made recently (Jacks 2020). Toll road operator Transurban, which has been able to fund a large project pipeline thanks to the demand from Australian super funds for infrastructure assets (Boyd 2018), has also made use of unsolicited proposals, including the AUD 6.7 billion West Gate Tunnel (commenced in 2017 and originally scheduled for completion in 2022) and the AUD 1 billion

Table 12.3 PPP case illustrations from Victoria, Australia

Projects	Investor(s)	Role	Source
Biosciences Research Centre Casey Community Hospital Melbourne Convention Centre	Caisse de dépôt et placement du Québec	Equity investor (secondary market)	1
EastLink	Universities Superannuation Scheme (UK) APG (Netherlands) National Pension Service (Korea) ATP (Denmark) New Zealand Superannuation Fund, Teachers Insurance and Annuity Association of America	Equity investors (secondary market)	2
Peninsula Link	State Super (Australia) Officers Super Fund (Australia) Prime Super (Australia)	Equity providers	3
Southern Cross Station	IFM Investors (Australia)	Equity provider	4
Victorian Comprehensive Cancer Centre Project	UniSuper Ltd (Australia)	Equity provider	5
	IFM Investors (Australia) HEST Australia Ltd CARE Super Pty Ltd (Australia)	Debt providers	5
Western Roads Upgrade	Pensionskasse Des Bundes Publica (Switzerland) Teachers Insurance and Annuity Association of America	Long-term debt providers	5

Sources: 1. Plenary Group (2012, 2013), 2. Reuters (2011), 3. IJ Global (2011), 4. www.ifminvestors.com/investment-capabilities/infrastructure/asset-portfolio/ southern-cross-station, 5. Project summaries available at www.dtf.vic.gov.au/public -private-partnerships/partnerships-victoria-ppp-projects

CityLink–Tulla Widening project (completed in 2018). The evidence suggests that Australian PPP frameworks are capable of accommodating pension fund investment through unsolicited proposals. Nevertheless, the Southern Cross Station example indicates that a lack of clarity of investment opportunities and uncertain political commitment may be barriers to such investments.

International pension funds have been significant investors in Australian PPPs. Australia's domestic pension funds are also significant investors, but given that their assets are a high proportion of the country's GDP, they might be expected to play a more dominant role. The apparently strong interest from international funds and subdued interest from domestic funds reflects differences in pension fund systems.

The Australian pension fund system primarily consists of defined contribution schemes, in which pension fund members directly bear the risk of the performance of the fund's assets, and members can easily move their investment from one pension fund manager to another (Foster 2012a). These factors protect the Australian pension system against the risk of funds having insufficient assets to meet their liabilities, but diminish the attractiveness of long-term illiquid investments, such as infrastructure. Instead, Australian defined contribution schemes need to hold significant levels of liquid assets so that they can be converted to cash and paid out to any fund member who decides to move their investment to another fund manager. This 'portability' also provides an incentive for fund managers to focus on short-term returns in order to attract funds, further reinforcing the bias against long-term investments.

In contrast, many other countries have pension systems that primarily consist of defined benefit schemes, in which the fund itself bears the risk that the performance of its assets is insufficient to meet its defined liabilities to members. Defined benefit funds seek to mitigate this risk through investments that can provide long-term stable returns, such as investment in PPPs. As their benefit is pre-defined, there is no compelling reason for fund members in these schemes to move their funds to another manager. Thus, defined benefit funds typically need less liquidity than defined contribution funds and are less influenced by short-term returns, giving them greater scope to invest in PPPs.

The heterogeneous nature of the pension fund schemes thus results in different schemes having different investment incentives and different barriers to investment in PPPs. Simplistic suggestions of alignment between pension funds and PPPs overlook these differences.

The maturity of the Australian PPP market also provides opportunities to investigate the implications of pension fund involvement in PPPs beyond their initial investment. Where infrastructure is provided through PPPs, changes that government may wish to make to the physical infrastructure or the services that it provides may be constrained by the PPP contractual framework and the willingness, capacity and capability of the various private sector actors to implement the changes. At one end of a spectrum, investors such as some banks may see change as an opportunity for additional business, particularly where the change requires additional financing. At the other end, a passive investor may simply want a 'quiet life' collecting a steady return, and may be resistant to any change, particularly where the change introduces additional risk.

Evidence as to whether pension fund investors in PPPs are accepting of change, or resistant to it, can be sought by examining project examples. Among the most significant changes to PPP-provided infrastructure in Australia have been the Casey Hospital Expansion Project and the Melbourne Exhibition Centre Expansion Project, both in the state of Victoria. At the time of the expansion projects, the Canadian CDPQ pension fund was an equity investor in the project companies responsible for both of the original PPPs (Plenary Group 2012). The Casey Hospital PPP was originally contracted in 2002 at a value (in 2002 dollars) of AUD 120 million. In 2016, the government provided an additional AUD 135 million in capital funding for an expansion of the hospital (Department of Health and Human Services 2017). The Melbourne Convention Centre PPP, in which the private sector constructed a new convention centre and then provided facility management services for the centre and an adjacent exhibition centre, was originally contracted in 2004 at a value (in 2002 dollars) of AUD 367 million. In 2016, the government signed a contract for an expansion of the exhibition centre at a total cost (in 2016 dollars) of AUD 237 million (Department of Economic Development, Jobs, Transport and Resources 2017).

The contractual arrangements for both expansion projects are complex. Each involves a new PPP contract and project company for the expansion, interfacing with the contractual structure for the original PPP, together with new subcontracting and financing arrangements. This contrasts with the alternative approach of implementing changes through mechanisms within the original contract, which is the usual method for making less substantial changes in the infrastructure or services under a PPP contract (Foster 2012b).

In addition to its role as an equity investor in the original PPPs, the CDPQ is also an equity investor in the Casey Hospital Expansion (Department of Health and Human Services 2017), but not the Melbourne Exhibition Centre Expansion. It is unclear why this was the case, or whether the presence of this investor in the original PPPs affected government's ability to implement the expansions efficiently and effectively. Further research is needed to better understand how the presence of pension fund investors affected the expansions, and whether any reforms are required to ensure that governments have a sufficient degree of flexibility in PPPs financed by pension funds.

The Australian example illustrates that significant pension fund investment in infrastructure can occur without the need for major reforms to PPP frameworks, and thus provides support for the opposing voices who believe there are no overarching material failures in the infrastructure investment market. However, the pattern of investment also illustrates that the pension fund regulatory landscape does influence investment.

Canada

Canada is considered a leading global PPP market (Romoff 2017). Its pension fund system is broadly similar to Australia in size and in the proportion of funds invested in infrastructure. In 2017, it was reported that Canada's largest pension plans have invested CAD 87 billion in infrastructure (Dachis 2017).

As defined benefit schemes, Canadian pension funds require a long-term strategy of matching assets to future liabilities. The barriers to Canadian pension funds' investment in infrastructure therefore relate to longer-term risks. For example, a key risk for defined benefit schemes is the risk of a mismatch between the return on its investments and the long-term inflation rate (Foster 2012a). Consequently, Canadian pension funds are among the most active investors in PPPs globally. Paradoxically, however, they have been reluctant to invest in Canadian PPPs (Dachis 2017, Liang 2013).

Liang (2013) identified three barriers that Canadian pension funds face in Canadian PPP investment:

1. Historically, only a handful of Canadian PPP projects met Canadian pension funds' minimum size criteria.
2. Many Canadian public sector labour unions are vigorously opposed to PPPs, and pension funds have therefore seen reputational risk in investing in domestic PPPs.
3. Canadian governments' commitments to PPPs often change after elections, which has led to perceptions of political risk.

The significant presence of Canadian pension funds in the Australian PPP market is consistent with these barriers. Australian PPPs are on average larger than Canadian PPPs.[10] PPPs in Australia have bipartisan political support from the two major political parties, and have seen little visible opposition from labour unions in contrast to Canada.

The relative failure of Canada's mature PPP market to attract investment from its domestic pension funds provides a stark contrast with the position in

Australia, and illustrates that the barriers to pension fund investment in PPPs are idiosyncratic.

New Zealand

New Zealand's pensions landscape has features in common with both the Australian and Canadian models. There are three key elements (OECD 2017):

1. A universal flat-rate public pension. The Government has established the New Zealand Superannuation Fund as an investment vehicle to fund future liabilities under this scheme (New Zealand Superannuation Fund 2019). This is effectively analogous to Canadian defined benefit pension funds.
2. A voluntary government-subsidised retirement savings scheme known as KiwiSaver. This is effectively a defined contribution system, analogous to Australia's superannuation system.
3. Occupational pensions, which have diminished in importance as KiwiSaver has grown.

New Zealand's PPP market is small in comparison to those in Australia and Canada.[11] This limits the opportunities for domestic pension fund investment in New Zealand PPPs.

The primary source of pension fund investment in New Zealand PPPs has been through funds established by investment manager Morrison & Co. The New Zealand Superannuation Fund was the cornerstone investor in Morrison & Co.'s first Public Infrastructure Partners Fund, and the manager of the occupational pension fund for government employees was the cornerstone investor in the second fund (Morrison & Co. 2015). The first fund invested in three New Zealand PPPs, together with projects in Australia, while the second fund is focused solely on projects within New Zealand.

The role of Morrison & Co. as an intermediary between pension funds and PPPs illustrates the importance of an accommodative investment and financial markets framework in facilitating pension fund investment in PPPs.

As in Australia, pension funds have attempted to expand the New Zealand PPP market through the government's unsolicited proposals process. In April 2018, the New Zealand government received an unsolicited proposal from a joint venture of the New Zealand Superannuation Fund and the CDPQ for the exclusive delivery of the Auckland Light Rail network (Robertson and Twyford 2018).

In June 2019, the government directed the Ministry of Transport to lead a 'parallel process' to select a preferred Auckland Light Rail delivery partner from the government's transport agency and the joint venture. Although both potential partners delivered credible proposals, in June 2020 the government announced that it would end the parallel process. During the development and evaluation of the two proposals, the government clarified its objectives for Auckland Light Rail and identified changes needed within the current regulatory and legislative regime for such transport systems (Ministry of Transport 2020). This suggests that, as in Australia, a lack of clarity of investment opportunities and uncertain political commitment in New Zealand may be barriers to pension fund investments in PPPs through unsolicited proposals.

Discussion and future research directions

Infrastructure as an asset class

The enthusiasm for promoting pension fund investment in PPPs partially rests on an assumption that infrastructure is a new 'asset class' that has distinct and attractive investment characteristics, yet there is no theoretical backing for the proposition that infrastructure as a whole is a separate asset class (Inderst 2010). The performance of listed infrastructure companies indicates that listed infrastructure is not an asset class distinct from other listed investments (Blanc-Brude et al. 2016a). In contrast, unlisted infrastructure firms appear to exhibit unique revenue and profit dynamics (Blanc-Brude et al. 2016b) and a return per unit of risk that is superior to other major asset classes (Blanc-Brude and Gupta 2020). Nevertheless, even here risk and performance are not well understood, in part because unlisted infrastructure investors typically assess their returns against inappropriate benchmarks (Amenc et al. 2020).

The lack of clarity as to the nature and performance of infrastructure as an asset class implies a need for further research to validate whether PPP investments offer a compelling risk return outcome for pension funds that justifies governments undertaking reforms to promote such investment.

If PPPs do offer a superior investment outcome for pension funds, a further question is whether government receives a sufficient share of the benefits arising from the apparent natural synergy between PPPs and pension funds. Typically, a government would seek to capture a share of the benefits through a competitive tender process. If the superior return exhibited by infrastructure investments represents the share of the benefits captured by the investor, how does that compare to the benefit to government? Could governments run more effective tender processes that capture a greater share of the excess return?

If, rather than competing for PPPs in tender processes, pension funds are taking the initiative by submitting unsolicited proposals for PPPs, the absence of competition may result in the pension fund retaining all of the benefits of the superior investment outcome. In this context, it is notable that in both the Auckland Light Rail project and the Southern Cross Station project, the relevant governments ultimately rejected the pension funds' unsolicited proposals.

Flexibility and responsiveness

PPPs are long-term contracts that potentially constrain government's ability to respond to changing circumstances. To implement significant changes, government must not only negotiate with the private partner, but also with the private partner's investors and lenders, which may include pension funds. Jurisdictions with well-developed PPP frameworks have, through experience, developed contractual mechanisms that introduce a degree of flexibility and allow for variations in the physical infrastructure and the services (Foster 2012b). These mechanisms seek to overcome the disadvantage of inflexibility that is inherent in PPPs. The need for flexibility in PPPs has been highlighted by the COVID-19 pandemic, with some governments finding that PPP contracts are not inherently flexible and responsive to appropriately manage the impacts of the pandemic.[12]

Our Australian case study raises questions as to whether pension fund investment in PPPs affected government's ability to implement major infrastructure expansions efficiently and effectively. This suggests potential future research in the following areas:

- What impact does the presence of pension fund investors have on the flexibility and responsiveness of PPPs to deal with changing needs and circumstances?
- Are these impacts different for different types of pension funds (defined benefit funds and defined contribution funds)?

Conflicting government objectives

The potential for pension funds to invest in infrastructure projects creates the potential for conflicts to arise between government's management of its infrastructure program and its regulation of the pension fund framework. This potential may be exacerbated where the pension fund was established by the government itself.

In the Auckland Light Rail project, the New Zealand Superannuation Fund was effectively competing against the Transport Ministry for the project. The fund has a 'double arm's length' governance arrangement to ensure independence from government (New Zealand Superannuation Fund 2019), but even if this is the case, government infrastructure decision making may be distorted by a desire to provide opportunities to the fund that is intended to meet the government's future pension liabilities. This potential bias may or may not be beneficial, once all public interest considerations are taken into account.

Further research into the implications of pension fund investment in infrastructure and transparency of decision making are key actions that would provide greater assurance that governments are appropriately managing conflicts between their management of infrastructure programs and their regulation of their pension fund frameworks.

The presence of government pension fund bodies as investors in New Zealand PPPs creates a further conflict: Governments typically emphasise that PPPs have benefits in transferring risk to the private sector, yet if a government pension fund is an investor, the taxpayer may ultimately be taking back that transferred risk. For example, the New Zealand government may believe it has transferred PPP risks to the private sector, but if the project fails and the New Zealand Superannuation Fund consequently loses its investment and therefore has reduced capacity to meet the government's future pension commitments, the loss will fall back on New Zealand taxpayers. Hence further research is required into the potential for value for money to be compromised if a government-sponsored pension fund invests in the same government's PPPs.

Encouraging greater infrastructure investment

One of the most interesting lessons of the analysis undertaken in this chapter is its direct relevance to the analytical frameworks useful in analysing other public policy problems. While some of the pension fund–infrastructure investment debate no doubt revolves around the complexity of legislative requirements and regulatory rules, analytical frameworks such as Sabatier's 'Advocacy Coalition Framework' (Zaharidias 2014) are just as applicable to pension policy reform debates and decisions as any other more frequently discussed area of public policy. Powerful interest groups will, of course, always line up to lobby for changes to existing public policy arrangements. But several high-profile Australian former political leaders have now turned bankers and pension fund chairmen (see Davidson 2014),[13] so readers ought to be aware of Kingdon's (1984) 'Multiple Streams' model of policy decision making in which he warns that such people (called 'policy entrepreneurs') swim around in the soup in which public policy ideas float, and look for problems to which they can attach their pre-prepared solutions.

Conclusions

Unrealistic expectations on either side raise a risk of governments or pension funds being disappointed like Miss Havisham, left at the altar by a supposed partner for life who turned out to be only in it for his own gain. Care is needed on this matter. There nevertheless continues to be a common assumption that pension funds ought to play a greater active role in the provision of public infrastructure. So this matter deserves a place in our future research agenda.

The empirical case studies analysed in this chapter showed that significant pension fund investment in PPPs is already taking place in countries such as Australia, Canada and New Zealand. It also revealed little evidence of strong common barriers to greater pension fund investment in PPPs. It is therefore not even clear at this stage that encouraging increased infrastructure investments by pension funds is a desirable public policy outcome for citizens. We also analysed the observation that only modest success had been achieved so far in mobilising growing pools of pension funds to meet increasing infrastructure needs despite an apparent mutual attraction. This was seen as being due to stakeholders having very different goals and the complexity of the regulatory space in which governments, PPP contractors and pension funds are situated. Three arenas were seen as relevant here: the PPP framework, the investment and financial market framework and the pension fund framework.

So, where to now? Some questions within a future PPP pension research agenda can be answered straight away. For example, would enabling pension funds to invest more strongly in infrastructure help to close the national infrastructure gap? No. As Foster (2012a, 6) said, 'pension fund investment in infrastructure is a form of financing, and hence is only the "answer" to meeting infrastructure needs if the key constraint holding back government infrastructure programs is a limit on the availability of finance, not a limit on the available funding'. The reality for most governments today is that funding availability is the primary constraint on infrastructure delivery, not financing, so working harder to mobilise pension fund investment in PPPs will not, in itself, close the infrastructure gap for governments. Likewise, we also now know that any policy changes to mobilise pension funds will be contingent on the context of a particular country, and that any policy or regulatory changes need to carefully balance the benefits of removing barriers to PPP investment against the fiduciary and prudential protections legally required in pension funds.

These observations nonetheless still leave a vast space for future PPP pension research. At the outset, there is first a need for some solid case-study-based research into the outcomes of existing pension investments in PPPs, including each of the various stakeholders. Second, future research could make the case whether reforms aiming to mobilise pension funds are desirable for a particular jurisdiction, and the ways in which proposed reforms might sensibly address the various layers of regulatory safeguards currently operating. Third, there is the overarching question of whether greater pension fund investment in infrastructure offers citizens a lower cost of capital, in the end, than alternative sources of capital. Fourth, and acknowledging continuing controversies over PPP transparency and decision making, there is the matter of improving transparency arrangements in both the public and private sectors in order to assure citizens that both governments and their private pension partners are operating in ways that are in the public's interest and not just their own. This leaves a wide PPP pension research agenda indeed.

Notes

1. The title of this chapter was inspired by the Charles Dickens novels *Great Expectations* and *A Tale of Two Cities*. The two metaphorical cities here were government and pension funds, and this title highlighted that the interests of these two cities were not necessarily aligned. Indeed, despite the common assumption that pension fund investment in infrastructure provides great outcomes for both governments and pension funds, this is not yet supported by strong evidence. It is possible that the best of times for government and taxpayers may be the worst of times for pension funds, and vice versa. We are therefore left unsure as to whether pension funds should regard PPPs as safe houses for long-term investments or just another wild market frontier (which was the original heading for this chapter).
2. In a traditional defined benefit pension plan, workers accrue a promise of a regular monthly payment from the date of their retirement. The payment is commonly based on a formula linked to an employee's wages or salary and years of tenure at the sponsoring firm. In a defined contribution pension plan, it is the contributions rather than the benefit that are fixed. The pension benefit is not known in advance, as it depends on the contributions made and the investment returns earned on the plan balances (Broadbent et al. 2006).
3. The simple average pension size in 2019 was 55 per cent of GDP.

4. The extent to which long-term infrastructure contracts (PPPs) have required up-front finance to be privately provided has differed over time and across countries. Early advocates in the United Kingdom and Australia, for instance, insisted on all initial finance being privately provided. But this was not the case in countries such as Canada, where public financing always played a significant role. More recently, mixed public and private financing has also been used (for example, in the Melbourne Metro Tunnel project in Victoria, Australia; Melbourne Metro Rail Authority 2018), and even full public financing has been trialled for the initial construction prior to the sale of the infrastructure to the private sector for longer-term operation (for example, in the WestConnex project in New South Wales, Australia; Government of New South Wales 2015).

5. PPPs have been known as 'PFI and PF2' projects in the United Kingdom. The PFI and PF2 Frameworks applied only to government-pays PPPs (the predominant form of PPP in the United Kingdom), not user-pays PPPs, hence the United Kingdom's published statistics potentially understate the total level of PPP investment.

6. One prominent example of this is the exaggerated claim of IPA (c.2010, 11) that 'PPPs around the world deliver lifecycle cost savings of around 30 per cent.' A more balanced assessment would at a minimum have acknowledged that such cost-savings claims have been heavily contested for decades.

7. Foster (2012a) notes, as have many others, that while public infrastructure is most often funded through government payments (for example, availability payments), it can also be funded by the users of a facility, such as occurs with toll roads. Foster also notes that irrespective of who ultimately funds a facility, it can be financed through either the private sector capital or public sector government borrowings.

8. Pollitt and Hupe (2011) termed some words used in public life 'magic', because of their linguistic appeal. Concepts like 'governance', 'accountability' and 'harmonisation' enjoy pervasive use in public life because of their high levels of abstraction, broad scope and great flexibility. They have an overwhelmingly positive and progressive connotation and are used by many practitioners and academics, and yet they dilute, obscure or deny the traditional social science concerns with conflicting interests and logics because they imply a degree of consensus. 'Nation building' is another magic concept – these words provide a vocabulary for discussion and debate and help marshal enthusiasm and energy towards new policy directions. We all inherently support these terms – a better world is surely possible through more 'nation building'! But as Windholz and Hodge (2012) warn, using these words does not dissolve the differences existing between traditional interest groups. Such differences are unmasked eventually. As decision making rolls on, one must move from abstraction (illusion) to detailed policy actions. And when this occurs, the initial personal conceptions we all willingly read into the project become visible and differences begin to appear. As reform decision making proceeds, our initial policy enthusiasm is seen for what it is: enthusiasm (Windholz and Hodge 2012).

9. The ideas of 'regulatory space' and 'regulatory frameworks' in this chapter encompass a broad notion of regulation as outlined in Hodge (2020). This includes the legal requirements operating on all corporations, the requirements of independent regulatory agencies overseeing securities, investments, prudential responsibilities and corporate behaviour, and, as well, a wide range of non-legal influences.

10. In 2017, Canada had 267 PPPs with a total value of CAD 123 billion, an average of CAD 461 million (approximately AUD 484 million) per project (Romoff 2017).

The State of Victoria, Australia, has undertaken 32 PPPs with a total value of AUD 30.1 billion, an average of AUD 941 million per project (Department of Treasury and Finance 2018).

11.   As at July 2020, New Zealand had five operational PPP projects and three in construction (Infrastructure Commission 2020).

12.   For example, in the United Kingdom, government identified a need to revise contract requirements/standards (including scope changes where necessary) and moderate payment and performance mechanism regimes where appropriate to maintain public services during the emergency period (Infrastructure and Projects Authority 2020).

13.   Davidson (2014, 7) lists several people as 'seeking rents' for investment banks and superannuation funds, including: 'ex-Treasurer and Prime Minister, Paul Keating, and ex-Finance Minister, Lindsay Tanner, who are employed by global investment banker, Lazard; ex-Victorian state premiers, Steve Bracks (who chairs the CBUS fund) and John Brumby (who chairs the Motor Traders of Australia super fund); and [Sir] Rod Eddington ... is now the chairman of Infrastructure Australia which promotes private financing of infrastructure'. An alternative view is that these individuals genuinely believe (rightly or wrongly) that, by applying their public sector standing and expertise in their roles in the pension sector, they are delivering positive outcomes for society.

References

AirRail Melbourne (2019) A world-class airport rail link, available at: www .airrailmelbourne.com.au/#documents.

Amenc, N., Blanc-Brude, F., Gupta, A., and Lum, L. (2020) *Infrastructure Investors Should Abandon Absolute Return Benchmarks*, EDHEC Infrastructure Institute – Singapore.

Association for Consultancy and Engineering (2012) Pensions and infrastructure: Balancing risk, reward, return and market conditions, available at: www.acenet.co .uk/economics.

Blanc-Brude, F. (2012) *Pension Fund Investment in Social Infrastructure: Insights from the 2012 Reform of the Private Finance Initiative in the United Kingdom*, EDHEC-Risk Institute, available at: www.edhec.edu/sites/www.edhec-portail.pprod .net/files/publications/pdf/edhec-publication-pension-fund-investment-in-social -infrastructure-f_1332412681078.pdf.

Blanc-Brude, F., and Gupta, A. (2020) 3 Things We Learned About Infrastructure Investment During COVID-19, Webinar (28 April 2020).

Blanc-Brude, F., Hasan, M., and Whittaker, T. (2016b) *Revenue and Dividend Payouts in Privately-Held Infrastructure Investments*, EDHEC Infrastructure Institute – Singapore.

Blanc-Brude, F., Whittaker, T., and Wilde, S. (2016a) *Searching for a Listed Infrastructure Asset Class*, EDHEC Infrastructure Institute – Singapore.

Boyd, B. (2018) Transurban and Challenger are winners from compulsory superannuation. *Australian Financial Review*, 13 February, available at: www.afr .com/chanticleer/transurban-and-challenger-are-winners-from-compulsory -superannuation-20180213-h0vzv3.

Broadbent, J., Palumbo, M., and Woodman, E. (2006) *The Shift from Defined Benefit to Defined Contribution Pension Plans: Implications for Asset Allocation and Risk Management*, Paper prepared for a Working Group on Institutional Investors, Global Savings and Asset Allocation established by the Committee on the Global Financial System, available at www.bis.org/publ/wgpapers/cgfs27broadbent3.pdf.

CDPQ (Caisse de dépôt et placement du Québec) (2018) *Annual Report*, available at: www.cdpq.com/en/performance/annual-reports/2018.

Clark, G.L., Monk, A.H.B., Orr, R., and Scott, W. (*c.*2011) *The New Era of Infrastructure Investing*, Stanford Global Projects Center working paper, available at: https://gpc.stanford.edu/sites/g/files/sbiybj8226/f/wp065_0.pdf.

Colquhoun, L. (2011) Australian pension funds reluctant to invest in infrastructure: The government needs to structure more attractive deals, *Financial Times*, August 14, available at: www.ft.com/content/a937b3f6-bf32-11e0-898c-00144feabdc0.

Dachis, B. (2017) *New and Improved: How Institutional Investment in Public Infrastructure can Benefit Taxpayers and Consumers*, C.D. Howe Institute, Toronto, available at: www.cdhowe.org/sites/default/files/attachments/research_papers/mixed/Commentary%20473.pdf.

Davidson, K. (2014) The wolves of finance. *D!SSENT*, Autumn/Winter, 2–9.

Department of Economic Development, Jobs, Transport and Resources (2017) *Melbourne Exhibition Centre Expansion Project: Project Summary*, available at: www.dtf.vic.gov.au/sites/default/files/2018-02/Melbourne%20Exhibition%20Centre%20Expansion%20Project%20Summary%20-%20February%202018.pdf.

Department of Health and Human Services (2017) *Casey Hospital Expansion Project: Project Summary*, available at: www.dtf.vic.gov.au/sites/default/files/2018-01/Casey-Hospital-Expansion-Project-Summary-November-2017.pdf.

Department of Treasury and Finance (n.d.) Finalised proposals, available at: www.dtf.vic.gov.au/market-led-proposals/finalised-proposals.

Department of Treasury and Finance (2018) Public private partnerships, available at: www.dtf.vic.gov.au/infrastructure-investment/public-private-partnerships.

Department of Treasury and Finance (2019) Market led proposals, available at: www.dtf.vic.gov.au/infrastructure-investment/market-led-proposals.

Dickens, C. (1850) *David Copperfield: The Personal History, Adventures, Experience and Observation of David Copperfield the Younger of Blunderstone Rookery*, Bradbury & Evans, London.

Duke, J. (2020) Super funds say policy stability key to more infrastructure investment, *Sydney Morning Herald*, June 10.

Dunn, J. (2019) Nation-building funded by super funds, *Australian Financial Review*, June 26.

EY and Financial Services Council (2014) *Superannuation Investment in Infrastructure: Steps to Further Efficiency*, 2014, available at: https://fsc.org.au/resources-category/research-report/1136-ey-fsc-report-super-investment-in-infrastructure-2014-final-7be9-1/file.

Foster, R. (2012a) *Promoting Pension Fund Investment in Public-Private Partnerships: Frameworks and Critical Issues*, unpublished working paper delivered at PPP scholars' network meeting, available at: https://fosterinfrastructure.com/documents/Working%20Paper%20-%20Pension%20Fund%20Investment%20in%20PPPs%20-%20Richard%20Foster%20-%20August%202012.pdf.

Foster, R. (2012b) *Study of Contractual Clauses for the Smooth Adjustment of Physical Infrastructure & Services through the Lifecycle of PPP Cycle*, available at: www

.gihub.org/resources/publications/comparative-study-of-contractual-clauses-for
-the-smooth-adjustment-of-physical-infrastructure-and-services/.

Government of New South Wales (2015) *WestConnex Updated Strategic Business Case*, available at: www.westconnex.com.au/media/yejnwxmw/westconnex-updated_strategic _business_case.pdf.

Hellowell, M. (2010) The UK's Private Finance Initiative: History, Evaluation, Prospects, in *International Handbook on Public–Private Partnerships*, edited by G.A. Hodge, C. Greve and A.E. Boardman. Cheltenham, UK and Northampton, MA, USA: Edward Elgar Publishing, pp. 307–332.

Hilton, A. (2012) Here's how to solve pension problem, Ed, *London Evening Standard*, July 17.

HM Treasury and Infrastructure and Projects Authority (2018) *Private Finance Initiative and Private Finance 2 Projects: 2017 Summary Data*, available at: https:// assets.publishing.service.gov.uk/government/uploads/system/uploads/attachment _data/file/696091/PFI_and_PF2_projects_2017_summary_data_March_2018_web .pdf.

Hodge, G., and Greve, C. (2019) *The Logic of Public–Private Partnerships: The Enduring Interdependency of Politics and Markets*. Cheltenham, UK and Northampton, MA, USA: Edward Elgar Publishing.

Hodge, G.A. (2020) What Should Every Public Servant Know About Regulation?, in *The Palgrave Handbook of the Public Servant*, edited by H. Sullivan and H. Dickinson. Cham: Springer. https://link.springer.com/content/pdf/10.1007/978-3 -030-03008-7_1-1.pdf.

IJ Global (2011), Peninsular Link: Way to recovery, available at: https://ijglobal.com/ articles/120227/peninsular-link-way-to-recovery.

Inderst, G. (2010) Infrastructure as an asset class. *EIB Papers*, 15 (1): 70–104.

Industry Super Australia (2018) *Should Superannuation Funds Do More Direct Lending?*, paper presented at Melbourne Money and Finance Conference 2018, 9 July, available at: www.industrysuper.com/media/should-superannuation-funds-do -more-direct-lending/.

Infrastructure and Projects Authority (2020) *Supporting Vital Service Provision in PFI/ PF2 (And Related) Contracts during the COVID-19 Emergency*, available at: https:// assets.publishing.service.gov.uk/government/uploads/system/uploads/attachment _data/file/878059/2020_04_02_PFI_and_COVID19_final.docx.pdf.

Infrastructure Commission (2020), PPP projects, available at: https://infracom.govt.nz/ major-projects/public-private-partnerships/ppp-projects/.

Infrastructure Partnerships Australia (*c*2010) *The Role of Superannuation in Building Australia's Future*. Sydney, 44pp.

Jacks, T. (2020) Andrews defends decision to ditch airport rail tunnel proposal, *The Age*, 21 November, available at: www.theage.com.au/national/victoria/andrews -defends-decision-to-ditch-airport-rail-tunnel-proposal-20201121-p56gnu.html.

Kingdon, J. (1984) *Agendas, Alternatives and Public Policies*. New York, NY: Addison Wesley Longman.

Liang, A. (2013) *Canadian Pension Funds' Investments in Canadian Public Private Partnership: Benefits, Barriers and Policy Actions*, available at: www.researchgate .net/publication/260944331_Canadian_Pension_Funds'_Investments_in_Canadian _Public_Private_Partnership_Benefits_Barriers_Policy_Actions.

Melbourne Metro Rail Authority (2018) *Tunnel and Stations Public Private Partnership Project Summary*, available at: www.dtf.vic.gov.au/sites/default/files/2018-02/Metro

%20Tunnel%20PPP%20Project%20Summary%20-%2021%20February%202018 .pdf.

Ministry of Transport (2020) Auckland Light Rail Project, available at: www.transport .govt.nz/land/auckland/atap/auckland-light-rail/.

Morrison & Co. (2015) H.R.L. Morrison & Co. Public Infrastructure Partners Fund II First Close, available at: https://hrlmorrison.com/assets/attachments-folder/PIP -Fund-II-Financial-Close.pdf.

Myer, R. (2020) Superannuation funds want to invest in infrastructure, but there's one thing missing, *Thenewdaily*, June 14, available at: https://thenewdaily.com.au/ finance/superannuation/2020/06/14/superannuation-funds-infrastructure/.

New Zealand Superannuation Fund (2019) *Annual Report*, available at: www .nzsuperfund.nz/publications/annual-reports.

OECD (2011) *Pension Funds Investment in Infrastructure: A Survey*, available at: www .oecd.org/futures/infrastructureto2030/48634596.pdf.

OECD (2017) *Pensions at a Glance 2017: Country Profiles – New Zealand*, available at: www.oecd.org/els/public-pensions/PAG2017-country-profile-New-Zealand.pdf.

OECD (2019) Annual Survey of Large Pension Funds and Public Pension Reserve Funds, available at: www.oecd.org/finance/private-pensions/survey-large-pension -funds.htm.

OECD (2020) Pension Markets in Focus 2020, available at: www.oecd.org/finance/p ensionmarketsinfocus.htm.

Orr, R.J. (2009) Pensions and Infrastructure: The Path to Common Ground, *Working Paper #51*, May, Collaboratory for Research on Global Projects, Stanford University, available at: https://gpc.stanford.edu/sites/g/files/sbiybj8226/f/wp051_0.pdf.

Penguin English Dictionary (2004) "Pension fund". Harmondsworth: Penguin.

Plenary Group (2012) The Caisse and Plenary Group partner on five Australian PPP projects, available at: https://plenarygroup.com/news-and-media/news/2012/the -caisse-and-plenary-group-partner-on-five-australian-public-private-partnership -projects.

Plenary Group (2013) CDPQ invests $32m in Melbourne's Biosciences Research Centre, available at: https://plenarygroup.com/news-and-media/news/2013/the -caisse-invests-au$32-million-in-melbournes-biosciences-research-centre-along -with-plenary-group.

Pollitt, C., and Hupe, P. (2011) Talking about government: The role of magic concepts. *Public Management Review*, 13 (5): 641–658.

Reuters (2011) Australia's ConnectEast agrees to $2.3 billion bid from CP2, available at: www.reuters.com/article/us-conecteast/australias-connecteast-agrees-to-2-3-billion -bid-from-cp2-idUSTRE76K7VH20110721.

Robertson, G., and Twyford, P. (2018) Auckland light rail a step closer, available at: www.beehive.govt.nz/release/auckland-light-rail-step-closer.

Romoff, M. (2017) Building on success: PPPs in a new era of Canadian infrastruc- ture, available at: https://blogs.worldbank.org/ppps/building-success-ppps-new-era -canadian-infrastructure.

Shaikh, F. (2012) CBI urges Osborne to focus on growth goals in budget, Business News, Reuters, available at: https://cn.reuters.com/article/uk-britain-budget-cbi -idUKTRE81L00620120222.

Toscano, N. (2020) Top super fund dumps coal miners as emissions cuts intensify. *The Sydney Morning Herald*, 9 July.

Weaven, G. (2012) How government can enrol funds to boost infrastructure projects. *The Australian*, 1 May, available at: www.theaustralian.com.au/business/wealth/

how-government-can-enrol-funds-to-boost-infrastructure-projects/story-e6frgac6
-1226343109879.
Windholz, E., and Hodge, G. (2012) The magic of harmonisation: A case study of occupational health and safety in Australia. *Asia Pacific Journal of Public Administration*,
34 (2): 212–237.
Zaharidias, N. (2014) Ambiguity and Multiple Streams, in *Theory of the Policy Process*,
edited by P.A. Sabatier and C.M. Weible, 3rd ed. Boulder, CO: Westview Press,
pp. 25–58.

13 The public–private partnership market maturity research frontier

Carter B. Casady

Introduction

As countries continue to grapple with the economic fallout of the Covid-19 pandemic, public–private partnerships (PPPs) are being widely touted as a recovery mechanism to 'build back better' and close the global infrastructure gap (Baxter and Casady 2020). Many of the same oft-cited benefits are espoused, especially the ability of PPPs to bundle various infrastructure project lifecycle phases (for example, design, construction, financing, operations, and maintenance) and shift risk via long-term contracts to private consortiums (Casady and Geddes 2016, World Bank 2017b). However, the PPP research terrain has long been a contested arena and extensive debate persists about overall PPP efficacy (see, for example, Teisman and Klijn 2002, Hodge and Greve 2007, Hodge and Greve 2010, Hodge and Greve 2017). Assessments of PPP programmatic performance have also been complicated by widespread differences in PPP regulatory regimes, agency formation, and business climates across Europe, North America, Asia, Latin America, and Africa (Van den Hurk et al. 2015, Casady and Peci 2020). Additionally, while some low- to middle-income countries are now only beginning to embrace PPPs and develop their own PPP programs, others, like the United Kingdom, the forefather of PPP as a policy, have seen PPP fall out of favor (Verhoest et al. 2013, Davies 2018).

In recent years, multilateral development banks and other international financing organizations have played an increasingly significant role in supporting PPP projects in emerging markets. Recognizing that past PPP failures stem from limited public sector capacity, lack of political will, and perceived legitimacy and trust issues (see, for example, Delhi, Palukuri, and Mahalingam 2010; Mahalingam 2010; Mahalingam et al. 2011; Jooste, Levitt, and Scott 2011; Jooste and Scott 2012; Van den Hurk et al. 2015; Verhoest et al. 2015; Opara et al. 2017; Soecipto and Verhoest 2018), these organizations have been building the capacity of national governments and promoting good governance through reforms of key enabling institutional factors and regulatory conditions. This institutional focus emphasizes the fact that private participation in infrastructure (PPI) investment is 'highly sensitive to conditions such as freedom from corruption, rule of law, quality of regulations, and the number of disputes in a sector' (PPIAF 2016, 26–27; Moszoro et al. 2014). Although many of these conditions predate modern conceptions of PPP and generally promote economic development, these factors tend to 'drive the viable formation of partnerships' when 'coupled with local geography, political conditions, and capital market sophistication' (Eggers and Startup 2006, as cited in Casady et al. 2018, 5).

Naturally, many countries have recognized this sensitivity of PPP markets to broader institutional[1] factors and begun to improve their regulatory and investment environments. However, scholars have only recently started to unpack the significance of institutional settings for PPP market maturity (Casady et al. 2018; Hodge, Greve, and Biygautane 2018; Casady et al. 2019; Casady 2020). Some scholars (see, for example, Pessoa 2010; Wankuan, Yongheng, and Youqiang 2010; Liu et al. 2013; Chou and Pramudawardhani 2015; Muhammad and Johar 2017, and so on) have demonstrated that 'a lack of institutional capacity, weak governance systems, and unclear or unsuitable rules and regulations ... [make] PPI arrangements more ineffective in practice' (Pessoa 2010, 1). Others have focused on critical success factors that support PPP programs (Zhang 2005; Matos-Castaño, Mahalingam, and Dewulf 2014; Chou and Pramudawardhani 2015; Opara et al. 2017). For instance, Matos-Castaño et al. (2014) found the emergence and stabilization of PPP programs was contingent on trust, political legitimacy, and organizational capacity. Chou and Pramudawardhani (2015) also observed that PPP programmatic outcomes depend on adequate governmental capacity, transparent procurement procedures, favorable governance, and stable macroeconomic, political, and social conditions. Opara et al. (2017, 77) further demonstrate that 'strong political leadership support for [PPPs], a favorable policy environment, and effective organizational capacity are pre-requisite factors for the successful implementation of [PPPs].'

Unsurprisingly, these institutional dimensions have become increasingly important considerations for PPP preparation, execution, and management because they 'require more rigour in establishing the explanatory factors and evaluating the extent of their contribution ... [to] the success of PPP projects' (Muhammad and Johar 2017, 9130). However, quantifying and analyzing many of these factors remains difficult because data is limited on the subject.

Consequently, few studies have been able to reasonably measure PPP market maturity, despite growing evidence which suggests the ability of countries to deliver sustainable, long-term PPP projects is associated with enabling investment environments (PPIAF 2016). This chapter thus attempts to build on current global representations of PPP market requirements by addressing the following questions:

1. What is PPP market maturity?
2. What data is available to measure it?

To address these questions, we begin by unpacking the theoretical dimensions of PPP market maturity using Casady et al.'s (2020) conceptual model of PPP institutional capabilities: legitimacy, trust, and capacity. Next, we highlight a few available data sources which have already enabled scholars to begin analyzing various dimensions of PPP market maturity. Finally, we discuss new research frontiers scholars may be able to explore using these novel sources.

What is PPP market maturity?

Although global interest in PPPs continues to rise, Hodge and Greve (2017) note that the overall performance of PPP projects and programs remains widely contested. Despite decades of research on PPPs, questions about their efficacy endure because 'the potential causal factors behind why [PPPs] may be capable of producing better performance compared with traditional arrangements' are still not well understood (Hodge and Greve 2017, 56). However, what ultimately denotes superior performance remains an elusive empirical conundrum for many PPP scholars.

The same can also be said for PPP market maturity. What makes PPP markets 'mature' can be a perplexing language game (McConnell 2010), and the term 'maturity' is often used quite loosely to describe a certain degree of national PPP programmatic performance (Casady 2020). As a result, although a number of studies have scrutinized the effects of institutional settings on PPP programs (see, for example, Jooste et al. 2011; Scott, Levitt, and Orr 2011; Matos-Castaño, Dewulf, and Mahalingam 2012; Yang, Hou, and Wang 2013; Matos-Castaño et al. 2014; Opara et al. 2017; Casady 2020; Casady et al. 2020), no uniform meaning for a 'mature' PPP market exists.

Yet, common thematic elements across the literature do offer some scholarly consensus. For instance, Eggers and Startup (2006) at Deloitte originally

devised a three-stage, PPP market maturity curve to illustrate the sophistication of PPP development observed across the world. Likely intended as 'a neat
marketing strategy to boost continued demand for PPP advisory services' (see
Hodge and Greve 2019, 140), this conceptual model stresses the importance
of improving the capacity of government to execute and manage PPPs so
they can 'move up the PPP maturity curve more rapidly and leapfrog to more
advanced stages of maturity' (Eggers and Startup 2006, 6). Matos-Castaño et al.
(2014) also suggest that PPP markets 'emerge' and 'stabilize' towards maturity
because of underlying institutional capabilities. Likewise, Opara et al. (2017)
stress that 'program permanence/continuity' is directly influenced by institutional environments. Casady (2020, 4; emphasis added) further surmises that
'[t]he *sustained* and *stable* mobilization of private investment in infrastructure
through PPPs' is a clear indicator of mature PPP market performance.

Among these studies, institutional settings appear to be a common driver
of PPP programmatic development, stability, and permanency. This evokes
classical notions of institutionalization, a process that 'connotes stability over
time' (Scott 2014, 26) and reflects a program's 'own distinctive history, the
people who have been in it, the groups it embodies and the vested interests they
have created, and the way it has adapted to its environment' (Selznick 1957,
16). Moreover, because these settings tend to mature over time via the ongoing
structuration of organizational fields (Scott and Meyer 1994; see also Jooste et
al. 2011, Jooste and Scott 2012), institutionalization may be the best theoretical
lens we have for assessing PPP market maturity.

Theorizing PPP market maturity: an institutional perspective

Fortunately, some emerging frameworks are now beginning to define PPP
market maturity more succinctly. One such framework put forward by
Casady et al. (2020) describes PPP institutional maturity using three critical
components:

1. Legitimacy – the 'generalized perception or assumption that the actions
    of an entity are desirable, proper or appropriate within some socially con-
    structed system of norms, values, beliefs and definitions' (Suchman 1995,
    574);
2. Trust – 'a disposition and attitude concerning the willingness to rely upon
    the actions of or be vulnerable towards another party, under circumstances

of contractual and social obligations, with the potential for collaboration' (Edkins and Smyth 2006, 84); and

3. Capacity – 'the ability of actors [that is, governments] to structure and govern PPP projects' (Matos-Castaño et al. 2014, 53).

For any PPP market, codification of PPP procurement procedures as well as supportive legal frameworks is one of the first steps governments take to legitimize their PPP programs (Tvarnø 2006, Brinkerhoff and Brinkerhoff 2011). The development of PPP legal frameworks is crucial because these laws create 'a general sense ... that a given policy decision has been formulated in acceptable ways, through justifiable procedures' (see, for example, Hult and Walcott 1990, 63–67). Without such rules, structures, and processes, the PPP market could not function. Thus, a country's regulatory regime often serves as a primary indicator of PPP legitimacy, making it a critical component of market maturity (Casady 2020).

Similarly, trust in PPPs, both from the government and the public, generally dictates their viability as an alternative project delivery mechanism. Opara et al. (2017, 77) specifically stress that 'relevant [PPP] policy measures and committed political support by field actors' often 'enables or disenables [PPP] outcomes.' Warsen et al. (2018) also note that perceived PPP project performance is significantly correlated with trust and management. Thus, the willingness of governments and the public to engage in these long-term, relational contracts can be viewed as a precondition for PPP market maturity as well (Casady et al. 2020).

Finally, the development of PPP market maturity comes down to institutional capacity. PPPs need 'aggressive management by a strong, competent government' (Kettl 2011, 6). This competence stems from training, documented experience, adherence to best practices, and the utilization of PPP-enabling organizations (for example, PPP units, project development funds). Within PPP-enabling fields, the relative strength and weakness (or absence) of these institutions (see, for example, Jooste et al. 2011, Jooste and Scott 2012) ultimately dictates the degree to which governments can design, execute, and manage PPPs.

Overall, these 'institutional environment elements ... are mutually re-enforcing with synergistic effects' (Opara et al. 2017, 77), meaning the preparation, procurement, and management of PPP contracts depends on the government's ability to properly align incentives, cultivate and sustain a trustworthy stakeholder network, and legitimize its PPP processes (Salamon and Elliott 2002; South, Levitt, and Dewulf 2015). When taken together, they create a framework which has proven to be quite useful because of its simplicity in signifying different dimensions of the PPP institutional environment or enabling field. However, quantifying and analyzing these institutional conditions remains an ongoing challenge.

Measuring PPP market maturity: where is the data?

Casady (2020) was the first to attempt to quantify and analyze these institutional capabilities. Using Casady et al.'s (2020) conceptual model of PPP institutional maturity, they operationalized the framework using six underlying institutional constructs:

- C1: Regulatory Regime – The extent to which relevant regulatory frameworks incentivize PPP utilization and/or reduce barriers to PPP execution;
- C2: Market Transparency – The degree of publicness/openness surrounding PPP procurement, bid documents, contractual changes, and evaluations;
- C3: Political and Social Will – The level of political/public support for PPP delivery;
- C4: Market Reliability – The conduciveness of the political/business environment surrounding PPP project development and implementation;
- C5: Institutional Support – The extent to which government agencies, public institutions, and inter-governmental organizations enable PPP procurement and contract management; and
- C6: Governance Mechanisms – The degree to which governments have implemented market-oriented governance mechanisms for managing PPP projects.

These 'super conditions/categories' were theoretically derived from the literature. The sub-indicators used to operationalize them were also combined based on their thematic content as well as other logical procedures. Figure 13.1 portrays the relationship of these conditions to the original components of PPP institutional maturity proposed by Casady et al. (2020).

Using qualitative comparative analysis (QCA), Casady (2020) was able to demonstrate that strong regulatory regimes, political and social will, and market reliability are necessary conditions for PPP market maturation. But these conditions are alone not sufficient to produce the outcome of interest. For some countries, governance mechanisms appear to be sufficient for more mature PPP markets while a combination of institutional support and the

Source: Casady (2020)

Figure 13.1 Operationalized PPP market maturity model

absence of market transparency underpins others.[2] The path-dependence of these findings suggest that legitimacy (that is, regulatory regimes) and trust (that is, political and social will, and market reliability) are essential but alone not sufficient for a mature functioning PPP market, while capacity (that is, mature governance mechanisms and/or institutional support) is sufficient but not necessary.[3] These results reinforce the importance and interdependence of legitimacy, trust, and capacity as critical institutional capabilities for PPP market maturity, but such an analysis was only possible because new data sources on PPP institutional quality emerged in recent years.

The EIU Infrascope Index

The Economist Intelligence Unit's (EIU) Infrascope Index (see, for example, EIU 2017a, 2017b, 2018a, 2019) is one such source, offering some of the first detailed institutional data on PPP markets around the world. Commissioned by the Inter-American Development Bank, Millennium Challenge Corporation, and European Bank for Reconstruction and Development, the index was originally created to identify recent regulatory, institutional, and business environment developments enabling PPP implementation. It now serves as a 'benchmarking tool that evaluates the capacity of countries to implement sustainable and efficient public-private partnerships (PPPs) in key infrastructure sectors, principally transport, electricity, water and solid waste management' (EIU 2018b). Dating back to 2009, the index gradually evolved over the years, becoming more granular and offering a larger geographical coverage. As of 2019, the index covered 67 emerging markets and developing economics (EMDEs) across Latin America and the Caribbean (LAC); Central and Eastern Europe, the Middle East, and Africa (CEMA); and the Asia-Pacific region (APAC) (see Figure 13.2).

What makes this index particularly useful is its rich data on PPP institutional support structures and programmatic outcomes in EMDEs. The index specifically includes information on:

1. Enabling laws and regulations,
2. The institutional framework,
3. Operational maturity,
4. The investment and business climate, and
5. Financing facilities for infrastructure projects.

Within these domains, the underlying sub-indicators of the Infrascope ultimately enabled Casady (2020) to construct institutional conditions for a QCA analysis, thereby opening new possibilities for research on PPP market maturity.

Benchmarking infrastructure development

More recently, the World Bank started benchmarking the institutional quality of countries to prepare, procure, and manage PPP projects. This benchmarking was specifically 'designed to encourage and support governments in improving the quality of regulatory frameworks governing large infrastructure projects' (World Bank 2020, 1). Beginning with a pilot back around 2015, the World Bank, like the EIU Infrascope, gradually updated its methodology, deepened its data granularity, and expanded its geographical coverage (World Bank 2017a, 2018, 2020). In its 2020 publication titled *Benchmarking Infrastructure Development*, the World Bank updated its assessment of the preparation, procurement, and contract management of PPPs (including the management of unsolicited proposals) for 140 countries.[4] The report also

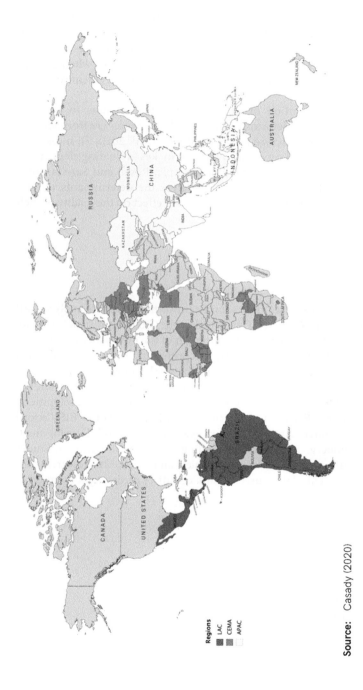

Source: Casady (2020)

Figure 13.2 EIU Infrascope Index coverage

assessed similar preparation, procurement, and contract management capabilities for traditional public investment (TPI) in 40 pilot countries. This addition of TPI measures opens new avenues to compare PPPs like-for-like with conventional projects. This data allows scholars to begin examining whether these institutional variables have different effects on various procurement routes.

While the ultimate intention of this benchmarking remains to 'support evidence-based regulatory reforms to improve the enabling environment for developing quality infrastructure projects' (World Bank 2020, 7), measuring each country's institutional capabilities for PPP makes evaluating elements of PPP market maturity more tractable. For example, Rosell and Saz-Carranza (2020) recently used this information to analyze the determinants of PPP policies and found that transparency has a positive effect on the quality of such policies.

InfraCompass

Finally, another new tool that may soon begin to help scholars analyze PPP market maturity is *InfraCompass*. Developed by the Global Infrastructure Hub, *InfraCompass* objectively quantifies the strength of the infrastructure enabling environment for 81 countries, collectively representing 93 per cent of global gross domestic product and 86 per cent of the world population. Developed for infrastructure policymakers, this tool currently aggregates data from the World Bank, the Organisation for Economic Co-operation and Development, the World Economic Forum, the International Monetary Fund, BIS Oxford Economics, the United Nations Conference on Trade and Development, IJ Global, Bloomberg, S&P Global, Trading Economics, Centre d'Études Prospectives et d'Informations Internationales, and in-country research conducted by Deloitte. This data is used to rank countries across eight themes:

1. Governance,
2. Regulatory frameworks,
3. Permits,
4. Planning,
5. Procurement,
6. Activity,
7. Funding capacity, and
8. Financial markets.

These themes are derived from 41 underlying metrics of institutional quality. Taken together, these thematic areas allow governments and policy specialists to assess a country's institutional strengths and weaknesses and identify opportunities for reform, thereby bolstering market maturity and improving both public and private infrastructure investment (Global Infrastructure Hub 2020a). More information on the construction of InfraCompass can be found in its *Technical Appendix* (Global Infrastructure Hub 2020b).

New frontiers: the opportunity set for PPP market maturity research

Overall, as the PPP field has broadened, deepened, and sharpened, new research frontiers have emerged to propel the discipline forward. While issues around PPP efficacy persist, new areas of inquiry focused on PPP institutions have surfaced. PPP market maturity is one of these new frontiers. Although scholarship on this subject remains relatively nascent, the emergence of novel data on PPP-enabling environments has generated a new opportunity set for PPP market maturity research.

However, when exploring these new frontiers, scholars should proceed with caution. With these new global databases, there is an equal risk that they may hide as much as they reveal. Widespread differences in how PPPs are prepared, procured, and managed exist across countries. Different histories, cultural practices, and habits/routines also matter and actively shape the places of power, process, and political influence that define PPPs.

In the immediate term, some scholars may be able to build on the work of Rosell and Saz-Carranza (2020) as well as Casady (2020) to explore the institutional determinants of PPP markets. By attempting to validate these initial findings as part of a broader theory-building research agenda, the PPP academic community may be able to finally build some definitional consensus around market maturity and performance. Additionally, other scholars may seek to analyze the temporal order of institutional development as a means of prioritizing strategic reform in PPP programs. Moreover, future research could explore how changes in these institutional conditions over time ultimately affect PPP market outcomes. More importantly, these research avenues lend themselves to both quantitative and qualitative types of investigation.

Moving forward, scholars should look to examine how project and programmatic outcomes influence the (in)formal institutionalization of PPP policies. At the same time, scholars should pay particular attention to growing government emphasis on 'the political and governance strengths of [PPPs] over the promised traditional utilitarian project benefits' such as efficiency, risk-transfer, and lifecycle costing (Hodge and Greve 2017, 70). Part of this work should pursue an 'expose' view of PPPs because PPPs, like other organizational forms, 'are not the rational creatures they pretend to be but vehicles for embodying (sometimes surreptitious) values' (Perrow 1986, as cited by Scott 2014, 25). At a minimum, future research on PPP market maturity should continue to 'challeng[e] mainstream interpretations of what PPPs *are* and what their proliferation *means*' because doing so will highlight 'the Western-centric nature of prevailing [PPP] wisdom' (Jones and Bloomfield 2020, 1; original emphasis).

Notes

1.   When referring to institutions, we adopt Scott's (2014, 56) omnibus definition of institutions as the 'regulative, normative, and cultural-cognitive elements that, together with associated activities and resources, provide stability and meaning to social life'.
2.   According to Casady (2020), this second pathway has two possible explanations. The first is institutional support (that is, capacity) may insulate countries from perverse conditions like nascent or weak market transparency. The second suggests certain countries may exploit the absence of external transparency to deliver PPP projects.
3.   QCA is a configurational analysis. Unlike statistical analyses of 'independent variables' which are hampered by collinearity, it is expected in QCA that some conditions may be related to one another. This is actually part of Boolean set logic underpinning these types of analyses (Thomas, O'Mara-Eves, and Brunton 2014).
4.   Further details, methodological information, and the complete dataset is available here: http://bpp.worldbank.org.

References

Baxter, D., and Casady, C.B. (2020) Proactive and strategic healthcare public-private partnerships (PPPs) in the coronavirus (COVID-19) epoch. *Sustainability*, 12 (12): 5097.

Brinkerhoff, D.W., and Brinkerhoff, J.M. (2011) Public–private partnerships: Perspectives on purposes, publicness, and good governance. *Public Administration and Development*, 31 (1): 2–14.

Casady, C.B. (2020) Examining the institutional drivers of public-private partnership (PPP) market performance: A fuzzy set qualitative comparative analysis (fsQCA). *Public Management Review*, 23 (7): 981–1005.

Casady, C.B., Eriksson, K., Levitt, R.E., and Scott, W.R. (2018) Examining the state of public-private partnership (PPP) institutionalization in the United States. *Engineering Project Organization Journal*, 8 (1): 177–198.

Casady, C.B., Eriksson, K., Levitt, R.E., and Scott, W.R. (2019). (Re)Assessing Public–Private Partnership Governance Challenges: An Institutional Maturity Perspective, in *Public–Private Partnerships for Infrastructure Development: Finance, Stakeholder Alignment, Governance*, edited by R.E. Levitt, W.R. Scott and M. Garvin. Cheltenham, UK and Northampton, MA, USA: Edward Elgar Publishing, pp. 188–204

Casady, C.B., Eriksson, K., Levitt, R.E., and Scott, W.R. (2020) (Re)defining public-private partnerships (PPPs) in the New Public Governance (NPG) paradigm: An institutional maturity perspective. *Public Management Review*, 22 (2): 161–183.

Casady, C.B., and Geddes, R.R. (2016) *Private Participation in US Infrastructure: The Role of PPP Units*. Washington, DC: American Enterprise Institute.

Casady, C.B., and Peci, F. (2020) The institutional challenges of public-private partnerships (PPPs) in transition economies: Lessons from Kosovo. *Economic Research-Ekonomska Istraživanja*, 34 (1): 1–17.

Chou, J.-S., and Pramudawardhani, D. (2015) Cross-country comparisons of key drivers, critical success factors and risk allocation for public-private partnership projects. *International Journal of Project Management*, 33 (5): 1136–1150.

Davies, R. (2018, October 29) Hammond abolishes PFI contracts for new infrastructure projects. *The Guardian*.

Delhi, V.S.K., Palukuri, S., and Mahalingam, A. (2010) *Governance Issues in Public Private Partnerships in Infrastructure Projects in India*. Paper presented at the Engineering Project Organizations Conference, South Lake Tahoe, CA.

Economist Intelligence Unit (EIU) (2017a) *Evaluating the Environment for Public-Private Partnerships in Eastern Europe, Central Asia and the Southern and Eastern Mediterranean: The 2017 Infrascope*. New York, NY: EIU.

Economist Intelligence Unit (EIU) (2017b) *Evaluating the Environment for Public-Private Partnerships in Latin America and the Caribbean: The 2017 Infrascope*. New York, NY: EIU.

Economist Intelligence Unit (EIU) (2018a) *Evaluating the Environment for Public-Private Partnerships in Asia: The 2018 Infrascope*. New York, NY: EIU.

Economist Intelligence Unit (EIU) (2018b) *Measuring the Enabling Environment for Public-Private Partnerships in Infrastructure*. New York, NY: EIU.

Economist Intelligence Unit (EIU) (2019) *Evaluating the Environment for Public-Private Partnerships in Latin America and the Caribbean: The 2019 Infrascope*. New York, NY: EIU.

Edkins, A.J., and Smyth, H.J. (2006) Contractual management in PPP projects: Evaluation of legal versus relational contracting for service delivery. *Journal of Professional Issues in Engineering Education and Practice*, 132 (1): 82–93.

Eggers, W.D., and Startup, T. (2006) *Closing the Infrastructure Gap: The Role of Public-Private Partnerships*. Deloitte Research Study. New York, NY: Deloitte.

Global Infrastructure Hub (2020a) *InfraCompass 2020*. Sydney: GI Hub.

Global Infrastructure Hub (2020b) *Technical Appendix*. Sydney, Australia: GI Hub.

Hodge, G., and Greve, C. (2010) Public-private partnerships: Governance scheme or language game? *Australian Journal of Public Administration*, 69: S8–S22.

Hodge, G., and Greve, C. (2019) Market development and public–private partnerships, in *The Logic of Public–Private Partnerships? The Enduring Interdependency of Politics and Markets*, edited by G. Hodge and C. Greve. Cheltenham, UK and Northampton, MA, USA: Edward Elgar Publishing, pp. 137–160.

Hodge, G., Greve, C., and Biygautane, M. (2018) Do PPP's work? What and how have we been learning so far? *Public Management Review*, 20 (8): 1105–1121.

Hodge, G.A., and Greve, C. (2007) Public-private partnerships: An international performance review. *Public Administration Review*, 67 (3): 545–558.

Hodge, G.A., and Greve, C. (2017) On public–private partnership performance: A contemporary review. *Public Works Management & Policy*, 22 (1): 55–78.

Hult, K.M., and Walcott, C.E. (1990) *Governing Public Organizations: Politics, Structures, and Institutional Design.* Pacific Grove, CA: Brooks/Cole Pub Co.

Jones, L., and Bloomfield, M.J. (2020) PPPs in China: Does the growth in Chinese PPPs signal a liberalising economy? *New Political Economy*, 25 (5): 829–847.

Jooste, S.F., Levitt, R.E., and Scott, W.R. (2011) Beyond 'one size fits all': How local conditions shape PPP enabling field development. *Engineering Project Organization Journal*, 1 (1): 11–25.

Jooste, S.F., and Scott, W.R. (2012) The public–private partnership enabling field: Evidence from three cases. *Administration & Society*, 44 (2): 149–182.

Kettl, D.F. (2011) *Sharing Power: Public Governance and Private Markets.* Washington, DC: Brookings Institution Press.

Liu, J., Love, P., Davis, P.R., Smith, J., and Regan, M. (2013) Performance measurement framework in PPP projects. In *P3BooK 2013: Proceedings of International Conference on PPP Body of Knowledge in Preston, UK, University of Central Lancashire, Lancashire*, pp. 55–64.

Mahalingam, A. (2010) PPP experiences in Indian cities: Barriers, enablers, and the way forward. *Journal of Construction Engineering and Management*, 136 (4): 419–429.

Mahalingam, A., Rajan, T., Seddon, J., Santosh, V., and Srinivasan, S. (2011) Creating an enabling ambient environment for PPPs. Chennai: IIT-Madras & Centre for Development Finance.

Matos-Castaño, J., Dewulf, G., and Mahalingam, A. (2012) The complex interplay between the institutional context and PPP project outcomes. In *Proceedings of the Engineering Project Organization Conference*, pp. 10–12.

Matos-Castaño, J., Mahalingam, A., and Dewulf, G. (2014) Unpacking the path-dependent process of institutional change for PPPs. *Australian Journal of Public Administration*, 73 (1): 47–66.

McConnell, A. (2010) *Understanding Policy Success: Rethinking Public Policy.* Basingstoke: Palgrave Macmillan.

Moszoro, M., Araya, G., Ruiz-Nuñez, F., and Schwartz, J. (2014) Institutional and political determinants of private participation in infrastructure. In *Public Private Partnerships for Transport Infrastructure: Renegotiations, How to Approach Them and Economic Outcomes.* Washington, DC: ITF Roundtable, pp. 121–148.

Muhammad, Z., and Johar, F. (2017) A conceptual framework for evaluating the success of public-private partnership (PPP) projects. *Advanced Science Letters*, 23 (9): 9130–9134.

Opara, M., Elloumi, F., Okafor, O., and Warsame, H. (2017) Effects of the institutional environment on public-private partnership (P3) projects: Evidence from Canada. *Accounting Forum*, 41 (2): 77–95.

Pessoa, A. (2010) *Reviewing PPP Performance in Developing Economies.* FEP Working Papers 362, Universidade do Porto, Faculdade de Economia do Porto.

Public-Private Infrastructure Advisory Facility (PPIAF) (2014) *PPIAF Supports the Institutional and Policy Environment for PPPs in Jordan.* Washington, DC: World Bank.

Public-Private Infrastructure Advisory Facility (PPIAF) (2016) *The State of PPPs: Infrastructure Public-Private Partnerships in Emerging Markets & Developing Economies 1991–2015.* Washington, DC: World Bank.

Rosell, J., and Saz-Carranza, A. (2020) Determinants of public–private partnership policies. *Public Management Review*, 22 (8): 1171–1190.

Salamon, L.M., and Elliott, O.V. (2002) *The Tools of Government: A Guide to the New Governance.* Oxford: Oxford University Press.

Scott, W.R. (2014) *Institutions and Organizations: Ideas, Interests, and Identities.* Thousand Oaks, CA: SAGE.

Scott, W.R., Levitt, R.E., and Orr, R.J. (eds) (2011) *Global Projects: Institutional and Political Challenges.* Cambridge: Cambridge University Press.

Scott, W.R., and Meyer, J.W. (1994) *Institutional Environments and Organizations: Structural Complexity and Individualism.* Thousand Oaks, CA: SAGE.

Selznick, P. (1957) *Leadership in Administration.* New York, NY: Harper & Row.

Soecipto, R.M., and Verhoest, K. (2018) Contract stability in European road infrastructure PPPs: How does governmental PPP support contribute to preventing contract renegotiation? *Public Management Review*, 20 (8): 1145–1164.

South, A.J., Levitt, R.E., and Dewulf, G.P.M.R. (2015) Dynamic stakeholder networks and the governance of PPPs. In *Proceedings of the 2nd International Conference on Public-Private Partnerships.*

Suchman, M.C. (1995) Managing legitimacy: Strategic and institutional approaches. *Academy of Management Review*, 20 (3): 571–610.

Teisman, G.R., and Klijn, E.-H. (2002) Partnership arrangements: Governmental rhetoric or governance scheme? *Public Administration Review*, 62 (2): 197–205.

Thomas, J., O'Mara-Eves, A., and Brunton, G. (2014) Using qualitative comparative analysis (QCA) in systematic reviews of complex interventions: A worked example. *Systematic Reviews*, 3 (1): 1–14.

Tvarnø, C.D. (2006) Denmark: Public-private partnerships from a Danish perspective. *Public Procurement Law Review*, 15: 98–108.

Van den Hurk, M., Brogaard, L., Lember, V., Helby Petersen, O., and Witz, P. (2015) National varieties of public–private partnerships (PPPs): A comparative analysis of PPP-supporting units in 19 European countries. *Journal of Comparative Policy Analysis: Research and Practice*, 18 (1): 1–20.

Verhoest, K., Carbonara, N., Lember, V., Helby Petersen, O., Scherrer, W., and Van den Hurk, M. (2013) *Public Private Partnerships in Transport: Trends & Theory P3T3.* Discussion Papers Part I. COST. https://citeseerx.ist.psu.edu/viewdoc/download?doi =10.1.1.669.1347&rep=rep1&type=pdf.

Verhoest, K., Helby Petersen, O., Scherrer, W., and Soecipto, R.M. (2015) How do governments support the development of public private partnerships? Measuring and comparing PPP governmental support in 20 European countries. *Transport Reviews*, 35 (2): 118–139.

Wankuan, Z., Yongheng, Y., and Youqiang, W. (2010) An empirical study on key factors influencing the performance of public-private partnerships (PPP) in some transitional countries. *Journal of Public Management*, 3: 16.

Warsen, R., Nederhand, J., Klijn, E.-H., Grotenbreg, S., and Koppenjan, J. (2018) What makes public-private partnerships work? Survey research into the outcomes and the quality of cooperation in PPPs. *Public Management Review*, 20 (8): 1165–1185.

World Bank (2017a) Benchmarking Public-Private Partnerships Procurement 2017: Assessing Government Capability to Prepare, Procure, and Manage PPPs. Washington, DC: IBRD/World Bank.

World Bank (2017b) Public Private Partnerships Reference Guide: Version 3. Washington, DC: IBRD/World Bank.

World Bank (2018) Procuring Infrastructure Public-Private Partnerships Report 2018: Assessing Government Capability to Prepare, Procure, and Manage PPPs. Washington, DC: IBRD/World Bank.

World Bank (2020) Benchmarking Infrastructure Development 2020: Assessing Regulatory Quality to Prepare, Procure, and Manage PPPs and Traditional Public Investment in Infrastructure Projects. Washington, DC: IBRD/World Bank.

Yang, Y., Hou, Y., and Wang, Y. (2013) On the development of public–private partnerships in transitional economies: An explanatory framework. *Public Administration Review*, 73 (2): 301–310.

Zhang, X. (2005) Critical success factors for public–private partnerships in infrastructure development. *Journal of Construction Engineering and Management*, 131 (1): 3–14.

14 The determinants of PPP uptake in Europe: a mixed methods approach[1]

Moritz Liebe

Introduction

After almost three decades of research into public–private partnerships (PPPs), we can now look at a rich, multifaceted body of literature around this phenomenon. As the introduction to this edited volume convincingly demonstrates, the research agenda evolved far beyond the concept itself. However, if we look at how the body of research has grown over time, we can see that comparative research is somewhat underrepresented (Hodge et al. 2018). This fact should not come as a surprise; PPPs are a very complex construct with different meanings and are embedded in different political and historical settings. Given the high number of variables that require consideration, generalisations across many cases are, therefore, a conceptual challenge – in particular, if we want to quantify our findings. Even if we succeed, we usually have to pay the price of sacrificing contextual information. Methodological advancements may offer us a way forward. For instance, qualitative comparative analysis (QCA) has become fashionable in PPP research in the past five to ten years as a means to conduct large-N comparative studies (cf. the Introduction, Casady 2020, Krumm 2014). This chapter will demonstrate the added value of applying a mixed methods design, which combines a quantitative large-N and a qualitative small-N analysis. Concurrent triangulation will allow us to look at the broad canvas of correlations and patterns without giving up a looking glass to spot the small differences and understand the causal mechanisms at work.

One topic suitable for a mixed methods design is the question of what factors determine the variation in uptake of PPPs. This question has been deliberated repeatedly – albeit inconclusively – in previous publications but primarily as single case studies. Comparative research can add to our understanding of the determinants of PPPs by establishing whether a factor also applies to other jurisdictions. Moreover, the quantitative approach allows us to weigh the relative importance of such factors for the uptake of PPPs. By contrast, the qualitative approach gives us the opportunity to prod deeper where the quantitative analysis can only scratch the surface.

In this chapter, we will put five broad hypotheses concerning the reasons for PPP uptake in the Member States of the European Union (EU) to the test. These hypotheses concern the public finances, the performance of the public sector, the predominant economic policies, and the political and economic institutions of the country. The quantitative analysis is a time-series-cross-sectional analysis (panel analysis) on PPP deals concluded in 23 EU Member States within the years 1990–2008. In addition to the panel analysis, a qualitative analysis of PPP uptake in Germany and France has been conducted. Those two sets of analysis will be the main body of the chapter; due to space constraints, findings from the case studies will be presented in a more complementary fashion. Beforehand, the rationale for using a mixed methods approach and its operationalisation will be spelt out.

The rationale for applying a concurrent triangulation design

The appeal of comparative research is that it allows us to make inferences about the absence or presence of certain variables for a particular outcome. We can approach a comparison from two sides: either through quantitative large-N analysis (LNA) across many cases and a higher level of abstraction or qualitative small-N analysis (SNA) across few cases but with a higher degree of detail and contextual information. Both methods differ with respect to their logic of inquiry and focus on different forms of causality. LNA is probabilistic in its outlook and interested in the relative 'effect of causes'; SNA and qualitative research are more interested in the 'causes of effects' and rather deterministic (Della Porta 2008, 204). SNA allows for a close inspection of a few cases to better understand the mechanisms through which a causal factor is operating, something an LNA cannot deliver. The costs are a higher possibility of selection bias, lack of formality and replicability, and 'weak empirical leverage' (Gerring 2007, 6). By contrast, the inclusion of many cases and random sampling in LNA yields a higher external validity and confidence in the generalisations drawn from the analysis. Further, a quantitative analysis is superior to an SNA in its ability to assess the relative effect of rival explanations and control variables simultaneously; something which SNA would overlook due to its own logic of case selection (Lieberman 2005). However, proponents of the small-N approach argue that there is a danger of a conceptual overstretch in LNA and that this type of analysis is prone to measurement error (Gerring 2007). Suppose we adopt a problem-centred logic (as opposed to philosophical dogma). In that case, there is little which speaks against combining both logics of inquiry to mitigate the shortcomings of each approach and benefit from their advantages (Creswell 2009). Proponents of mixed methods have developed a rich repertoire of inquiry strategies that help researchers combine different methods or research questions. The most common form is a concurrent triangulation approach (Creswell 2003). Concurrent triangulation keeps the data collection and the analysis stage separate, and the findings of each are only compared after completion (Watkins and Gioia 2015). The approach usually delivers substantiated findings but poses a challenge regarding the interpretation of discrepant findings due to separate processes of data collection and analysis (Creswell 2009).

Theorising and operationalising the study of variation in uptake of PPPs

There are many accounts as to why governments decide to resort to PPPs for infrastructure procurement and public service provision. A publication by the European PPP Expertise Centre (EPEC 2015) lists no fewer than 15 arguments in favour of PPPs. Essentially two themes reoccur in the literature repeatedly: investment under budgetary constraints and public sector reforms. Both are linked to the same goal of improved microeconomic efficiencies. The pre-financing through the private sector may facilitate the additional investment in times of scarce public resources (Winch et al. 2012; for a discussion of why PPPs may be attractive under real and rule-imposed borrowing constraints see Buso et al. 2017). The relevance of these factors has been confirmed in previous comparative research. A qualitative cross-country analysis by Onishi and Winch (2012) identified additionality as the main driver for PPP use. Krumm (2014) finds a significant bivariate correlation between the mean of deficit levels of EU Member States and PPP uptake; his subsequent QCA analysis found a less pronounced effect. Based on these observations, we arrive at this hypothesis:

Hypothesis 1: PPPs are more likely to be adopted in the light of budgetary constraints.

The concept of PPPs with its incentive structure to account for life-cycle costs of projects and competitive tendering resounds with the principles of New Public Management (Grimsey and Lewis 2004, Yescombe 2007). PPPs offer a tool to run public services on business management principles, namely output controls, performance standards and financial incentives. The changes initiated through the introduction of PPPs can lead to further public sector reforms to ensure a level playing field. More ambitious reformers understand PPPs as a part of a wider project to redefine the role of the state. In their vision, the state should withdraw from the role of a service provider and act instead as a regulator and guarantor of services. In light of accounts, which understand PPPs as a solution to introduce more efficient public services, a second hypothesis can be presented as follows:

Hypothesis 2: PPPs are more likely to be adopted in the light of underperforming public services.

Whereas most government policy papers and private sector publications treat PPPs as a functional response to policy problems, it is not clear that they can be understood as an apolitical, neutral tool. Instead, if we consider that PPPs affect and benefit social and economic interests disproportionally and challenge established practices, then the introduction of the new procurement method becomes political. In fact, several pundits understand PPPs as a tool to reinforce neoliberal principles (Fine 2020, Hearne 2006). The question, therefore, is what motivates policymakers to initiate such a change? The literature on public choice offers a possible answer: policymakers are guided by their desire to maximise their utility (Butler 2012). In this context, utility is derived by policymakers advancing either particular policies or their careers; often, both interests overlap. Irrespective of the motive, politicians will, if they want to stay in the political arena, pursue policies that resound with the political preferences of the electorate they represent. Following from this assumption on the general behaviour of politicians and bearing in mind that PPPs are perceived to be a tool of liberal economics, we can state the following hypothesis:

Hypothesis 3: PPPs are adopted when politicians who pursue liberal economic policies are in power.

Irrespective of the policies decision-makers pursue, their actions are guided, enabled or constrained by established practices – also commonly referred to as institutions. New Institutionalism includes different strands of analysis that stress how institutions affect the preferences of actors operating within institutions. There are two ways that institutions may shape the decision-making process leading to the introduction of PPPs. On the one hand, the necessary provisions have to be channelled through the political system to gain approval. On the other hand, the new concept will have to fit into the economic system or be adjusted accordingly to be successfully adopted. Two types of literature can substantiate what new institutionalism spells out in general terms: veto player theory and the Varieties of Capitalism (VoC) literature.

Veto player theory builds on the observation that laws and policies seldom resemble the original policy proposals. The reason for the divergence is to be found in the political institutions and the number of veto players which can uphold a policy proposal. Therefore, for agenda-setters to be successful, they will have to accommodate policy preferences of actors occupying veto point positions. The likelihood for policy change hinges on the number of players, the relative influence of these players, and the decision-making rules within institutional veto players (Stoiber 2006, Tsebelis 2010). In fact, Krumm (2014) argues that the presence or absence of possible veto players within government was the most influential factor in the variation in PPP uptake. Based on the observation of veto player theory, we can arrive at the following proposition:

Hypothesis 4: The number of veto players determines the likelihood of PPP uptake.

In recent years, the research on PPPs turned to the study of institutions to understand why PPPs are used and under what conditions their usage becomes permanent (Casady in Chapter 13 of this volume provides one framework on the roles of institutions; insights for PPPs in Europe are provided in Mota and Moreira 2015, and Krumm 2014). Whether or not PPPs find appeal in a country may also be a matter of how well they fit into its economic institutions. Scholars of comparative capitalism and VoC have engaged with how domestic economies differ, what factors contribute to their relative success and how they respond and adjust to economic challenges. In Hall and Soskice's (2002) seminal work on VoC, the authors found that the marked difference between capitalist economies is how firms organise their relations with competitors, the workforce and other actors. They distinguish between the ideal types of liberal market economies (LMEs) – where firms organise their relations mainly through contracting and stand in competition – and coordinated market economies (CMEs), where firms organise their relations through more informal and relational modes of cooperation. Countries not fulfilling the criteria of these ideal types can be classified as mixed market economies (MMEs), which display both forms of cooperation and therefore are at a disadvantage as they cannot benefit to the same degree from complementarities. Often the state has to step in to mitigate those shortcomings. Economic institutions are sticky because they are fine-tuned systems, where institutions in one sphere of cooperation, like governance on a firm level, complement other institutions such as vocational training; that is, one institutional arrangement will increase the returns from another. Hypothetically, PPPs offer both systems of cooperation a means to emulate some features of the other (Hodge and Greve 2019). In LME countries, they allow for the introduction of a relational arrangement embedded in a market-based mechanism. In countries with a coordinative mode of cooperation, PPPs present a way of introducing market mechanisms. Based on the observation of VoC scholars that liberal and coordinated market economies will likely respond to economic challenges with their preferred mode of cooperation, the following hypothesis can be stated:

Hypothesis 5: The uptake of PPPs is determined by the mode of cooperation of a country's economy.

Operationalisation

Data from the European Investment Bank (Kappeler 2012), which covers PPP activity across 25 countries since 1990, offers the possibility to apply a panel data analysis. For two reasons, we limit the analysis to a sub-sample of 23 EU Member States and a study period of 19 years. First, the analysis is cut off in 2008 due to considerations on how best to account for the distorting effects of the global financial crisis on financing conditions and the perception of PPPs by the public. Second, neither Luxembourg nor Lithuania recorded PPP activity in the study period, and we gain no analytical leverage from their inclusion. A negative binomial regression model[2] is applied to the number of signed PPP deals as a dependent variable.[3] A Hausman test[4] confirmed that the estimator can be further specified as a random effect model. Therefore the analysis can make full use of the time- and space-related information. To address possible problems of aggregate trends and stationarity, the model required the modification of the dependent variables by introducing a lag or a first difference, respectively. A potentially problematic outlier for the analysis is the UK, as it holds by far the largest market share. Subsequently, several models are presented below – a model without the UK and a separate time-series analysis of the UK. Naturally, the UK time-series model omits several time-invariant variables and therefore only allows comparison on a limited set of variables.

The quantitative inquiry is guided in broader terms by the hypotheses outlined above. However, to establish a link between the available data and the explanandum, we break down these hypotheses further. This variable selection is not only a matter of convenience but also owes to the fact that not only is the phenomenon under study multifaceted, but so are some of the regressors. The following passage spells out how the hypotheses will be operationalised and tested. Governments can be constrained in their financial room for manoeuvre in a short-term and a long-term fashion. Consequently, the model incorporates a measure of the annual deficit relative to GDP (Deficit) and the overall debt level relative to GDP (Debt) (European Commission 2015). The second guiding hypothesis states that PPPs are more likely to be adopted in the context of underperforming public services. The performance of public services is operationalized in this chapter through the ICRG Quality of Government indicator (QualGovt) (Teorell et al. 2015). The question of whether the use of PPPs is determined by governments pursuing liberal economic policies is put to the test with an indicator measuring ideological complexion (LeftRight), which is derived from Seki and Williams (2014) and Volkens et al. (2014). Veto points may affect the government's autonomy to pursue its policies – constraining factors may be the presence of coalition partners (Parties) and the overall power it holds (Type) (Seki and Williams 2014), as well as the institutional constraints embedded in a country's political system (InstConstraint) (Henisz 2002, continued in Teorell et al. 2015). The final proposition developed above is that there is a marked difference between the uptake of PPPs and the mode of cooperation within a country's economic system. We account for this factor in two ways: employment of Jahn's (2016) index of corporatism (Corporatism)[5] and the introduction of a nominal variable reflecting the different clusters of countries.[6] The estimator is completed by several control variables which were used in previous studies (Hammami et al. 2006, Krumm 2014): the size of the population (Population), gross added value per capita (GDP), gross fixed capital formation (GCF), and the size of the construction and finance sector, respectively. The quantitative estimator can be summarised as follows:

$$PPP_{num} = \beta_0 + \beta_1 Population(\log)_{i,t} + \beta_2 \Delta GDP_t + \beta_3 \Delta GCF_i + \beta_4 Finance_{i,t-1}$$

$$+ \beta_5 \Delta Construction_i + \beta_6 \Delta Debt_i + \beta_7 Deficit_{i,t-1} + \beta_8 QualGovt_{i,t-1}$$

$$+ \beta_9 InstConstra\,\mathrm{int}_{i,t-1} + \beta_{10} Type_{i,t-1} + \beta_{11} Corporatism_{i,t-1} + \mu_{i,t}$$

An SNA, which considers the process by which modern infrastructure PPPs were introduced in France and Germany, complements the aforementioned model. Two considerations guide the specific choice of cases. First, France and Germany are close approximate cases of an MME and a CME. Second, the two cases fulfil many criteria of a most similar case selection strategy, which expects cases to vary on independent variables but are similar with regard to intervening or possible spurious variables (Burnham 2008). Germany and France are the largest and second-largest Member States of the EU in terms of population and the size of the economy. Both countries show a very similar development with regard to GDP per capita and average debt levels.

The determinants and mechanisms of PPP uptake in Europe

Over 25 years (1990–2015), some 1786 projects amounting to €338.1 bn were procured through PPPs in the EU Member States; within the study period of the quantitative analysis (1990–2008), 1209 projects were signed with a capital value of €235.8 bn (Kappeler 2012, Vandeburie 2016). Measured by relative market share, the most active countries in PPP procurement were the larger EU Member States. However, smaller countries such as Greece and Portugal would rank very high if one were to compare the capital invested through PPPs with a country's population, its economic strength (expressed in GDP), and public investment (gross fixed capital formation of the state). Irrespective of the viewing angle, the UK consistently sticks out as a leader in PPP adoption. What catches the eye is that the Member States with a low infrastructure endowment also invest a larger share of infrastructure through PPPs relative to their gross fixed capital investment. By expressing PPP activity in this way, one can also see that CMEs consistently rank lower than the Member States with other VoC.

Panel analysis

The qualitative difference in PPP uptake in the EU Member States respective to their mode of economic cooperation and the outlier position of the UK informed the decision to conduct and present the LNA along those categories. Table 14.1 depicts the negative binominal model by categorical variable and country groups. The first model presents the data for the EU with a detailed account of different categories of the regressors. This model serves mainly as a reference point. Models two and three show the results of the panel analysis excluding the UK and the time-series model of the UK, respectively. Model four introduces a VoC variable to the EU model.

At first sight, demographic factors seem to play a relevant role in the PPP uptake on the continent. However, the effect size is more apparent than real since the regressor is the logarithm of the population (in 1000) variable. Likewise, the influence of infrastructure investment (GFC) seems negligible; the effect is small and becomes insignificant when the UK is excluded from the equation. The control variables regarding the potential influence of the industry, however, deliver interesting results. In the UK, a 1 per cent increase in the share of the finance industry relative to overall gross added value results in a decrease in the log number of PPPs by 0.979, which can be explained by the fact that the finance sector contracted relative to other sectors of the

Table 14.1   Negative binominal model by categorical variable and country groups

Variables	(1) EU	(2) EU without UK	(3) UK	(4) VoC
Population (1000; log)	1.3434***	1.0670***	11.27	1.2321***
	(0.0000)	(0.0000)	(16.37)	(0.0000)
GDP p.c.	0.1030	-0.1327	0.507***	-0.1534
	(0.6709)	(0.6387)	(0.0651)	(0.5598)
GFC/GDP	-0.0010***	0.0280	-0.0606	0.0081
	(0.9960)	(0.8966)	(0.112)	(0.9640)
Corporatism				
Very low level	baseline	baseline	omitted	baseline
Low level	-0.2199	1.7706**		-0.2395
	(0.5642)	(0.0016)		(0.6750)
Medium level	-0.0504	2.3758***		0.0924
	(0.8707)	(0.0000)		(0.8952)
High level	0.4205	2.8296***		0.9400
	(0.3426)	0.0000)		(0.3025)
Quality of gov't				
Good	baseline	baseline		baseline
Very good	0.5169	0.3774	baseline	0.3110
	(0.0688)	(0.1435)		(0.2780)
Excellent	0.0868	-0.9303**	-0.330***	-0.0385
	(0.7900)	(0.0059)	(0.113)	(0.9157)

	(1)	(2)	(3)	(4)
Variables	EU	EU without UK	UK	VoC
Left–right				
Left	baseline	baseline		baseline
Left–centre	0.1497	-0.1944		0.0390
	(0.7878)	(0.6000)		(0.9291)
Centre	-0.2159	-0.7469	baseline	-0.3971
	(0.7051)	(0.0659)		(0.3819)
Right–centre	-0.5575	-0.8701		-0.5075
	(0.3533)	(0.0595)		(0.2962)
Right	-0.9681	-1.3021*	-0.546***	-1.0038*
	(0.1137)	(0.0205)	(0.147)	(0.0459)
Gov't parties	1.1114*	0.7864	omitted	1.1250*
	(0.0180)	(0.0832)		(0.0108)
Type of gov't				
Single-party gov't	baseline	baseline	omitted	baseline
Coalition gov't	-0.0723	1.1352		0.5268
	(0.9302)	(0.1733)		(0.5636)
Surplus coalition	2.8985***	3.9601***		3.2986***
	(0.0001)	(0.0000)		(0.0000)
Single-party minority	-0.8178**	-0.1628		-0.4831
	(0.0075)	(0.5417)		(0.0976)
Multi-party minority	-3.9014***	-2.3657*		-3.3619***
	(0.0001)	(0.0154)		(0.0006)
Gov't parties * Type				
Coalition gov't	-1.2108*	-1.0985*	omitted	-1.1995*
	(0.0232)	(0.0346)		(0.0235)

	(1)	(2)	(3)	(4)
Variables	EU	EU without UK	UK	VoC
Surplus coalition	-1.8371***	-1.6794***		-1.9152***
	(0.0003)	(0.0006)		(0.0000)
Pol. constraint	-4.2620***	-3.4468***	0.482	-3.4343**
	(0.0002)	(0.0010)	(3.337)	(0.0047)
Net lending	0.1243***	0.0994**	-0.173***	0.1087**
	(0.0000)	(0.0040	(0.0228)	(0.0010)
Debt/GDP	-0.0015	-0.0147	0.105***	-0.0166
	(0.9665)	(0.7561)	(0.0254)	(0.6732)
Finance	0.5867***	0.3967***	-0.979***	0.2886***
	(0.0000)	(0.0000)	(0.193)	(0.0009)
Construction	0.3586	0.2468	-1.506***	0.3536
	(0.1122)	(0.2837)	(0.351)	(0.1005)
VoC				
LME				baseline
MME				-1.2051
				(0.0709)
CME				-1.9598**
				(0.0015)
NMS (New Member State)				-2.1430***
				(0.0002)
PPP numbers			0.00154	
			(0.00371)	
Constant	-14.2745***	-12.8298***	-121.2	-10.7294***
	(3.040)	(0.0000)	(178.2)	(0.0000)
Observations	312	299	13	312

	(1)	(2)	(3)	(4)
Variables	EU	EU without UK	UK	VoC
Number of countries	23	22		23
AIC (Akaike information criterion)	801.2259	634.7126	101.7006	789.1163

Notes: GFC, GDP, Construction and Debt were first-differenced. The remaining variables are lagged by one time unit. GFC = Gross fixed capital formation; GDP = Gross domestic product. Robust standard errors in parentheses. *** p<0.001, ** p<0.01, * p<0.05

economy in the period 1997–2004. A similar picture presents itself with regard to the construction industry. By contrast, there is a significant correlation between the log number of PPPs and the size of the finance industry on the continent, whereas the size of the construction industry does not have a significant effect. A central point of the debate in the PPP literature is the degree to which the level of public indebtedness or public deficits affects the use of PPPs. The estimate delivered somewhat unexpected results, though. Whereas our assumptions are met in the UK, and the likelihood of PPP uptake increases with a higher debt level and a higher public annual deficit, we can observe the reverse on the continent. Surprisingly, a positive net lending figure[7] corresponds to a higher expected count of PPP projects – even though the effect is fairly small. The effect of debt levels seems to be marginal and non-significant. The quality of government appears to be a significant predictor of PPP numbers on both accounts (the UK and the rest of Europe). The expected difference in log count of PPPs in the UK was 0.33 lower when the quality of government is rated 'excellent' than when it is rated 'very good'; this result is highly significant. A similar picture presents itself when we consider the PPP developments in the rest of Europe. The expected log count of PPPs is 0.377 times higher when the quality of government is rated 'very good' as opposed to 'good', and 0.930 lower when the quality of government is ranked 'excellent' rather than 'good'. Expressed in other terms: the expected mean count of PPP projects if all cases were set at a 'good' level of quality is 1.06; for a 'very good' level the number is 1.54, and for an 'excellent' level only 0.417. The difference between the two lower criteria is significant. Of course, the question arises how those findings relate to the hypothesis that governments will engage more with PPPs to improve and reform public services. The lower expected numbers of PPPs in governments with an excellent ranking vis-à-vis governments that perform less well seems to confirm the hypothesis partially. The lower expected count of PPP projects in countries with only a 'good' rating in the quality of government appears to contradict the assumption. Still, it would confirm another strand of the PPP literature which stresses the importance of a well-functioning public service to make PPPs work. As expected from the knowledge about the development of the Public Finance Initiative projects in the UK and the fact that the New Labour Government heavily championed this new policy, it does not come as a surprise that the analysis of PPP use in the UK finds that there is an expected difference in ideological complexion. Also, in the rest of Europe, we can observe differences, whereas the further a government leans to the right, the lower the expected count in PPPs. The 'left–right' variable is a borderline significant predictor for PPP use as a chi-square test on the elements of the variable indicates (chi-square: 9.27; $p > 0.0546$) and the difference between a government pursuing leftist policies to more centrist and right-wing governments with respect to PPP use. A possible explanation for this finding is the claim frequently made in the literature that PPPs are an alternative means to privatisation policies; whereas PPPs stand for private sector involvement and the use of private finance, they can be regarded as the lesser evil compared to privatisation, where the public side relinquishes its control (Savas 2000). The political constraints variable, which reflects the institutional veto points of a political system, shows a very high significant effect on PPP use in an expected direction; that is, with greater constraints, the expected number of PPPs would decrease. If we consider the relative power of a government, we see a mixed picture. The number of parties in a government seems to play a role but only for the model that accounts for the EU as a whole. The relative power of a government versus its opposition has stronger influence. PPP usage is most likely to happen in surplus coalitions instead of minority governments and even a single-party government. At first sight, the finding that the incidence rate of PPPs increases with more than one party in power appears to contradict the assumption that PPPs are less likely to occur with more parties being involved in government. The lower expected log count in PPPs with single-party government may confirm the claim in the literature that PPPs are the second-best solution for providing more efficient public services or infrastructure. A single-party government may have to find fewer compromises and may be more able to pursue privatisation strategies or raise taxes to finance the new endeavour. By testing the effect of different levels of corporatism in a country's economic system on the continent, we find that the expected log PPP number increases in a linear fashion, the higher the level of corporatism is. This finding stands in contrast with another result we obtain when we treat belonging to a particular type of market economy as a predictor variable. The predicted number of PPPs is markedly higher in LMEs, were we to assume all countries in our sample fall in this category. However, what is also apparent is that the predicted number of projects in the MME category is higher than the number in other groups (2.22 versus 1.04 in CME and 0.87 in

NMS). At this point, we can return to the discrepancy between the finding on corporatism and the VoC variable. Upon closer inspection, 'low' and 'very low' levels of corporatism are only found in the transition economies of the new EU Member States so that effectively the corporatism regressor is reflected in the marginal difference in PPP uptake between NMS and the remaining types of economies.

France

France experimented with the introduction of design-build-finance-operate models in the 1990s. However, the procedures of granting contracts were too opaque; this, in turn, led to a de facto ban on contractual PPPs (Bergère 2016). In 2002 a neo-Gaullist government initiated a series of private sector-inspired reforms and reformed the procurement rules in general. A small working group, led by the Liberal MP and PPP proponent Alain Madelin, was in charge of drafting the *contrat de partenariat*, or CP (Batiactu 2004). The CP was not presented as a stand-alone law to parliament but was embedded in a general law to simplify the legal procurement canon. This allowed the government to circumvent possible veto points: the new law granted the government permission to introduce PPP contracts and to require changes in adjacent regulations by simple ordinance, thus avoiding lengthy parliamentary debates. Senator Jean-Pierre Sueur of the opposition Socialist Party criticised the law for going almost unnoticed through parliament and the Senate due to its technical appearance 'under the guise of "administrative simplification"' (Sueur 2003). The Socialist Party failed in its appeal to the Council of State and Constitutional Council. Whereas liberal reformers like Madelin, Grand d'Esnon and Novelli embraced the new CP, there were also critical positions in the neo-Gaullist government party. In particular, the former finance minister Jean Arthuis saw PPPs as a tool to avoid borrowing constraints (Orange 2005; Rey-Lefebvre and Clavreul 2012).[8] PPP uptake was still slow because the current legislation required procuring authorities to demonstrate that projects were so urgent and complex that alternative procurement methods would be an insufficient alternative.

PPP received a new lease of life in 2007 when Sarkozy became President and ordered his Prime Minister François Fillon to develop a plan to boost the use of PPPs. He explicitly requested that the legal framework should be based on the work of the government's PPP task force and the work of the Institut de la Gestion Déléguée (IGD), an industry body concerned with the promotion of PPPs (Le Président de la République de France 2007; see also Defawe 2007). The legal foray picked up on the possible additionality element in PPPs. It made them part of a wider investment and growth programme, which resounded well with France's demand-led outlook, which is so characteristic of MMEs. With the advent of the global financial crisis, PPPs were made a part of the government's stimulus plan (Bouvet-Guiramand and Cuello 2012, Campagnac 2012). By linking PPPs to economic growth and stressing the urgency, the UMP-led Fillon government and the Sarkozy presidency could introduce changes to the legal framework without encountering institutional obstacles. The PPP promotion on macroeconomic grounds met a temporarily silent political opposition that was unwilling to oppose measures to revive the economy. During Hollande's presidency, the government's view on PPPs was constantly swinging between outright scepticism and tentative embracement by more moderate actors in the government. Despite criticism from members of the Radical Left, the government under Valls was never willing to let go of PPP entirely (Lagoutte 2014). Whilst PPPs were placed under review domestically (culminating in a new single law in 2019), the French government actively promoted PPPs internationally and backed the ambitions of the French Institute of International Legal Experts and the Confederation of International Contractors Association to establish the UN International PPP Specialist Centre for Policies, Laws and Institutions in Paris. All these engagements suggest that the PPP development in France has not yet come to an end; in fact, France remains the second-largest procurer of PPPs in Europe (EPEC 2020).

Germany

The introduction of PPP laws in Germany and the creation of a framework conducive for their usage has been a long and, at times, incoherent development. Even more than ten years after passing the PPP Acceleration Act (2005), the policy is not second nature to procuring authorities. Despite a considerable infrastructure backlog (Kommission Zukunft der Verkehrsinfrastrukturfinanzierung 2012, Reidenbach et al. 2008), serious economic difficulties for the German construction industry in the 2000s (European Construction Industry Federation 2008) and promotional efforts by the finance industry (Bressler 2009, Sack 2009), the PPP idea only gradually took hold. Additionality arguments had their appeal, and it is certainly no coincidence that the first comprehensive PPP legislation was initiated in 2001 when Germany had serious economic and fiscal difficulties. However, there are reasons to argue that the additionality argument was not the decisive driver for introducing PPPs. First, a large part of the projects was done through the forfeiting financing model, where the project costs become a public financial liability after the construction phase (Daube et al. 2008, Partnerschaften Deutschland 2019). Second, PPPs were used by poor and rich regional governments and local authorities alike (Mause and Krumm 2011). The decision to intensify efforts and create a comprehensive framework for PPPs was carried by a new reformist zeitgeist: a new cast of (social democratic) politicians, notably Chancellor Schröder (SPD), Peer Steinbrück (SPD) in North Rhine-Westphalia and Roland Koch (CDU) in Hesse, entered the political stage as innovators and business-friendly reformers. In particular, the Social Democrats sought to change the role of the state vis-à-vis its citizens and propagated the idea of a 'guarantor' and 'enabling state' which would withdraw from the production of public services (Sack 2004). The idea of public–private cooperation became a credo of the government and PPPs a part of the public sector reform agenda. The success of the initiatives to establish a legal and institutional framework for PPPs from 2001 onwards and the subsequent institutionalisation hinged on the political acceptance of the new concepts. However, rather than mustering political support through consensus-building deliberations, the social democratic government strategically excluded possible opposing actors from the agenda-setting and legal drafting process by establishing working groups outside parliament (Sack 2009). By this means, they managed to bypass less-well-informed formal veto players. The exclusion of critical voices allowed the passing of relevant legislation. However, the fact that the law was written without considering the opinion of other stakeholders means that PPPs remain contested – in particular since the reformers who embraced PPPs so wholeheartedly have left the political stage. Specifically, the courts of auditors play an important role now. Even though the courts of auditors were involved in the initial drafting process, their proposals were not considered in the final legal draft of the PPP Acceleration Act. Consequently, the PPP legal framework included provisions that are not best practice and are now repeatedly criticised by the courts of auditors (Adamek and Otto 2008). The open critique of PPP practices by the courts of auditors has consequences insofar as it supports the arguments of other critical groups of actors such as the parliamentary factions of the Social Democrats and the Green Party; that is, representatives of parties who brought the initial legislation on its way. Another defining factor for the relative success and low uptake rate can be found in how well PPPs square Germany's economic institutions and modes of cooperation. Prior to the arrival of contractual PPPs, Germany already used its own form of public–private cooperations at the local level through its public enterprises (Ambrosius 2013). Therefore, the need to find other organisational models to solve problems of hierarchical market relations was less pronounced. The German economic system is characterised through close links between public authorities and other public and private economic actors to coordinate the functioning of its economy. Also, the economy heavily relies on small and medium-sized enterprises (SMEs) for economic success. Both these aspects are potentially harmful to the PPP policy itself. Intimate relations ensured greater access of SMEs to projects but were potentially harmful to microeconomic efficiency savings. Further, the close links between the actors can be a deterrent for potentially beneficial outside competition and expertise (Greive 2016). Another reason why PPPs never received the attention hoped for by their promotors can be found in the economy's focus on export-led growth (which is more common in CMEs; Hope and Soskice 2016). Subsequently, investment in human capital and research and reforms improving cost and price competitiveness took precedence over public infrastructure investment in economic policy decision-making in the past 20 years. Because public infra-structure investment only played a subordinate role in the public debate about what determines the country's economic success, PPPs could never be linked to a salient topic and therefore receive broader backing.

Conclusions

The decision to employ a mixed methods approach naturally increases the likelihood of becoming entangled in contradictions, not least because the studies are based on different assumptions about causality. Indeed, Table 14.2, which compares the results, shows that the two approaches do not always speak with the same voice. This is not necessarily a bad thing: consistencies increase our confidence in the results; discrepancies give us an incentive to prod deeper. Both sets of analysis above have highlighted, and at the same time re-confirmed, due to the concurrent triangulation approach, that economic and political institutions are significant determinants as to whether countries will introduce and use PPPs. Moreover, we can distil from those findings possible inroads for future research agendas. One insight from the panel analy-sis is that there might be a difference between PPPs' usage and the mode of economic cooperation (hierarchical, cooperative, state-led). The application of the VoC approach might also deliver valuable insights if applied to other regions of the world. The VoC literature departed from its initial European focus in recent years, and PPP research could make use of those advancements. The panel analysis also highlighted that there is a marked difference between the UK and the rest of the European countries as to why PPP usage varied. It suggests that the UK might be an 'exceptional, not paradigmatic' (Clifton et al. 2003, 88) case and consequently this might affect how we interpret pre-vious insights from the literature. The SNA demonstrated that a successful legal initiative to introduce a supporting framework for PPPs depends on the agency of potent political champions and that for PPPs to be accepted as an alternative long-term solution, the PPP arrangements have to be in congru-ence with the established domestic economic pattern. The introduction to this volume previously made a reference to a body of literature that is concerned

Table 14.2 Similarities and differences in findings between panel analysis and case studies

	Panel analysis	France	Germany
Control variables			
GDP per capita	UK: pos. relationship	€27,965 (s.e.: 0.56; Ø 1990–2008)	€28,038 (s.e.: 0.48; Ø 1990–2008)
Supporting industry	EU w/o UK: correlation between the size of the financial industry and likelihood of PPP use.	National champions in construction and finance with international PPP experience. PPPs were promoted primarily by the IGD, a body representing major construction companies. The finance sector joined the IGD in the period 2004-06.	National champions in construction and finance with international PPP experience. The construction industry, which was in crisis at the turn of the millennium, exerted a strong influence. Strong lobbying efforts by the banking sector.
Hypothesis 1: PPPs are more likely to be adopted in the light of budgetary constraints			
Net lending/GDP	UK: higher public deficit correlated with PPP uptake. EU: PPP use expected to be higher when the public deficit is lower.	Average deficit was -3.42 per cent; average debt level at 56.6 per cent. The first attempt to introduce a PPP law coincides with an economic downturn and problems to adhere to the EU's deficit criteria. There are indications, but no conclusive proof, that the off-balance advantage was used deliberately.	Average deficit was -2.72 per cent; average debt level at 56.4 per cent. The discussion intensified when Germany had problems meeting the EU's deficit criteria, but evidence suggests this was not a decisive driver.
Debt/GDP	UK: pos. correlation between debt levels and PPP uptake.		
Net gov't capital stock/GDP	No effect.	Stable (55.44 per cent; Ø 1990–2001) but increasingly a greater need for investment in maintenance and social infrastructure (which informed the development of a precursor of the CP). Tackling the backlog was linked to the growth strategy under Sarkozy.	In decline (49.77 per cent, Ø 1990–2001). Germany has a considerable infrastructure backlog, and even though the banks made the point that PPPs could be a remedy, this aspect never entered the mainstream discourse.

	Panel analysis	France	Germany
Hypothesis 2: PPPs are more likely to be adopted in the light of underperforming public services			
Public sector performance/ efficiency	Where public services have an excellent performance, the expected PPP count is significantly lower.	Sarkozy entered office in 2007, intending to reform the state. The argument of the IGD to employ PPPs as a tool gets picked up but does not enter the subsequent discourse – quite different from the growth argument.	The Social Democratic Party entered power in 1999 intending to transform public administration towards an 'enabling' state. PPP fit the bill and the initiative for a PPP law was partially informed by those reform efforts.
Hypothesis 3: PPPs are adopted when politicians who pursue liberal economic policies are in power			
Ideological complexion and party numbers	The further a government leans to the right on a left–right spectrum, the less likely PPPs are used.	Early PPP laws were insufficient (1997–2002: left-centre complexion; major party: PS; parties: five). Liberal reformers pushed PPPs from 2002 onwards. PPPs found appeal among centre-right and centre-left politicians alike. Extra push under Sarkozy (2002–2007: right-wing dominance, major party: UMP, two parties; 2007–2012: Right-centre complexion, major party: UMP, 2 parties). Critical voices became louder during the presidency of Hollande, in particular from the Radical Left (2012–2018: Left-centre complexion, major party: PS, three parties).	The Kohl government preferred privatisation and financing arrangements (1987–1998: centre-right, major party: CDU/CSU, two parties). PPP laws launched under the Schröder government (1998–2005: left-centre complexion, major party: SPD, two parties). PPPs gained support across the spectrum from business-friendly politicians; parties: two). The momentum was upheld in the grand coalition (2005–09, two parties). In the wake of the financial crisis, parts of the SPD and the Green Party started to distance themselves from PPPs. The Merkel government(s) (major party: CDU/CSU, two parties) acknowledged PPPs as an option but did not relaunch plans for legal reforms for PPPs.

Panel analysis		France	Germany
Hypothesis 4: The number of veto players determines the likelihood of PPP uptake			
Power fragmentation	EU: The more a government is constrained in its power (type of government), and by institutional veto points, the less likely PPPs are used.	Phases of high power concentration: 1988-1993, 1995-1997, 2002 to today. Phases of fragmented power: 1993-1995 and 1997-2002. PPPs gained real momentum under the *dirigiste* leadership of Sarkozy. PPPs were embedded in the country's recovery plan. This narrative temporarily silenced the opposition.	Power is fragmented most of the time due to the veto power of the Bundesrat and federal system. Power is more concentrated during phases of matching majorities in both chambers: 1990-1991, 1998-1999, 2005-2010. The Schröder government strategically excluded possible opposing actors from the agenda-setting and legal drafting process. This allowed the laws to pass but had detrimental effects on ownership in subsequent years.
Hypothesis 5: The uptake of PPPs is determined by the mode of cooperation of a country's economy			
Mode of cooperation	The predicted PPP numbers are significantly higher in LMEs and MMEs as opposed to CMEs and the transition economies in the new EU Member States.	Mixed Market Economy Increasing drift to demand-led growth model in 2000s (net export/GDP, 1990-99: 1.29 (s.e. 0.38); 2000-08: -0.3 (s.e. 0.43)) PPPs were promoted as part of an investment and growth strategy and embedded in the recovery plan.	Coordinated Market Economy Public enterprises as part of the economic model reduce the need for other relational models. A high share of SMEs is present in the construction sector. They gradually started to oppose PPPs, and their role needed to be acknowledged in contracts. Export-led growth model (net export/GDP, 1990-99: 0.54 (s.e. 0.22); 2000-08: 4.42 (s.e. 0.70)), which means that infrastructure investments are not given the same standing as in France.

Notes: s.e. = standard error; Ø = average. Figures expressed as averages over the period 1990-2008, unless stated otherwise
Source: European Commission (2015)

with the language and linguistics of PPPs; the findings above suggest that there is more room for systematic discourse analysis regarding how PPPs can be or have been brought in congruence with established practices. One stumbling block to understanding the policy process is the fact that in some jurisdictions, most certainly in our case studies, many decisions and discussions took place in small fora and back rooms. After such a long time, it may be hard to obtain the relevant information to reconstruct those processes – particularly after the liquidation of PPP institutions and task forces in the wake of the global financial crisis. However, one silver lining is that in the coming years, information will become publicly available and moved to archives (in particular in the UK, where the embargo has been reduced to twenty years). Here a potentially large field of research might emerge.

Notes

1. This chapter draws on the so far unpublished results of Liebe (2017).
2. Discrete count variables can be also estimated with a Poisson model. However, the data does not meet the Poisson model's assumption of congruence of variance (137.62) and mean (2.77) due to the high number of years without a project in the dataset (300 out of 437 observations). A negative binominal model does not rely on those assumptions and is therefore employed in this analysis. For the analysis STATA 14 was used and the GLM (Generalized Linear Model) estimator with a log link function and a negative binominal family was employed. The GLM estimator rather than STATA's xtnbreg function has been used because the latter does not report robust standard errors. To operationalise the GLM estimator an alpha value was obtained by running every equation with a simple negative binomial estimator (nbreg) first.
3. The data provided by the European Investment Bank contains a simple count on signed contracts and PPP engagement expressed through 'aggregate financing needs of PPPs' (Kappeler 2012). Both measurements show overdispersion. A hyperbole sine transformation on capital volume to achieve a more normal distribution was not successful. Hence, the analysis will only make use of the count variable by employing a negative binominal model, which performs better in the light of the presence of excess zeros. For more information on the criteria by which PPP projects were chosen, please consult EPEC (2020).
4. A Hausman test was conducted on the full model and on each set of hypotheses separately. The test of the full model and most of the sub-models returned results which suggested that a random-effect model is feasible. The exceptions were the model which tested only the control variables and the model which tested the effect of the size of financial and construction sector, respectively, on PPP uptake. Both sub-models did not meet the asymptotic assumption of the Hausman test; that is, suggesting problems of collinearity. The results suggest that the submodel containing the control variables alone should be best treated as a fixed effect model; for the the the other models it safe to run use random effects.

5. Hall and Gingerich (2009) establish that there is a high correlation between indices of corporatism and the VoC concept.
6. Following Hall and Gingerich (2009), the countries are sorted into the following categories. The UK and Ireland are LMEs. Portugal, Spain, France, Italy and Greece are categorised as MMEs. Germany, Austria, the Benelux and the Nordic countries are labelled as CMEs. The remaining countries are placed into the New Member State category (NMS), acknowledging that the four Visegrad states are leaning towards a more coordinated mode of capitalism (Hancké et al. 2007). This element of the analysis has to be considered with an extra degree of caution because the UK, as a LME, might distort the findings.
7. To interpret the coefficient correctly one has to know that the deficit variable ranges from a negative to a positive value (min: -31.2, max: 7, mean: -2.78). Ergo we would assume that a lower deficit is correlated with a lower incident rate of PPPs – the analysis, however, suggests the opposite.
8. A comment of Bergère (2013) of MAPPP, the government's PPP task force, on the challenges for future projects due to change in international accounting regimes suggests that the government knowingly used the accounting loophole.

References

Adamek, S., and Otto, K. (2008) *Der gekaufte Staat: Wie Konzernvertreter in deutschen Ministerien sich ihre Gesetze selbst schreiben.* Köln: Kiepenheuer & Witsch.

Ambrosius, G. (2013) Die Entwicklung Öffentlich-Privater Partnerschaften seit den 1980er Jahren, die fördernden und die hindernden Faktoren. *Der moderne staat,* 6(2): 321–344.

Batiactu (2004) Les PPP: 'une vraie révolultion culturelle' selon Alain Madelin. *Batiactu* [online]. www.batiactu.com/edito/ppp-vraie-revolution-culturelle-selon -alain-madelin-17172.php (accessed 30 May 2021).

Bergère, F. (2013) PPP challenges and initiative in France. Presentation at the 6th annual OECD meeting on Public-Private Partnerships, Paris, 15–16 April.

Bergère, F. (2016) Ten years of PPP: An initial assessment. *OECD Journal on Budgeting,* 15 (1): 31–123.

Bouvet-Guiramand, M., and Cuello, J. (2012) Public Private Partnerships in France, in *The Principles of Project Finance,* edited by R. Morrison. Burlington, VT: Gower Publishing, pp. 389–398.

Bressler, S (2009) *Public private partnership im Bank- und Börsenrecht durch Beleihung mit einer Anstaltsträgerschaft.* Dissertation. Frankfurt a. M.: Lang.

Burnham, P. (2008) *Research Methods in Politics.* Basingstoke: Palgrave Macmillan.

Buso, M., Marty, F., and Tran, P. (2017) Public-private partnerships from budget constraints: Looking for debt hiding? *International Journal of Industrial Organization,* 51: 56–84.

Butler, E. (2012) *Public Choice: A Primer.* London: Inst. of Economic Affairs.

Campagnac, E. (2012) The Challenges of Implementing New Forms of PPP, in *Taking Stock of PPP and PFI Around the World,* edited by G.M. Winch, M. Onishi and S. Schmidt. London: ACCA, pp. 36–44.

Casady, C.B. (2020) Examining the institutional drivers of public-private partnership (PPP) market performance: A fuzzy set qualitative comparative analysis (fsQCA).

Public Management Review. https://doi.org/10.1080/14719037.2019.1708439 (accessed 30 May 2021).

Clifton, J., Comín, F., and Díaz Fuentes, D. (2003) *Privatisation in the European Union: Public Enterprises and Integration.* Dordrecht and Boston, MA: Kluwer Academic Publishers.

Creswell, J.W. (2003) *Research Design: Qualitative, Quantitative, and Mixed Methods Approaches.* Thousand Oaks, CA: SAGE.

Creswell, J.W. (2009) *Research Design: Qualitative, Quantitative, and Mixed Methods Approaches.* Los Angeles, CA: SAGE.

Daube, D., Vollrath, S., and Alfen, H.W. (2008) A comparison of Project Finance and the Forfeiting Model as financing forms for PPP projects in Germany. *International Journal of Project Management,* 26 (4): 376–387.

Defawe, P. (2007) Nicolas Sarkozy demande une loi pour développer le recours au PPP. *Le Moniteur* [online]. www.lemoniteur.fr/article/exclusif-nicolas-sarkozy-demande -une-loi-pour-developper-le-recours-au-ppp.1923224 (accessed 30 May 2021).

Della Porta, D. (2008) Comparative Analysis: Case-oriented Versus Variable-oriented Research, in *Approaches and Methodologies in the Social Sciences: A Pluralist Perspective,* edited by D. Della Porta and M. Keating. Cambridge: Cambridge University Press, pp. 198–222.

European Commission (2015) *Annual Macro-Economic Database: AMECO,* updated 5 May 2015. Brussels: European Commission.

European Construction Industry Federation (2008) *Construction Activity in Europe.* Brussels: FIEC.

European PPP Expertise Centre (EPEC) (2015) *PPP Motivations and Challenges for the Public Sector: Why (Not) and How.* www.eib.org/attachments/epec/epec_ppp _motivations_and_challenges_en.pdf (accessed 30 May 2021).

European PPP Expertise Centre (EPEC) (2020) *Review of the European PPP Market in 2019.* www.eib.org/en/publications/epec-market-update-2019 (accessed 30 May 2021).

Fine, B. (2020) Situating PPPs, in *Critical Reflections on Public Private Partnerships,* edited by J. Gideon and E. Unterhalter. Abingdon: Routledge, pp. 26–38.

Gerring, J. (2007) The Conundrum of the Case Study, in *Case Study Research: Principles and Practices,* edited by J. Gerring. Cambridge: Cambridge University Press, pp. 1–13.

Greive, M. (2016) Dobrindt wegen Bau-Partnerschaften abgewatscht. *Die Welt* [online]. www.welt.de/politik/deutschland/article150540370/Dobrindt-wegen-Bau -Partnerschaften-abgewatscht.html (accessed 30 May 2021).

Grimsey, D., and Lewis, M.K. (2004) *Public Private Partnerships: The Worldwide Revolution in Infrastructure Provision and Project Finance.* Cheltenham, UK and Northampton, MA, USA: Edward Elgar Publishing.

Hall, P.A., and Gingerich, D.W. (2009) Varieties of capitalism and institutional complementarities in the political economy: An empirical analysis. *British Journal of Political Science,* 39 (3): 449–482.

Hall, P.A., and Soskice, D. (2002) *Varieties of Capitalism: The Institutional Foundations of Comparative Advantage.* Oxford: Oxford University Press.

Hammami, M., Ruhashyankiko, J.-F., and Yehoue, E.B. (2006) *Determinants of Public-Private Partnerships in Infrastructure.* IMF Working Paper 06/99. www .imf.org/en/Publications/WP/Issues/2016/12/31/Determinants-of-Public-Private -Partnerships-in-Infrastructure-19086 (accessed 30 May 2021).

Hancké, B., Rhodes, M., and Thatcher, M. (2007) Introduction, in *Beyond Varieties of Capitalism: Conflict, Contradictions, and Complementarities in the European Economy*, edited by B. Hancké, M. Rhodes and M. Thatcher. Oxford: Oxford University Press, pp. 3–38.

Hearne, R. (2006) Neo-liberalism, public services and PPPs in Ireland. *Progress in Irish Urban Studies*, 2: 1–14.

Henisz, W.J. (2002) The institutional environment for infrastructure investment. *Industrial and Corporate Change*, 11 (2): 355–389.

Hodge, G., and Greve, C. (2019) *The Logic of Public–Private Partnerships: The Enduring Interdependency of Politics and Markets*. Cheltenham, UK and Northampton, MA, USA: Edward Elgar Publishing.

Hodge, G., Greve, C., and Biygautane, M. (2018) Do PPPs work? What and how have we been learning so far? *Public Management Review*, 20 (8): 1105–1121.

Hope, D., and Soskice, D. (2016) Growth models, varieties of capitalism, and macroeconomics. *Politics & Society*, 44 (2): 209–226.

Jahn, D. (2016) Changing of the guard: Trends in corporatist arrangements in 42 highly industrialised societies from 1960 to 2010. *Socio-Economic Review*, 14 (1): 47–71.

Kappeler, A. (2012) *PPPs and their Financing in Europe: Recent Trends and EIB Involvement*. ECON Note, Luxembourg: European Investment Bank (EIB). www .eib.org/attachments/efs/econ_note_2012_ppp_and_financing_in_europe_en.pdf (accessed 30 May 2021).

Kommission Zukunft der Verkehrsinfrastrukturfinanzierung (2012) Bericht der Kommission (Daehre Kommission): Zukunft der Verkehrsinfrastrukturfinanzierung. www.vifg.de/_downloads/service/Bericht-Daehre-Zukunft-VIF-Dez-2012.pdf (accessed 30 May 2021).

Krumm, T. (2014) Vetospieler als Prädiktor für Policy-Wandel: Ein Test anhand von öffentlich-privaten Partnerschaften im internationalen Vergleich. *Politische Vierteljahresschrift*, 55 (1): 445–471.

Lagoutte, C. (2014) Manuel Valls veut relancer les partenariats public-privé. *Le Figaro* [online]. www.lefigaro.fr/conjoncture/2014/09/02/20002-20140902ARTFIG00013 -manuel-valls-veut-relancer-les-partenariats-public-prive.php (accessed 30 May 2021).

Le Président de la République de France (2007) *Letter from the President of the Republic to the Prime Minister: 01.10.2007.* www.fondation-igd.org/files/pdf/Lettre_PR_PM .pdf (accessed 13 June 2016).

Liebe, M. (2017) *The Spread of Public-Private Partnerships in Europe: A Political Economy Analysis*. Dissertation, University of Luxembourg.

Lieberman, E.S. (2005) Nested analysis as a mixed-method strategy for comparative research. *American Political Science Review*, 99 (3): 435–452.

Mause, K., and Krumm, T. (2011) Public–private partnershipping as a tool of government: Exploring its determinants across German states. *German Politics*, 20 (4): 527–544.

Mota, J., and Moreira, A. (2015) The importance of non-financial determinants on public–private partnerships in Europe. *International Journal of Project Management*, 33 (7): 1563–1575.

Onishi, M., and Winch, G.M. (2012) Cross-country Case Analysis, in *Taking Stock of PPP and PFI Around the World*, edited by G.M. Winch, M. Onishi and S. Schmidt. London: ACCA, pp. 16–25.

Orange, M. (2005) En 2004, le gouvernement a allégé procédures destinées à garantir la moralité de la vie publique. *Le Monde* [online]. www.lemonde.fr/societe/article/

2005/05/16/en-2004-le-gouvernement-a-allege-les-procedures-destinees-a-garantir-la-moralite-de-la-vie-publique_650212_3224.html (accessed 30 May 2021).

Partnerschaften Deutschland (2019) *Überblick zu ÖPP-Projekten im Hoch- und Tiefbau in Deutschland.* www.ppp-projektdatenbank.de/fileadmin/user_upload/191231_OEPP-Markt_ab_2002.pdf (accessed 30 May 2021).

Reidenbach, M., Bracher, T., Grabow, B., Schneider, S., and Seidel-Schulze, A. (2008) *Investitionsrückstand und Investitionsbedarf der Kommunen: Ausmaß, Ursachen, Folgen und Strategien.* Berlin: Dt. Inst. für Urbanistik.

Rey-Lefebvre, I., and Clavreul, L. (2012) Hôpital Sud Francilien: Les collectivités ne peuvent plus se passer des PPP. *Le Monde* [online]. www.lemonde.fr/societe/article/2012/01/23/les-collectivites-ne-peuvent-plus-se-passer-des-ppp_1633288_3224.html (accessed 30 May 2021).

Sack, D. (2004) *PPP im ,aktivierenden Staat'.* Paper presented at the conference Stand und Perspektiven der politikwissenschaftlichen Verwaltungsforschung, University of Koblenz, Koblenz, 23–25 September 2004.

Sack, D. (2009) *Governance und Politics: Die Institutionalisierung öffentlich-privater Partnerschaften in Deutschland.* Baden-Baden: Nomos-Verl.-Ges.

Savas, E. (2000) *Privatisation and Public-Private Partnerships.* Seven Bridges, NY: Chatham House Publishers.

Seki, K., and Williams, L.K. (2014) Updating the Party Government data set. *Electoral Studies,* 34: 270–79.

Stoiber, M. (2006) *Different Types of Veto Players and the Fragmentation of Power.* Paper presented at the 64th Annual Meeting of the Midwest Political Science Association, Chicago, IL, 20–23 April.

Sueur, J.-P. (2003) La machine à corruption est en marche. *Le Monde* [online]. www.lemonde.fr/archives/article/2003/06/02/la-machine-a-corruption-est-en-marche-par-jean-pierre-sueur_322413_1819218.html (accessed 30 May 2021).

Teorell, J., Dahlberg, S., Holmberg, S., Rothstein, B., Hartmann, F., and Svensson, R. (2015) *The Quality of Government Standard Dataset,* version Jan 2015. Gothenburg: Quality of Government Institute, University of Gothenburg.

Tsebelis, G. (2010) Veto Player Theory and Policy Change: An Introduction, in *Reform Processes and Policy Change: Veto Players and Decision-Making in Modern Democracies,* edited by T. König, G. Tsebelis and M. Debus. New York, NY: Springer, pp. 3–18.

Vandeburie, T. (2016) *Market Update 2011–2015.* Underlying data for market update reports. Answer to a request for data to the European PPP Expertise Centre (EPEC).

Volkens, A., Lehmann, P., Merz, N., Regel, S., and Werner, A. (2014) *The Manifesto Data Collection: Manifesto Project (MRG/CMP/MARPOR),* Version 2014b. Berlin: Wissenschaftszentrum Berlin für Sozialforschung.

Watkins, D., and Gioia, D. (2015) *Mixed Methods Research.* Oxford: Oxford University Press.

Winch, G.M., Onishi, M., and Schmidt, S. (2012) *Taking Stock of PPP and PFI Around the World.* London: ACCA. https://study.sagepub.com/sites/default/files/ACCA%20on%20PPPs%20around%20the%20world.pdf (accessed 30 May 2021).

Yescombe, E.R. (2007) *Public-Private Partnerships: Principles of Policy and Finance.* Amsterdam: Butterworth-Heinemann.

15 Institutional work in policy transfers: a case study of PPP adoption in Germany[1]

Micaela Mihov

Introduction

During the 1990s, the United Kingdom (UK) developed the Private Finance Initiative (PFI), a form of cooperation between the public and private sectors for the joint planning, delivery, financing and maintenance of public building infrastructure. This project delivery model has been adopted in the public infrastructure repertoire of many European countries, including Germany. German politicians grasped the UK PFI model as an opportunity to build new social municipal infrastructure with limited public resources during the late 1990s (Schwalb 2011). Today, public–private partnerships (PPPs) are a public procurement option used in Germany. However, the contemporary German PPP model differs strongly from what national policymakers envisioned more than 20 years ago. Compared to the UK PFI model, PPPs in Germany are small in size, mainly use a forfeiting model[2] instead of project finance and are mostly contracted by medium-sized enterprises.

As in the case of the PFI model, transferring practices and policies from foreign national contexts has been an important approach for countries looking to catch up in the delivery of public services and modernise existing public administration processes (Dolowitz and Marsh 1996). However, transfer processes between countries with considerably different political economy contexts and histories can be complicated and lead to unintended consequences (Benson 2009). PPP authors have previously suggested that differences in the state-market nexus of a country can explain to what extent PPPs are adopted (Greve and Mörth 2010, Hodge and Greve 2019). Combining insights from the policy transfer literature (De Jong et al. 2002, Dolowitz and Marsh 2000) with the theory of institutional work (Lawrence and Suddaby 2006), this chapter aims to shed light on how German public infrastructure field actors impacted the PPP adoption process in Germany.

Policy transfer authors investigate how policies, practices or ideas spread from one context to another. They attempt to understand how policy entrepreneurs engaged in the transfer process and what effects it has on policymaking (Ellison 2017). Institutional work authors study the purposive actions of various elite and more ordinary actors with different resources at hand to create, maintain and disrupt institutions (Battilana et al. 2009, Lawrence and Suddaby 2006, Pemer and Skjolsvik 2017). Institutional work adopts an endogenous view of social conventions, rules and criteria, maintaining that actors within organisations and fields can contribute towards their change and continuity (Oliveira 2013). Hence, by combining the entrepreneurial policy transfer perspective with the analysis of institutional work activities of various reflexive actors, the guiding research question is: How have public infrastructure field actors shaped the transfer process of the UK PFI model to Germany?

Theoretical underpinnings: policy transfers and institutional work

Despite some research on the impact of institutional structures on PPP transfer and adoption in various local contexts (Jooste et al. 2011, Koppenjan and De Jong 2017, Matos-Castaño et al. 2014, Sheppard and Beck 2016, Van den Hurk et al. 2015, Verhoest et al. 2015), an in-depth analysis of national public infrastructure actors and their actions in shaping PPP adoption has been missing. This chapter uses insights from the policy transfer approach (De Jong et al. 2002) combined with the institutional work perspective (Lawrence and Suddaby 2006) to explore how various public infrastructure actors influenced the transfer process of the UK PFI model to Germany.

Policy transfers: goodness of fit and institutional bricolage

The reasons for the occurrence of policy transfers are varied and usually relate to catching up in regionalisation, industrialisation and modernisation or solving problems with tools for which information on potential outcomes or experiences already exist (Dolowitz and Marsh 1996, Marsh and Sharman 2009). Policy actors can engage in transferring policy structures, contents, goals, instruments, administrative techniques and organisations, as well as softer institutions such as ideology, attitudes and negative lessons (Dolowitz and Marsh 1996, Wolman 1992).

There are two different perspectives on institutional transfer processes. The goodness-of-fit perspective in the policy transfer literature emphasises that historical, cultural, bureaucratic or even political particularities can make the adoption of foreign practices problematic (De Jong et al. 2002). Therefore institutional 'fit' might not exist between specific policies and contexts given the institutional distance between countries. The institutional bricolage perspective on policy transfers maintains that these institutional obstacles can, to some extent, be overcome through policymakers engaging in resourceful improvisation (Hendry and Harbone 2011). Domestic policy actors engage in bricolage efforts by piecing together ideas from the new policy with existing ideas in order to create goodness of fit between the transferred policy and the national institutional context (Lanzara 1998).

While the goodness-of-fit lens emphasises that the local context of the transferred policy as well as the host context matter and can constrain transfers, the institutional bricolage lens maintains that fit can be cobbled together by policy actors or other social entrepreneurs (De Jong 2013, De Jong et al. 2002). This chapter adopts an institutional work lens that explores activities by institutionally embedded actors in response to a policy transfer process in order to better understand how goodness of fit impacts policy transfers and how institutional bricolage can succeed.

Regulative, normative and cognitive institutional work

Institutional work authors understand institutions as 'products of human action and reaction motivated by idiosyncratic personal interests and agendas for institutional change preservation' (Lawrence et al. 2009, 6). Institutional work authors maintain that all action is embedded in institutional structures and that actors actively shape whether and how institutions are created, maintained or disrupted. As a result of studying day-to-day work efforts by which actors influence their institutional surroundings, the institutional work literature is interested in the ordinary activities of various institutional workers that attempt to shape their institutional environment through the institutional resources they have at hand.

To analyse different types of activities, this chapter uses the institutional work taxonomy of regulative institutional work, normative institutional work and cognitive institutional work (Jolly et al. 2016, Lawrence and Suddaby 2006, Perkmann and Spicer 2008). Regulative institutional work involves political activities by policymakers or interest group associations to address rules or regulations. Normative institutional work involves actors, mainly the media or civil society organisations, but also others, attempting to change or maintain culturally shaped beliefs, assumptions, norms and behaviours. Cognitive institutional work is a type of analytical and technical work that involves actors

Table 15.1   The three types of institutional work

Type of institutional work effort	Examples of institutional creation	Examples of institutional maintenance	Examples of institutional disruption	Type of actors
Regulative: Political activities associated with addressing formal rules and regulations	Advocacy Vesting	Enabling Policing	Disconnecting sanctions and rewards	Politicians, industry associations, trade unions, advocacy organisations
Normative: Cultural activities associated with mobilising public rhetoric and propagating norms or ideologies	Constructing identities Changing normative associations	Valorising Demonising Mythologising	Dissociating moral foundations	Media, civil society organisations, consumer groups, ordinary citizens
Cognitive: Technical activities associated with analytical theorising to address thought processes and problems	Mimicking Theorising Educating	Embedding Routinising	Undermining assumptions and beliefs	Professional associations, consultancies, universities, independent think-tanks

Source: Adapted from Jolly et al. 2016, Lawrence and Suddaby 2006, Perkmann and Spicer 2008

engaging in chains of cause and effect and problem solving in the institutional change or maintenance process. Table 15.1 offers an overview of the three types of institutional work.

Theories of institutional change postulate that successful adoption occurs when the regulative, normative and cognitive institutional pillars are modified simultaneously (Campbell 2004, Scott 1995). For example, Berthinier-Poncet (2013) studies the complementary effect of regulative, normative and cognitive institutional work for institutionalising new practices. He maintains that addressing all three institutional work dimensions encourages establishing an institutional environment that improves cooperation. Accordingly, 'political practices [regulative institutional work] benefit the building of the cluster's legitimacy', 'normative practices facilitate the emergence of institutional trust', and 'cognitive practices participate to the constitution of architectural knowledge' (Berthinier-Poncet 2013, 20). Each of these three dimensions fulfils a different task in the institutionalisation process and therefore the three pillars complement each other.

Institutional work sequences

Discussion in the institutional change and institutional work literatures has focused on whether and how sequences of regulative, normative and cognitive institutional pillars occur (Alnesafi and Al-Omari 2018, Chacar et al. 2018, Chiwamit et al. 2014, Hoffman 1999, Nicklich and Fortwengel 2017, Oliveira 2013, Perkmann and Spicer 2008). For example, Hoffman's (1999) sequential analysis contends that while regulative institutional work is more easily malleable and actors can address this pillar at an early stage of institutional change, cognitive institutions are more entrenched and, hence, more difficult to modify. Others have studied institutionalisation processes from the perspective of mature and emerging fields (Chacar et al. 2018, Greenwood and Suddaby 2006, Maguire et al. 2004). These authors argue that the greater the maturity of the field is, the more likely institutional change will be introduced by a change in norms and ideas before new regulations can be enacted. Nicklich and Fortwengel (2017), who study the institutionalisation of German apprenticeship programmes in the security services industry, also acknowledge that institutional work efforts might prevail at different times in the institutionalisation process. This can lead to phases where institutional work is insufficient, and policies cannot become fully institutionalised.

Exploring how institutional work efforts may occur sequentially is significant for understanding the process of PPP adoption in the German public infrastructure field. Policymakers or organisational managers often attempt to adopt new institutions from foreign contexts without understanding the underlying domestic currents which push and pull institutional layers in unexpected directions. As a result of insufficient capacity-building, PPP adoption efforts through institutional bricolage can fail (Koppenjan and De Jong 2017). However, the failed bricolage attempt can, at times, create something unanticipated but useful for the institutionalisation process (Lawrence and Suddaby 2006). It is imperative to analyse the work efforts used by actors to create new institutions or maintain or disrupt existing ones. This chapter focuses on Germany to explore the role of institutional work processes when transferring PPP policies, practices and ideas between country contexts.

Table 15.2   Overview of interviews

Actor category	Interviewee codes
Public officials (federal, state and municipal level)	PO1; PO2; PO3; PO4; PO5; PO6; PO7; PO8; PO9; PO10; PO11
Construction companies (large companies and SMEs)	CONL1; CONL2; CONL3; CONL4; CONL5; CONL6; CONSME1; CONSME2; CONSME3
Banks (corporate and public banks)	BANKC1; BANKC2; BANKC3; BANKP1; BANKP2; BANKP3; BANKP4; BANKP5; BANKP6
Advisers	ADV1; ADV2; ADV3; ADV4; ADV5; ADV6; ADV7; ADV8; ADV9; ADV10; ADV11; ADV12; ADV13
Interest group associations (SMEs, public banks, trade unions, construction companies, architects, municipalities, court of auditors)	IGSME1; IGSME2; IGSME3 IGBANKREG1; IGTRADEU1; IGTRADEU2; IGCONL1; IGARCH1; IGMUNICIPAL1; COURTAUDIT1

Method

Similar to other continental European countries, Germany has a long tradition of providing public infrastructure in the conventional way whereby the state entrusts individual private companies with the construction and, occasionally, the operation of public infrastructure. Thus, the emergence of the UK PFI life-cycle model in the 1990s, with the bundling of tasks and the use of private sector finance, was an innovation with repercussions for the whole German public infrastructure field and actors.

This chapter uses data collected from 52 semi-structured in-depth interviews with German public and private sector infrastructure professionals to analyse how actors shaped the PPP transfer process. These actors include public officials; managing directors of small- to medium-sized companies (SMEs) and large construction companies; senior corporate and public bankers; advisers; and members of interest group associations, including construction companies, banks, public trade unions, architects, municipalities and courts of auditors (see Table 15.2). The collected interview data offers an insight into the multiple and diverse work efforts of these actors in shaping the transfer process of PPPs in Germany from the late 1990s until 2019. As part of the data triangulation method, the interview findings were complemented by an analysis of various government and business reports and documents as well as newspaper articles.

The methodology follows Langley's (1999) recommendations for process research to analyse the data. It uses various sense-making activities to understand the collected qualitative data fully. In the first step, using a narrative strategy and temporal bracketing the relevant events and activities of the key actors in the German PPP adoption process were identified (ibid.). In a second step, the key PPP actors that emerged from the first stage were identified and categorised depending on their involvement or interest in PPP projects. In a third step, the NVivo software was used to code the interview data according to the actors and themes that emerged as highly relevant for the specific group of interviewees. In a fourth step, the interview data was coded according to evidence of regulative institutional work, normative institutional work or cognitive institutional work in the form of first-order codes that were advanced into second-order themes (Gioia et al. 2013). In a final step, the findings were visually mapped according to actors and time periods to establish what type of work effort occurred at which point in time and to what intensity.

Findings: the three phases in the German PPP adoption process

In 1989, the reunification of West and East Germany worsened the already difficult financial situation of West Germany. As part of the East German reconstruction process, new roads, public utilities, commercial areas and housing had to be built (Grömling 2008). The German government was compelled to find a way to build new and modernise existing public infrastructure with limited public resources. Public officials and politicians in the German federal government were aware of the PFI model in the UK (Schwalb 2011), which ultimately set off a policy transfer process starting in the late 1990s. In the following, the identified three phases of PPP adoption in Germany, which we have author labelled 'implantation' (the late 1990s to 2007), 'irritation' (2008–2014) and 'transcendence' (2015–2019), are explained in more detail. The findings show that in each phase, public and private actors used different activities of institutional work, which impacted the PPP adoption process in distinctive ways.

Phase I: implantation – the attempt by policymakers and lobbyists to embed contractual PPPs in Germany

From the late 1990s until 2007, politicians, banks, large construction companies and international consultancies engaged in regulative institutional work, including defining, lobbying, vesting and developing new alliances to internalise the foreign transplant of 'PPPs' in Germany. Public officials and politicians exchanged ideas with the British government to learn about the UK's experiences with this procurement model. At the same time, German banks and the construction industry, which had already worked on PPPs abroad, lobbied federal government politicians to change laws to facilitate the use of the PFI model in Germany. Together with the national PPP lobby, policymakers used the UK PFI experience as a blueprint for building institutional capacity for PPPs in their domestic context (Willems and Van Dooren 2016).

During that period, the PPP Acceleration Act was introduced, and a national German PPP unit called Partnerschaften Deutschland (Partnerships Germany) formed. The core task of this new German PPP unit was to offer consultancy services to public authorities and bring PPP know-how into the public infrastructure field. It was structured as a half-public/half-private organisation, similar to the British Partnerships UK (PUK), to 'accelerate the PPP procurement process in Germany and further methodologically improve the public procurement competence' (IFD 2007, 77).

German policymakers engaged in limited cognitive institutional work by theorising: 'the naming of new concepts and practices so that they might become a part of the cognitive map of the field' (Lawrence and Suddaby 2006, 226). They started using the acronym ÖPP for the German words for 'public–private partnerships', Öffentlich-Private Partnerschaft, to internalise the PFI model and delineate ÖPP from other types of PPPs. One head of unit from a German state ministry emphasised during an interview: 'ÖPP was in Germany what the PFI initiative was for England. We actually understood PPP as PFI, so we Germanized it to ÖPP so as not to confuse people about what we mean' (PO3). Although cognitive institutional work was enacted in the form of naming PPPs 'ÖPP', it did not fully clarify the meaning of PPPs in the eyes of citizens, the media or even municipalities. There was still misunderstanding and confusion in the public infrastructure field about what ÖPP was and how its implementation would affect Germany's infrastructure provision.

Actors did not engage in any normative institutional work to legitimise the use of PPPs among the wider public infrastructure procurement community. Normative institutional work involves mobilising public discourse, building visions or propagating professional norms and ideologies (Jolly et al. 2016). Hence, policy actors did not address how PPPs will be used and implemented in the daily work of public infrastructure field actors. During the interviews, public officials and some bank and construction company managers admitted that they might have approached the formation of a PPP market too casually. Municipal public officials, architects, SMEs and the German civil society were

Table 15.3   Institutional work in the implantation phase (late 1990s to 2007)

Type of institutional work	Intensity	Work efforts	Actors
Regulative	Strong	Defining, lobbying, vesting and developing new alliances	Banks and construction industry associations, politicians, advisers
Normative	Weak	Discounting moral foundations	
Cognitive	Moderate	Some theorising work	

not actively involved in this institutional capacity-building process. Table 15.3 summarises the institutional work efforts by the different actors during the implantation phase.

Phase II: irritation – the emergence of a PPP legitimacy struggle between PPP supporters and opponents

From 2008 until 2014, there was a phase of irritation since public infrastructure actors felt antagonised by the ÖPP implant. PPP critical actors started delegitimising the PPP model while PPP supporters hardened their stance through overly optimistic PPP reports and by constructing normative networks. Both groups of actors appealed to morality and norms to persuade the public to take on a position for or against PPPs.

The interviews indicate that for many municipalities, which heard about the PPP model through the newly formed PPP unit Partnerships Germany or their respective state governments, the first reaction was, 'if the private sector takes on sovereign tasks, something will go wrong' (PO9). The long-term outsourcing of the infrastructure maintenance phase to a private company worried some municipalities. As a manager of a construction company working with PPPs emphasised, on the part of municipalities there was 'simply total incomprehension of the whole PPP concept'. This quickly resulted in resistance through, for example, PPP-opposing local politicians putting a discussion point, 'Assessing our PPP position', on the agenda of town hall meetings. Ultimately, this meant that the PPP model was put into question.

At the same time, SMEs started raising concerns about the PPP model. In Germany, there is a principle of 'lot allocation' (Hattenhauer and Gall 2012).

Services have to be separated by quantity (partial lots) and by area of expertise (specialist lots). For example, different buildings of one larger school project have to be tendered as individual projects to contract out to different construction companies. Specialist lots imply a narrow understanding of areas of expertise, meaning that a painter should have a painting contract and a plumber a plumbing contract. In theory, this ensures that SME craft businesses can participate in public tenders and effectively safeguards their jobs. In a PPP project, various tasks are bundled and provided by one private partner or a consortium of private partners undermining the promotion of SMEs through partial and specialist lots. For this reason, SMEs, particularly local craft businesses, regarded PPPs as 'SME-unfriendly' (ZDB 2016).

Towards the mid-2000s, two civil society organisations with anti-PPP agendas started gaining the attention of the German media. One of them was the German branch of the Association for the Taxation of Financial Transactions and Citizens' Action (Attac). In 2003, it formed a working group on privatisation intending to fight 'privatisation and public-private partnerships in the various areas of public services and public goods' (Sander 2016). From their perspective, the German PPP policy agenda represented a back-door privatisation program. Large German media outlets started using the critiques made by civil society organisations or public trade unions, which also feared the privatisation aspect, to position themselves against PPPs. This was a backlash for the political PPP agenda since many politicians and public officials were hopeful that they had built sufficient support for the PPP concept by establishing a sound legal and regulatory framework for PPPs (BANKP1; IGBANKREG1).

However, PPP supporters, mainly construction companies and banks, were not engaging actively with the critique of the PPP model. They called for better communication of PPP benefits. The rhetoric of 'it's not the PPP model, it's the critics, they do not understand it' (IGSME2) started to become a common explanation for the absent 'PPP revolution' that some supporters had hoped for. Some PPP actors took on a defensive attitude and propagated their positive PPP examples to show the 'truth' about PPPs and to convince public authorities and the media of PPPs' financial value and economic efficiency.

These tensions in the public infrastructure field point towards an apparent lack of fit between the implanted UK PPP model and the norms and habits of embedded actors in the German political economy context. In the previous PPP implantation phase, institutional work efforts acted as irritants to the established public infrastructure field. During this tense period involving persuasion activities, actors did not engage in regulative institutional work and only engaged to a limited extent in cognitive institutional work. The focus was

Table 15.4   Institutional work in the irritation phase (2008–2014)

Type of institutional work	Intensity	Work efforts	Actors
Regulative	Weak	Lack of addressing laws or regulations	Media, civil society organisations, trade unions, SME construction companies, municipalities
Normative	Strong	Legitimisation struggle involving defending existing ways of 'doing things', demonising, valorising, constructing normative networks	
Cognitive	Moderate	Some work on creating linkages between new and existing practices	

not on clarifying misunderstandings, adapting the PPP model or providing more explicit templates of PPPs, but on 'winning' the debate on whether PPPs are 'good' or 'bad' and protecting one's own best interests. Table 15.4 provides a summary of these findings.

Phase III: transcendence – the collective effort to abstract ÖPP from its Anglo-Saxon roots

In the transcendence phase between 2015 and 2019, actors began surpassing their own mental constraints regarding the meaning and relevance of the contractual PPP model for Germany. Market actors with enough PPP expertise and knowledge started restructuring their cognitive map associated with PPPs. The initial Anglo-Saxon assumptions and ideas slowly started to diminish and, instead, actors began to consider the needs of the German public infrastructure field. Normative institutional work efforts started to fade, and also regulative institutional work efforts were not very pronounced from 2015 onwards. Emotions and justification for or against PPPs gave way to a more balanced understanding of the PPP model. The PPP debate began to normalise around actors' attempts to provide a clearer and more transparent template of PPPs for the German public infrastructure field.

Construction companies, advisers and banks started engaging in mimicry, which meant actors trying to 'associate the practices they propose as a continuation of current and taken-for-granted ones to make them appear accessible' (Monteiro and Nicolini 2015, 69). In particular, the life-cycle element of PPPs was used by public and private PPP supporters to claim that PPPs by design offer a more sustainable use of public resources. In the early 2010s, sustainable public resource management, not least due to the development of the United Nations' Sustainable Development Goals, became politically very important and PPP actors saw a way of linking these discourses directly to PPPs (PO6).

In the German PPP market, PPP actors – municipalities, construction companies, advisers and banks – theorised and crafted a new understanding of PPPs by relabelling and redefining them. Public officials, especially politicians and employees from public construction departments, stopped using the term 'PPP' or 'ÖPP'. Instead, they started referring to these types of projects simply as 'general contractor models', 'sustainability contracts', 'alternative public procurement contracts' and 'life-cycle projects'. These new labels made it easier for the public and private sector to gain political support for PPP projects.

A group of actors that started changing their attitude towards PPPs were public sector trade unions, who initially fully supported Attac and other civil society groups against PPPs and privatisation. However, in recent years there have been cases where they have sought to make concessions on some aspects of private sector involvement in public infrastructure. In 2010, for example, the public sector trade union ver.di signed a collective trade agreement with the city of Hanover, stating that:

> Irrespective of whether the PPP referred to in the annexe of this collective agreement include a transfer of duties, with this agreement the parties accept that there will be no further PPPs in the future. (City of Hanover 2010)

In 2015, ver.di and Hanover signed a new collective agreement for public sector employees with a different PPP paragraph:

> The city of Hanover promises to realize such projects [PPPs] without a subsequent operation and structural maintenance. This means that the operation and structural maintenance always remain with the city of Hanover, this form of implementation applies to all procurement procedures. (City of Hanover 2016)

Instead of insisting on 'no further PPPs in the future', as in 2010, this new collective agreement in 2015 allows PPPs, although only if the operation and maintenance are not part of the PPP project contract. Hence, public maintenance and operation workers will not receive private sector contracts. This was a significant change from 2010 because ver.di no longer categorically opposed

Table 15.5   Institutional work in the transcendence phase (2015–2019)

Type of institutional work	Intensity	Work efforts	Actors
Regulative	Moderate	Some defining work	Construction companies (large and SMEs), banks, public officials, trade unions
Normative	Weak	Subsiding legitimisation struggle	
Cognitive	Strong	Active theorising, mimicking and educating	

PPPs as before, but merely the elements that would directly affect its members. This example illustrates how normative institutional work efforts associated with 'demonising' the PPP model in its entirety have given way to a position towards PPPs that is still critical but also more nuanced.

At the end of 2016, Partnerships Germany was transformed into PD – Berater der öffentlichen Hand GmbH, dropping its previous name of ÖPP Deutschland AG and Partnerships Germany. It also became fully owned by the public sector. Hence, it no longer had a private ownership component and was no longer working towards proliferating the number of PPP projects. It became an all-round public advisory agency, helping public organisations in all their investment endeavours. Good public infrastructure governance, instead of the PPP model, became the mandate of this in-house consultancy.

Discussions around PPPs gradually normalised in the public infrastructure field during the transcendence phase. SMEs in particular, relying on the German lot allocation principles, realised that they would not have to fear the PPP model, since traditional public procurement remained the dominant public procurement model. At the same time, the PPP supporters had by 2015 become more nuanced in their positions towards the value of PPPs. They no longer promoted PPPs as a 'superior' public procurement model. The struggles of PPP supporters and opponents in the irritation phase had left marks on the PPP model. While PPPs became part of the German public procurement repertoire, they neither became the primary form of providing infrastructure nor a duplicate of the British PFI model as expected in the 1990s. Table 15.5 portrays the institutional work efforts of the key actors in the transcendence phase.

Discussion: the impact of the institutional work sequence on the PPP transfer process

The impact of the three phases of 'implantation', 'irritation' and 'transcendence' on the transfer process of PPPs in Germany is discussed below. It takes a closer look at the relationship between institutional work sequences and policy transfer processes. As depicted in Table 15.6, during each phase of the German PPP transfer process, one institutional work effort dominated over the other two, which resulted in a stepwise adoption and adaptation of the PPP phenomenon in the German public infrastructure field.

First attempt at institutional bricolage through regulative institutional work

During the early 1990s, large construction companies, banks and the German federal government identified a window of opportunity or an 'institutional corridor' (Cleaver 2012) to reshape institutions associated with public infrastructure procurement and adopt the PPP concept. This institutional bricolage attempt involved entrepreneurial actors combining foreign and existing institutions to embed the foreign practice of PPPs (De Jong et al. 2002). While laws were adapted to fit PPPs, the PPP concept itself was not adapted. German public and private actors were aware of many differences between the German public infrastructure field and the UK PFI concept. However, it was expected that adapting German public procurement laws and forming the PPP-enabling organisation Partnerships Germany would suffice to embed the Anglo-Saxon PPP model.

As discussed above, the German PPP unit was designed to resemble the British PPP unit and had a mandate to look actively for potential PPP projects. German corporate banks, such as Deutsche Bank and Commerzbank, expected a substantial rise in their project finance business and large construction companies expected PPP megaprojects in the infrastructure construction sector. Actors had clear PPP structures in mind, which were inspired by Anglo-Saxon practices. While institutional bricolage occurred at the PPP policy level based on reaching goodness of fit between the German regulatory framework and contractual PPPs, there was a copying of PPP project structures and governance arrangements from the UK context. The German government pursued a strategy of building PPP policy fit by adapting German laws and creating Partnerschaften Deutschland. However, the pursuit of the British understanding of project structures and market goals resulted in discrepancies in the German public infrastructure field. Despite efforts of institutional bricolage

Table 15.6 Institutional work efforts and transfer outcomes in the German PPP adoption case

Phase	Period	Type of work and intensity	Exemplary quote	Key actors	Transfer outcome
Implantation	1990s–2007	Regulative: strong	'And interestingly enough, back then, the PPP Acceleration Act was developed with us, the private sector. Imagine this, we as a private bank sat with many others at the table and discussed this law [...] today, this kind of private participation would hardly exist.' (BANKC1)	Federal public officials, politicians, banking and construction industry associations, legal advisers	First bricolage attempt: politicians together with large construction companies, banks and advisers adjusted laws and organisations to embed the Anglo-Saxon PPP model in the German public infrastructure field.
		Normative: weak	'We under prioritized the danger of conflicts of interest, we saw that, but we said, "We are building that now, no matter what" [...] the financial crisis had not unfolded back then, there was a spirit of optimism.' (PO1)		
		Cognitive: moderate	'And then we really used this working group to ask ourselves "Why does it not work so well with PPPs in Germany? What do we have to do to improve that?"' (ADV1)		

Phase	Period	Type of work and intensity	Exemplary quote	Key actors	Transfer outcome
Irritation	2008–2014	Regulative: weak	'Until 2010 everything went quite well, there were indeed the first critical clues, but not as intensive, as later in 2011/2012, then it really started to fall apart. Steinbrück was not there anymore, there was no one who was willing to follow in his footsteps as a representative of the [PPP] task force. There was a political vacuum and some critical stakeholders used that to crush PPPs.' (CONSME1)	Media, civil society movements, public trade unions, SME construction companies, municipalities, courts of auditors	Surfacing lack of goodness of fit: a normative debate between PPP supporters and PPP opponents on the necessity for PPPs in the German public infrastructure environment sets in due to a mismatch between the Anglo-Saxon PPP ideas and the German conception of public good provision.
		Normative: strong	'Well, I know that we had projects where well-known PPP opponents were invited to the district council, who should then talk about PPPs to try and ruin the project.' (BANKP5)		
		Cognitive: moderate	'We wrote to mayors all over Saxony-Anhalt and tried to share our experiences with them, to show how infrastructure procurement can be done differently. But after 50 letters and phone calls we didn't get a single appointment.' (CONSME3)		

Phase	Period	Type of work and intensity	Exemplary quote	Key actors	Transfer outcome
Transcendence	2015–2019	Regulative: moderate	'We do not have a lobby anymore. I am in the PPP working group in Berlin. But 80% of the time they speak about highway projects, no time is spent talking about PPPs in building construction.' (CONL3)	Construction companies (large and SMEs), municipalities, state officials, public trade unions	Second bricolage attempt and emerging goodness of fit: industry actors begin to work on conceptualising PPPs vis-à-vis traditional public procurement in Germany by redefining the meaning of PPPs for German public infrastructure field.
		Normative: weak	'We have tried for years to fight it or to do some persuasive work, but in the meantime – I do not want to say we are over it – but we know the counterarguments by heart. We also know the opponents' arguments by heart [...] it is important to convince those who really want to do it that it can work and show them how it can work.' (PO7)		
		Cognitive: strong	'Procuring public infrastructure is no longer black or white. PPPs can be more efficient and feasible, but traditional public procurement can be too. We take on a case-by-case approach.' (CONSME1)		

between the German institutional context and the British PFI ideas, there was no thorough conceptualisation of PPPs in the German public infrastructure field.

On the one hand, the German government's strategy of building PPP policy fit through adapting German laws and forming Partnerschaften Deutschland but, on the other hand, following a British understanding of project structures and market goals created a mismatch in the public infrastructure field. Although institutional bricolage between the British PFI ideals and the German institutional context was attempted from the beginning, there was no clear conceptualisation of PPPs for the German public infrastructure field. Entrepreneurial actors did not attempt to provide a clear template of PPPs vis-à-vis traditional German public procurement and legitimise the use of PPPs for the actors responsible for the implementation of PPPs (for example, municipalities). Overall, the institutional bricolage attempt in the implantation phase did not establish goodness of fit between the contractual PPP model and the German institutional environment.

Surfacing lack of goodness of fit and strong normative institutional work

After the institutional 'shock' (Pemer and Skjolsvik 2017) that had occurred due to the PPP implantation process, German public infrastructure procurement actors were at odds with the PPP concept and there was no longer the opportunity for an objective discussion. As a result of the lack of goodness of fit between the PPP phenomenon and the German public infrastructure field, a legitimisation struggle arose (De Jong et al. 2002). Municipalities and cities were not involved in the PPP policymaking process during the implantation phase but were informed about the outcomes afterwards. Public trade unions, SME construction companies and municipalities could not provide any input to the PPP debate initially because there was no forum for their involvement. This proved fatal for the intensive 'regulative bricolage' efforts of the federal government, advisers and business associations.

With the confusion about why PPPs should be used and how they would benefit individual groups of actors and society, many actors began following critical reports on failing PFI projects in the UK. They began associating the negative connotations of 'privatisation' and 'unconscious capitalism' with the German PPP model. PPP opponents and supporters worked on evoking emotions in other actors to delegitimise or legitimise PPPs by conjuring feelings such as fear, shame, pride or a sense of duty (Moisander et al. 2016, Voronov and Vince 2012). This perpetuated the lack of goodness of fit, which was mirrored in the many misunderstandings between market actors, the public upheavals and the hesitance of municipalities to engage in PPP projects.

The transfer process of PPPs to Germany emphasises that mature institutional fields, such as the German public infrastructure field, have enshrined rules and regulations, cultures, ways of working and norms (Chacar et al. 2018, Greenwood and Suddaby 2006, Maguire et al. 2004). To a certain extent, the strong normative institutional work efforts by PPP supporters and opponents were the result of institutional entrepreneurs having to 'simultaneously de-institutionalise pre-existing cognitive understandings, social norms, and regulations, as well as mobilize support for new cognitions, norms, and rules' (Fortwengel and Jackson 2016, 897). Conventional public procurement, the use of public finance and public sector employees and the lot allocation principle have been integral components of the German public infrastructure field (Brandstaett 2000, Hattenhauer and Gall 2012). Hence, implementing a practice with new institutional underpinnings to disrupt these formal and informal institutions could not be achieved merely by setting up new laws and regulations at the policy level.

Second bricolage attempt through cognitive institutional work and emerging goodness of fit

The second wave of institutional bricolage created goodness of fit, since PPP supporters to a large extent abandoned their Anglo-Saxon PPP blueprints. PPP supporters began working on redefining PPPs, relabelling them and educating actors on a more nuanced understanding of PPPs as 'one procurement variant out of many'. Using private finance in the form of project finance or circumventing the debt brake was no longer considered a crucial element of PPPs. Instead, a broader definition and understanding of the PPP phenomenon emerged. An example of this is the PPP light model or three-phases model, where the public contractor either waives technical or infrastructural facility management services (see the previous example of the collective trade agreement between ver.di and Hanover) or takes over the long-term financing beyond the construction phase (Partnership Germany 2019, STB Web 2013). While previously private finance was considered the key element that made PPPs more attractive than traditional public procurement, the life-cycle approach and the private sector expertise were regarded as the key benefits of PPPs. Overall, groups of actors which were initially marginalised in the PPP policymaking process gained a better understanding of the role of PPPs for the German public infrastructure field.

The above institutional work efforts have in recent years created the basis for a normalisation of the PPP debate in Germany and, simultaneously, the partial acceptance of a German version of the PPP model that combines UK PFI ideas with domestic public infrastructure field practices. Today, most building construction PPP projects in Germany do not require private finance, are tailored to smaller building construction projects with municipalities, encourage the integration of SME construction companies and use the national PPP unit as an optional public procurement adviser. Hence, this second bricolage attempt at the cognitive level, which re-adapted the meaning of PPPs to the German public infrastructure procurement context, gave rise to goodness of fit (De Jong et al. 2002).

The findings demonstrate that addressing cognitive institutional aspects created a culturally supported basis of legitimacy that became less questioned (Hoffman 1999, 353). Addressing informal institutions, such as cultural traits, work habits and customs, by theorising on what public infrastructure means and how PPPs fit into the field helped with the institutionalisation of the PPP concept. As De Jong and Stoter (2009) emphasise, actors can engage in regulative activities through enforcing new laws or creating organisations which enforce new rules, but 'if the informal institutions are not transformed [...] such transplants will merely be a dead letter and will not enjoy any acceptance or functionality' (2009, 318).

The case of goodness of fit with PPPs in Germany does not mean that the institutional work life-cycle of PPPs in Germany has ended in a transcendence phase. The term 'goodness of fit' might signal a state of equilibrium; however, institutions are constantly in flux. The process through which practices become embedded needs to be comprehended 'as an issue of dynamic fit between practice and adopter' (Ansari et al. 2010, 68). There are still tensions in the German public infrastructure field regarding the use of PPPs, not least due to the intense clashes between PPP supporters and opponents between 2008 and 2014. These tensions will continue to exist and possibly create new institutional dynamics. Adoption and goodness of fit should be understood as an evolving process and not as a constant.

Concluding remarks and future research

In the past decades, PPP best practices from different country contexts and transmitted by international organisations and private consultants have tempted policymakers to develop PPP policies, change laws and establish

PPP units according to foreign blueprints. The focus has been on 'enabling' and 'building capacity' for PPPs (Jooste et al. 2011, Matos-Castaño et al. 2014, Mu et al. 2010, Van den Hurk et al. 2015). However, as this chapter emphasises, this regulatory policy perspective is merely one component of the complex national adoption process of PPPs. Theoretical assumptions about the adoption of PPPs cannot be made without exploring key institutional actors embedded in the PPP implementation process. Researchers interested in the PPP–institutional theory nexus should further explore the regulative, normative and cultural-cognitive foundations of the public infrastructure field. As organisational and strategic management scholars (Ansari et al. 2010, Gond and Boxenbaum 2013, Hoffman and Ventresca 1999, Scott 1995) argue, embedding or diffusing practices 'is influenced by technical, cultural, and political factors' (Ansari et al. 2010, 68). Acknowledging the versatility of institutional workers with different resources, interests and emotions to create, maintain or disrupt institutions (Lawrence and Suddaby 2006, Voronov and Vince 2012) is crucial to understand the opportunities and constraints in the institutionalisation of the PPP model.

Hodge and Greve (2018) have previously emphasised that PPP research has often focused on analysing PPPs from the perspective of governments while ignoring economic interest groups and their stakes in the delivery of PPPs. A recent strand of literature has started studying multiple embedded actor dynamics in the delivery of public infrastructure. Authors use an institutional work lens to argue that PPP policy reform requires that new values match ingrained institutions of governments, businesses and public administration (Biygautane et al. 2020, Biygautane and Micelotta 2019). While this chapter offers a lens to investigate the impact of private actors on PPP policies and projects, further research and rich case study material are required.

The PPP case of Germany represents one instance where institutional work sequences occurred because the government initially did not involve necessary stakeholders in the policy process, which led to the absence of a normative and cognitive foundation for PPPs in the public infrastructure field. This case study supports some of the existing but limited literature on the occurrence of institutional work sequences (Alnesafi and Al-Omari 2018, Berthinier-Poncet 2013, Chiwamit et al. 2014, Nicklich and Fortwengel 2017, Oliveira 2013, Perkmann and Spicer 2008). However, the determinants of why institutional work sequences occur have been insufficiently studied and the explanation of a work sequence presented in this thesis is only one example. The PPP literature would benefit from more in-depth case studies of institutional work when exploring transfers to non-Anglo-Saxon contexts with fundamentally different legal, cultural and public administration roots (De Jong et al. 2002).

The particular context of the findings suggests that further research is required to broaden the findings and generalise them across similar and dissimilar countries. For example, studies on other countries with state–market relationships similar to Germany's coordinated market economy (Hall and Soskice 2001), such as Austria, Belgium or the Netherlands, could yield insights into whether identical institutional work sequences occurred in their public infrastructure fields when implementing PPPs. Conversely, in less developed economies, with weak regulatory frameworks, engaging merely in regulative work to establish an operational framework for PPPs might not result in normative work with intense clashes between actors such as in Germany. Here, further research could explore dependent market economies of Central and Eastern Europe (CEE) (Nölke and Vliegenthart 2009). Countries in CEE are marked by weaker regulatory and public governance frameworks than their Western European neighbours. These countries also rely on lending from the European Investment Bank or the European Bank for Reconstruction and Development to finance their public infrastructure. Studying PPPs in CEE or other non-Anglo-Saxon contexts where PPPs have been deployed – for example, in China's authoritarian capitalist system (Witt and Redding 2014) – could generate insights into institutional work efforts of other actors, such as the European Union or state-owned enterprises.

PPP authors should further examine the relationship between PPP transfers to different political economy contexts and the role of institutional work sequences. This should allow researchers to investigate other boundary conditions of PPP adoption, such as the strength of public governance frameworks, the type of state–market relationship or the amount of development finance. In this way, the impact of variation within institutional orders and across different groups of actors on the PPP phenomenon can be better understood.

Notes

1. This chapter is based on the PhD thesis of the author (Mihov 2020), awarded by King's College London in May 2020.
2. In a forfeiting model the private party of a PPP project sells the claim for payments (resulting from the contract with the public party) to the bank after the construction phase has finished. The bank instead of the private party owns the claim for repayment by the public sector. The forfeiting model usually involves a non-recourse element, meaning that the public party must repay the bank the total sum of the loan even in a case where the private party is not complying with the output specifications. See Daube et al. (2008) for an exploration of the forfeiting model in comparison to project finance.

References

Alnesafi, A., and Al-Omari, A. (2018) Exploring the development of the accounting profession in Kuwait: an institutional work analysis. *Problems and Perspectives in Management*, 16 (3): 285–301.

Ansari, S.M., Fiss, P.C., and Zajac, E.J. (2010) Made to fit: how practices vary as they diffuse. *Academy of Management Review*, 35 (1): 67–92.

Battilana, J., Leca, B., and Boxenbaum, E. (2009) How actors change institutions: towards a theory of institutional entrepreneurship. *Academy of Management Annals*, 3 (1): 65–107.

Benson, D. (2009) *Constraints on Policy Transfer*. University of East Anglia, Centre for Social and Economic Research on the Global Environment (CSERGE) Working Paper EDM, No. 09–13. Norwich: CSEGRE.

Berthinier-Poncet, A. (2013) Cluster governance and institutional dynamics: a comparative analysis of French regional clusters of innovation. Presentation at the Economics and Management of Networks Conference.

Biygautane, M., Clegg, S., and Al-Yahya, K. (2020) Institutional work and infrastructure PPPs: the role of religious symbolic work and power in implementing PPP projects. *Accounting, Auditing & Accountability Journal*, 33 (5).

Biygautane, M., and Micelotta, E. (2019) Actors, institutions and organisations: how policy games affect the implementation of public-private partnerships (PPPs) in Kuwait. EGOS Conference 2019, Sub-theme 59: Actor-centered institutionalism – comparing actors, contexts, interactions and change. Edinburgh.

Brandstaett, T. (2000) *Prozeßmanagement in der kommunalen Verwaltu-g – Möglichkeiten und Grenzen für die Übertragung eines Organisationskonzeptes*. Köln: Josef Eul Verlag.

Campbell, J.L. (2004) *Institutional Change and Globalization*. Princeton, NJ: Princeton University Press.

Chacar, A.S., Celo, S., and Hesterly, W. (2018) Change dynamics in institutional discontinuities: do formal or informal institutions change first? Lessons from rule changes in professional American baseball. *Business History*, 60 (6): 728–753.

Chiwamit, P., Modell, S., and Yang, C.L. (2014) The societal relevance of management accounting innovations: economic value added and institutional work in the fields of Chinese and Thai state-owned enterprises. *Accounting and Business Research*, 44 (2): 144–180.

City of Hanover (2010) Tarifvertrag zur Beschäftigungssicherung der Beschäftigten der Landeshauptstadt Hannover. *Collective Agreement between the City of Hannover and ver.di*. https://e-government.hannover-stadt.de/lhhSIMwebdd.nsf/A47A9AED3419 9048C125772F0032CF45/$FILE/1268-2010_Anlage1.pdf.

City of Hanover (2016) Tarifvertrag zur Beschäftigungssicherung der Beschäftigten der Landeshauptstadt Hannover. *Collective Agreement between the City of Hannover and ver.di*. https://e-government.hannover-stadt.de/lhhsimwebre.nsf/DS/0291-2016N1.

Cleaver, F. (2012) *Development through Bricolage: Rethinking Institutions for Natural Resource Management*. Abingdon: Routledge/Earthscan.

Daube, D., Vollrath, S., and Alfen, H. W. (2008) A comparison of Project Finance and the Forfeiting Model as financing forms for PPP projects in Germany. *International Journal of Project Management*, 26: 376–387.

De Jong, M. (2013) China's art of institutional bricolage: selectiveness and gradualism in the policy transfer style of a nation. *Policy and Society*, 32 (2): 89–101.

De Jong, M., Lalenis, K., and Mamadouh, V. (2002) *The Theory and Practice of Institutional Transplantation: Experiences with the Transfer of Policy Institutions.* Dordrecht: Kluwer Academic Press.

De Jong, M., and Stoter, S. (2009) Institutional transplantation and the rule of law: how this interdisciplinary method can enhance the legitimacy of international organisations. *Erasmus Law Review,* 2 (3): 311–330.

Dolowitz, D., and Marsh, D. (1996) Who learns what from whom: a review of the policy transfer literature. *Political Studies,* 44 (2): 343–357.

Dolowitz, D.P., and Marsh, D. (2000) Learning from abroad: the role of policy transfer in contemporary policy making. *Governance,* 13 (1): 5–24.

Ellison, N. (2017) Politics, power and policy transfer. *Journal of Asian Public Policy,* 10 (1): 8–24.

Fortwengel, J., and Jackson, G. (2016) Legitimizing the apprenticeship practice in a distant environment: institutional entrepreneurship through inter-organizational network. *Journal of World Business,* 51: 895–909.

Gioia, D.A., Corley, K.G., and Hamilton, A.L. (2013) Seeking qualitative rigor in inductive research: notes on the Gioia methodology. *Organizational Research Methods,* 16 (1): 15–31.

Gond, J.P., and Boxenbaum, E. (2013) The glocalisation of responsible investment: contextualisation work in France and Quebec. *Journal of Business Ethics,* 115: 707–721.

Greenwood, R., and Suddaby, R. (2006) Institutional entrepreneurship in mature fields: the big five accounting firms. *Academy of Management Journal,* 49 (1): 27–48.

Greve, C., and Mörth, U. (2010) Public–private partnerships: the Scandinavian experience, in *International Handbook on Public–Private Partnerships,* edited by G.A. Hodge, C. Greve and A.E. Boardman. Cheltenham, UK and Northampton, MA, USA: Edward Elgar Publishing, pp. 439–455.

Grömling, M. (2008) *Reunification, Restructuring, Recessions and Reforms – The German Economy over the Last Two Decades.* Wirtschaftswissenschaftliche Beiträge des Lehrstuhls für Volkswirtschaftslehre, insbes. Wirtschaftsordnung und Sozialpolitik. Nr. 102.

Hall, P.A., and Soskice, D. (2001) *Varieties of Capitalism.* Oxford: Oxford University Press.

Hattenhauer, D., and Gall, S. (2012) Der Grundsatz des Gebotes der losweisen Vergabe und dessen Ausnahmen. *Newsletter Vergaberecht,* 11(1).

Hendry, C., and Harbone, P. (2011) Changing the view of wind power development: more than 'bricolage'. *Research Policy,* 40: 778–789.

Hodge, G.A., and Greve, C. (2018) Contemporary public–private partnership: towards a global research agenda. *Financial Accounting & Management,* 34: 3–16.

Hodge, G.A., and Greve, C. (2019) *The Logic of Public–Private Partnerships: The Enduring Interdependency Between Politics and Markets.* Cheltenham, UK and Northampton, MA, USA: Edward Elgar Publishing.

Hoffman, A.J. (1999) Institutional evolution and change: environmentalism and the U.S. chemical industry. *Academy of Management Journal,* 42 (4): 351–371.

Hoffman, A.J., and Ventresca, M.J. (1999) The institutional framing of policy debates: economics versus the environment. *American Behavioral Scientist,* 42 (8): 1368–1392.

IFD (2007) *Finanzstandort Deutschland Bericht Nr. 3. Report Nr. 3.* www.dia-vorsorge .de/wp-content/uploads/2015/12/2007-07-15_Finanzstandort-Deutschland.pdf.

Jolly, S., Spodniak, P., and Raven, R.P.J.M. (2016) Institutional entrepreneurship in transforming energy systems towards sustainability: wind energy in Finland and India. *Energy Research & Social Science,* 17: 102–118.

Jooste, S.F., Levitt, R., and Scott, R. (2011) Beyond 'one size fits all': how local conditions shape PPP-enabling field development. *Engineering Project Organization Journal*, 1: 11–25.

Koppenjan, J., and De Jong, M. (2017) The introduction of public–private partnerships in the Netherlands as a case of institutional bricolage: the evolution of an Anglo-Saxon transplant in a Rhineland context. *Public Administration*, 96 (1): 171–184.

Langley, A. (1999) Strategies for theorising from process data. *Academy of Management Review*, 24 (4): 691–710.

Lanzara, G.F. (1998) Self-destructive processes in institution building and some modest countervailing mechanisms. *European Journal of Political Research*, 33: 1–39.

Lawrence, T.B., and Suddaby, R. (2006) Institutions and institutional work, in *The SAGE Handbook of Organization Studies*, edited by S.R. Clegg, C. Hardy, T.B. Lawrence and W.R. Nord. London: SAGE, pp. 215–254.

Lawrence, T.B., Suddaby, R., and Leca, B. (2009) *Institutional Work: Actors and Agency in Institutional Studies of Organisation*. Cambridge: Cambridge University Press.

Maguire, S., Hardy, C., and Lawrence, T.B. (2004) Institutional entrepreneurship in emerging fields: HIV/AIDS treatment advocacy in Canada. *Academy of Management Journal*, 47 (5): 657–679.

Marsh, D., and Sharman, J.C. (2009) Policy diffusion and policy transfer. *Policy Studies*, 30 (3): 269–288.

Matos-Castaño, J., Mahalingam, A., and Dewulf, G. (2014) Unpacking the path-dependent process of institutional change for PPPs. *Australian Journal of Public Administration*, 73 (1): 47–66.

Mihov, M. (2020) *Making It Fit: The Role of Institutional Work in the Transplantation of the Anglo-Saxon Public-Private Partnership Model to Germany*. Doctoral dissertation. London: King's College London.

Moisander, J.K., Hirsto, H., and Fahy, K.M. (2016) Emotions in institutional work: a discursive perspective. *Organisation Studies*, 37 (7): 963–990.

Monteiro, P., and Nicolini, D. (2015) Recovering materiality in institutional work prizes as an assemblage of human and material entities. *Journal of Management Inquiry*, 24 (1): 61–81.

Mu, R., De Jong, M., and Heuvelhof, E.T. (2010) Public-private partnerships for expressways in China: an agency theory approach. *European Journal of Transport and Infrastructure Research*, 10 (1): 42–62.

Nicklich, M., and Fortwengel, J. (2017) Explaining the puzzling stagnation of apprenticeships in Germany's security services: a case of insufficient institutional work? *Journal of Professions and Organization*, 4: 302–323.

Nölke, A., and Vliegenthart, A. (2009) Enlarging the varieties of capitalism: the emergence of dependent market economies in East Central Europe. *World Politics*, 61 (4): 670–702.

Oliveira, S. (2013) Institutional work for new modes of evaluation: emerging culture of assessment in evaluating sustainability in architecture. 29th EGOS Colloquium Subtheme 53: Behaviour, Management and Work. Montreal, 4–7 July.

Partnership Germany (2019) PPP project database for Germany. Online project search tool. www.ppp-projektdatenbank.de/index.php?id=9.

Pemer, F., and Skjolsvik, T. (2017) Adopt or adapt? Unpacking the role of institutional work processes in the implementation of new regulations. *Journal of Public Administration Research and Theory*, 138–154.

Perkmann, M., and Spicer, A. (2008) How are management fashions institutionalised? The role of institutional work. *Human Relations*, 61 (6): 811–844.

Sander, H. (2016) Die Zukunft von Attac – Stärken, Probleme, Handlungsoptionen. *Rosa-Luxemburg Foundation*. 03/2016.

Schwalb, L. (2011) *Kreative Governance? Public Private Partnerships in der lokalpolitischen Steuerung*. Berlin: Springer Verlag.

Scott, W.R. (1995) *Institutions and Organizations: Theory and Research*. Thousand Oaks, CA: SAGE.

Sheppard, G., and Beck, M. (2016) The evolution of public–private partnership in Ireland: a sustainable pathway? *International Review of Administrative Sciences*, 84 (3): 1–17.

STB Web (2013) Trendwend: 'ÖPP-Light'-Projekte überholen klassische ÖPP-Projekte. www.stb-web.de/news/article.php/id/5659/.

Van den Hurk, M., Brogaard, L., Lember, V., Petersen, O.H., and Witz, P. (2015) National varieties of public–private partnerships (PPPs): a comparative analysis of PPP-supporting units in 19 European Countries. *Journal of Comparative Policy Analysis: Research and Practice*, 18 (1): 1–20.

Verhoest, K., Petersen, O.H., Scherrer, W., and Soecipto, R.M. (2015) How do governments support the development of public private partnerships? Measuring and comparing PPP governmental support in 20 European countries. *Transport Reviews*, 35 (2): 118–139.

Voronov, M., and Vince, R. (2012) Integrating emotions into the analysis of institutional work. *Academy of Management Review*, 37 (1).

Willems, T., and Van Dooren, W. (2016) (De)politicization dynamics in public–private partnerships (PPPs): lessons from a comparison between UK and Flemish PPP policy. *Public Management Review*, 18 (2): 199–220.

Witt, M.A., and Redding, G. (2014) China: authoritarian capitalism, in *The Oxford Handbook of Asian Business Systems*, edited by M.A. Witt and G. Redding. Oxford: Oxford University Press. 11–32.

Wolman, H. (1992) Understanding cross national policy transfers: the cases of Britain and the US. *Governance: An International Journal of Policy and Administration*, 5 (1): 27–45.

ZDB (2016) *Bericht zum Forschungsvorhaben ÖPP- Infrastrukturprojekte und Mittelstand*. Ausgeführt durch die Technische Universität Braunschweig. www.zdb.de/zdb-cms.nsf/res/TUBS_Forschungsbericht_ZDB.pdf/$file/TUBS_Forschungsbericht_ZD B.pdf.

16

High speed, high cost: the problematic procurement of Ireland's National Broadband Plan

Dónal Palcic and Eoin Reeves

Introduction

The COVID-19 pandemic has brought the importance of quality broadband infrastructure into sharp focus for governments and citizens around the world. It has become abundantly clear that fast and reliable broadband is a fundamental requirement for education, health, commerce and other aspects of modern life. Governments therefore face big decisions in relation to how broadband infrastructure should be provided. These include decisions about broadband technology, the precise roles of the state and private sector in delivering infrastructure, and how infrastructure and services should be regulated, funded and financed.

In Ireland, the government launched the tendering process for a National Broadband Plan (NBP) to deliver high-speed broadband to every premise in the country in December 2015. Seven months later it was announced that the government had chosen to procure the NBP using the so-called 'gap funding' commercial stimulus model of public–private partnership (PPP). Under the gap funding approach the government contracts with a private sector partner to finance, design, build, own and operate the broadband infrastructure, with the government providing the minimum amount necessary in the form of a subsidy to facilitate the delivery of the project.

The subsequent history of the NBP procurement has been highly controversial as it was beset by a series of issues that led to long delays in the signing of a contract and a massive increase in the size of the government subsidy, which is now estimated to cost at least €2.2 billion (EC 2019). The principal problems that arose during the procurement process included:

1. The announcement by one of the bidders (Eir – the incumbent former state-owned telecoms company) that it would deliver high-speed broadband to approximately 300,000 homes within the original NBP intervention area.
2. The subsequent withdrawal of two shortlisted bidders, which left just one remaining bidder in the process.
3. Significant cost escalation and delays in the procurement process, with the delays compounded by the resignation of the government minister with responsibility for the NBP due to allegations of inappropriate private meetings with the last remaining bidder.

The events that have transpired since the launch of Ireland's NBP raise important questions that we seek to address in this chapter. These cover the rationale for the regulatory choice made by the government (the gap funding model) and whether the chosen model has been workable. We also examine the conduct of the procurement process, the factors (economic, political and institutional) that contributed to the significant escalation in cost and protracted nature of the procurement process, and the ultimate impact of changes to ownership and competition in the telecommunications market that were instigated over 20 years ago. To examine these questions we utilise the transaction cost regulation (TCR) framework based on the contributions of Williamson (1975, 1999) and Spiller (2013), which elucidate the contractual hazards that affect the governance of infrastructure regulation and the interaction between private investors and government. The next section provides some important historical background and context before we move on to describe our framework and present our analysis.

Background: the development of broadband infrastructure in Ireland

The rationale for Ireland's NBP can be explained by the historically slow rollout of broadband services and the current low stock and quality of broadband infrastructure, particularly in rural areas, relative to other countries at similar stages of economic development. Figure 16.1 illustrates the growth in Ireland's fixed-line broadband penetration rate before 2020. It shows how Ireland has lagged the rest of Western Europe in relation to the historical rollout of broadband services and was still ranked next to last for fixed broadband penetration rates in 2019.

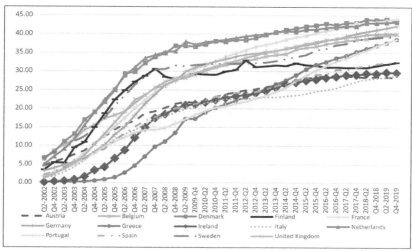

Source: Organisation for Economic Co-operation and Development (OECD) Broadband Statistics Portal, www.oecd.org/digital/broadband/broadband-statistics/

Figure 16.1 Fixed broadband penetration rate (subscriptions per 100 inhabitants)

Regarding the quality of Ireland's broadband infrastructure, Figure 16.2 shows how Ireland is significantly behind most OECD countries in terms of the rollout of fibre-to-the-premises (FTTP) broadband connections. As of June 2020, just 13.5 per cent of total fixed broadband connections in Ireland were fibre, compared to an OECD average of 29.2 per cent. In rural areas, the comparative situation is even less favourable, with European Union (EU) figures showing the percentage of rural premises in areas served by FTTP in Ireland to be one of the lowest in the EU at just 2.7 per cent in 2018, compared to an EU average of 14.2 per cent.[1]

In order to gain a more complete understanding of how the stock and quality of Ireland's broadband infrastructure has perennially trailed behind that of its peers, it is necessary to examine the historical development of the fixed-line telecommunications sector. Prior to 1999 the sector was regulated through public ownership in the form of a monopoly state-owned commercial enterprise. Since full privatisation in July 1999, the sector has operated under

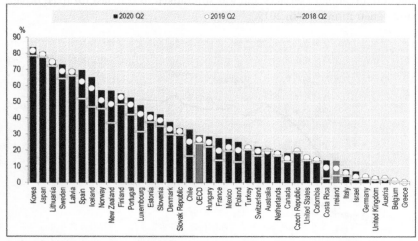

Source: OECD Broadband Statistics Portal, www.oecd.org/digital/broadband/broadband-statistics/

Figure 16.2   Percentage of fibre connections in total fixed broadband, June 2020

a system of discretionary regulation with the former incumbent operator (renamed Eir in 2015) still the dominant player in the fixed-line market. As privatisation roughly coincided with the advent of the internet age, the public demand for investment in the fixed-line network increased. These demands were not, however, sufficiently met by the newly privatised company, which went through a number of ownership changes, including highly leveraged buyouts by private equity groups that resulted in significantly increased debt levels and the company going into examinership[2] in 2012 (Palcic and Reeves 2013).

Low levels of capital investment by the incumbent prior to 2012, along with the stifling of competition in the fixed-line market, had grave consequences for the rollout of broadband services in Ireland, particularly in rural areas. In an effort to correct the market failure that emerged, successive Irish governments responded by implementing a number of small-scale market-oriented broadband schemes over the 2003–2012 period. These included the Metropolitan Area Networks (MANs) programme and the National Broadband Scheme (NBS). Both of these programmes were essentially PPP-style interventions in that they either involved co-funding with the private sector or a concession agreement to operate the infrastructure once it was constructed.[3]

As part of the EU's Digital Agenda for Europe published in 2010, all member states were required to publish a national broadband plan by 2012 which set out how the EU's broadband targets would be achieved. These targets included speeds of 30Mbps to be available to all households by 2020, with 50 per cent of households subscribing to speeds of 100Mbps. Ireland's NBP, published in August 2012, stated that the total cost of meeting EU targets would be €350 million, with the government co-funding half of this investment along with the private sector. In December 2015, an updated NBP stated that €275 million in public funds was earmarked to deliver the plan, and a contract notice was issued to procure the NBP using a gap funding model of PPP. Over the next four years there were repeated delays in the procurement process, which was marred by controversy. In addition, the projected cost of the NBP escalated considerably, with the cost of subsidy to the Exchequer estimated at between €2.2 and €2.9 billion when the final contract was signed in December 2019 (EC 2019).

In order to examine the issues that arose during the complex procurement of the plan, we utilise a TCR framework (Spiller 2010, 2013) to illuminate the contracting hazards that slowed down the procurement process and led to significant increases in the cost of public subsidy. The next section describes our framework in more detail before we explore the key developments that underpinned the cost escalation and delays observed in Ireland's NBP procurement process.

Theoretical framework

TCR theory provides a framework for studying the governance features of the interaction between governments and private investors and focuses especially on utility sectors such as telecommunications. TCR sees regulation and regulatory contracts as governance structures, with the precise regulatory choice (for example, state-owned enterprise or PPP) explained by the need to cope with the hazards that arise in interactions between governments and private investors. There are two fundamental pillars to TCR, namely (a) transaction cost economics (TCE) and (b) positive political theory.

Transaction cost economics

Like Commons (1932–33) and Coase (1937), Williamson (1999, 312) emphasises the transaction as the unit of analysis and posits that 'transactions, which differ in their attributes, are aligned with their governance structures' so as to effect an economising of transaction costs (that is, the costs of using the market including finding trading partners, agreeing contracts and monitoring performance). In other words, we expect the chosen approach to organising economic activity to be the one that minimises the magnitude of transaction costs. The original TCE framework focused on contracting between private firms. However, given the differences between public-private contracting and contracting between private entities, the original TCE framework has been extended in order to illuminate interactions between public and private contractors (Spiller 2011, 2013; Williamson 1976, 1999).

Obermann (2007) describes how parties to public-private contracts incur transaction costs arising from finding information and negotiating and finalising contracts. These costs arise at different stages of the procurement lifecycle and include those incurred when appraising capital investment decisions (for example, cost-benefit analysis) and comparing different procurement alternatives as well as organising and participating in tendering processes (O'Nolan and Reeves 2018). Transaction cost theory describes how the level of transaction costs is determined by the characteristics of the transaction (Williamson 1975, 1985). These include: asset specificity, frequency, uncertainty and complexity.

Large-scale infrastructure projects are generally complex in engineering and technological terms. The specifications of contracts for infrastructure projects such as motorways, bridges and renewable energy assets are generally detailed and costly. In addition, the long-term nature of infrastructure projects creates uncertainty and difficulties around the prediction of future events and their consequences. The combination of complexity and uncertainty poses hazards and raises the potential for contracting parties to incur significant transaction costs especially under conditions of incomplete contracting where parties are locked into an agreement (Boardman and Hewitt 2004, Obermann 2007).

The hazard of asset specificity arises because infrastructure assets often tend to have low (or zero) value outside their original intended use. Contracting parties that make significant (sunk cost) investments are therefore susceptible to opportunistic behaviour by their trading partners. Transaction costs may be incurred due to the interaction between opportunism, uncertainty, small numbers of bidders and bounded rationality (Williamson 1975). Where opportunism and contractual hold-up is likely, special governance is required to limit such conduct. When considering which regulatory option (ranging from fully public to fully private delivery) is most appropriate, the main propositions from TCE are neatly summarised by Gómez-Ibáñez, who states that:

> From this perspective the most intrusive forms of government involvement are justified when transaction costs are relatively high, so that even a crude approximation is an improvement. Private contracts are appropriate if transaction costs are low, concession contracts might be justified if transaction costs are moderate, and discretionary regulation or public enterprise could be justified only if transaction costs are extremely high and less intrusive remedies impractical. (Gómez-Ibáñez 2003, 23)

Positive political theory

In public infrastructure projects the interactions between government and private contractors have significant political dimensions. Spiller (2011, 2013) draws on positive political theory to examine the full extent of hazards associated with those interactions. He places strong emphasis on two types of opportunism that apply in cases of public–private contracting, namely governmental and third-party opportunism.

Scope for opportunistic behaviour by governments derives from private sector investments in specific infrastructure assets that involve significant levels of sunk costs. Such investments can make private contractors vulnerable to opportunistic behaviour (hold-up) by their public sector clients. In extreme cases, governmental opportunism can occur through outright expropriation of assets. Examples of more indirect forms of opportunism include where the government changes the rules of the game by altering investment requirements or regulated prices. Governance schemes that do not limit the potential for governmental opportunism can therefore create strong inefficiencies and sub-standard performance. Poor quality, underinvestment and high prices lead, eventually, to more conflicts between the operator and the government (Spiller 2010, 150).

Concerns about appropriate use of public monies in the context of public contracting can also introduce specific hazards with implications for contractual governance. The requirement for probity (a high standard of integrity) in public sector transactions is emphasised by Williamson (1999). Third-party opportunism presents a hazard to probity because 'interested parties' such as politicians, citizens or rival bidders have incentives to challenge the probity of public–private interactions in order to derive political or economic benefit. Political benefits may be accrued by third parties who succeed in undermining public officials by such challenges. In economic terms, third parties may also benefit from the cancellation of contracts resulting in displacement of the incumbent (O'Nolan and Reeves 2018, Spiller 2013).

To summarise, the TCR framework sheds light on the economic and political dynamics associated with public–private contracting and provides an appropriate framework for the analysis of the governance of contractual relations in infrastructure PPPs. In particular, it illuminates the nature of governance by emphasising contractual hazards and 'assessing real people, in real environments, within real institutions' (Spiller 2013, 232).

NBP: regulatory choice and procurement

Although the NBP was first announced in August 2012, a decision on the choice of regulatory model was not finalised until 2016. The final decision was based on an analysis conducted by international consultants KPMG and published in an 'ownership report' in December 2015 (KPMG 2015). The ownership report examined five potential options ranging from fully public to fully private as follows:

1. Public sector build, finance, own and operate through the creation of a new public enterprise;
2. Public sector finance and own with private sector design, build and operate (operating concession model);
3. Corporate joint venture between State and private sector;
4. Private sector finance, build and operate with asset reversion to public sector at contract end (full concession model);
5. Private sector build, finance, own and operate with asset retained by private sector at contract end (gap funding model).

The ownership report stated that only the full concession DBFO (design, build, finance, operate) model and the gap funding model were being considered for the delivery of the NBP, with the main difference between the two being the fact that the private sector retains ownership of the asset under the gap funding model. The preference for these private sector solutions to the market failures in the broadband market followed an established pattern whereby successive governments adopted various forms of PPP-style interventions in the broadband market after the full privatisation of Eircom in 1999. For example, the MANs programme mentioned previously involved the government funding the rollout of the network infrastructure with a concession agreement for the operation of the networks once they were completed. The NBS programme involved the government co-funding the rollout of mobile broadband infrastructure in rural areas as part of a relatively short-term gap funding agreement (the scheme commenced in 2008 and expired in 2014).

Table 16.1   National Broadband Plan timeline

Date	Event
August 2012	Publication of the NBP, which set a target of a minimum 30Mbps download speed for all citizens and a projected total cost of €350 million to deliver high-speed broadband to those areas without access to such speeds, with the state providing half of this amount.
December 2015	An updated NBP is published committing the government to meeting a minimum 30Mbps download speed for all households by 2020, with €275 million in Exchequer funds earmarked for the plan. The government announces that it will adopt either a PPP-style concession agreement or a gap funding commercial stimulus model for a period of 25 years to deliver the infrastructure. A contract notice for the NBP is issued in the *Official Journal of the EU*.
July 2016	Government announces it will proceed with a gap funding model for the NBP. Three bidders are shortlisted: Eir (the incumbent operator), Siro (a joint venture between Vodafone and the ESB, the state-owned electricity company) and a third bidder made up of a consortium of investors and firms led by Enet (the operator of the MANs).
April 2017	The Minister for Communications announces a commitment deal with Eir to remove 300,000 premises from the NBP intervention area, leaving 542,000 covered by the NBP.
September 2017	One of the three shortlisted bidders, Siro, withdraws from the competition, stating that there was no longer a business case for bidding for the contract.
January 2018	The incumbent operator, Eir, withdraws from the competition, citing concerns in relation to increasing uncertainty about regulatory and pricing issues.
September 2018	The final tender is received from the sole remaining bidder. The tender reveals that the composition of the consortium, now led by Granahan McCourt, has changed significantly since bidders were shortlisted in 2016.
October 2018	The Minister for Communications is forced to resign after it is revealed that he attended a number of private dinners and meetings with the CEO of Granahan McCourt.
November 2018	A review of the NBP procurement process finds that the process was not compromised by the minister's actions and could proceed as planned.
May 2019	The Granahan McCourt led consortium is selected as preferred bidder following review of tender by a new minister.

Date	Event
July 2019	A parliamentary committee that examined the NBP publishes a report that is highly critical of the plan.
November 2019	The NBP contract is signed with Granahan McCourt, with an estimated cost of subsidy to the Exchequer of between €2.2 and €2.9 billion.

In July 2016, the government announced its decision to proceed with a gap funding commercial stimulus model for the NBP. Under this model, the private sector operator is subsidised through capital grants, which are paid during deployment and over the operational life of the contract. The grant amount should be the minimum amount necessary for the private sector to deliver the project while also making an acceptable rate of return, and is subject to clawback mechanisms that track actual versus forecast financial performance during network build and operations and at contract expiry. The private sector partner bears the risk associated with wholesale network deployment, operation and exploitation over the 25-year contract term and beyond, and the payments of capital grants (upfront and during operation) are subject to the operator meeting the performance standards in the contract.

Once the gap funding model was formally adopted, three bidders were shortlisted and invited to participate in dialogue. Thereafter the procurement process was beset by difficulties, delays and a considerable increase in the cost of subsidy to the Exchequer. Table 16.1 summarises some of the key developments during the procurement of the plan. The major issues were the removal of 300,000 premises from the NBP intervention area by the incumbent legacy network operator when it signed a commitment deal with the government, the withdrawal of two bidders from the competition for the contract, the resignation of the minister with responsibility for the delivery of the project after allegations of inappropriate private communications with the sole remaining bidder, and a significant escalation in the estimated cost of delivering the project.

Explaining the events observed

Many of the difficulties and controversies with the procurement process described in the previous section can be understood in terms of the contracting hazards elucidated by TCE and TCR. The key reasons for most of the issues experienced concern: (1) opportunistic behaviour by the former national fixed-line operator through exploiting its incumbency advantage, (2) the removal of competitive tension from the procurement process with the withdrawal of the two main bidders for the contract and (3) the political dynamics that surrounded the latter stages of the tendering process. We address each of these issues separately below.

The role of Eir

One of the key obstacles to progressing the NBP as per the government's plans has been the dominant role played by Eir and the fixed-line telecoms infrastructure that it controls. This can be traced back to the impact of the privatisation of the firm in 1999. While privatising the incumbent national telecoms operator was not unusual in a European context in the 1990s, the manner in which the Irish government did so is unique. Ireland was the only European country to sell its entire stake in the national operator when floating the company on the stock market in July 1999. The fact that the government did not retain a minority stake or a golden share left it powerless to prevent a number of undesirable takeovers of the company from 2001 onwards.

In total, Eir has undergone seven changes in ownership since its initial public offering in 1999. However, the most damaging of these from a national perspective were two separate highly leveraged buyouts (LBOs) by private equity groups in 2001 and 2006. These LBOs resulted in the build-up of unsustainable levels of debt which severely hindered the capacity of the company to invest in its fixed-line network (Palcic and Reeves 2013). Although Eir began to invest significantly in urban areas from 2013 onwards, Ireland's NBP was essentially a necessary response to the historical lack of investment by Eir in its fixed-line infrastructure, particularly outside of major urban centres. However, in seeking to address the digital divide issue in rural areas it is very difficult to find a solution that does not directly involve Eir, or indirectly involve access to the fixed-line infrastructure that it owns. European state aid rules in particular make any intervention by a government seeking to address a market failure extremely difficult since incumbents can opportunistically exploit such rules to frustrate any plan that might threaten their natural monopoly position. This was certainly the case when one examines the actions of Eir after the NBP was first announced and the procurement process for the plan commenced.

Prior to the publication of the tender at the end of 2015, Eir announced that it could provide high-speed broadband services to 300,000 premises within the proposed intervention area. While a deal with the company was rejected at the time, it was unsurprising when Eir proceeded to develop more concrete plans to invest in these premises while the NBP procurement process was underway. Under state aid rules the government had no choice but to allow these 300,000 premises be removed from the intervention area once Eir signed a commitment agreement in April 2017. Importantly, the premises included in the commitment agreement with Eir were the most commercially viable in the intervention area. Additionally, it transpired that the rollout of high-speed broadband infrastructure to the rest of the intervention area would have to traverse Eir's existing and new fibre infrastructure, ensuring that Eir would benefit in terms of revenue from access charges. Because of the commitment agreement with Eir, one of the other main bidders for the contract – Siro – subsequently withdrew from the NBP competition, stating that it was no longer commercially viable to proceed. Some months later, Eir itself announced its decision to withdraw from the competition for the contract.

Removal of competition

The decision to only consider a PPP or gap funding approach was based on KPMG's claim that the gap funding model involved the lowest cost of government subsidy, with the full concession PPP model the second cheapest of the five options considered. When the government announced in July 2016 that it was opting for the gap funding model, the decision was justified entirely on the basis of it involving the lowest cost to the Exchequer. The principal justification for the gap funding model being cheapest was the assumption that there would be strong competition among established industry players for the contract. This assumption was based on the expectation that the model would (1) incentivise full integration of the NBP network with the existing business and infrastructure of bidders for the contract, thereby enabling efficiencies; and (2) incentivise bidders through long-term ownership to invest in the network and diversify, thereby further increasing revenues and future-proofing the network. The report assumed that these incentives 'would attract the greatest level of "strategic value" from bidders in a competitive procurement process, thereby driving down the level of public subsidy required' (KPMG 2015, 58).

The ownership report's assumption that there would be strong competition among industry players with substantial assets that they could leverage was highly questionable since only two companies fit this description: Eir and the ESB (the state-owned electricity utility with substantial telecoms assets as part of its Siro joint venture with Vodafone). Indeed, the report highlights that one of the risks with the gap funding option was the strong likelihood that it would favour a large existing infrastructure owner, such as Eir or Siro, which could reinforce the incumbency advantage of such companies in the market. Since the report effectively acknowledges that there would be only two realistic bidders for the contract, its subsequent recommendation to pursue a gap funding model as the most competitive and therefore lowest-cost option for the state is difficult to understand. Whether this recommendation was the result of ideological bias against a more public solution to the NBP or a naïvely optimistic view of the level of competition that would emerge for the contract is impossible to say. However, it is worth noting that the decision aligned with a historical pattern of interventions favouring private-led solutions to the market failure that emerged post-privatisation.

Unfortunately, the sequence of events that followed the tendering of the NBP contract in December 2015 led to all competitive tension, which is a necessary condition for successful procurement, being removed from the process. This absence of competition 'for the market' created a contractual hazard that undermined the procurement process and led to a significant escalation in the expected cost of subsidy to the government. This outcome is unsurprising given the fundamental importance of competition as a factor that justifies the use of market-oriented regulation such as PPP. The advantage of the concession/PPP approach to infrastructure regulation is that 'market forces are involved, because a concession is usually awarded through competitive bidding. A competitive award should ensure that the infrastructure supplier is driven to offer terms that reflect his costs and no more' (Gómez-Ibáñez 2003, 30).

While the economic literature provides no clear guidance on the question of the desired level of competition for concession/PPP contracts, there is general consensus that a minimum of two bidders is a fundamental condition for ensuring efficient outcomes. This is described clearly by Sappington and Stiglitz (1987), who devise a privatisation theorem where three objectives (namely economic efficiency, equity and rent extraction) can be achieved when 'two or more risk-neutral firms (agents) who have symmetric beliefs about the least cost production technology' bid for the contract (1987, 569). Threats to real competition include bidders possessing advantageous information, high entry costs, collusion and loss-leading behaviour. Moreover, a low number of bidders (which is common for large infrastructure contracts) can result in some associated pitfalls, such as higher transaction costs due to post-contractual lock-in and contract renegotiations where firms seek to extract higher profits (Engel et al. 2014, Lonsdale 2005, Williamson 1975).

In the case of the NBP, the KPMG Ownership Report explicitly identified competition as an advantage of both PPP models (concession and gap funding) compared to the other three alternatives (corporate joint venture, DBO model and state-owned enterprises). Given the events that have unfolded it is evident that the advice provided to government was based on a gross underestimation of the risks attendant to the PPP/gap funding model. The withdrawal of all but one remaining bidder from the competition for the contract created an *ex ante* bilateral monopoly that increased the risk of opportunistic behaviour by the bidder (both *ex ante* and *ex post*) and severely diminished the potential to achieve value for money. Moreover, it increased the scope for third-party opportunism and politicisation of the procurement process. The risk of such developments was not given any attention in the KPMG Ownership Report even though there was evidence in 2015 that Eir had plans to invest in a significant number of premises within the intervention area. While the then minister rejected Eir's initial plan to invest in these premises in 2015, it should have raised serious concerns that Eir would exploit its incumbent advantage and develop more concrete investment plans to invest in the area in the near future, thereby increasing the risk that there would be less competition for the contract and a higher subsidy required.

Political dynamics

A full understanding of the nature of public–private interactions, governance structures and related hazards necessitates an appreciation of the political dynamics that apply in the regulatory context. In the case of the NBP, a number of political developments impacted the procurement process and created obstacles to its completion. First, the choice of regulatory model (that is, PPP/gap funding model) reflected an inherent political preference for mainly market-led solutions to market failures in the telecommunications sector. This preference can be traced back to the decision to privatise the state-owned telecommunications monopoly in 1999, and it has characterised subsequent interventions in the broadband market such as the MANs and NBS programmes described previously. This political preference for pro-market approaches to regulation was also evident during the assessment of the regulatory alternatives contained in the KPMG Ownership Report that essentially reduced the detailed analysis to two PPP-type alternatives: concession DBFO or gap funding DBFOO (design, build, finance, own, operate).

Although it is to be expected that political preferences will influence regulatory choice, the difficulties encountered during the conduct of the procurement process became increasingly political in nature following the decision in April 2017 to reduce the intervention area by 300,000 homes. This decision was followed by a series of officially announced delays to the procurement over the following two years. Moreover, the subsequent withdrawal from the bidding process of Siro (September 2017) and then Eir (January 2018) resulted in the procurement process becoming the subject of intense public scrutiny and increased the scope for third-party opportunism.

Following the submission of the final bid from the only remaining bidder in September 2018, it was revealed that the composition of the bidding consortium had changed and was now led by US private equity group Granahan McCourt. When details of earlier private meetings and dinners between the relevant minister and the CEO of Granahan McCourt became public, the minister resigned in response to demands from political competitors and other 'interested' parties. This resulted in further delays and the establishment of a review of the NBP process by the independent process auditor for the contract. Although the review (published in November 2018) found that the process was not compromised by the minister's actions, the final decision on the award of the NBP contract was postponed until Easter 2019. In the meantime the government encountered further high-profile controversy around the procurement of public infrastructure as the expected cost of delivering a National Children's Hospital escalated from an initial estimate of €983 million to €1.73 billion. The ensuing public outcry and political controversy resulted in the minority government pushing out a final announcement on the award of the NBP contract and the establishment of an inquiry by a parliamentary committee into the plan. Despite the publication of a report by the committee that was highly critical of the NBP procurement process, the government eventually signed off on a contract with the remaining bidder in December 2019, a full four years after the contract was originally tendered.

The drawn-out procurement process can therefore be partly attributed to the political dynamics that played out over the 48-month procurement period. It is evident that the former state-owned monopoly, Eir, used its market power to act opportunistically and capture approximately 40 per cent of the original intervention area, which led to the withdrawal of the other main bidder for the contract (Siro). With the principal justification (that is, competition) for the use of the PPP model undermined, the scope for political opportunism was greatly enhanced and subsequent actions by interested parties created significant delays for the procurement of the NBP.

Discussion and conclusion

Ireland's National Broadband Plan, which aims to roll out high-speed broadband services to every premises in the country, is the biggest (in terms of cost) infrastructure contract to be signed in the history of the state. It is now over eight years since the publication of the initial NBP, which was originally envisaged to cost €350 million (including €175 million of public finance). Following the decision to proceed with a gap funding model and a procurement process plagued by delays and controversy, it is now anticipated that the cost of the public subsidy will amount to at least €2.2 billion. In addition, the department responsible for procuring the NBP has had to put in place a costly governance structure to monitor the NBP contract, which is projected to cost up to €10 million per year and include up to ten permanent civil servants, as well as the outsourcing of specialist advice to external consultants (Joint Committee on Communications, Climate Action and Environment 2019).

It is worth asking whether the experience in Ireland is similar to that of other European countries that implemented NBPs. Like-for-like comparisons are not feasible given that every country is different in terms of important factors such as the historical development of their telecommunications sectors, prevailing broadband technologies and population densities in rural areas. Some European countries initially opted for fibre-to-the-cabinet (FTTC) solutions in rural areas, whereas others have opted for FTTP solutions similar to Ireland. However, a review of all NBPs that have been reported to the European Commission to date found that Ireland has by far the highest average cost of subsidy per premises passed of any EU country (EC 2020).[4] A major factor in the higher cost observed for Ireland (outside of the lack of competition for the NBP contract) was the decision to go with a FTTP solution for the vast majority of the premises in the intervention area. A mixed FTTP/wireless solution where fixed wireless access was provided for the most remote and difficult-to-access premises would have led to significantly reduced cost and levels of subsidy. Indeed, in New Zealand, which has a low population density similar to Ireland, the ultrafast broadband plan rolled out by the government there will see FTTP provided to up to 87 per cent of premises in the country by 2023, with enhanced wireless access used for the remaining 13 per cent of premises (Milner 2020).

This chapter uses the TCR framework devised by Williamson and Spiller to deepen our understanding of how the procurement of Ireland's NBP unfolded. The objective is to explore the workings of the procurement of the PPP-style gap funding model, which was chosen after a detailed analysis of five regulatory alternatives ranging from a new state-owned enterprise to the gap funding model under which the private sector is contracted to build, finance, own and operate the infrastructure. The case study approach we adopt is valuable as it 'allows one to examine how the interplay of economics, politics, and institutions affects regulatory commitment and performance' (Gómez-Ibáñez 2003, 13). The TCR framework permits this approach given its two underlying pillars of TCE and positive political theory. Whereas TCE provides a suitable framework for understanding the choice of regulatory model (for example, PPP or state-owned enterprise), the positive political theory pillar recognises the political dimensions of regulatory choice and provides a lens for understanding the political dynamics associated with interactions between government and the private sector.

Overall, the TCR framework provides useful insights that aid our understanding of Ireland's NBP procurement. This case confirms a fundamental proposition of TCE by demonstrating how market-led approaches to procuring complex infrastructure projects are not suitable where transaction costs are extremely high. The time delays and enormous cost escalation witnessed in this case suggest that a state-owned enterprise approach was justified. This case also highlights how opportunistic behaviour by key economic actors can undermine public procurement. Eir's market power (a legacy of earlier privatisation decisions) gave it enormous scope for opportunistic behaviour which it fully exercised when it made the move to provide services to 300,000 premises in the intervention area.

This case also demonstrates the relevance of the political theory pillar of TCR. For example, Spiller (2010) highlights how the essence of public contracts is their publicity. In reasonably working democratic societies, mechanisms are available to allow interested third parties, including political opponents, to scrutinise public procurement and seek to hold public decision makers to account. The case of Ireland's NBP provides a salient example of how political opponents can take full advantage of the available instruments of accountability (for example, establish an independent inquiry) to question the probity of public agents (for example, a government minister). We do not argue that the behaviour of public opponents in the NBP case was purely self-seeking and opportunistic. However, this episode of the NBP procurement highlights the incentives for third parties to challenge the process, thereby creating hazards that affect how public (and PPP) procurement plays out.

TCR also emphasises the interaction between the particular hazards associated with specific sectors and the institutional environment in which they operate. Telecommunications sectors around the globe are currently challenged to provide accessible and equitable broadband, especially in the post-COVID-19 world. However, the rollout of broadband infrastructure raises sector-specific regulatory and procurement challenges that are elucidated in this chapter. Our study shows how the legacy of privatisation policies in the telecommunications sector and the power of previously state-owned incumbents can have considerable influence on how regulatory choices such as PPP play out.

In addition, the Irish NBP experience adds to the existing evidence that shows the importance of good governance when governments are considering the regulatory choices that are available. The appraisal of regulatory options and ultimate choice of the PPP (gap funding) model in this case provides lessons for other countries aiming to roll out high-speed broadband infrastructure at a large scale. In this case, the appraisal of regulatory options by international management consultants KPMG provided little evidence to support its recommendation to rule out a state-owned approach. Moreover, it underestimated the risks (hazards) associated with the gap funding model, especially those concerning competition for the contract (small numbers exchange), and opportunistic behaviour by firms, especially the former state-owned monopoly.

This raises questions about the role of private sector advisors, especially the big accounting and consultancy firms, that advise governments on policy and projects. Shaoul et al. (2007, 481) describe how a small number of large accountancy and consultancy firms are:

> advising governments on policy and projects via their staff, who they second or loan to government [...] advising the private sector firms that tender for PFI [Private Finance Initiative] projects; acting as advisors on public bodies; lobbying for the expansion of the policy internationally; and sponsoring research on PFI/PPP. Furthermore, in some cases, the firms or their sister companies are equity stakeholders or major subcontractors in PFI contracts.

The role of these firms and their relationships with government raise important questions about conflicts of interest, the quality and objectivity of the advice they provide and the interests their advice serves.

In conclusion, we emphasise that this chapter was written at a time when the provision of reliable broadband infrastructure and services has become a COVID rallying cry around the world. In this context, the Irish NBP experience provides valuable insights into the economic, political and governance challenges faced by governments seeking to provide universal access to high-speed broadband services. Our case study highlights the nature of economic and political hazards that give rise to significant transaction costs in the context of an extensive rollout of broadband infrastructure. It lends support to the fundamental proposition of TCE which suggests that market-led regulatory options such as PPP are less likely to be suitable when these economic and political hazards are salient. The Irish NBP case provides a stark example of where these hazards were underestimated and provides important lessons for policymakers in other jurisdictions seeking to achieve timely and cost-efficient delivery of vital broadband infrastructure and services.

Notes

1. Source: European Commission, Digital Economy & Society Scoreboard.
2. Examinership is the corporate rescue process used in Ireland for an insolvent company that protects it from creditors for a period of up to 100 days while an appointed examiner investigates whether a rescue package can be put together for the firm or whether the company's assets should be liquidated.
3. The MANs programme involved the construction of 'middle mile' fibre optic networks in approximately 90 cities and towns in Ireland, while the NBS involved the delivery of basic mobile broadband services to rural areas without any broadband service (approximately 10 per cent of the country at the time). See Palcic and Reeves (2011) for more detail on these interventions.
4. The report found that the average cost of subsidy per premises passed for Ireland's NBP was €5,500. The next highest average cost of subsidy per premise passed was €3,958 for Denmark and €3,084 for Austria, with all other countries reporting significantly lower average subsidies (EC, 2020: 49).

References

Boardman, A.E., and Hewitt, E.S. (2004) Problems with contracting out government services: lessons from orderly services at SCGH. *Industrial and Corporate Change*, 13 (6): 917–929.

C&AG (2011) *Report on the Accounts of the Public Services 2010, Volume 2*. Dublin: Comptroller & Auditor General.

Coase, R.H. (1937) The nature of the firm. *Economica*, New Series, 4(16): 386–405.

Commons, J.R. (1932–33) The problems of correlating law economics and ethics. *Wisconsin Law Review*, 8 (1): 3–26.

DCENR (2008a) *Value for Money and Policy Review of the Group Broadband Schemes*. Dublin: Department of Communications, Energy and Natural Resources.

DCENR (2008b) *Value for Money and Policy Review of the Metropolitan Area Networks (Phase I)*. Dublin: Department of Communications, Energy and Natural Resources.

EC (2019) *Decision on State Aid SA.54472 (2019/N) – Ireland: National Broadband Plan*. Brussels: European Commission. https://ec.europa.eu/competition/state_aid/cases1/201951/282707_2118156_159_2.pdf.

EC (2020) *The Role of State Aid for the Rapid Deployment of Broadband Networks in the EU*. Brussels: European Commission.

Engel, E., Fischer, R., and Galetovic, A. (2014) Risk and public-private partnerships. *CESifo DICE Report*, 12 (3): 3–7.

Gómez-Ibáñez, J.A. (2003) *Regulating Infrastructure: Monopoly, Contracts, and Discretion*. Cambridge, MA: Harvard University Press.

Joint Committee on Communications, Climate Action and Environment (2019) *Report of the Joint Committee on an Investigation to Examine the National Broadband Plan Process Thus Far and How Best to Proceed and the Best Means to Roll Out Rural Broadband*. Dublin: Houses of the Oireachtas.

KPMG (2015) *Ownership Report: National Broadband Intervention Strategy*. Dublin: KPMG.

Lonsdale, C. (2005) Post-contractual lock-in and the UK private finance initiative (PFI): the cases of the national savings and investments and the Lord Chancellor's department. *Public Administration*, 83 (1): 67–88.

Milner, M. (2020) Ultra-fast broadband: the New Zealand experience. *Journal of Telecommunications and the Digital Economy*, 8 (2): 31–55.

National Development Plan 2000–2006 (1999) Dublin: Stationery Office.

Obermann, G. (2007) The role of the state as guarantor of public services: transaction cost issues and empirical evidence. *Annals of Public and Cooperative Economics*, 78 (3): 475–500.

O'Nolan, G., and Reeves, E. (2018) The nature of contracting hazards in public–private partnerships: evidence from Ireland. *International Journal of Public Administration*, 41 (15): 1205–1216.

Palcic, D., and Reeves, E. (2011) *Privatisation in Ireland: Lessons from a European Economy*. Basingstoke: Palgrave Macmillan.

Palcic, D., and Reeves, E. (2013) Private equity leveraged buyouts in European tele-coms: the case of Eircom. *Telecommunications Policy*, 37: 573–582.

Sappington, D.E.M., and Stiglitz, J.E. (1987) Privatization, information and incentives. *Journal of Policy Analysis and Management*, 6 (4): 567–585.

Shaoul, J., Stafford, A., and Stapleton, P. (2007) Partnerships and the role of financial advisors: private control over public policy? *Policy and Politics*, 35 (3): 479–495.

Spiller, P.T. (2010) Regulation: a transaction cost perspective. *California Management Review*, 52 (2): 147–158.

Spiller, P.T. (2011) Basic Economic Principles of Infrastructure Liberalization: A Transaction Cost Perspective, in *International Handbook of Network Industries: The Liberalization of Infrastructure*, edited by M. Finger and R.W. Künneke. Cheltenham, UK and Northampton, MA, USA: Edward Elgar Publishing, pp. 11–25.

Spiller, P.T. (2013) Transaction cost regulation. *Journal of Economic Behaviour & Organization*, 89 (C): 232–242.

Williamson, O.E. (1975) *Markets and Hierarchies: Analysis and Antitrust Implications*. New York, NY: Free Press.

Williamson, O.E. (1976) Franchise bidding for natural monopolies – in general and with respect to CATV. *Bell Journal of Economics*, 7 (1): 73–104.

Williamson, O.E. (1985) *The Economic Institutions of Capitalism*. New York, NY: Free Press.

Williamson, O.E. (1999) Public and private bureaucracies: a transaction cost economics perspective. *Journal of Law, Economics, and Organization*, 15 (1): 306–342.

PART IV

Conclusion

17 Common themes for a PPP research agenda

Graeme A. Hodge and Carsten Greve

Introduction

This concluding chapter outlines what we have learned from the various chapters about infrastructure PPPs and the ways they are governed today. Many insights are certainly visible within each of the chapters, but rather than summarise each of these individually, we will take more of a meta-view of the terrain covered in order to articulate broad future research directions. This will point to common themes that have become visible across the whole volume.

This closing chapter outlines six themes in our public–private partnership (PPP) research journey to date. For each theme, we outline where we appear to have moved from, where we have now landed and why research interest in this theme is likely to continue. We then discuss some of the dynamics of future directions.

Themes in the research agenda

To us, there have been six themes throughout the research journey presented in the present volume. The PPP research agenda has moved:

1. From few traditional research methods such as case studies and surveys to a wider and more diverse menu in terms of our research methodology (towards fresh research approaches),
2. From well-known theoretical approaches to new lenses in terms of our theoretical approach (towards new theories on the block),
3. From a belief in market superiority to renewed government strength as the dominant meta-assumption operating in the political economy (towards public–private balance),

4. From an era of New Public Management (NPM) to an era of financialisation as the dominant technical ethos operating in the political economy (towards financialised everything),
5. From a focus on contracts and projects to governance as dominant political research questions (towards stronger governance), and
6. From understanding PPPs as a sophisticated Western infrastructure technique to a broader global development perspective for all countries (towards a global phenomenon).

And in each case, we have moved into new domains in which there are opportunities for new research to grow. Each of these themes deserves discussion.

1.   Methodology: towards fresh research approaches

We have firstly been progressively moving towards a wider menu of research approaches. And whilst strong traditional surveys and case studies will no doubt remain relevant for potential research studies, such approaches are now being supplemented by fresh new methods. These include techniques such as qualitative comparative analysis (QCA), Q methodology and experiments, as argued by Warsen (Chapter 3). Her comment, quite rightly, was that not only will these methods bring a greater diversity to our scholarship, they also have the potential to address new questions. Warsen notes examples of her own work which adopted QCA and Qsort methods (as well as using surveys), whilst Casady (in Chapter 13) noted his research, which also used QCA. Liebe (Chapter 14) also reminded us that a greater use of mixed methods is also a sensible direction for future research. He argued that mixed methods 'add value' through their ability to combine quantitative large-N methods with qualitative small-N studies. This allows one 'to look at the broad canvas of correlations and patterns without giving up a looking glass to spot the small differences and understand the causal mechanisms at work'.

There has also been a resurgence of interest in drawing research conclusions from existing studies and analyses through systematic approaches in order to provide more reliable meta-analytic conclusions. All of these approaches are being employed with newfound enthusiasm and perhaps even fanfare at times when scholars believe that the new approach they have taken offers greater rigour than previous methods.[1] Alongside this, there has also been a renewed enthusiasm in adopting global databases. Both Bertelli and Woodhouse (Chapter 5), and Casady (Chapter 13) are examples here. Without doubt, the methodological debates of the past half century will continue[2] as we better understand the weaknesses as well as the more widely advertised strengths of both new methodological approaches and new databases.

There will be a need to heed Liebe's message and increasingly both use mixed methods and adopt stronger triangulation procedures in order to learn, as we have long done, from multiple methods. Researchers will always need to 'join the dots'. And as he says, there is little which speaks against combining different logics of inquiry to mitigate the shortcomings of each approach and benefit from their advantages. Without doubt, these developments have widened the ways in which PPPs can now be studied.

2.   Theoretical approaches: towards new theories on the block

Interestingly, as Wang et al. (2017) showed in a literature review in *Public Management Review*, the theoretical approaches employed in analysing PPPs over the past four and a half decades have actually been impressively wide. Traditionally powerful lenses such as transaction cost economics, principal–agent theory and NPM have all featured strongly. But so have lenses such as network-oriented perspectives, as well as institutionalist and governance approaches. These have not monopolised our ways to think, however. Organisational sense-making, sustainability and policy transfer also featured in the lenses summarised by Wang et al., albeit less frequently. But if we were to take a 'meta-view' of theoretical approaches, what might we discern?

Klijn presented us (in Chapter 2) with a new take on PPP theories. He acknowledged by way of context that partnerships between the public and private sectors go back centuries, and that even the same version of a PPP transforms 'in line with the (political) culture in a country'. Importantly, he also articulated three fundamentally different theoretical foundations for PPPs: an economic monitoring game (where we check for opportunistic behaviour and investigate information completeness in contracts), complex network collaboration (where we take more of a governing perspective and study how tensions between conflict and cooperation are resolved and how trust is nurtured) and sensemaking orientations (where we think more about how PPP work is framed inside organisations, the frames used by different actors, and how they cooperate, solve problems, and learn and adapt to make sense of their world). The possible alternative lenses within each of these three categories of theoretical approaches is wide. We clearly have important choices to make.

What this volume has demonstrated is a willingness to take up an even wider net of potential theoretical approaches in our research. Several examples were discussed. Sturup's continuing work on psychology was noted in Chapter 6, and Zwalf mapped some behaviourial science frontiers in Chapter 7. Both exemplified an interesting new vein of analysis at the individual level. At a broader level, Mihov's research (Chapter 15) was a wonderful example of how to combine insights from both the policy transfer literature and the institutional work literature in order to better understand how the practices of public infrastructure actors are shaped not only by government policy, but also by norms and by culture when the PPP idea is adopted. She used two theoretical domains in her research, institutional transplantation and institutional work, to study the German PPP adoption process.

Liebe's chapter (Chapter 14) on comparative political economy was also interesting from a theoretical perspective. It appealed to a wide range of theories in formulating hypotheses for its mixed methods analysis. These included NPM, Public Choice, New Institutionalism and Varieties of Capitalism. In a parallel vein, Casady (in Chapter 13) drew his theoretical inspiration from institutional theory in order to more carefully conceptualise, quantify and then analyse the crucial dimensions of PPP market maturity.

Vinogradov and Shadrina covered much theoretical ground in Chapter 4. Their impressively ambitious aim was to join economics thinking to the public administration discipline, and in doing so, not only point to gaps in coverage but also call for a comprehensive theory of PPPs as institutions. Importantly, they conclude that theorising the existence, role and operation of PPPs from an economics perspective still has a long way to go. To them, PPPs still need to 'earn attention as institutions that serve some purpose differently from and better than other existing arrangements' (whether this is the public provision of public goods or outsourcing this provision) in order for progress in this direction to occur. Theirs was a provocative challenge. And they contributed one step towards this challenge in presenting their own PPP model.

Importantly, too, each of the above authors developed their thinking from a solid knowledge of foundational work undertaken through previous decades. They explicitly acknowledged the shoulders of the giants on which they built their own work: Alchian, Demsetz, Boardman and Vining, Hart, Iossa, Megginson, Stiglitz, Williamson, Coase, North and Ostrom in economics, for example; or Koppenjan, Bovaird, Klijn, McGuire and Agranoff, Parker, Broadbent and Laughlin, Linder, Brinkerhoff, DiMaggio and Powell, Scott, Grimsey and Lewis, Hall, Dolowitz and Marsh, and Pierson in public policy and management. In this context, it is of little surprise that there are strong reasons to continue adopting those traditional lenses (such as institutionalist ideas) which are reliable and trustworthy, as well as developing these theories further. The analysis of Christensen and Greve (Chapter 8) aimed to show the renewed interest in governance by the state in infrastructure projects and policies is a case in point here. They adopted the arguments of institutionalisation and institutional change in their analysis, illustrated by the Organisation for Economic Co-operation and Development's (OECD's) major focus on the wider lens of infrastructure governance, which aimed for a more pragmatic approach, and thereby demonstrated yet another way to refresh our views. Mihov's institutional work perspective in Chapter 15 broke new ground in PPP studies by demonstrating how the PPP institution in Germany changed over time as the original focus on the Public Finance Initiative (PFI) model in Britain's centralised system of government got translated into a much more pragmatic use and adoption in Germany's federalised system of government.

Today's breadth of potential research approaches is thus nothing short of spectacular. So, which are the most promising new kids on the block? And how can these approaches be adopted to answer some of the priority questions for the age? Whatever one's personal views on this, we certainly observe that new theoretical approaches mean that the PPP research arena is still alive and kicking. And it is also being carried further by a younger cohort of energetic and capable researchers.

3.   Dominant political-economy assumption: towards public–private balance

Reflecting over the past three decades is illuminating. We saw initial infrastructure PPP research born in the 1990s when governments were being increasingly reformed under the guise of the NPM (Hood, 1991) and catchphrases such as 'steering, not rowing'. The metaphor of 'steering, not rowing' evolved from the writing of Savas (1987), when he said 'the role of government is to steer, not to man the oars' during the privatisation debate, but it was popularised through the American version of NPM known as 'Reinventing Government' (Osborne and Gaebler, 1992). During this period, most public sector activities were being reformed to match private sector approaches. We built up a love of the market, of competition and of efficiency. The desire was to discipline governments to stay out of commerce (Roberts, 2010), and governments tended to worship the apparent power of the efficient market hypothesis. PPPs were seen as part and parcel of the NPM movement by some, but for others PPPs represented a middle way or third way between governments and markets (see Klijn, 2010 for this perspective).

But PPP research was also tossed about amongst the winds of global shifts in thinking over the past three decades. This brash era of market worship was punctuated by several market crashes, the largest of which was the 2007/08 global financial crisis. Trust in governments and in institutions more generally continued a downwards trend. Warnings of global catastrophe in not wrestling effectively with climate change grew progressively louder. Political leadership was found wanting across traditionally stable Western liberal countries such as the USA, as Trumpism and an increasingly influential social media produced echo chambers of stupidity as well as offering windows of increased transparency to assist the public interest. And the most recent COVID-19 global pandemic has again reminded us that our own continued biological (and financial) health is not guaranteed. It remains simply an assumption. All of these dynamics left us one step further along the road into the 'Risk Society' as foreseen by the prescient German sociologist Ulrick Beck (Beck, 1986, 1992).

Within this background context, PPP research directions shifted noticeably. PPP research was initially located in an environment which prioritised an assumption of market superiority married inside an engineering and finance narrative. This narrative, laced with early hope and excitement around the power of reinventing infrastructure delivery, assumed, naively, that this reinvention was certain and was good for everyone. An international army of consultant advisors spread the simple good news. Decades of experience, though, revealed lessons which were more accurate. We gradually understood that infrastructure PPPs were not the same everywhere, and that even identical legal and contractual arrangements worked quite differently in different countries. So, the marketing salesmanship of a long-term infrastructure contract PPP panacea was false. The reality was, as Klijn says in Chapter 2 for the case of the PFI (design, build, finance and operate) version, 'as in all policy transfers, the core ideas of PPP were ... adopted and implemented differently'. Put another way, PPPs meant very different things in different places, for different reasons. We learned that risk-constrained PPPs with public as well as private finance worked more reliably than the more aggressive Australian ('risk everything', testosterone-charged) PPPs. And in this volume, we were also again reminded (Chapter 14) that PPPs in places such as Germany do not even adopt private finance at all, are much smaller than those in other Western countries and work through small and medium-sized enterprises (SMEs) rather than international construction giants.

Overall then, a search for a new public–private balance was taken though this time. And it was a different balancing act in different countries. Moreover, as fast as the PPP idea swirled around Western liberal economies, it also spread to the development context. But that is a story for another theme later in this chapter.

4.   Dominant technical ethos: towards financialised everything

The central place of both finance and economics to the PPP phenomenon has not changed over the past three decades, but a shift in the narrative has occurred. As Stafford, Smyth and Almeida argued (in Chapter 11), we have moved from a space in which we were devoted to the tenets of NPM towards the frameworks, language and beliefs stemming from financialisation. Our movement was from a time when the financial foundations of infrastructure investment policy were invisible and implied to an era where they are now explicit and visible. And the private finance school dominated analyses globally for most of this period (Hodge and Greve, 2021).

Stafford, Smyth and Almeida observe that financialisation has become the driving force in today's PPPs, and a topic of controversy. Instead of arguing about whether PPPs are a part of NPM or not, the bigger question now concerns the effects of increased financialisation. To what extent should we expect the market to work for us, as citizens, or should it be the other way around? And even if we get a clear answer to such a politically loaded question, exactly where should the line be drawn? Trade-offs between democratic (political) control and market forces remain. And how to best balance values such as effectiveness, fairness, due process, transparency, flexibility and accountability whilst aiming for efficient solutions will always remain for all levels of decision making.

In the case of pension funds, Foster and Hodge (Chapter 12) revealed that the pension funds are already large investors in PPPs around the world. They remained somewhat hesitant, though, to recommend that governments reform pension fund regulatory arrangements in order to exert greater political influence over this source of finance. In part, this was because pension funds are simply an upfront financing option and not a viable solution to governments' real problem – their own limited capacity to fund everything suggested by interest groups or the community more generally. But this hesitancy was also due to the strict legal requirements requiring pension fund boards and executives to act in the best interests of their long-term pension holders – not the interests of the current government in power.

There is also little doubt that financialisation can play an influential role in how cities are planned and shaped. Indeed, Siemiatycki (Chapter 9) comments that the geography and planning disciplines have generally been quite critical of infrastructure PPPs because of 'the ways in which PPPs drive social inequality and put private profit ahead of public benefit'. Whilst the early triumphant view of the PPP brand has waned, a new frontier is taking place with fresh rationales aiming for collaborative advantage, new urban development PPP types and new actors. This has left researchers with the task of working harder to look at the 'responses and resistance to the financialization of urban infrastructure'. The overall view from the perspective of city planning is therefore that 'reinvigorating the place of meaningful partnerships and collaboration in city building is as important as ever to tackle the most pressing urban challenges'.

Of course, in one sense, the acknowledgement that financialisation is a central theme to the future of PPPs is hardly news. It follows the pioneering work of many authors, such as Jean Shaoul, Jane Broadbent, Richard Laughlin, Istemi Demirag, Mark Hellowell and Veronica Vecchi, as well as many others. But it again reminds us that new research will inevitably build on the careful work of those who have walked before us.

5.   Research focus: towards stronger governance

The fifth theme is the transition from focusing on contracts and projects towards a stronger and broader debate around better governing – whatever long-term infrastructure arrangements are chosen. There has been much written on this theme. As we said in the Introduction, Hodge and Greve (2018, 2019), for instance, ask simply 'How do governments govern their complex portfolio of PPP deals?' Likewise Klijn emphasised the need in his writing (Chapter 2) for long-term monitoring to check for opportunistic behaviour, and facilitating cooperation. Bertelli and Woodhouse (Chapter 5) viewed PPPs as 'an alternative to full public management' and 'as a governing mechanism [themselves] with political payoffs'. Sturup (Chapter 6) reminded us that PPP projects are something 'outside business as usual' and indeed create 'a state of exceptionalism'. Under this logic, perhaps we might ask whether we have already entered an era of governance exceptionalism.

Christensen and Greve (Chapter 8) trace the academic literature including the move from public management towards public governance. They also note the professional literature emanating from bodies such as the OECD and multilateral banks in their overwhelming emphasis on public governance frameworks for infrastructure. The change in narrative has been blatant – from contractual structures and detailed project design matters to broader issues that 'the governance of infrastructure' entails and a more balanced approach less ideologically bent towards market solutions. Some countries, like Denmark, are even reviving the state-owned enterprise model.

A primary study of governing infrastructure through a PPP was presented in this volume by Palcic and Reeves (Chapter 16). Their study of the Irish National Broadband Plan was instructive; including the opportunistic behaviour of the (privatised) incumbent fixed-line operator, the forced resignation of the responsible minister and a massive escalation in subsidy cost to government. They showed how quickly the Irish Broadband Plan escalated from being a procurement issue to a major governance failure amidst high political stakes, encompassing regulatory, management, procurement and policy components. We might be forgiven for asking whether this particular case study described the logical conclusion for a country subject to excessive financialisation.

The transition in research towards matters of public infrastructure governance has in some ways been gradual. Many scholars have long sought answers to important governance matters including decision making, transparency, public consultation, due process, citizen influence and public accountability. Indeed, both editors of this volume have always believed that governance of PPPs mattered. Hodge (2002, 16) argued that 'improved governance [was] now critical' some two decades ago, and Greve (2003) analysed a Danish PPP in which a local mayor ended up in prison and the municipality was put under administration – essentially unable to govern even itself! There were also strong accusations that PPPs in Australia at that time lacked legitimacy, and warnings that contract law had become a governance mechanism which lacked sufficient public accountability (Hodge, 2006). Two decades ago, the editors of this volume sounded more like lone voices in the wilderness. But times have changed and it is terrific to now see a wide range of such governance-related questions dominating discourses in PPP discussions. Research interests are also now more structured and interlinked, covering governance models (Levitt and Erikssen, 2016), rationalistic governance for the whole lifecycle (Wang et al., 2020), responsive governance to manage uncertainty (Dewulf and Garvin, 2020), and opportunistic behaviour in social networks (Wang et al., 2021), for example. Klijn and colleagues have demonstrated again and again that networks matter in infrastructure PPPs, which was witnessed lately in the Dutch 'Smarter governance of PPPs' research program.[3]

These more recent writings on governance stand on the shoulders of earlier efforts to raise the governance flag. An early example here is UNECE (2008), whose document *Guidebook on Promoting Good Governance in Public-Private Partnerships* explicitly recognised that 'governance objectives [were] not being promoted enough'. Their guidebook aimed 'to integrate good governance criteria into PPP processes' (p. 15) 'based on good governance principles' (p. 16). This work continues today (see Prats 2019). On the academic front, scholars ranging from North (1990) to Skelcher (2010) have also long contributed to the intellectual foundations of PPP governance as well.

6.   Expanding perspectives: towards a global phenomenon

The PPP phenomenon has progressively changed its shape over three decades. It has transmogrified from simply being a sophisticated Western infrastructure technique and a favoured infrastructure delivery policy to being a global development perspective with relevance to all countries. This transformation towards a global phenomenon has in many ways been inevitable as our professional and academic interests have moved from a select focus on Western countries to a focus on the developing world and a more global outlook. As others have noted, PPP is not a Western phenomenon anymore (if it ever was), but is now truly global.

This inevitability had several factors behind it. First, PPP has been transferred and spread around the world through globally influential consultants (cheekily termed the 'consultocracy' by Hood and Jackson, 1991). Paralleling the earlier transfer of its policy predecessor, privatisation, the early experiences of the UK, Canada and Australia were quickly followed by interest in OECD countries. Consultants eagerly spread the message of Western financiers and construction industries that 'modern capitalist governments now employ sophisticated PPPs – and so should you!' But PPPs have always had multiple grammars as Linder (1999) said, and the notion of PPP has thus long been an ambiguous shape-shifter in the public policy world. The phrase has therefore, secondly, taken on whatever meaning governments have wanted to give it – even whilst many professional groups have simultaneously pushed for greater technical clarity and consensus. The point here is that the PPP phraseology has become politically useful and this linguistic ambiguity has enabled governments to employ it to advantage. So, PPPs now seem to appear in countries ranging from the UK, Canada and Australia to China and Russia. But they are strikingly different and those assuming that a Chinese PPP is like a Canadian PPP is like a Russian PPP are either unfortunately naive or an advocate for an idea which they themselves misunderstand. The PPP language appeals to the ideal of public–private collaboration, whereas the project delivery mechanism refers to something far more specific to particular governance, legal and cultural assumptions. What this ambiguity does enable, however, is for all governments to speak the narrative of the collaborative ideal – marrying together a strong public sector and a strong private sector for the public good. This is the third reason why PPP as a global phenomenon was inevitable. The fourth influence on the 'globalisation' of PPPs lies in joining together the ambiguity of the partnership rhetoric with the ambiguity (as well as the importance) of governing well. Governance, and governing well, have become global concerns. And given the abovementioned shift towards improved PPP governance, it is little wonder that the world is now anchored on a new narrative of infrastructure governance.

Not surprisingly, we are therefore now witnessing an increasing interest in PPPs and in infrastructure governance in developing countries, and in most regions in the world, making PPP and infrastructure governance a global phenomenon. The breadth of the language now, thankfully, encompasses efforts to strengthen government administrative and policy capacity, improve the maturity of private markets across the economy and reduce corruption. It may also be that the breadth of the infrastructure governance language will invite an even broader array of public policy goals sought through PPPs in the future. The role of women in infrastructure development (Siemiatycki et al., 2020), as well as issues of sustainability and climate change (as Tvarnø and Denta suggest in Chapter 10) allude to this possibility.

Into this context has come the research agenda of Bertelli and Woodhouse (Chapter 5). Their research is fascinating because it goes much further than simply stating that 'politics matters' to PPPs. They study both advanced and transition economies using comparative, systematic and quantitative analytical methods and are able to observe the influence of 'veto players' in decision making, whether corruption influences PPP popularity, and how voters perceive PPPs. Interestingly, they also look at what they term 'partnership communities' (networked communities and private consortia) and rather than finding competitive markets, they find limited numbers of repeat agents delivering government projects. They doubt the 'market efficiency' argument of PPP advocates and claim provocatively that 'what efficiency is coming from PPPs seems clearly not to be because of market-style competition among partners'.

There remains much work to be done in strengthening our understanding of both the political context of PPPs as well as their political nature through such systematic empirical research methods.

Meta themes in the research agenda

Having articulated six themes which we have observed throughout the chapters of this book, we might logically ask whether this helps us think about the future of PPP research. We believe it does. Table 17.1 summarises the primary dimensions of these themes.

Reflecting back on these six themes, we can return to a bigger philosophical research picture. Over time, we have clearly begun the journey of adopting new methodological approaches to our PPP research as well as looking through fresh theoretical lenses (that is, themes 1 and 2, above). We have, in other words, been broadening our research philosophy. Next, we have witnessed shifts in both our assumptions as to sectoral superiority and the optimum place of each sector in the task of governing as well. An emphasis back towards effective public governance has occurred. This continuing historical battle between the rightful place of the public and private sectors has been complicated, though, by the dominant narrative of financialisation. Western societies appear to have moved from a period in which we believed that everything should be measured through performance indicators and targets towards a period in which we are now dominated by the idea that everything needs to be not only quantised, but also turned into equations and rationalised in a visible financialised calculus. In other words, and joining together themes 3 and 4, we have witnessed a complex shift in ideological context of the public and private sectors. Lastly, we have over time seen a greater interest in asking about matters of infrastructure governance, however this is being shared between the sectors, as our research hypotheses have gravitated towards matters of policy and governance. This move towards a stronger inquiry into infrastructure governance has occurred at the same time as the PPP phenomenon has progressively become a global narrative with a host of meanings relevant to the needs of individual developing countries. Our research questions and hypotheses have therefore changed.

Of course, all of these change dimensions have implications for our PPP research future. But they equally serve as an important reminder for PPP scholars. The logic of our reflection above provides a meta-construct for the issues tackled in this book. Figure 17.1 shows this meta-construct conceptually. We are all, as research scholars, no doubt proud of our findings on PPPs. But one's findings rely on us fully understanding the evolution of research support from three foundations: the intellectual lens/method through which one works (level 1), the ideological sectoral context in which one's thinking and one's case studies are being completed (level 2) and the research questions one is focusing on (level 3). In short, strong research findings (level 4) require strong foundations on all three underpinning levels.

Table 17.1 PPP research agenda themes and implications

Themes	Theme focus	Main time period	Movement		
				From:	To:
1. Towards fresh research approaches	Research method adopted	2010 to present		Few	Many
2. Towards new theories on the block	Theoretical lens chosen	2015 to present		Few well-known lenses	Many new and traditional lenses
3. Towards optimal public–private balance	Which sector governs?	2000 to present		Market superiority	Renewed public governance
4. Towards financialised everything	Dominant technical ethos	1990 to present		New Public Management	Financialisation
5. Towards stronger governance	Research questions/ hypotheses posed	2015 to present		Project-/ contract-focused	Policy/governance focused
6. Towards a global phenomenon	How is the PPP narrative interpreted?	2000 to present		PPP as sophisticated Western technology	PPP as many meanings for the development context

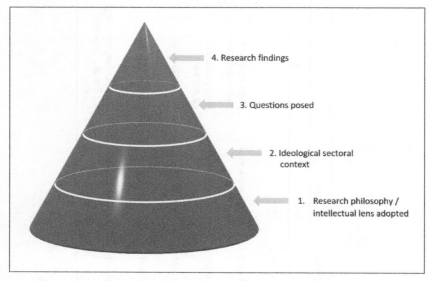

4. Research findings

3. Questions posed

2. Ideological sectoral
   context

1. Research philosophy /
    intellectual lens adopted

Figure 17.1   Meta-construct for this book

Some concluding thoughts for lifelong partnerships

For the past century and a half, those about to go through an English marriage ceremony and begin their marital partnership have been told by superstitious guests to wear 'something old, something new, something borrowed and something blue'.[4] According to old social traditions, one should wear something old in order to protect a baby (yet to be born), something new as a sign of optimism for the future, something borrowed from another happily married couple to provide good luck and something blue as a sign of purity and fidelity.

In parallel with this old saying, PPP researchers have long had the serious intellectual challenge of discerning just what is old in PPP debates, and what is new, as well as what is borrowed (through policy transfer) and how we differentiate all these things from what is 'blue' in terms of pure policy goals (as opposed to the voices of interest groups.) All these tasks remain challenges today and are worthy of some closing contemplation.

So, what is old, and offers protection, here? Clearly, traditional research methods and theoretical lenses will continue to be adopted by PPP scholars, as we continue to test the best optimum public–private balance. We are all subject to path dependency. But most professionals also want to hang on to the best of what we have had to date and do not wish to 'throw out the baby with the bath water' as we reform our public infrastructure delivery methods or revise our infrastructure governance mechanisms.

What is new and optimistic? The youthful energy and enthusiasm of new researchers is certainly visible. And as Liebe says in Chapter 14, we now have a heightened awareness of the multiplicity of research methods available, including their strengths and weaknesses. This is gratifying. And as Mihov comments in Chapter 15, future PPP research ought to be richer and more nuanced across a multidisciplinary narrative as a result – hopefully including new arenas of contestation. The increasing influence of the financialised world over all public policy matters is also new, however – both with its incessant narrative and through its interest groups. Looking at the UK, for example, one wonders who runs the country – the City of London financial centre or the British Parliament?[5] Our own reaction to this provocation matters, because if we blindly accept their infrastructure policy ideas, the resulting inequalities which seem to accompany these ideas may well also transfer. And the optimism of finance sector employees may not transfer to optimism for infrastructure users, citizens or taxpayers.

What is borrowed from another happily married couple for good luck? In the case of PPPs, perhaps this is the new research methods that have come into fashion and are now being applied to PPPs. Warsen's chapter brings us up to date on this, and the rise of more quantitative techniques using large databases as seen in the chapters by Bertelli and Woodhouse and Casady is another case in point.

What is blue and pure is the collaborative ideal. It has always been a worthy pursuit and remains a goal of most Western liberal economies and democracies. Its existence as an ideal is perhaps the most important thing to keep explicit.

There is no doubt the PPP research agenda will remain open, vibrant and fascinating. And individual research exercises will be determined by people whose time and hearts are being invested. The content of many research questions being asked in future may well vary from those of the past, and new research approaches and fresh lenses will hopefully be increasingly adopted. But the tensions between increasing financialisation and the need for stronger public governance will also test our intellectual prowess. This has already been so as the infrastructure governance narrative has progressively globalised. But there is also little doubt that the future research agenda for PPPs will be as exciting and engaging as it has been to date.

All of this, of course, shows a maturing research community, and a more sophisticated and progressive outlook to a topic which will not go away any time soon. It is certain that the language, research questions posed and the analytical methods adopted for infrastructure governance will increasingly tailor to an expanding constellation of surrounding concepts, hybrid organisations, networked communities, mega-projects, social impact bonds, public–private mixes and smart cities. Again, this will lead to a richer discourse. And yet, even given the immense structural implications of PPPs, the breadth of issues continually being debated and the variety of partnership forms around the globe, it may equally be that many of the biggest PPP questions will not be quickly resolved at all. This is perhaps part of the beauty and the challenge inherent for all scholars who continue to search for answers.

Notes

1.   One high-profile example of a new method advocated for PPP research has been fuzzy-set QCA (fsQCA). Often seen as a superior approach to social inquiry (Krogslund et al., 2015), this technique has become increasingly popular in PPP research (for example, Klijn et al., 2010; Kort et al., 2016; Verweij, 2015; Warsen 2019). We, too, have been excited by its promised ability to marry quantitative and qualitative data, and its appealing logic. In Chapter 3 of this volume, Warsen explicitly noted its strengths and acknowledged weaknesses. Interestingly though, Warsen's chapter appears to be the rare exception in PPP research. We have not observed any fsQCA-based PPP article over the past five years giving any serious acknowledgment or discussion of the published methodological debates now existing on fsQCA. The impressive work of Gerrits and Verweij (2018) acknowledges such debates, but nonetheless argues that QCA provides 'a more thorough understanding of the complex causality that has led to certain outcomes in infrastructure projects' (p. 116). Warsen's chapter noted four criticisms: Type I errors, the excessive sensitivity of results to parameter values and choices, neglect of measurement errors and aggregation bias. We suspect such QCA concerns deserve deeper consideration.
     Type I errors: Here, the concern is that fsQCA confirms relationships (that is, pathways to outcomes), when in fact there is none in the data. Braumoeller (2015) notes that whilst QCA results can appear compelling, 'scholars rarely if ever pay attention to the question of how likely they are to have occurred by chance' (p. 474). His re-analysis of one prominent fsQCA publication in political science 'demonstrate[d] that all four of the findings in the original article are plausibly the result of random chance' (p. 472). He argued that fsQCA effectively tested multiple hypotheses and that the fsQCA test statistic was inadequate. His conclusion was that 'even very strong QCA results may plausibly be the result of chance' (p. 471).
     Excessive sensitivity: Krogslund et al. (2015, 21) argued 'that fsQCA is an extraordinarily sensitive method whose results are worryingly susceptible to minor parametric and model specification changes'. It appeared to find complex connections

between variables, even for so called causal combinations containing randomly generated variables. On this matter, they concluded that 'fsQCA produces tenuous results'.

Measurement errors: Hug commented that 'many studies employ QCA inductively and gloss over possible measurement errors' and that using Boolean algebra can then 'lead to dramatically misleading inferences'. His overall view on measurement errors was clear: 'measurement error affects conclusions from QCA quite dramatically' (Hug, 2013, 257).

Aggregation bias: Braumoeller (2017, 243) argues that 'fsQCA analyses of the complex causes of necessary and sufficient conditions (Ragin 2000:234–38) incorporate two definitional assumptions that are individually innocuous but jointly worrisome': the cumulation assumption and the triangular data assumption. To him, these two assumptions 'can be problematic in combination' and 'they produce a form of aggregation bias' that has been a 'heretofore-unappreciated danger in fsQCA'.

Other critiques: We note two. Stockemer (2013) analysed data using both Ordinary Least Squares regression and fsQCA and concluded that 'fsQCA suggests complex configurations of conditions with low empirical coverage and high sensitivity to coding' (p. 86). Tanner (2014) compared several traditional policy evaluation methods against FsQCA policy evaluations. He argued that 'QCA adds little value to current methods of policy scholarship, and its contribution in fact falls far short, compared with present-day standard practices' because it does not 'deliver useful, credible insights for the policy research community' (p. 287). The conclusion of his article told the story: 'an unsuitable method' (p. 290).

Ongoing debate: Of course, critiques such as these are usually followed by a response. The response of Buche, Buche and Siewert (2016, 359) is an example. They charge that Stockemer's criticisms, for instance, were based on misconceptions of 'set-theoretical thinking in general' and 'a misinformed application throughout various steps of the fsQCA'. Stockemer's rebuttal also followed, arguing that fsQCA failed on three fronts: it 'fails in offering parsimonious, easily interpretable results; it fails in providing robust solutions; and it fails in providing solutions with high explanatory power or coverage' (Stockemer, 2016, 386).

The point of this commentary is not to suggest that researchers necessarily abandon fsQCA as a method for social scientific inquiry. We continue to greatly admire the work of our good colleagues, in the style of Rubin (2005, 329), when he extended the work of the famous statistician R.A. Fisher. But there is a need to reconcile such critiques of fsQCA against traditional methods, with care and humility as to the superiority of one research technique over others. Our point is that limitations in new statistical approaches are not always clear (Skaaning 2011). As Cooper and Glaesser (2011, 11) put it, all analytic techniques need to be used with an understanding of the main likely threats to validity. It 'is especially important to report these threats explicitly when, as with fsQCA, mathematics such as fuzzy sets and logic, whose properties are new to most social scientists, are embedded in easily available and easy-to-use software.'

2.   Even a quick skim across the debates between Configurational Comparative Methods (CCMs), such as QCA, and the Regressional Analytic Methods (RAMs) is instructive. Thiem, Baumgartner and Bol (2016, 742) observe that even after a quarter-century of debate in political science and sociology these two schools of scholars 'continue talking at cross purposes'. They comment that the misunderstandings dominating the debates concern algebraic systems, hypotheses classes,

and the concept of causal complexity, and are central, rather than peripheral, to the issue of research veracity. Importantly, they argue, too, that such misunderstandings exist as much within as between these two research communities.

To the authors of this concluding chapter, some of these misunderstandings appear to be wholly understandable. For a start, Thiem, Baumgartner and Bol's work, for instance, observes that because CCMs are based on the logic of Boolean algebra 'whereas RAMs work according to the laws of linear algebra', this 'give(s) rise to semantically incommensurable languages despite occasional resemblances in syntax' (2016, 765). Moreover, the propositional logic of Boolean algebra which underpins CCMs is nowhere near as commonly taught or understood as the linear algebra which is the foundation of RAMs. Less understandable and somewhat worrying, though, is the fact that long-term proponents of QCA such as Ragin, Schneider and Wagemann have been accused of inconsistently interpreting fundamental concepts such as 'necessity' in accordance with a Boolean definition (Thiem and Baumgarter 2016, 802). In a similar vein, Thiem and Baumgarter (2016, 805) comment that Ragin's fs/QCA software 'relies on an algorithmic routine – minimal disjunctivity – which is very useful in logic synthesis yet totally unsuitable for the purpose of causal data analysis'.

Thankfully, more recent debates between methodological scholars appear to have reinforced an attitude of increased care and cautiousness. On the one side, Thomann and Maggetti (2020), for example, seek to assist QCA scholars in carefully designing better studies, and outline multiple approaches to QCA studies and the various analytical choices to be made by researchers. On the other hand, Baumgartner and Thiem (2020, 279) evaluate QCA by conducting a battery of simulation tests, and caution QCA users. They qualify their support for its veracity, finding that 'QCA perform[ed] faultlessly in a series of methodologically appropriate tests, but only in conjunction with the parsimonious solution type' (p. 281). Importantly, they found 'the QCA method to be untrustworthy' when generating the conservative and intermediate solution types, despite these having long been recommended by methodologists such as Ragin, Schneider and Wagemann. To their minds, these evaluation results have serious implications and they call for 'a radical rethink on some hitherto central tenets of QCA methodology'.

So, with such debates continuing, where does this leave us as PPP scholars? For a start, we ought to remind ourselves that debates over qualitative versus quantitative research have a long history and will not be resolved in the short term. Secondly, this CCMs versus RAMs debate is also only one of the ongoing methodological debates occurring between scholars. We could add debates over Bayesian versus frequentist statistics, or between data versus algorithmic modellers to this (Thiem, Baumgartner and Bol, 2016, 767). Thirdly, perhaps it is time for us to take more seriously their warning to us (p. 765) that 'methodologists should thus stop arguing about the superiority of one set of methods in dealing with causal complexity, and instead begin to appreciate their distinct capabilities, leveraging respective strengths wherever apposite'. At a minimum, and fourthly, users of techniques such as QCA (and fsQCA) should tread more cautiously in future, employing the improvements suggested by QCA critics, as well as testing the robustness of their findings. After all, if the criticisms of scholars such as those mentioned above hold water, fsQCA results may be just as unreliable as the results from poor case studies, despite any initial appearance of a dazzling mathematical rationale.

3.   See https://smartgovernance-partnerships.org/.

4. See https://en.wikipedia.org/wiki/Something_old.
5. Paralleling the invisible but influential political power of financial centres in places such as London, New York and Hong Kong, the neutrality of multilateral investment banks has also long been a hot topic of debate. Interestingly, recent analyses of PPP advocacy from institutions such as the European Investment Bank have shown it to be an activist 'policy entrepreneur' rather than acting with neutrality (Liebe and Howarth, 2020).

References

Baumgartner, M., and Thiem, A. (2020) Often Trusted but Never (Properly) Tested: Evaluating Qualitative Comparative Analysis. *Sociological Methods & Research*, 49 (2), 279–311. https://doi.org/10.1177/0049124117701487.

Beck, U. (1986) *Risikogesellschaft*. Frankfurt: Suhrkamp.

Beck, U. (1992) *Risk Society: Towards a New Modernity*. London: SAGE.

Braumoeller, B.F. (2015) Guarding Against False Positives in Qualitative Comparative Analysis. *Political Analysis*, 23, 471–487. https://doi.org/10.1093/pan/mpv017.

Braumoeller, B.F. (2017) Aggregation Bias and the Analysis of Necessary and Sufficient Conditions in fsQCA. *Sociological Methods & Research*, 46 (2), 242–251. https://doi .org/10.1177/0049124116672701.

Buche, A., Buche, J., and Siewert, M. (2016) Fuzzy Logic or Fuzzy Application? A Response to Stockemer's 'Fuzzy Set or Fuzzy Logic?' *European Political Science*, 15, 359–378.

Cooper, B., and Glaesser, J. (2011) Paradoxes and Pitfalls in Using Fuzzy Set QCA: Illustrations from a Critical Review of a Study of Educational Inequality. *Sociological Research Online*, 16 (3), 8. www.socresonline.org.uk/16/3/8.html 10.5153/sro.2444.

Dewulf, G., and Garvin, M. (2020) Responsive Governance in PPP Projects to Manage Uncertainty. *Construction Management and Economics*, 38 (4), 383–397. https://doi .org/10.1080/01446193.2019.1618478.

Gerrits, L., and Verweij, S. (2018) *The Evaluation of Complex Infrastructure Projects: A Guide to Qualitative Comparative Analysis*. Cheltenham, UK and Northampton, MA, USA: Edward Elgar Publishing.

Greve, C. (2003) *When Public–Private Partnerships Fail: The Extreme Case of the NPM-Inspired Local Government of Farum in Denmark*. Paper for the EGPA Conference, 3–6 September, Oeiras, Portugal.

Hodge, G. (2006) Public Private Partnerships and Legitimacy. *University of New South Wales Law Journal*, 29 (3), 318–327.

Hodge, G., and Greve, C. (2019) *The Logic of Public–Private Partnerships: The Enduring Interdependency of Politics and Markets*. Cheltenham, UK and Northampton, MA, USA: Edward Elgar Publishing.

Hodge, G.A. (2002) Who Steers the State When Governments Sign Public-Private Partnerships? *Journal of Contemporary Issues in Business and Government*, 8 (1), 5–18.

Hodge, G.A., and Greve, C. (2018) Contemporary Public–Private Partnership: Towards a Global Research Agenda. *Financial Accountability and Management*, 34 (1), 3–16.

Hodge, G.A., and Greve, C. (2021) What Can Public Administration Scholars Learn from the Economics Controversies in Public-Private Partnerships? *Asia Pacific Journal of Public Administration*. https://doi.org/10.1080/23276665.2021.1939744.

Hood, C. (1991) A Public Management for All Seasons. *Public Administration*, 69 (Spring), 3–19.

Hood, C., and Jackson, M. (1991) *Administrative Argument*. Aldershot: Dartmouth.

Hug, S. (2013) Qualitative Comparative Analysis: How Inductive Use and Measurement Error Lead to Problematic Inference. *Political Analysis*, 21, 252–265. https://doi.org/10.1093/pan/mps061.

Klijn, E.-H. (2010) Public Private Partnerships: Deciphering Meaning, Message and Phenomenon in *International Handbook on Public–Private Partnerships*, edited by G.A. Hodge, C. Greve and A.E. Boardman. Cheltenham, UK and Northampton, MA, USA: Edward Elgar Publishing, pp. 68–80.

Klijn, E.-H., Steijn, B., and Edelenbos, J. (2010) The Impact of Network Management on Outcomes in Governance Networks. *Public Administration*, 88 (4), 1063–1082. https://doi.org/10.1111/j.1467-9299.2010.01826.x.

Kort, M., Verweij, S., and Klijn, E.-H. (2016) In Search for Effective Public-Private Partnerships: An Assessment of the Impact of Organizational Form and Managerial Strategies in Urban Regeneration Partnerships Using fsQCA. *Environment and Planning C: Government and Policy*, 34, 777–794. https://doi.org/10.1177/0263774X15614674.

Krogslund, C., Choi, D.D., and Poertner, M. (2015) Fuzzy Sets on Shaky Ground: Parameter Sensitivity and Confirmation Bias in fsQCA. *Political Analysis*, 23, 21–41. https://doi.org/10.1093/pan/mpu016.

Levitt, R.E., and Eriksson, K. (2016) Developing a Governance Model for PPP Infrastructure Service Delivery Based on Lessons from Eastern Australia. *Journal of Organization Design*, 5 (7), 1–8. https://doi.org/10.1186/s41469-016-0009-3.

Liebe, M., and Howarth, D. (2020) The European Investment Bank as Policy Entrepreneur and the Promotion of Public-Private Partnerships. *New Political Economy*, 25 (2), 195–212. https://doi.org/10.1080/13563467.2019.1586862.

Linder, S. (1999) Coming to Terms with the Public-Private Partnership: A Grammar of Multiple Meanings. *American Behavioural Scientist*, 43 (1), 35–51.

North, D.C. (1990) *Institutions, Institutional Change and Economic Performance*. Cambridge: Cambridge University Press.

Osborne, D., and Gaebler, T. (1992) *Reinventing Government: How the Entrepreneurial Spirit is Transforming the Public Sector*. Reading, MA: Addison-Wesley.

Prats, J. (2019) *The Governance of Public–Private Partnerships: A Comparative Analysis*. Inter-American Development Bank Technical Note 1616.

Ragin, C. (2000) *Fuzzy Set Social Science*. Chicago, IL: University of Chicago Press.

Roberts, A. (2010) *The Logic of Discipline*. Oxford: Oxford University Press.

Rubin, D.B. (2005) Causal Inference Using Potential Outcomes. *Journal of the American Statistical Association*, 100 (469), 322–331. https://doi.org/10.1198/016214504000001880.

Savas, E.S. (1987) *Privatization: The Key to Better Government*. Chatham, NJ: Chatham House Publishers.

Siemiatycki, M., Enright, T., and Valverde, M. (2020) The Gendered Production of Infrastructure. *Progress in Human Geography*, 44 (2), 297–314.

Skaaning, S.-E. (2011) Assessing the Robustness of Crisp-Set and Fuzzy-Set QCA Results. *Sociological Methods & Research*, 40 (2), 391–408. https://doi.org/10.1177/0049124111404818.

Skelcher, C. (2010) Governing Partnerships, in *International Handbook on Public–Private Partnerships*, edited by G.A. Hodge, C. Greve and A.E. Boardman. Cheltenham, UK and Northampton, MA, USA: Edward Elgar Publishing, pp. 292–306.

Stockemer, D. (2013) Fuzzy Set or Fuzzy Logic? Comparing the Value of Qualitative Comparative Analysis (fsQCA) versus Regression Analysis for the Study of Women's Legislative Representation. *European Political Science*, 12, 86–101.

Stockemer, D. (2016) Fuzzy Sets ... Too Fuzzy to Study Women's Representation in Parliament. *European Political Science*, 15, 379–388.

Tanner, S. (2014) QCA Is of Questionable Value for Policy Research. *Policy and Society*, 33 (3), 287–298. https://doi.org/10.1016/j.polsoc.2014.08.003.

Thiem, A., and Baumgarter, M. (2016) Back to Square One: A Reply to Munck, Paine, and Schneider. *Comparative Political Studies*, 49 (6): 801–806. https://doi.org/10.1177/0010414015626455.

Thiem, A., Baumgartner, M., and Bol, D. (2016) Still Lost in Translation! A Correction of Three Misunderstandings Between Configurational Comparativists and Regressional Analysts. *Comparative Political Studies*, 49 (6): 742–774. https://doi.org/10.1177/0010414014565892.

Thomann, E., and Maggetti, M. (2020) Designing Research with Qualitative Comparative Analysis (QCA): Approaches, Challenges, and Tools. *Sociological Methods & Research*, 49 (2), 356–386. https://doi.org/10.1177/0049124117729700.

UNECE (United Nations Economic Commission for Europe) (2008) *Guidebook on Promoting Good Governance in Public-Private Partnerships*. New York, NY: United Nations.

Verweij, S. (2015) Producing Satisfactory Outcomes in the Implementation Phase of PPP Infrastructure Projects: A Fuzzy Set Qualitative Comparative Analysis of 27 Road Constructions in the Netherlands. *International Journal of Project Management*, 33 (2015), 1877–1887.

Wang, H., Xiong, W., Wu, G., and Zhu, D. (2017) Public–Private Partnership in Public Administration Discipline: A Literature Review. *Public Management Review*, 20 (2), 293–316. https://doi.org/10.1080/14719037.2017.1313445.

Wang, N., Ma, M., and Liu, Y. (2020) The Whole Lifecycle Management Efficiency of the Public Sector in PPP Infrastructure Projects. *Sustainability*, 12 (3049), 1–17. https://doi.org/10.3390/su12073049.

Wang, X., Yin, Y., Deng, J., and Xu, Z. (2021) Opportunistic Behaviour Governance in PPP Projects: An Analysis Based on Trust Networks. *Advances in Civil Engineering*, 2021, Article 8899338. https://doi.org/10.1155/2021/8899338.

Warsen, R. (2019) *Explaining Trust in Public-Private Partnerships: A Qualitative Comparative Analysis (QCA) of 25 Public-Private Partnerships in the Netherlands and Belgium*. Paper delivered at the XXIII Annual Conference of the International Research Society for Public Management, 16–18 April, Wellington, New Zealand.

Index

Printed and bound by CPI Group (UK) Ltd, Croydon, CR0 4YY

16/04/2025